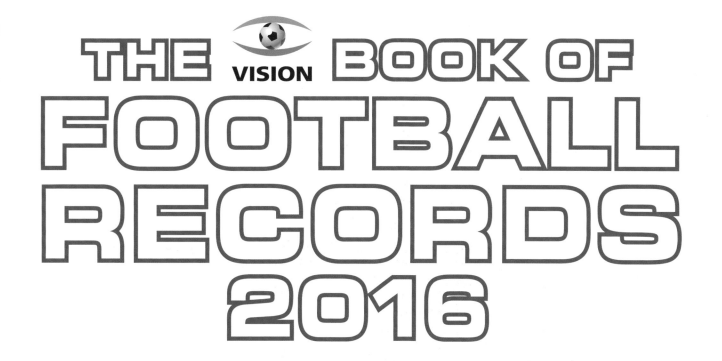

# THE VISION BOOK OF FOOTBALL RECORDS 2016

**BY CLIVE BATTY**

**VSP**

Published by Vision Sports Publishing in 2015

Vision Sports Publishing
19-23 High Street
Kingston upon Thames
Surrey
KT1 1LL

www.visionsp.co.uk

© Clive Batty

ISBN: 978-1909534-52-0

Editors: Paul Baillie-Lane and Jim Drewett
Design: Neal Cobourne
Kit images: David Moor, www.historicalkits.co.uk
All pictures: Getty Images

Printed and bound in Slovakia by Neografia
A CIP catalogue record for this book is available from the British Library

MIX
Paper from
responsible sources
FSC® C020353

All statistics in the *Vision Book of Football Records 2016* are correct up until the start of the 2015/16 season

# INTRODUCTION

Welcome to the 2016 edition of *The Vision Book of Football Records*. In the 12 months since the previous edition of this book appeared on the shelves there have been any number of exciting events on the pitch, both here in Britain and the wider football world. After a couple of seasons when they seemed to be on a downward spiral, Barcelona have re-established themselves as Europe's top club, scooping up a truly magnificent treble in 2015; little Bournemouth surprised everyone by winning promotion to the top flight for the first time in their 125-year history; and England's 'Lionesses' did the nation proud at the Women's World Cup, claiming third place and proving once and for all that girls most definitely can 'Bend It Like Beckham'.

Off the pitch, though, the past year has been memorable for all the wrong reasons with football's world body FIFA engulfed in a massive corruption scandal that has shocked, appalled and outraged fans around the globe. Allegations that some high-ranking officials were less interested in promoting the 'beautiful game' than in lining their own pockets have tarnished football's reputation, but hopefully the damage won't prove to be too great in the long term.

Bundles of cash stuffed inside a brown paper bag won't, however, get your club, star player or manager a place in this book. That has to be earned strictly on merit, through stand-out performances on the field of play. So, for example, our old friends Barnet and Bristol Rovers – both promoted back to League Two after short stays in the non-league wilderness – are included again, alongside all the other Football League and Premier League clubs, the top outfits in Scotland and the giants of the European game. In much the same way, up-and-coming young players like Fabian Delph, Jordan Henderson and Harry Kane have forced their way into the book for the very first time, taking their place alongside the more established Premier League stars and exciting new recruits from abroad such as Memphis Depay, Roberto Firmino and Bastian Schweinsteiger. There are entries, too, for the biggest international superstars such as Lionel Messi, Cristiano Ronaldo and Zlatan Ibrahimovic as well as the great names from the past, including the likes of Maradona, Matthews and Moore.

Meanwhile, all the other facts, figures, records and stats have been amended, revised and updated to take account of the many changes that have occurred in the footy world over the past year. As in previous editions, you will find entries for the leading football nations, the most important domestic and international competitions, the most prestigious individual prizes, and the leading managers both here and on the continent. All the entries are ordered alphabetically, which means that Jose Mourinho and Arsene Wenger have been kept some distance apart – a good thing, too, as the pair get on about as well as legendary cartoon characters Tom and Jerry (you can decide which is which!).

Nor is that all. There are also dozens of different individual entries for 'wild card' subjects as diverse as 'Corners' (did you know that a female international was the first player to score from two corners in the same match?), 'Friendlies' (the longest one ever lasted a really quite ridiculous 102 hours and finished 910–725!), 'Size' (can you guess who is the tallest Premier League player ever? – surprisingly, it's not the giraffe-like Peter Crouch) and 'Twitter' (Wayne Rooney will, no doubt, be thrilled to learn that he has almost as many followers on the social media site as the Dalai Lama!)

All in all, then, you ought to find enough inside these pages to keep yourself occupied throughout the entire season – and the 2015/16 campaign is certainly a long one, stretching from the Community Shield at the start of August to the final of Euro 2016 on 10th July... pretty much when the next edition of this book will be due out!

**CLIVE BATTY**

## ABANDONED MATCHES

A record three Football League fixtures were abandoned on 2nd November 2010. The League Two match between Cheltenham and Southend was called off after 66 minutes due to floodlight failure, while waterlogged pitches led to the abandonment of the Hartlepool-Notts County and Rochdale-Oldham League One fixtures after less than 10 minutes total playing time.

• The shortest ever English game took place in 1894, when a raging blizzard caused the match between Stoke and Wolves at the Victoria Ground to be called off after just three minutes. Only 400 hardy fans had braved the elements, and even they must have been secretly relieved when the referee, Mr Helme, called the game off.

• English referee Martin Atkinson abandoned the Euro 2016 qualifier between Serbia and Albania in October 2014 when a drone carrying a 'Greater Albania' flag flew over the stadium, sparking scuffles between the players and a pitch invasion by home fans. UEFA awarded Albania a 3-0 win, and deducted Serbia three points for the crowd trouble.

• On the last day of the 2014/15 Championship season hundreds of Blackpool fans invaded the pitch shortly after half time protesting against the club's owners, causing the Tangerines' home match against Huddersfield to be abandoned. The Football League later ruled that the score at the time, 0-0, should stand as the final result.

• In May 2015 the Copa Libertadores derby clash between Boca Juniors and River Plate was abandoned after Boca fans targeted four River players with pepper spray, causing them burns which required hospital treatment. The disgraceful attack led to Boca being thrown out of the competition.

---

## ABERDEEN

**Year founded:** 1903
**Ground:** Pittodrie Stadium (20,897)
**Nickname:** The Dons
**Biggest win:** 13-0 v Peterhead (1923)
**Heaviest defeat:** 0-9 v Celtic (2010)

Aberdeen were founded in 1903, following the amalgamation of three city clubs, Aberdeen, Orion and Victoria United. The following year the club joined the Scottish Second Division, and in 1905 the Dons were elected to an expanded First Division. Aberdeen have remained in the top flight ever since, a record shared with just Rangers and Celtic.

• The club was originally known as the Whites and later as the Wasps or the Black and Golds after their early strips, but in 1913 became known as the Dons. This nickname is sometimes said to derive from the involvement of professors at Aberdeen University in the foundation of the club, but is more likely to be a contraction of the word 'Aberdonians', the term used to describe people from Aberdeen.

• Aberdeen first won the Scottish title in 1955, before enjoying a trio of championship successes in the 1980s under manager Alex Ferguson. Before he moved on to even greater triumphs at Old Trafford, Fergie also led the Dons to four victories in five years in the Scottish Cup, which included a record run of 20 cup games without defeat between 1982 and 1985.

• The club's finest hour, though, came in 1983 when the Dons became only the second Scottish club (after Rangers in 1972) to win the European Cup Winners' Cup, beating Real Madrid 2-1 in the final. Later that year Aberdeen defeated Hamburg over two legs to claim the European Super Cup and remain the only Scottish side to win two European trophies.

• In 1984 Aberdeen became the first club outside the 'Old Firm' to win the Double, after finishing seven points clear at the top of the league and beating Celtic 2-1 in the Scottish Cup final.

• Aberdeen's record of 15 appearances in the Scottish Cup final (including seven wins) is only bettered by Celtic and Rangers.

• Scottish international defender Willie Miller has made more appearances for the club than any other player, an impressive 556 games between 1973 and 1990. Hotshot striker Joe Harper is the Dons' record goalscorer, with 205 during two spells at Pittodrie (1969-72 and 1976-81).

• Aberdeen's most capped player is Miller's long-time defensive partner and former Birmingham and Aston Villa boss Alex McLeish, who made 77 appearances for Scotland between 1977 and 1990.

• The Dons suffered their worst ever defeat in November 2010 when they were hammered 9-0 by Celtic, the biggest ever thrashing in the history of the Scottish Premiership.

> **HONOURS**
> *Division 1 champions* 1955
> *Premier Division champions* 1980, 1984, 1985
> *Scottish Cup* 1947, 1970, 1982, 1983, 1984, 1986, 1990
> *League Cup* 1956, 1977, 1986, 1990, 1996, 2014
> *European Cup Winners' Cup* 1983
> *European Super Cup* 1983

## ROMAN ABRAMOVICH

**Born:** Saratov, Russia, 24th October 1966

Chelsea owner Roman Abramovich has a fortune estimated at £8.5 billion and, since buying the Blues from previous owner Ken Bates in July 2003, he has invested hundreds of millions in the club – including over £800 million in transfer fees – in an attempt to establish the west Londoners as a dominant force in the English and European game.

• Abramovich's massive spending spree has been rewarded with four league titles and seven domestic cups, including the Double in 2010.

### IS THAT A FACT?

Down to nine men and trailing 4-1 in a Peruvian cup tie in October 2014, five players of Defensor Bolivar dropped to the ground faking injury in an attempt to get their match against Defensor La Bocana abandoned. The ref fell for the trick and called the game off, but the Peruvian FA were unimpressed and threw Bolivar out of the cup.

For many years his burning ambition to see Chelsea win the Champions League was frustrated – a failure which led Abramovich to sack a number of his managers – but the Blues finally managed to lift the biggest prize of all in 2012 following a dramatic penalty shoot-out against Bayern Munich.

• After starting out selling retread car tyres, Abramovich's business career took off when he began trading oil products out of Russia's largest refinery in western Siberia. He gradually acquired a controlling interest in Sibneft, the country's main oil company, before selling his share to the Russian government-controlled Gazprom for an eye-watering £7.4 billion in 2005.

• Abramovich enjoys a lifestyle befitting his billionaire status, owning a number of luxury homes, three yachts, a private Boeing 767 jet and a large collection of valuable works of art.

## AC MILAN

**Year founded:** 1899
**Ground:** San Siro (80,018)
**Nickname:** Rossoneri
**League titles:** 18
**Domestic cups:** 5
**European cups:** 14
**International cups:** 4

One of the giants of European football, the club was founded by British expatriates as the Milan Cricket and Football Club in 1899. Apart from a period during the fascist dictatorship of Benito Mussolini, the club has always been known as 'Milan' rather than the Italian 'Milano'.

• Milan were the first Italian side to win the European Cup, beating Benfica in the final at Wembley in 1963, and have gone on to win the trophy seven times – a record surpassed only by Real Madrid, with 10 victories.

• In 1986 the club was acquired by the businessman and future Italian President

Silvio Berlusconi, who invested in star players like Marco van Basten, Ruud Gullit and Frank Rijkaard. Milan went on to enjoy a golden era under coaches Arrigo Sacchi and Fabio Capello, winning three European Cups and four Serie A titles between 1988 and 1994. Incredibly, the club were undefeated for 58 games between 1991 and 1993, the third longest such run in top-flight European football history behind Celtic (62 games) and Steaua Bucharest (104 games).

• **Milan's San Siro Stadium, which they share with city rivals Inter, is the largest in Italy, with a capacity of over 80,000. The stadium has hosted the European Cup/Champions League final on three occasions – a total only matched by Rome's Stadio Olimpico among Italian venues.**

• Legendary defender Paolo Maldini made a Serie A record 647 league appearances for Milan between 1985 and 2009, and also played in a record 175 European club games.

### HONOURS
*Italian champions* 1901, 1906, 1907, 1951, 1955, 1957, 1959, 1962,1968, 1979, 1988, 1992, 1993, 1994,1996, 1999, 2004, 2011
*Italian Cup* 1967, 1972, 1973, 1977, 2003
*European Cup/Champions League* 1963, 1969, 1989, 1990, 1994, 2003, 2007
*European Cup Winners' Cup* 1968, 1973
*European Super Cup* 1989, 1990, 1994, 2003, 2007
*Intercontinental Cup* 1969, 1989, 1990
*Club World Cup* 2007

*AC Milan's Keisuke Honda is extremely reliable and has a good engine*

## ACCRINGTON STANLEY

**Year founded:** 1968
**Ground:** Crown Ground (5,057)
**Nickname:** The Stans
**Biggest win:** 10-1 v Lincoln United (1999)
**Heaviest defeat:** 2-8 v Peterborough (2008)

Accrington Stanley were founded at a meeting in a working men's club in Accrington in 1968, as a successor to the former Football League club of the same name which had folded two years earlier.

• **Conference champions in 2006, Stanley were promoted to the Football League in place of relegated Oxford United.** Ironically, when a financial crisis forced the old Accrington Stanley to resign from the League in March 1962, the club that replaced them the following season was Oxford!

• In 2011 the club finished a best ever fifth in League Two, but their hopes of promotion were dashed by Stevenage who beat them 3-0 on aggregate in the play-off semi-final.

• **The original town club, Accrington, were one of the 12 founder members of the Football League in 1888, but resigned from the League after just five years.**

• The Stans splashed out a club record £114,000 on Swansea midfielder Ian Craney in 2008, and two years later received a record £260,000 from Scunthorpe United for winger Bobby Grant.

> HONOURS
> *Conference champions 2006*

## AFC WIMBLEDON

**Year founded:** 2002
**Ground:** Kingsmeadow (4,850)
**Nickname:** The Dons
**Biggest win:** 9-0 v Chessington United (2004) and v Slough Town (2007)
**Heaviest defeat:** 0-5 v York City (2010)

AFC Wimbledon were founded in 2002 by supporters of the former Premiership club Wimbledon, who opposed the decision of the FA to sanction the 'franchising' of their club when they allowed it to move 56 miles north from their south London base to Milton Keynes in Buckinghamshire (the club later becoming the MK Dons).

• **In October 2006 an agreement was reached with the MK Dons that the honours won by the old Wimbledon would return to the London Borough of Merton. This was an important victory for the AFC fans, who view their club as the true successors to Wimbledon FC.**

• In their former incarnation as Wimbledon the club won the FA Cup in 1988, beating hot favourites Liverpool 1-0 at Wembley. Incredibly, the Dons had only been elected to the Football League just 12 years earlier, but enjoyed a remarkable rise through the divisions, winning promotion to the top flight in 1986. Dubbed the 'Crazy Gang' for their physical approach on the pitch and madcap antics off it, Wimbledon remained in the Premiership until 2000.

• **While rising through the non-league pyramid AFC went 78 matches undefeated between February 2003 and December 2004 – the longest unbeaten run in English**

*AFC Wimbledon's Adebayo 'The Beast' Akinfenwa scores for the Dons in the FA Cup against Liverpool*

senior football. Then, in 2011, AFC beat Luton Town on penalties in the Conference play-off final at Eastlands, securing a place in the Football League just nine years after their formation.

• With a capacity of just 4,850, the club's tiny Kingsmeadow Stadium is the smallest in the Football League.

> HONOURS
> *Division 4 champions 1983 (as Wimbledon FC)*
> *FA Cup 1988 (as Wimbledon FC)*
> *FA Amateur Cup 1963 (as Wimbledon FC)*

## AFRICA CUP OF NATIONS

The Africa Cup of Nations was founded in 1957. The first tournament was a decidedly small affair consisting of just three competing teams (Egypt, Ethiopia and hosts Sudan) after South Africa's invitation was withdrawn when they refused to send a multi-racial squad to the finals. Egypt were the first winners, beating Ethiopia 4-0 in the final in Khartoum.

• **With seven victories, Egypt are the most successful side in the history of the competition. After triumphing in Angola in 2010 following a 1-0 victory over Ghana in the final, the north Africans claimed a record three consecutive trophies. However, Ghana were the first country to win the tournament three times and, following their third success in 1978, were allowed to keep the original Abdel Abdullah Salem Trophy, named after the first president of the Confederation of African Football.**

• The final has been decided on penalties on eight occasions, with Ivory Coast winning the longest shoot-out 11-10 against Ghana in 1992.

• **The top scorer in the history of the competition is Cameroon striker Samuel Eto'o, who has hit a total of 18 goals in the tournament. Mulamba Ndaye of Zaire holds the record for the most goals in a single tournament, with nine in 1974.**

• Morocco were due to host the 2015 tournament, but refused to do so after expressing worries over the Ebola outbreak. The competition was moved to Equatorial Guinea and was won by Ivory Coast.

## AFRICAN FOOTBALLER OF THE YEAR

The African Footballer of the Year award was established by the Confederation of African Football in 1992, Nigerian striker Rashidi Yekini topping the first poll the following year.

• **Ivory Coast midfielder Yaya Toure has dominated the award in recent years, with a record four wins on the trot between 2011 and 2014. Legendary Cameroon striker Samuel Eto'o has also won the award four times, including a hat-trick between 2003 and 2005.**

• The first Premier League-based player to win the award was Arsenal striker Kanu in 1999. Altogether, players at English clubs have won the award a record nine times.

• **Players from eight different African countries have won the award, with Ivory Coast (six wins in total) enjoying the most success.**

## AGE

Legendary winger Sir Stanley Matthews is the oldest player to appear in the top flight of English football. 'The Ageless Wonder' had celebrated his 50th birthday five days before playing his last match for Stoke against Fulham in February 1965.

• **Matthews, though, was something of a spring chicken compared to Neil McBain, the New Brighton manager, who had to go in goal for his side's Division Three (North) match against Hartlepool during an injury crisis in 1947. He was 51 and 120 days at the time, the oldest player in the history of English football.**

• Manchester City goalkeeper John Burridge became the oldest player in the Premier League when he came off the bench at half-time in City's match against Newcastle in April 1995, aged 43. The youngest player is Fulham's Matthew Briggs, who was aged 16 years and 65 days when he made his debut for the Cottagers against Middlesbrough in May 2007.

• **The oldest international in British football is Wales' Billy Meredith, who played against England in 1920 at the age of 45. The youngest is Liverpool winger Harry Wilson, who was aged just 16 and 207 days when he made his debut for Wales as a sub against Belgium in 2013.**

• The oldest goalscorer in Premier

League history is Teddy Sheringham, who was aged 40 and 268 days when he hit the target for West Ham against Portsmouth on Boxing Day 2006. The youngest is James Vaughan, who was aged 16 and 270 days when he scored for Everton against Crystal Palace in 2005.

• The oldest player to appear at the World Cup is Colombia goalkeeper Faryd Mondragon, who played the last five minutes of his side's 4-1 victory against Japan at the 2014 tournament three days after his 43rd birthday. The youngest is Norman Whiteside, who was aged 17 and 41 days when he played for Northern Ireland against Yugoslavia in 1982.

• The oldest goalscorer in the Champions League is Francesco Totti, who celebrated his 38th birthday three days before scoring for Roma in a 1-1 draw at Manchester City on 30th September 2014.

• **The youngest player to appear in international football is Lucas Knecht who turned out for the Northern Mariana Islands against Guam two days after his 14th birthday in 2007. At the opposite end of the scale Barrie Dewsbury was 52 and 11 days when he played in Sark's 16-0 defeat by Greenland in 2003.**

## SERGIO AGUERO

**Born:** Quilmes, Argentina, 2nd June 1988
**Position:** Striker
**Club career:**
2003-06 Independiente 54 (23)
2006-11 Atletico Madrid 175 (74)
2011- Manchester City 120 (78)
**International record:**
2006- Argentina 66 (26)

In 2015 Sergio Aguero became the first Manchester City player to win the Premier League Golden Boot outright after topping the scoring charts with an impressive total of 26 goals.

• Known as 'El Kun' because of his resemblance to a Japanese cartoon character, Aguero became the youngest ever player to appear in Argentina's top flight when he made his debut for Independiente in 2003 aged just 15 years and 35 days. The previous record was set by the legendary Diego Maradona, Aguero's former father-in-law.

• Aguero moved on to Atletico Madrid in 2006 aged 17, helping the Spanish club win the inaugural Europa League in 2010. The following year he joined Manchester City for £38 million, to become the second most expensive player in British football history at the time. The fee proved to be a bargain as Aguero banged in 23 Premier League goals – including a dramatic title-clinching winner against QPR on the last day of the season – as City topped the table for the first time since 1968. Two years later he contributed another 17 goals as City won the title again. Aguero's total of 19 goals for City in European competition is a club record.

• A quicksilver attacker who possesses excellent close control, Aguero made his international debut for Argentina in a 2006 friendly against Brazil at Arsenal's Emirates Stadium. In 2008 he was a key figure in the Argentina team that won gold at the Beijing Olympics, but he endured heartache at the 2014 World Cup and the 2015 Copa America when he finished on the losing side in the final both times.

## AIR CRASHES

On 6th February 1958 eight members of the Manchester United 'Busby Babes' team, including England internationals Roger Byrne, Duncan Edwards and Tommy Taylor, were killed in the Munich Air Crash. Their plane crashed while attempting to take off in a snowstorm at Munich Airport, where it had stopped to refuel after a European Cup tie in Belgrade. In total, 23 people died in the crash, although manager Matt Busby and Bobby Charlton were among the survivors. Amazingly, United still managed to reach the FA Cup final that year, but lost at Wembley to Bolton Wanderers.

• The entire first team of Torino, the strongest Italian club at the time, were wiped out in an air disaster on 4th May 1949. Returning from a testimonial match in Portugal, the team's plane crashed into the Basilica of Superga outside Turin. Among the 31 dead were 10 members of the Italian national side and the club's English manager, Leslie Lievesley. Torino fielded their youth team in their four remaining fixtures and, with their opponents doing the same as a mark of respect, won a joint-record fifth consecutive league title at the end of the season.

• Eight members of Denmark's Olympic football squad were killed on 16th July 1960 when the plane they were travelling in crashed into the sea shortly

*'All together now: Blue Moon, you saw me standing alone...'*

after taking off from Copenhagen airport. Incredibly, the Danes still managed to claim the silver medal in the football tournament in Rome.

## AJAX

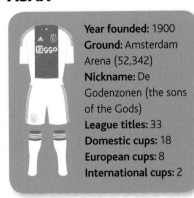

**Year founded:** 1900
**Ground:** Amsterdam Arena (52,342)
**Nickname:** De Godenzonen (the sons of the Gods)
**League titles:** 33
**Domestic cups:** 18
**European cups:** 8
**International cups:** 2

Founded in 1900 in Amsterdam, Ajax are named after the Greek mythological hero. The club is the most successful in Holland, having won the league a record 33 times and the Dutch Cup a record 18 times.

• Ajax's white shirts with a broad vertical red stripe are among the most iconic in world football. However, the club's original kit was very different – an all-black outfit with a red sash tied around the players' waists.

• The Dutch side's most glorious decade was in the 1970s when, with a team featuring legends like Johan Cruyff, Johan Neeskens and Johnny Rep, Ajax won the European Cup three times on the trot, playing a fluid system known as 'Total Football'. In 1995 a young Ajax team won the trophy for a fourth time, Patrick Kluivert scoring the winner in the final against AC Milan.

• **When Ajax beat Torino in the final of the UEFA Cup in 1992 they became only the second team, after Juventus, to win all three major European trophies.**

• During the 1971/72 season Ajax won a world record 26 matches on the trot in all competitions.

> **HONOURS**
> *Dutch League champions 1918, 1919, 1931, 1932, 1934, 1937, 1939, 1947, 1957, 1960, 1966, 1967, 1968, 1970, 1972, 1973, 1977, 1979, 1980, 1982, 1983, 1985, 1990, 1994, 1995, 1996, 1998, 2002, 2004, 2011, 2012, 2013, 2014*
> *Dutch Cup 1917, 1943, 1961, 1967, 1970, 1971, 1972, 1979, 1983, 1986, 1987, 1993, 1998, 1999, 2002, 2006, 2007, 2010*
> *European Cup/Champions League 1971, 1972, 1973, 1995*
> *European Cup Winners' Cup 1987*
> *UEFA Cup 1992*
> *European Super Cup 1973, 1995*
> *Intercontinental Cup 1972, 1995*

## ANIMALS

A dreary 0-0 draw between Liverpool and Tottenham in February 2012 was livened up when a grey and white tabby cat ran onto the Anfield pitch. A Twitter account purporting to be 'The Anfield Cat' was quickly set up and soon had more than 25,000 followers!

• **The most famous dog in football, Pickles, never appeared on the pitch but, to the relief of fans around the globe, discovered the World Cup trophy which was stolen while on display at an exhibition in Central Hall, Westminster, on 20th March 1966. A black and white mongrel, Pickles found the trophy under a bush while out for a walk on Beulah Hill in south London with his owner. He was hailed as a national hero but, sadly, later that same year he was strangled by his lead while chasing after a cat.**

• The World Cup also made an international celebrity of Paul, an octopus based at the Sea Life Aquarium in Oberhausen, Germany. During the 2010 finals in South Africa, the two-year-old cephalopod correctly predicted the result of all seven of Germany's games by choosing his favourite food, mussels, from one of two boxes marked with the national flag of the competing teams. Before the final between Holland and Spain, Paul's choice of breakfast snack suggested that the trophy would

*Anyone for cricket? This pesky grasshopper landed on Colombia's James Rodriguez just before he was about to take a penalty in the 2014 World Cup*

## IS THAT A FACT?

The Belgian first division match between Zulte Waregem and Lokeren in 2010 was briefly interrupted when a duck waddled onto the pitch. Zulte striker Mahamadou Habib Habibou eventually caught the uninvited guest but didn't endear himself to the crowd when he casually threw the bird over the advertising hoardings.

be heading to Madrid rather than Amsterdam... and, yet again, the amazing 'psychic' octopus was spot on!

• The start of Oldham's pre-season friendly with Blackburn Rovers in July 2015 was delayed after a swarm of bees settled on one of the goalposts. The invaders were eventually disposed of by a local beekeeper who managed to persuade them to fly into a cardboard box.

• When a dog ran onto the pitch during a lower league match in Argentina between San Juan and Bella Vista in June 2013, visiting winger Jose Jimenez decided to take matters into his own hands, grabbing the mutt by the scruff of the neck and throwing it back into the crowd. Unfortunately, he only managed to hurl the poor animal against a high metal fence, sparking a near riot on the pitch and outrage on the home terraces. Eventually the referee was able to restore order by showing Jimenez the red card.

## APPEARANCES

Goalkeeping legend Peter Shilton holds the record for the most Football League appearances, playing 1,005 games between 1966 and 1997. His total was made up as follows: Leicester City (286 games), Stoke City (110), Nottingham Forest (202), Southampton (188), Derby County (175), Plymouth (34), Bolton (1) and Leyton Orient (9). Shilton is followed in the all-time list by Tony Ford (931 appearances, 1975-2001), who holds the record for an outfield player.

• Manchester United assistant manager Ryan Giggs holds the Premier League appearance record, with a total of 632 appearances between 1992 and 2014. Brad Friedel holds the consecutive games record with 310 for Blackburn,

Aston Villa and Tottenham between August 2004 and October 2012.

• Between 1946 and 1955 Harold Bell was ever present for Tranmere in a record 375 consecutive league games.

• Since making his debut in 1992 Sao Paulo goalkeeper Rogerio Ceni has played an incredible 1,184 games for the Brazilian outfit. No other player in the world has made as many competitive appearances for the same team.

• Spanish midfield maestro Xavi holds the record for the most appearances in the Champions League with 151 for Barcelona from 1998 to 2015.

## ARGENTINA

**First international:** Uruguay 2 Argentina 3, 1901
**Most capped player:** Javier Zanetti, 145 caps (1994-2011)
**Leading goalscorer:** Gabriel Batistuta, 56 goals (1991-2002)
**First World Cup appearance:** Argentina 1 France 0, 1930
**Biggest win:** 12-0 v Ecuador, 1942
**Heaviest defeat:** 1-6 v Czechoslovakia (1958) and v Bolivia (2009)

Outside Britain, Argentina is the oldest football nation on the planet. The roots of the game in this football-obsessed country go back to 1865, when the Buenos Aires Football Club was founded by British residents in the Argentine capital. Six clubs formed the first league in 1891, making it the oldest anywhere in the world outside Britain.

• Losing finalists in the first World Cup final in 1930, Argentina had to wait until 1978 before winning the competition for the first time, defeating Holland 3-1 on home soil. Another success, inspired by brilliant captain Diego Maradona, followed in 1986 and Argentina came close to retaining their trophy four years later, losing in the final to West Germany. After a 24-year wait they reached the final again in 2014, but narrowly lost to Germany.

• Argentina's oldest rivals are neighbours Uruguay. The two countries first met in 1901, in the first official international to be played outside Britain, with Argentina winning 3-2 in Montevideo. In the ensuing years the two sides have played each other 180 times, making the Argentina-Uruguay fixture the most played in the history of international football.

• With 14 victories to their name, Argentina have the second best record in the Copa America. In 2015 Messi and co. had a great chance to match Uruguay's record 15 wins in the competition, but they lost on penalties in the final to hosts Chile.

### HONOURS
**World Cup winners** *1978, 1986*
**Copa America winners** *1921, 1925, 1927, 1929, 1937, 1941, 1945, 1946, 1947, 1955, 1957, 1959, 1991, 1993*
**World Cup Record**
*1930 Runners-up*
*1934 Round 1*
*1938 Did not enter*
*1950 Did not enter*
*1954 Did not enter*
*1958 Round 1*
*1962 Round 1*
*1966 Quarter-finals*
*1970 Did not qualify*
*1974 Round 2*
*1978 Winners*
*1982 Round 2*
*1986 Winners*
*1990 Runners-up*
*1994 Round 2*
*1998 Quarter-finals*
*2002 Round 1*
*2006 Quarter-finals*
*2010 Quarter-finals*
*2014 Runners-up*

## ARSENAL

**Year founded:** 1886
**Ground:** Emirates Stadium (60,361)
**Previous name:** Dial Square, Royal Arsenal, Woolwich Arsenal
**Nickname:** The Gunners
**Biggest win:** 12-0 v Ashford United (1893) and v Loughborough Town (1900)
**Heaviest defeat:** 0-8 v Loughborough Town (1896)

### IS THAT A FACT?

Arsenal's 4-0 thrashing of Aston Villa in 2015 was the most emphatic victory in an FA Cup final at the new Wembley and the biggest win in the final since Manchester United beat Chelsea by the same score in 1994.

Founded as Dial Square in 1886 by workers at the Royal Arsenal in Woolwich, the club was renamed Royal Arsenal soon afterwards. Another name change, to Woolwich Arsenal, followed in 1891 when the club turned professional. Then, a year after moving north of the river to the Arsenal Stadium in 1913, the club became simply 'Arsenal'.

• One of the most successful clubs in the history of English football, Arsenal enjoyed a first golden period in the 1930s under innovative manager Herbert Chapman. The Gunners won the FA Cup for the first time in 1930 and later in the decade became only the second club to win three league titles on the trot. The first was the club Chapman managed in the 1920s, Huddersfield Town.

• Arsenal were the first club from London to win the league, topping the table in 1931 after scoring an incredible 60 goals in 21 away matches – an all-time record for the Football League.

• When they thrashed Aston Villa 4-0 in the 2015 FA Cup final Arsenal became the most successful ever club in the competition, with 12 victories to their name – one more than Manchester United. No fewer than six of those cup triumphs were achieved during the long run of current manager Arsene Wenger, who also led the Gunners to the Double in both 1998 and 2002. The north Londoners had also won the Double in 1971, and their total of three Doubles is only matched by Manchester United.

• Wenger's greatest triumph, though, came in the 2003/04 season when his team were crowned Premier League champions after going through the entire campaign undefeated. Only Preston North End had previously matched this feat, way back in 1888/89, but they had only played 22 league games compared to the 38 of Wenger's 'Invincibles'.

• The following season Arsenal extended their unbeaten run to 49 matches – setting an English league record in the process – before crashing to a bad-tempered 2-0 defeat against Manchester United at Old Trafford on 24th October 2004.

• One of the stars of that great Arsenal side was striker Thierry Henry, who is the Gunners'

*Alex Oxlade-Chamberlain learned this levitating trick from magician David Blaine*

all-time leading scorer with 228 goals in all competitions in two spells at the club between 1999 and 2012. The former fans' favourite is also the most capped Arsenal player, appearing 81 times for France during his time with the club.

• In 1989 Arsenal won the closest ever title race by beating Liverpool 2-0 at Anfield in the final match of the season to pip the Reds to the championship on goals scored (the two sides had the same goal difference). But for a last-minute goal by Gunners midfielder Michael Thomas, after Alan Smith had scored with a second-half header, the title would have stayed on Merseyside.

• Irish international defender David O'Leary made a club record 722 first-team appearances for Arsenal between 1975 and 1993.

• Arsenal endured a nightmare season in 1912/13, finishing bottom of Division One and winning just one home game during the campaign – an all-time record. However, the Gunners returned to the top flight in 1919 and have stayed there ever since – the longest unbroken run in the top tier.

• Arsenal tube station on the Piccadilly Line is the only train station in Britain to be named after a football club. It used to be called Gillespie Road, until Herbert Chapman successfully lobbied for the name change in 1932.

• Three years later, on 14th December 1935, Arsenal thrashed Aston Villa 7-1 at Villa Park. Incredibly, centre-forward Ted Drake grabbed all seven of the Gunners' goals to set a top-flight record that still stands to this day.

• Arsenal have played more games in the FA Cup (435) and won more (233) than any other club.

• Arsenal's most expensive signing is German midfielder Mesut Ozil, who cost the Gunners £42.4 million when he joined them from Real Madrid in September 2013. The club's record sale is Cesc Fabregas, who boosted the Gunners' coffers by £25.4 million when he signed for Barcelona in 2011.

• Previously famed for being a rather dull team who specialised in 1-0 victories, Arsenal have become the great entertainers in the Wenger era. Proof of the Gunners' attacking prowess came when they established an English league record by scoring in 55 consecutive matches between 2001 and 2002.

• The Gunners have a host of celebrity supporters, including novelist Nick Hornby, 'Jonathan Creek' actor Alan Davies and rapper Jay-Z. Prince Harry is also a fan, as, apparently, is his grandmother. In 2007 a Buckingham Palace spokesman surprised the football world by revealing that "Her Majesty has been fond of Arsenal for over 50 years."

HONOURS
***Division 1 champions*** *1931, 1933, 1934, 1935, 1948, 1953, 1971, 1989, 1991*
***Premier League champions*** *1998, 2002, 2004*
***FA Cup*** *1930, 1936, 1950, 1971, 1979, 1993, 1998, 2002, 2003, 2005, 2014, 2015*
***League Cup*** *1987, 1993*
***Double*** *1971, 1998, 2002*
***Fairs Cup*** *1970*
***European Cup Winners' Cup*** *1994*

# ASTON VILLA

**Year founded:** 1874
**Ground:** Villa Park (42,788)
**Nickname:** The Villans
**Biggest win:** 13-0 v Wednesbury Old Athletic (1886)
**Heaviest defeat:** 0-8 v Chelsea (2012)

One of England's most famous and distinguished clubs, Aston Villa were founded in 1874 by members of the Villa Cross Wesleyan Chapel in Aston, Birmingham. The club were founder members of the Football League in 1888, winning their first title six years later.

• The most successful team of the Victorian era, Villa became only the second club to win the league and FA Cup Double in 1897 (Preston North End were the first in 1889). Villa's manager at the time was the legendary George Ramsay, who went on to guide the Villans to six league titles and six FA Cups – a trophy haul which has only been surpassed by Liverpool's Bob Paisley and, more recently, former Manchester United boss Sir Alex Ferguson.

• Ramsay is also the second longest serving manager in the history of English football, taking charge of the Villans for

an incredible 42 years between 1884 and 1926. Only West Brom's Fred Everiss has managed a club for longer, racking up 46 years' service at the Hawthorns.

• Although they slipped as low as the old Third Division in the early 1970s, Villa have spent more time in the top flight than any other club apart from Everton (105 seasons compared to the Toffees' 113). The two clubs have played each other 200 times to date, making Aston Villa v Everton the most played fixture in the history of league football.

• Villa won the last of their seven league titles in 1980/81, when manager Ron Saunders used just 14 players throughout the whole campaign – equalling Liverpool's record set in 1965/66. The following season Villa became only the fourth English club to win the European Cup when they beat Bayern Munich 1-0 in the final in Rotterdam.

• In 1961 Villa won the League Cup in the competition's inaugural season, beating Rotherham 3-2 in a two-legged final. The Villans are the joint-second most successful side in the tournament behind Liverpool with five triumphs, and have won more games (135) and scored more goals (457) in the competition than any other club.

• In two spells at Villa Park defender Steve Staunton won a club record 64 caps for the Republic of Ireland between 1991 and 2002.

• Stalwart defender Charlie Aitken made more appearances for the club than any other player, turning out in 657 games between 1959 and 1976. Villa's all-time top goalscorer is Billy Walker, who found the back of the net an incredible 244 times between 1919 and 1933.

• Walker helped Villa bang in 128 league goals in the 1930/31 season, a record for the top flight which is unlikely ever to be broken. In the same campaign Tom 'Pongo' Waring scored a club record 49 league goals.

• Before FA Cup semi-finals moved to Wembley, Villa Park staged a record 55 of these fixtures. The stadium has also hosted 16 England internationals and was the first venue to be used by the national team in three different centuries.

• Villa's biggest league win came back in 1892 when they thrashed Accrington Stanley 12-2 in Division One – no side

ASTON VILLA

has scored more goals in a top-flight fixture. Six years earlier, though, the club recorded their biggest ever victory in the FA Cup, humiliating Wednesbury Old Athletic 13-0.

• **Villa splashed out a club record £18 million on Sunderland striker Darren Bent in 2011. Four years later the Villans received a club record £32.5 million when striker Christian Benteke moved to Liverpool.**

*Aston Villa players get together regularly for group bonding sessions*

• Famous Villa fans include punk violinist Nigel Kennedy, Prince William and David Cameron, who is a nephew of former club chairman Sir William Dugdale.

*Returning to Atletico Madrid has clearly been a hair-raising experience for Fernando Torres*

## ATLETICO MADRID

**Year founded:** 1903
**Ground:** Estadio Vicente Calderon (54,960)
**Previous names:** Athletic Club de Madrid, Athletic Aviacion de Madrid
**Nickname:** El Atleti
**League titles:** 10
**Domestic cups:** 10
**European cups:** 5
**International cups:** 1

The club was founded in 1903 by breakaway members of Madrid FC (later Real Madrid). In 1939, following a merger with the Spanish air force team, the club became known as Athletic Aviacion de Madrid before becoming plain Atletico Madrid eight years later.

• Atletico are the third most successful club in Spanish football history with 10 La Liga triumphs under their belt. The most recent of these came in 2014 when Atleti drew 1-1 at runners-up Barcelona on the last day of the season to become the first side for a decade to break the Barca/Real Madrid duopoly.

• Atletico have enjoyed European success in recent years, winning the Europa League in both 2010 and 2012 to become the first club to claim European football's newest competition

on two occasions. Atleti also reached the Champions League final in 2014 but lost 4-1 after extra-time to city rivals Real Madrid.

• Over the last decade Atletico have made a habit of selling their star striker to English clubs in mega-money deals with Fernando Torres (£20 million to Liverpool in 2007), Sergio Aguero (£38 million to Manchester City in 2012) and Diego Costa (£32 million to Chelsea in 2014) all leaving the Spanish capital for the Premier League.

### HONOURS
***Spanish League winners*** *1940, 1941, 1950, 1951, 1966, 1970, 1973, 1977, 1996, 2014*
***Spanish Cup*** *1960, 1961, 1965, 1972, 1976, 1985, 1991, 1992, 1996, 2013*
***European Cup Winners' Cup*** *1962*
***Europa League*** *2010, 2012*
***European Super Cup*** *2010, 2012*
***Intercontinental Cup*** *1974*

## ATTENDANCES

The Maracana Stadium in Rio de Janeiro holds the world record for a football match attendance, 199,854 spectators having watched the final match of the 1950 World Cup between Brazil and Uruguay. Most of the fans, though, went home in tears after Uruguay came from

behind to win 2-1 and claim the trophy for a second time.

• The biggest crowd at a match in Britain was for the first ever FA Cup final at Wembley in 1923. The official attendance for the match between Bolton and West Ham was 126,047, although, with thousands more fans gaining entry without paying, the actual crowd was estimated at 150,000-200,000. The record official attendance for a match in Britain is 149,547, set in 1937 for Scotland's 3-1 victory over England in the Home International Championship at Hampden Park.

• In 1948 a crowd of 83,260 watched Manchester United entertain Arsenal at Maine Road (United's temporary home in the post-war years after Old Trafford suffered bomb damage), a record for the Football League. The following year, on 27th December 1949, the 44 Football League games played that day were watched by a record aggregate of 1,272,815 fans – an average of 28,913 per match.

• On 15th April 1970 the biggest crowd ever to watch a European Cup tie, 135,826, crammed into Hampden Park in Glasgow to see Celtic beat Leeds United 2-1 in the semi-final second leg.

• Celtic's arch rivals Rangers hold the British record for a league match attendance. On 2nd January 1939 a vast crowd of 118,567 piled through the Ibrox turnstiles to see the Gers defeat Celtic 2-1.

• A record average crowd of 68,991 watched the 52 matches at the 1994 World Cup in the USA.

| AVERAGE CHAMPIONSHIP HOME ATTENDANCES 2014/15 | |
|---|---|
| 1. Derby County | 29,231 |
| 2. Norwich City | 26,342 |
| 3. Brighton & Hove Albion | 25,644 |
| 4. Leeds United | 24,051 |
| 5. Nottingham Forest | 23,492 |
| 6. Wolverhampton Wanderers | |
| | 22,418 |
| 7. Sheffield Wednesday | 21,992 |
| 8. Cardiff City | 21,123 |
| 9. Ipswich Town | 19,602 |
| 10. Middlesbrough | 19,562 |

## LEIGHTON BAINES

**Born:** Kirkby, 11th December 1984
**Position:** Defender
**Club career:**
2002-07 Wigan Athletic 145 (4)
2007- Everton 262 (23)
**International record:**
2010- England 30 (1)

When Everton left-back Leighton Baines crossed for Steven Naismith to head in against Manchester City on 10th January 2015 it was his 45th Premier League assist – a record for the competition for a defender.

• Baines began his career at Wigan, with whom he rose from the third tier to the Premier League in just three seasons between 2003 and 2005. A £6 million switch to Everton followed in 2007, and two years later Baines helped the Toffees reach the FA Cup final, but he had to settle for a runners-up medal after a 2-1 defeat by Chelsea.

• Voted into the PFA Premier League Team of the Year in both 2012 and 2013, Baines is the first player in Premier League history to have taken more than 10 penalties and scored them all. He finally failed from the spot in October 2014 when Manchester United keeper David de Gea saved his penalty.

• An attack-minded player who is known for his ability to whip in dangerous crosses from the left side, Baines won his first England cap in a 3-1 friendly win over Egypt at Wembley in March 2010. He scored his first international goal in a 5-0 rout of Moldova in September 2012 and was England's first-choice left-back at the 2014 World Cup in Brazil.

## GARETH BALE

**Born:** Cardiff, 16th July 1989
**Position:** Winger
**Club career:**
2006-07 Southampton 40 (5)
2007-13 Tottenham Hotspur 146 (22)
2013- Real Madrid 58 (28)
**International record:**
2006- Wales 50 (17)

Gareth Bale became the most expensive player in football history when he moved from Tottenham to Real Madrid for a world record transfer fee of £86 million in August 2013. The Welshman enjoyed a brilliant first season in the Spanish capital, scoring in Real's victories in both the Copa del Rey final and the Champions League final. Bale's second year at the Bernabeu was rather less successful, but he did score for Real in their Club World Cup final victory over Argentina's San Lorenzo.

• Bale began his career at Southampton, where he became the second youngest player to debut for the club (behind Theo Walcott) when he appeared in a 2-0 win against Millwall in the Championship in April 2006. The following season his outstanding displays for the Saints earned him the Football League Young Player of the Year award.

• In the summer of 2007 Bale joined Tottenham for an initial fee of £5 million. Incredibly, he failed to feature on the winning side for Spurs in his first 24 league games – a Premier League record – but once he had buried that jinx his form rapidly improved, and he was soon being hailed as one of the most exciting talents in the game.

• Bale enjoyed an outstanding season with Spurs in 2010/11 and at the end of the campaign he was named PFA Player of the Year – only the fourth Welshman to receive this honour. He was also the only Premier League player to be voted into the UEFA Team of the Year for 2011. He had an even better season in 2012/13, picking up both Player of the Year gongs and the PFA Young Player of the Year award – only the second player, after Cristiano Ronaldo, to collect this individual treble.

• When Bale scored his first international goal, in a 5-1 home defeat by Slovakia in 2006, he become his country's youngest ever scorer aged 17 and 35 days. In June 2015 he won his 50th cap, a milestone he celebrated in great style by scoring the winner against Belgium in a vital Euro 2016 qualifier.

*Gareth Bale, the world's most expensive player*

## IS THAT A FACT?

Serial bad boy El-Hadji Diouf was investigated by police in September 2009 after allegedly making a racist comment to a white ball boy during Blackburn's 3-0 defeat at Everton. The Rovers striker defended himself afterwards, saying the ball boy had thrown the ball to him "like a bone to a dog".

### BALL BOYS

Ball boys developed from a gimmick employed by Chelsea in the 1905/06 season. To emphasise the extraordinary bulk of the team's 23-stone goalkeeper, William 'Fatty' Foulke, two young boys would stand behind his goal. They soon proved themselves useful in retrieving the ball when it went out of play, and so the concept of the ball boy was born.

• Amazingly, a ball boy scored a goal in a match between Santacruzense and Atletico Sorocaba in Brazil in 2006. Santacruzense were trailing 1-0 when one of their players fired wide in the last minute. Instead of handing the ball back to the Atletico goalkeeper, the ball boy kicked it into the net and the goal was awarded by the female referee despite the angry protests of the Atletico players.

• Manchester City ball boys were strongly reprimanded by the fourth official in December 2008 after one of them threw the ball at, rather than to, Manchester United's Cristiano Ronaldo as he waited to take a corner at the Etihad.

• Armenia striker Gevorg Ghazaryan was sent off in September 2012 after kicking a stray ball at a ball boy during a World Cup qualifier away to Bulgaria. The ball boy, Bozhidar Atanasov, was also dismissed for swearing at Ghazaryan, but was unrepentant afterwards, saying, "The fourth official shouted, 'You, out!' But it was the coolest day of my life!"

• Seventeen-year-old Swansea ball boy Charlie Morgan helped his side reach the League Cup final in 2013 by falling on top of the ball when Chelsea's Eden Hazard wanted to take a corner kick. Frustrated at the lad's refusal to return the ball quickly, Hazard kicked it out from under him and was promptly shown a red card that pretty much ended Chelsea's chances of overhauling a two-goal deficit from the first leg.

### BALLS

The laws of football specify that the ball must be an air-filled sphere with a circumference of 68-70cm and a weight before the start of the game of 410-450g. Before the first plastic footballs appeared in the 1950s, balls were made from leather and in wet conditions would become progressively heavier, sometimes actually doubling in weight.

• Most modern footballs are made in Pakistan, especially in the city of Sialkot, and are usually stitched from 32 panels of waterproofed leather or plastic. In the past child labour was often used in the production of the balls but, following pressure from UNICEF and the International Labour Organisation, manufacturers agreed in 1997 not to employ underage workers.

• Adidas have supplied the official ball for the World Cup since 1970. The ball for the 2014 tournament in Brazil, the Brazuca, was considered vastly superior to its predecessor, the Jabulani, which was widely thought to be the worst in the competition's history, its unpredictable trajectory attracting much criticism from players, managers and fans.

• Nike are the official supplier of balls for the Premier League, taking over the role from Mitre in 2000. A winter 'Hi-Vis' yellow ball has been used in the league since the 2004/05 season.

• Nike are also the official supplier of

*Nike's new Serie A ball goes especially well with pink boots!*

balls for the FA Cup, and in the 2013/14 season the company introduced a new 'mango' ball for the competition. Hull's James Chester was the first player to score in the final with the mango ball, netting in his side's 3-2 defeat by Arsenal in 2014.

• Remarkably, the ball burst during both the 1946 and 1947 FA Cup finals at Wembley – an unlikely coincidence which was probably caused by the poor quality of leather available after the Second World War.

## MARIO BALOTELLI

**Born:** Palermo, Italy, 12th August 1990
**Position:** Striker
**Club career:**
2005-06 Lumezzane 2 (0)
2007-10 Inter Milan 59 (20)
2010-12 Manchester City 54 (20)
2013- 14 AC Milan 43 (26)
2014- Liverpool 15 (1)
2015- AC Milan (loan)
**International record:**
2010- Italy 33 (13)

One of the most unpredictable players in world football, Liverpool striker Mario Balotelli endured a difficult first season at Anfield, scoring just one Premier League goal, after joining the Reds from AC Milan for £16 million. He was subsequently loaned back to AC Milan in August 2015. Previously, Balotelli had played a big part in Manchester City's recent successes, being voted Man of the Match when they beat Stoke in the 2011 FA Cup final, and then helping the club win a first Premier League title the following year.

• Arguably, though, Balotelli is more famous for his madcap antics off the pitch than for anything he has done on the field of play. These include setting off fireworks in his bathroom, throwing darts at a youth team player and turning his garden into a quad bike course.

• The son of Ghanaian immigrants to Sicily who was cared for by foster parents as a child, Balotelli rose to prominence with Inter Milan. In November 2008 he became the club's youngest ever scorer in the Champions League when, aged 18 years and 85 days, he netted in a 3-3 draw against Cypriot outfit Anorthosis Famagusta. He helped Inter win consecutive Serie A titles between 2008 and 2010, but his lax attitude to training and volatile personality did not impress then Inter boss Jose Mourinho and he was sold to City for £23.5 million in August 2010.

• In the same year Balotelli became the first black player to represent Italy at full international level when he played in a 1-0 friendly defeat against Ivory Coast. Two years later he starred for the Azzurri at Euro 2012, scoring both Italy's goals in their 2-1 semi-final defeat of Germany. However, Balotelli was less effective at the 2014 World Cup, despite scoring Italy's winner in their opening match against England.

## BARCELONA

**Year founded:** 1899
**Ground:** Nou Camp (99,786)
**Nickname:** Barça
**League titles:** 23
**Domestic cups:** 27
**European cups:** 17
**International cups:** 2

One of the most famous and popular clubs in the world, Barcelona were founded in 1899 by bank worker Joan Gamper, a former captain of Swiss club Basel. The club were founder members and first winners of the Spanish championship, La Liga, in 1928 and have remained in the top flight of Spanish football ever since.

• For the people of Catalonia, Barcelona is more like a national team than a mere club. As former manager Bobby Robson once succinctly put it, "Catalonia is a country and FC Barcelona is their army."

*Barcelona are the only club to have won the Treble twice*

*Everton fans are banking on Ross Barkley to pay dividends*

• Along with Ajax, Juventus, Bayern Munich and Chelsea, Barcelona are one of just five clubs to have won three different European trophies: the European Cup/Champions League, the European Cup Winners' Cup (a record four times) and the Fairs Cup (Barça being the first winners of the competition in 1958).

• **With a capacity of 99,786, Barcelona's Nou Camp Stadium is the largest in Europe. Among the stadium's many facilities are a museum which attracts over one million visitors a year, mini training pitches and a chapel for the players.**

• For many years Barcelona played second fiddle to bitter rivals Real Madrid. Finally, in the 1990s, under former player-turned-coach Johan Cruyff, Barça turned the tables on the team from the Spanish capital, winning four La Liga titles on the trot between 1991 and 1994. Cruyff also led the Catalans to a first taste of glory in the European Cup, Barcelona beating Sampdoria at Wembley in 1992. The club have since won the Champions League on four more occasions, most recently beating

Juventus 3-1 in the 2015 final to become the first European club to win the treble twice (the first occasion was in 2009).

• **With 27 victories to their name, Barcelona have won the Copa del Rey (the Spanish version of the FA Cup) more times than any other club.**

HONOURS
*Spanish League* 1929, 1945, 1948, 1949, 1952, 1953, 1959, 1960, 1974, 1985, 1991, 1992, 1993, 1994, 1998, 1999, 2005, 2006, 2009, 2010, 2011, 2013, 2015
*Spanish Cup* 1910, 1912, 1913, 1920, 1922, 1925, 1926, 1928, 1942, 1951, 1952, 1953, 1957, 1959, 1963, 1968, 1971, 1978, 1981, 1983, 1988, 1990, 1997, 1998, 2009, 2012, 2015
*European Cup/Champions League* 1992, 2006, 2009, 2011, 2015
*European Cup Winners' Cup* 1979, 1982, 1989, 1997
*Fairs Cup* 1958, 1960, 1961
*European Super Cup* 1992, 1997, 2009, 2011, 2015
*Club World Cup* 2009, 2011

## ROSS BARKLEY

**Born:** Liverpool, 5th December 1993
**Position:** Midfielder
**Club career:**
2010- Everton 76 (8)
2012 Sheffield Wednesday (loan) 13 (4)
2013 Leeds United (loan) 4 (0)
**International record:**
2013- England 13 (0)

Hailed by Everton manager Roberto Martinez as "a mix of Paul Gascoigne and Michael Ballack", Ross Barkley is one of the most exciting young English players in the Premier League.

• **After joining Everton as an 11-year-old, Barkley recovered from a triple leg fracture when he was 16 to make his debut against QPR in 2011, before spending much of the next year on loan at Sheffield Wednesday and Leeds United.**

• A strong player who loves to drive forward from midfield, Barkley scored his first goal for Everton in a 2-2 draw at Norwich on the opening day of the

2013/14 season with a long-range strike. His eye-catching performances during the rest of the campaign saw him shortlisted for the PFA Young Player of the Year award, although he was eventually pipped to top spot by Chelsea's Eden Hazard.

• Barkley played for England at all levels from Under-16 to Under-21, helping his country win the Under-17 European Championships in 2010 after a 2-1 victory over Spain in the final. He won his first full cap as a sub against Moldova in September 2013 and the following year was included in Roy Hodgson's England squad for the 2014 World Cup.

## BARNET

**Year founded:** 1888
**Ground:** The Hive Stadium (5,100)
**Previous name:** Barnet Alston FC
**Nickname:** The Bees
**Biggest win:** 7-0 v Blackpool (2000)
**Heaviest defeat:** 1-9 v Peterborough United (1998)

Founded in 1888, Barnet spent more than a hundred years in non-league football before finally gaining promotion to the Football League after winning the Conference in 1991. The Bees have since twice suffered the agony of losing their league status, but claimed the Conference title in both 2005 and 2015 to become the first club ever to win the fifth tier of English football on three occasions.

• Barnet may not be London's most high-profile club, but some famous names have been associated with the Bees over the years. Legendary England marksman Jimmy Greaves played for Barnet at the end of his career in the late 1970s, while fellow internationals Ray Clemence, Alan Mullery and Tony Cottee have all managed the club at some point.

• In 1994/95 striker Dougie Freedman scored a Bees best 24 league goals during the season. His goalscoring feats made him a hot property and he soon moved on to Crystal Palace for a club record £800,000.

• In 1946 the first live televised football match was broadcast by the BBC from Barnet's old Underhill Stadium. Around 75 minutes of the Bees' fixture with Wealdstone were screened before the broadcast was pulled because it got too dark!

HONOURS
*Conference champions* 1991, 2005, 2015
*FA Amateur Cup* 1946

## BARNSLEY

**Year founded:** 1887
**Ground:** Oakwell (23,009)
**Previous name:** Barnsley St Peter's
**Nickname:** The Tykes
**Biggest win:** 9-0 v Loughborough United (1899)
**Heaviest defeat:** 0-9 v Notts County (1927)

Founded as the church team Barnsley St Peter's in 1887 by the Rev Tiverton Preedy, the club changed to their present name a year after joining the Football League in 1898.

• **The Tykes have spent more seasons (76) in the second tier of English football than any other club and had to wait until 1997 before they had their first taste of life in the top flight. Unfortunately for their fans, it lasted just one season.**

• The Yorkshiremen's finest hour came in 1912 when they won the FA Cup, beating West Bromwich Albion 1-0 in a replay. The club were nicknamed 'Battling Barnsley' that season as they played a record 12 games during their cup run, including six 0-0 draws, before finally getting their hands on the trophy. Barnsley came close to repeating this feat in 2008, but were beaten in the semi-finals by fellow Championship side Cardiff City after they had sensationally knocked out Liverpool and cup holders Chelsea.

• **The youngest player to appear in the Football League is Barnsley striker Reuben Noble-Lazarus, who was 15 years and 45 days old when he faced Ipswich Town in September 2008. Afterwards, Barnsley boss Simon Davey joked Noble-Lazarus would be rewarded with a pizza as he was too young to be paid!**

• Stalwart defender Barry Murphy made a club record 514 league appearances for the Tykes between 1962 and 1978.

HONOURS
*Division 3 (N) champions* 1934, 1939, 1955
*FA Cup* 1912

## BAYERN MUNICH

**Year founded:** 1900
**Ground:** Allianz Arena (75,000)
**Nickname:** The Bavarians
**League titles:** 25
**Domestic cups:** 17
**European cups:** 7

The biggest and most successful club in Germany, Bayern Munich were founded in 1900 by members of a Munich gymnastics club. Incredibly, when the Bundesliga was formed in 1963, Bayern's form was so poor they were not invited to become founder members of the league. But, thanks to the emergence in the mid-1960s of legendary players like goalkeeper Sepp Maier, sweeper Franz Beckenbauer and prolific goalscorer Gerd Muller, Bayern rapidly became the dominant force in German football. The club won the Bundesliga for the first time in 1969 and now have a record 25 German championships to their name.

• **In 1974 Bayern became the first German club to win the European Cup, defeating Atletico Madrid 4-0 in the only final to go to a replay. Skippered by the imperious Beckenbauer, the club went on to complete a hat-trick**

**TOP 10**

**GERMAN CUP WINS**

| | | |
|---|---|---|
| 1. Bayern Munich | 17 wins |
| 2. Werder Bremen | 6 wins |
| 3. Schalke | 5 wins |
| 4. Cologne | 4 wins |
| 5. Nuremberg | 4 wins |
| 6. Eintracht Frankfurt | 4 wins |
| 7. Borussia Dortmund | 3 wins |
| Hamburg | 3 wins |
| Stuttgart | 3 wins |
| Borussia Monchengladbach | 3 wins |

of victories in the competition – the last time a club has won Europe's top prize three times on the spin.

• In winning the Bundesliga title in 2012/13, Bayern set numerous records, including highest points total (91), most wins (29) and best goal difference (+80). They then beat Borussia Dortmund 2-1 at Wembley in the first all-German Champions

League final, before becoming the first ever German team to win the Treble when they beat Stuttgart 3-2 in the final of the German Cup.

• **With over 250,000 registered fans, Bayern have the second largest membership of any club in the world after Benfica.**

• Champions League records held by Bayern Munich include biggest aggregate wins in the knock-out stages (12-1 v Sporting Lisbon in 2009) and semi-final (7-0 v Barcelona in 2013) and the fastest ever goal in the competition, scored by Roy Makaay after just 10 seconds against Real Madrid in 2007.

*Despite shaving most of his hair off, Bayern Munich's Arturo Vidal still suffered from terrible dandruff*

HONOURS
*German championship* 1932, 1969, 1972, 1973, 1974, 1980, 1981, 1985, 1986, 1987, 1989, 1990, 1994, 1997, 1999, 2000, 2001, 2003, 2005, 2006, 2008, 2010, 2013, 2014, 2015
*German Cup* 1957, 1966, 1967, 1969, 1971, 1982, 1984, 1986, 1998, 2000, 2003, 2005, 2006, 2008, 2010, 2013, 2014
*European Cup/Champions League* 1974, 1975, 1976, 2001, 2013
*European Cup Winners' Cup* 1967
*UEFA Cup* 1996
*Club World Cup* 2013

## FRANZ BECKENBAUER

**Born:** Munich, Germany, 11th September 1945
**Position:** Defender
**Club career:**
1964-77 Bayern Munich 427 (60)
1977-80 New York Cosmos 105 (19)
1980-82 Hamburg 28 (0)
1983 New York Cosmos 29 (2)
**International record:**
1965-77 West Germany 103 (14)

Germany's greatest ever player, Franz Beckenbauer's elegant playing style and outstanding leadership qualities earned him the nickname 'Der Kaiser' ('The Emperor'). Having started out as a midfielder, Beckenbauer created and defined the role of the offensive 'sweeper' in the late 1960s, turning defence into attack with surging runs from the back.

• **Beckenbauer enjoyed huge success at both club and international level. He captained Bayern Munich to three consecutive victories in the European Cup between 1974 and 1976, matching Ajax's treble earlier in the decade. As skipper of West Germany, Beckenbauer led his country to victory in the 1972 European Championships, and two years later he cemented his reputation as a national icon by collecting the World Cup trophy after a 2-1 defeat of the Netherlands in the 1974 final in Munich.**

• His consistent performances won him the European Footballer of the Year award in 1972 and 1976 – the first German player to win the award twice. He was also voted German Footballer of the Year a record four times: in 1966, 1968, 1974 and 1976.

• More success followed for Beckenbauer in the late 1970s after he accepted a lucrative offer to play in America, his New York Cosmos side winning the NASL Soccer Bowl in 1977, 1978 and 1980.

• Beckenbauer was appointed manager of West Germany in 1986 and when, four years later, his country triumphed at Italia '90 'Der Kaiser' became the first man to both captain and coach a World Cup-winning team. Later, in 1996, he led Bayern Munich to glory in the UEFA Cup, before becoming the driving force behind Germany's successful bid to host the 2006 World Cup.

## DAVID BECKHAM

**Born:** Leytonstone, 2nd May 1975
**Position:** Midfielder
**Club career:**
1993-2003 Manchester United 265 (62)
1995 Preston North End (loan) 5 (2)
2003-07 Real Madrid 116 (13)
2007-12 LA Galaxy 98 (18)
2009 AC Milan (loan) 18 (2)
2010 AC Milan (loan) 11 (0)
2013 Paris St Germain 10 (0)
**International record:**
1996-2009 England 115 (17)

One of the most famous names on the planet, David Beckham's fame extends far beyond the world of football. Yet, for all the interest in his marriage to Spice Girl Victoria Beckham, his fashion sense, his eye-catching haircuts and tattoos, it shouldn't be forgotten that his celebrity status stems primarily from his remarkable ability on the ball.

• **A superb crosser of the ball and free kick expert, at his peak Beckham was probably the best right-sided midfielder in the world. He twice came close to winning the World Player of the Year award, finishing as runner-up in 1999 and 2001.**

• Beckham enjoyed huge success with his first club Manchester United, winning six Premiership titles, two FA Cups and, as the final leg of the Treble, the Champions League in 1999. However, his glamorous lifestyle began to irritate United boss Sir Alex Ferguson, and the deteriorating relationship between the pair led to Beckham's departure to Spanish giants Real Madrid in 2003.

*David Beckham celebrates the fact that he is England's highest capped outfield player*

• **As one of Real's 'galacticos', Beckham was part of a team which was much hyped but frequently failed to deliver. He eventually won the Spanish title with Real in 2007, shortly before making a lucrative move to Major League Soccer in the USA with LA Galaxy, with whom he twice won the MLS championship. In 2013, shortly before announcing his retirement from the game, he enjoyed a brief spell with Paris St Germain, helping them to win the French league to become the first**

British player to win titles in four different countries.

• One of just nine England centurions and the only Three Lions player to have scored at three different World Cups, Beckham captained his country from 2000 to 2006. After being sent off against Argentina at the 1998 World Cup he was made the scapegoat for England's elimination from the competition, but famously bounced back to score the winning goal from the penalty spot against the same opposition at the 2002 tournament in Japan and South Korea.

• Beckham's England career appeared to be over when he was dropped from the squad by new manager Steve McClaren in 2006. However, he was recalled the following year and was rewarded with his 100th cap by McClaren's successor, his former Real boss Fabio Capello, against France in 2008. The following year he became England's most capped outfield player, beating the old record set by the great Bobby Moore, when he won his 109th cap against Slovakia. Sadly for Beckham, injury ruled him out of the 2010 World Cup, effectively ending his international career.

## TOP 10

### HIGHEST CAPPED ENGLAND PLAYERS

| | Player | Caps |
|---|---|---|
| 1. | Peter Shilton (1970-90) | 125 |
| 2. | David Beckham (1996-2009) | 115 |
| 3. | Steven Gerrard (2000-14) | 114 |
| 4. | Bobby Moore (1962-73) | 108 |
| 5. | Ashley Cole (2001-14) | 107 |
| 6. | Bobby Charlton (1958-70) | 106 |
| | Frank Lampard (1999-2014) | 106 |
| 8. | Billy Wright (1946-59) | 105 |
| | Wayne Rooney (2003- ) | 105 |
| 10. | Bryan Robson (1980-91) | 90 |

# BELGIUM

*People who say nothing interesting ever comes out of Belgium clearly haven't watched Kevin De Bruyne and the rest of the lads in action recently*

## BENFICA

**Year founded:** 1904
**Ground:** Estadio Da Luz, Lisbon (65,647)
**Nickname:** The Eagles
**League titles:** 34
**Domestic cups:** 28
**European cups:** 2

## BELGIUM

**First international:** Belgium 3 France 3, 1904
**Most capped player:** Jan Ceulemans, 96 caps (1977-91)
**Leading goalscorer:** Bernard Voorhoof (1928-40) and Paul Van Himst (1960-74), 30 goals
**First World Cup appearance:** Belgium 2 Germany 5
**Biggest win:** Belgium 10 San Marino 1, 2001
**Heaviest defeat:** England amateurs 11 Belgium 2, 1909

A rising force in the world game, Belgium are yet to win a major trophy but they came mighty close in the 1980 European championships in Italy. After topping their group, ahead of the hosts, England and Spain, Belgium went straight through to the final against West Germany where they were unfortunate to go down 2-1 in a close encounter.

• Belgium's best performance at the World Cup came in 1986 when, after beating the USSR and Spain in the earlier knock-out rounds, they lost 2-0 to a Diego Maradona-inspired Argentina in the semi-finals. After losing 4-2 in the third place match to France, Belgium had to be content with fourth spot at the tournament.

• Following an impressive World Cup qualifying campaign, a young Belgian side featuring the likes of goalkeeper Thibaut Courtois, Manchester City skipper Vincent Kompany and Chelsea midfielder Eden Hazard, were given top-seed status in the draw for the 2014 World Cup. The Belgians lived up to their billing, reaching the last eight for only the second time in their history before bowing out to Argentina.

• Hosts Belgium won the 1920 Olympic football tournament, despite the final against Czechoslovakia being abandoned after 40 minutes when the Czechs walked off the pitch in protest at the sending-off of one of their players. To the fury of the Czechs, the Olympic committee decided that the score at the time – 2-0 to Belgium – should stand as the final result.

Portugal's most successful club, Benfica were founded in 1904 at a meeting of 24 football enthusiasts in south Lisbon. The club were founder members of the Portuguese league in 1933 and have since won the title a record 34 times.

• With 270,000 registered members, Benfica is officially the biggest club in the world, ahead of Bayern Munich and Barcelona.

• Inspired by legendary striker Eusebio, Benfica enjoyed a golden era in the 1960s when the club won eight domestic championships. In 1961 Benfica became the first team to break Real Madrid's dominance in the European Cup when they beat Barcelona 3-2 in the final. The following year, the trophy stayed in Lisbon after the Eagles sensationally beat Real 5-3 in the final in Amsterdam.

• In 1972/73 Benfica went the whole season undefeated – the first Portuguese team to achieve this feat – winning a staggering 28 and drawing just two of their 30 league matches.

The great Eusebio struck 40 goals that season to top the European scoring charts as Benfica were crowned champions once again.

• Benfica hold the record for the biggest ever aggregate win in the European Cup/Champions League with an astonishing 18-0 thrashing of Luxembourg minnows Stade Dudelange in 1965.

HONOURS

*Portuguese championship* 1936, 1937, 1938, 1942, 1943, 1945, 1950, 1955, 1957,1960, 1961, 1963, 1964, 1965, 1967, 1968, 1969,1971, 1972, 1973, 1975,1976, 1977, 1981, 1983, 1984, 1987, 1989, 1991, 1994, 2005, 2010, 2014, 2015

*Portuguese Cup* 1930, 1931, 1935, 1940, 1943, 1944, 1949, 1951, 1952, 1953, 1955, 1957, 1959, 1962,1964, 1969, 1970, 1972, 1980, 1981,1983, 1985, 1986, 1987, 1993, 1996, 2004, 2014

*European Cup* 1961, 1962

## CHRISTIAN BENTEKE

**Born:** Kinshasa, DR Congo, 3rd December 1990
**Position:** Striker
**Club career:**
2007-09 Genk 10 (1)
2009-11 Standard Liege 18 (3)
2009-10 Kortrijk (loan) 34 (15)
2010- 11 Mechelen (loan) 18 (6)
2011-12 Genk 37 (19)
2012-15 Aston Villa 88 (42)
2015- Liverpool
**International record:**
2010- Belgium 24 (7)

When he moved from Aston Villa to Liverpool for £32.5 million in July 2015 Christian Benteke became the most expensive player ever to leave Villa Park and the Reds' second most expensive player ever.

• But for Benteke's goals in the second half of the 2014/15 season Villa would surely have been

relegated from the Premier League for the first time. The powerfully-built Belgian was on target 11 times in the last three months of the campaign, one of a number of Villa players to be completely revitalised under new boss Tim Sherwood. Benteke's best season with the club, though, was in 2012/13 when he scored 19 league goals – a record tally for a Villa player in a single Premier League campaign.

• Born in DR Congo, Benteke fled to Belgium as a child with his family to escape the dictatorial regime of President Mobutu. He played for a number of Belgian clubs, including Genk and Standard Liege, before joining Villa for £7 million from Genk in August 2012.

• **Benteke made his debut for Belgium against Bulgaria in 2010. Injury deprived him of a chance to shine at the 2014 World Cup but he has since regained his place in the national side at the expense of Romelu Lukaku.**

## KARIM BENZEMA

**Born:** Lyon, France, 19th December 1987
**Position:** Striker
**Club career:**
2004-09 Lyon 112 (43)
2009- Real Madrid 188 (87)
**International record:**
2007- France 77 (25)

Real Madrid striker Karim Benzema is easily the highest-scoring French forward in the history of La Liga, with a total of 87 goals for the Spanish giants.

• **A strong and powerful runner who can shoot accurately with both feet,** Benzema rose to prominence with his hometown club, Lyon, enjoying a superb season in 2008/09 when he was voted Ligue 1 Player of the Year. He then moved on to Real for £30 million, but initially struggled in the Spanish capital, gaining weight and famously being described as 'listless' by then manager Jose Mourinho.

• Benzema's form picked up, though, and in 2014 he played a key role in Real's record 10th Champions League success after they beat city rivals Atletico Madrid 4-1 in the final in Lisbon. In the same year he was voted French Player of the Year for the third time. In

*£32.5 million Christian Benteke is Liverpool's second most expensive player ever*

September 2014 Benzema scored Real Madrid's record 1,000th goal in European competition when he notched his side's fifth in a 5-1 Champions League group stage hammering of Basle.

• **After missing out on the 2010 World Cup due to his poor club form, Benzema was desperate to do well at the tournament four years later in Brazil. He didn't disappoint, finishing as France's top scorer with three goals.**

## GEORGE BEST

**Born:** Belfast, 22nd May 1946
**Died:** 25th November 2005
**Position:** Winger
**Club career:**
1963-74 Manchester United 361 (138)
1975 Stockport County 3 (2)
1975-76 Cork Celtic 3 (0)
1976-77 Fulham 33 (7)
1977-78 Los Angeles Aztecs 55 (27)
1978-79 Fort Lauderdale 26 (6)
1979-80 Hibernian 22 (3)
1980-81 San Jose Earthquakes 56 (28)
1983 Bournemouth 4 (0)
**International record:**
1964-78 Northern Ireland 37 (9)

Possibly the greatest natural talent in the history of the British game, George Best was a football genius who thrilled fans everywhere with his dazzling dribbling skills, superb ball control and goalscoring ability.

• **Best left his native Northern Ireland as a youngster to play for Manchester United, making his debut at Old Trafford in 1963 when aged just 17. His most memorable achievements were all packed into the next five years as he helped fire United to two league titles in 1965 and 1967 and to glory in the European Cup in 1968, Best scoring the vital second goal against Benfica at Wembley. In 1968 he was also named Footballer of the Year and European Footballer of the Year.**

• Dubbed 'The Fifth Beatle' for his long hair and good looks, Best was the first footballer to become famous outside the game. He cashed in on his celebrity status by opening a chain of boutiques, appearing in a number of TV ads and dating a seemingly never-ending series of Miss World winners.

• **In 1970 Best scored six goals to set a still-unbeaten United record as the Red Devils thrashed Northampton**

**8-2 in an FA Cup fifth-round tie at the Cobblers' old County Ground. "I was so embarrassed that I played the last 20 minutes at left-back," he said years later.**

• There appeared to be no limit to what he might achieve, but Best's career nosedived in the 1970s as his hard-drinking, glamorous lifestyle inevitably took its toll. Sacked by Manchester United for repeatedly missing training sessions, Best played for a succession of lesser clubs in Britain and the USA, only occasionally showing flashes of his old brilliance. He eventually ended his playing career in the low-key environment of Dean Court, making four appearances for third-tier Bournemouth in 1983.

• **Easily the finest player ever to represent Northern Ireland, Best never appeared in the final stages of the World Cup or European Championships. Yet he remains idolised in his home country, his standing summed up by the popular Belfast saying: "Maradona good, Pelé better, George Best".**

• After a long battle with alcoholism, Best died in November 2005. His passing was marked by a minute's applause at grounds up and down the country – the first British player to receive this continental-style tribute.

## BIRMINGHAM CITY

**Year founded:** 1875
**Ground:** St Andrew's (30,016)
**Previous name:** Small Heath Alliance, Small Heath, Birmingham
**Nickname:** The Blues
**Biggest win:** 12-0 v Nottingham Forest (1899), Walsall Town Swifts (1892) and Doncaster Rovers (1903)
**Heaviest defeat:** 1-9 v Blackburn Rovers (1895) and Sheffield Wednesday (1930)

*Birmingham City – Britain's first ever European finalists*

Founded in 1875 as Small Heath Alliance, the club were founder members and the first champions of the Second Division in 1892. Unfortunately, Small Heath were undone at the 'test match' stage (a 19th-century version of the play-offs) and failed to gain promotion to the top flight.

• **The club had to wait until 2011 for the greatest day in their history, when the Blues beat hot favourites Arsenal 2-1 in the League Cup final at Wembley, on-loan striker Obafemi Martins grabbing the winner in the final minutes to spark ecstatic celebrations among Birmingham's long-suffering fans.** City had previously won the competition back in 1963 after getting the better of arch-rivals Aston Villa over a two-legged final, although that achievement was hardly comparable as half the top-flight clubs hadn't even bothered to enter.

• However, on the final day of the 2010/11 season Birmingham were relegated from the Premier League, to become only the second club (after Norwich City in 1985) to win a major domestic trophy and suffer the drop in the same campaign. It was the 12th time in their history that the Blues had fallen through the top-flight trapdoor, a record of misery unmatched by any other club.

• **In 1956 Birmingham became the first club to reach the FA Cup final without playing a single tie at home, the Midlanders winning at Torquay, Leyton Orient, West Brom and Arsenal before seeing off Sunderland in the semi-final at Hillsborough. Perhaps, though, their tricky route to Wembley caught up with them, as they lost in the final to Manchester City.**

• On 15th May 1955 Birmingham became the first English club to compete in Europe when they drew 0-0 away to Inter Milan in the inaugural competition of the Fairs Cup.

**IS THAT A FACT?**
In 1960 Birmingham City became the first British club to reach a European final when they faced Barcelona over two legs to decide the destiny of the Fairs Cup. Sadly for Blues fans, their team lost 4-1 on aggregate.

• **England international Joe Bradford scored a club record 249 league goals for the Blues between 1920 and 1935.**

• The Blues' youngest ever player is club legend Trevor Francis, who was aged just 16 and 139 days when he made his debut against Cardiff City in 1970. Francis went on to score 133 goals for the Brummies before he became the first British player to be sold for £1 million when he joined Nottingham Forest in 1979.

HONOURS
*Division 2 champions* 1893, 1921, 1948, 1955
*Second Division champions* 1995
*League Cup* 1963, 2011
*Football League Trophy* 1991, 1995

## BLACKBURN ROVERS

**Year founded:** 1875
**Ground:** Ewood Park (31,367)
**Nickname:** Rovers
**Biggest win:** 11-0 v Rossendale United (1884)
**Heaviest defeat:** 0-8 v Arsenal (1933)

Founded in 1875 by a group of wealthy local residents and ex-public school boys, Blackburn Rovers joined the Football League as founder members in 1888. Two years later the club moved to a permanent home at Ewood Park, where they have remained ever since.

• **Blackburn were a force to be reckoned with from the start, winning the FA Cup five times in the 1880s and 1890s. Of all league clubs Rovers were the first to win the trophy, beating Scottish side Queen's Park 2-1 in the final at Kennington Oval in 1884. The Lancashire side went on to win the cup in the two following years as well, setting a record which still stands by remaining undefeated in 24 consecutive games in the competition between 1884 and 1886.**

• Rovers won the cup again in 1890, 1891 and 1928 to make a total of six triumphs in the competition. In the first of these victories they thrashed Sheffield Wednesday 6-1 in the final, with left winger William Townley scoring three times to become the first player to hit a

hat-trick in the final.

• **The club have won the league title three times: in 1912, 1914 and, most memorably, in 1995 when, funded by the millions of local steel magnate Jack Walker and powered by the deadly 'SAS' strikeforce of Alan Shearer and Chris Sutton, Rovers pipped reigning champions Manchester United to the Premiership title.** The team soon broke up, though, and Rovers were relegated from the top tier just four years later.

• Derek Fazackerley made the most appearances for Blackburn, turning out in 596 games between 1970 and 1986. The club's all-time leading scorer is Simon Garner, with 168 league goals between 1978 and 1992, although Alan Shearer's incredible record of 122 goals in just 138 games for the club is arguably more impressive.

• **Defender Walter Crook made a club record 208 consecutive league appearances for Blackburn between 1934 and 1946 – and but for the unfortunate intervention of World War II his total would have been even higher.**

• In 1955 Rovers striker Tommy Briggs scored a club record seven goals in a single match in an 8-3 thrashing of Bristol Rovers at Ewood Park.

HONOURS
*Division 1 champions* 1912, 1914
*Premier League champions* 1995
*Division 2 champions* 1975
*FA Cup* 1884, 1885, 1886, 1890, 1891, 1928
*League Cup* 2002

## BLACKPOOL

**Year founded:** 1887
**Ground:** Bloomfield Road (17,338)
**Nickname:** The Seasiders
**Biggest win:** 10-0 v Lanerossi Vincenza (1972)
**Heaviest defeat:** 1-10 v Small Heath (1901)

Founded in 1887 by old boys of St John's School, Blackpool joined the Second Division of the Football League in 1896. The club merged with South Shore in 1899, the same year in which Blackpool lost their league status for a single season.

• Blackpool's heyday was in the late 1940s and early 1950s when the club reached three FA Cup finals in five years. The Seasiders lost in the finals of 1948 and 1951 but lifted the cup in 1953 after defeating Lancashire rivals Bolton 4-3 in one of the most exciting Wembley matches ever. Although centre-forward Stan Mortensen scored a hat-trick, the match was dubbed the 'Matthews Final' after veteran winger Stanley Matthews, who finally won a winners' medal at the grand old age of 38.

• An apprentice at the time of the 'Matthews Final', long-serving right-back Jimmy Armfield holds the record for league appearances for Blackpool, with 569 between 1952 and 1971. Now a match summariser for BBC Radio Five Live, Armfield is also Blackpool's most capped player, having played for England 43 times. In 2011 a nine-foot-high statue of the Seasiders legend was unveiled outside Bloomfield Road.

• The club's record scorer is Jimmy Hampson, who hit 248 league goals between 1927 and 1938, including a season best 45 in the 1929/30 Second Division championship-winning campaign.

• Blackpool are the only club to have gained promotion from three different divisions via the play-offs, most recently rising from the Championship to the Premier League in 2010 after a thrilling 3-2 win over Cardiff City at Wembley. However, the following year Blackpool dropped back down to the Championship, despite scoring 55 league goals – a record for a relegated Premier League club.

• Blackpool conceded a top-flight record 125 goals in 1930/31 but, amazingly, just managed to avoid relegation to Division Two by

**IS THAT A FACT?**
Blackpool were relegated from the Championship in 2014/15 after picking up just 26 points – the joint-worst total for the second tier since Cambridge went down with two points fewer in 1984.

finishing a point ahead of Leeds United (who only conceded 81 goals).

> HONOURS
> *Division 2 champions* 1930
> *FA Cup* 1953
> *Football League Trophy* 2002, 2004

## BOLTON WANDERERS

**Year founded:** 1874
**Ground:** The Macron Stadium (28,723)
**Previous name:** Christ Church
**Nickname:** The Trotters
**Biggest win:** 13-0 v Sheffield United (1890)
**Heaviest defeat:** 1-9 v Preston North End (1887)

The club was founded in 1874 as Christ Church, but three years later broke away from the church after a disagreement with the vicar and adopted their present name (the 'Wanderers' part stemmed from the fact that the club had no permanent home until moving to their former stadium, Burnden Park, in 1895).

• Bolton were founder members of the Football League in 1888, finishing fifth at the end of the campaign. The Trotters have since gone on to play more seasons in the top flight without ever winning the title, 73, than any other club.

• The club, though, have had better luck in the FA Cup. After defeats in the final in 1894 and 1904, Bolton won the cup for the first time in 1923 after beating West Ham 2-0 in the first Wembley final. In the same match, Bolton centre-forward David Jack enjoyed the distinction of becoming the first player to score a goal at the new stadium. The Trotters went on to win the competition again in 1926 and 1929.

• In 1953 Bolton became the first, and so far only, team to score three goals in normal time in the FA Cup final yet finish as losers, going down 4-3 to a Stanley Matthews-inspired Blackpool. In 1958 Bolton won the cup for a fourth time, beating Manchester United 2-0 in the final at Wembley. Since then major honours have eluded the club, although the Trotters were runners-up in the League Cup in 1995 and 2004.

• In 1993, while they were in the third tier, Bolton became the last club from outside the top two flights to knock out the reigning FA Cup holders when they beat Liverpool 2-0 at Anfield in a third-round replay. The following season Wanderers, by then in the second tier, accounted for the holders again, beating Arsenal 3-1 in a fourth-round replay at Highbury.

• The club's top scorer is legendary centre-forward Nat Lofthouse, who notched 285 goals in all competitions between 1946 and 1960. The Trotters' appearance record is held by another England international of the same era, goalkeeper Eddie Hopkinson, who turned out 578 times for the club between 1952 and 1970.

• Bolton have an impressive record in continental competition, suffering just two defeats in 18 UEFA Cup matches between 2005 and 2008.

> HONOURS
> *Division 2 champions* 1909, 1978
> *First Division champions* 1997
> *Division 3 champions* 1973
> *FA Cup* 1923, 1926, 1929, 1958
> *Football League Trophy* 1989

## BOOTS

The first record of a pair of football boots goes back to 1526 when Henry VIII, then aged 35, ordered "45 velvet pairs and one leather pair for football" from the Great Wardrobe. Whether he actually donned the boots for a royal kick-around in Hampton Court or Windsor Castle is not known.

• Early leather boots were very different to the synthetic ones worn by modern players, having hard toe-caps and protection around the ankles. Studs were originally prohibited, but were sanctioned after a change in the rules in 1891. Lighter boots without ankle protection were first worn in South America, but did not become the norm in Britain until the 1950s, following the example of England international Stanley Matthews who had a lightweight pair of boots made for him by a Yorkshire company.

• Herbert Chapman, later Arsenal's manager, is believed to be the first player to wear coloured boots, sporting a yellow pair in the 1900s. White boots first became fashionable in the 1970s when they were worn by the likes of Alan Ball (Everton), Terry Cooper (Leeds) and Alan Hinton (Derby County). In 1996, Liverpool's John Barnes was the first player to wear white boots in an FA Cup final.

• **Boots, or rather the lack of them, became a major issue at the 1950 World Cup. After qualifying for the tournament for the first time, India pulled out of the finals after their players were refused permission to play barefoot!**

• In 2013 Cristiano Ronaldo signed a world record £8 million-a-year sponsorship deal with his boot manufacturers Nike. Sergio Aguero's £1.25 million-a-year deal with Puma is the most lucrative in the Premier League.

## BOURNEMOUTH

**Year founded:** 1899
**Ground:** Dean Court (11,464)
**Previous name:** Boscombe, Bournemouth and Boscombe Athletic
**Nickname:** The Cherries
**Biggest win:** 11-0 v Margate (1970)
**Heaviest defeat:** 0-9 v Lincoln City (1982)

The Cherries were founded as Boscombe FC in 1899, having their origins in the Boscombe St John's club, which was formed in 1890. The club's name changed to Bournemouth and Boscombe FC in 1923 and then to AFC Bournemouth in 1971, when the team's colours were altered to red-and-black stripes in imitation of AC Milan.

• **Any similarity to the Italian giants was not obvious, though, until the 2014/15 season when the Cherries won promotion to the top flight for the first time in their history, clinching the Championship title in some style with a 3-0 victory at Charlton on the final day of the campaign.**

• The Cherries' attack-minded team set a new record for the second tier by scoring 50 goals on their travels. They also set a new club record for goals scored in a season, with 115 in total in all competitions.

• **Perhaps Bournemouth's biggest hero was their young manager Eddie Howe, who in two spells at the club had overseen their rise from the depths of League Two to the heady heights of the Premier League. His efforts were acknowledged in May 2015**

when he was named the first Football League Manager of the Decade at the Football League awards.

• The club recorded their biggest ever win in the FA Cup, smashing fellow seasiders Margate 11-0 at Dean Court in 1970. Cherries striker Ted MacDougall scored nine of the goals, an all-time record for an individual player in the competition. It was also in the cup that Bournemouth won their most famous ever victory, beating holders Manchester United 2-0 at Dean Court in the third round in 1984.

• **Bournemouth were the first ever winners of the Football League Trophy (then known as the Associate Members' Cup) in 1984, beating Hull City 2-1 in the final at Boothferry Park.**

• The club's record scorer is Ron Eyre (202 goals between 1924 and 1933), while striker Steve Fletcher pulled on the Cherries' jersey an amazing 628 times in two spells at Dean Court between 1992 and 2013.

**HONOURS**
*Championship champions* 2015
*Division 3 champions* 1987
*Football League Trophy* 1984

'Ok, heads down everyone and maybe they'll think we're AC Milan'

## BRADFORD CITY

**Year founded:** 1903
**Ground:** Valley Parade (25,136)
**Nickname:** The Bantams
**Biggest win:** 11-1 v Rotherham United (1928)
**Heaviest defeat:** 1-9 v Colchester United (1961)

Bradford City were founded in 1903 when a local rugby league side, Manningham FC, decided to switch codes. The club was elected to Division Two in the same year before they had played a single match – a swift ascent into the Football League which is only matched by Chelsea.

• City's finest hour was in 1911 when they won the FA Cup for the only time in the club's history, beating Newcastle 1-0 in a replayed final at Old Trafford. There were more celebrations in Bradford in 1929 when City won the Third Division (North) scoring 128 goals in the process – a record for the third tier.

• In 2013 Bradford City became the first club from the fourth tier of English football to reach a major final at Wembley, losing 5-0 to Swansea City in the League Cup. Two years later the Bantams pulled off possibly the biggest FA Cup shock ever, coming back from 2-0 down to beat Chelsea 4-2 in the fourth round at Stamford Bridge.

• Sadly, City will forever be associated with the fire that broke out in the club's main stand on 11th May 1985 and killed 56 supporters. The official inquiry into the tragedy found that the inferno had probably been caused by a discarded cigarette butt which set fire to litter under the stand. As a permanent memorial to those who died Bradford added black trimming to their shirt collars and sleeves.

• Loyal right-back Ces Podd, an international player with Saint Kitts and Nevis, made a club record 502 league appearances for the Bantams between 1970 and 1984.

HONOURS
*Division 2 champions* 1908
*Division 3 (N) champions* 1929
*Division 3 champions* 1985
*FA Cup* 1911

## BRAZIL

**First international:** Argentina 3 Brazil 0, 1914
**Most capped player:** Cafu, 142 caps (1990-2006)
**Leading goalscorer:** Pelé, 77 goals (1957-71)
**First World Cup appearance:** Brazil 1 Yugoslavia 2, 1930
**Biggest win:** Brazil 14 Nicaragua 0, 1975
**Heaviest defeat:** Brazil 1 Germany 7, 2014

The most successful country in the history of international football, Brazil are renowned for an exciting, flamboyant style of play which delights both their legions of drum-beating fans and neutrals alike.

• **Brazil is the only country to have won the World Cup five times. The South Americans first lifted the trophy in 1958 (beating hosts Sweden 5-2 in the final) and retained the prize four years later in Chile. In 1970, a great Brazilian side featuring legends such as Pelé, Jairzinho, Gerson and Rivelino thrashed Italy 4-1 to win the Jules Rimet trophy for a third time. Further triumphs followed in 1994 (3-2 on penalties against Italy after a dour 0-0 draw) and in 2002 (after beating Germany 2-0 in the final).**

• Brazil is the only country to have appeared at every World Cup (a total of 20) since the tournament began in 1930. The South Americans have also recorded the most wins (70) at the finals. Less impressively, Brazil suffered the heaviest ever defeat by a host nation when they were trounced 7-1 by Germany in the semi-finals of the 2014 tournament.

• **Between February 1993 and January 1996 Brazil set a new world record when they were undefeated for 35 consecutive internationals.**

• With eight wins to their name, Brazil are the third most successful side in the history of the Copa America (behind

# TOP 10

**BRAZIL GOALSCORERS**

| | | |
|---|---|---|
| 1. | Pele (1957-71) | 77 |
| 2. | Ronaldo (1994-2011) | 62 |
| 3. | Romario (1985-2005) | 55 |
| 4. | Zico (1976-86) | 48 |
| 5. | Neymar (2010- ) | 44 |
| 6. | Bebeto (1985-98) | 39 |
| 7. | Rivaldo (1993-2003) | 35 |
| 8. | Jairzinho (1964-82) | 33 |
| 9. | Ronaldinho (1999-2013) | 33 |
| 10. | Ademir (1945-53) | 32 |

*Brazil: The World's best ever football team – just don't mention the Germans!*

Uruguay and Argentina, who have won the trophy 15 and 14 times respectively). Brazil last won the tournament in Venezuela in 2007, beating neighbours Argentina 3-0 in the final.

• **Brazil have the best record of any nation in the Confederations Cup, winning the trophy four times – most recently in 2013, when they trounced Spain 3-0 in the final in Rio de Janeiro.**

*There's a warm glow around Brentford's Griffin Park these days...*

HONOURS

*World Cup winners 1958, 1962, 1970, 1994, 2002*
*Copa America winners 1919, 1922, 1949, 1989, 1997, 1999, 2004, 2007*
*Confederations Cup winners 1997, 2005, 2009, 2013*
**World Cup Record**
*1930 Round 1*
*1934 Round 1*
*1938 Semi-finals*
*1950 Runners-up*
*1954 Quarter-finals*
*1958 Winners*
*1962 Winners*
*1966 Round 1*
*1970 Winners*
*1974 Fourth place*
*1978 Third place*
*1982 Round 2*
*1986 Quarter-finals*
*1990 Round 2*
*1994 Winners*
*1998 Runners-up*
*2002 Winners*
*2006 Quarter-finals*
*2010 Quarter-finals*
*2014 Fourth place*

# BRENTFORD

**Year founded:** 1889
**Ground:** Griffin Park (12,300)
**Nickname:** The Bees
**Biggest win:** 9-0 v Wrexham (1963)
**Heaviest defeat:** 0-7 v Swansea Town (1926), v Walsall (1957) and v Peterborough (2007)

Brentford were founded in 1889 by members of a local rowing club. After playing at a number of different venues, the club settled at Griffin Park in 1904.
• **The club enjoyed its heyday in the decade before the Second World War.**

In 1929/30 Brentford won all 21 of their home games in the Third Division (South) to set a record which remains to this day. Promoted to the First Division in 1935, the Bees finished in the top six in the next three seasons before being relegated in the first post-war campaign. After plunging into the Fourth Division in 1962, Brentford became the first team to have played all the other 91 clubs in the Football League.
• **Brentford enjoyed their best season since those glory days in 2014/15 when they reached the Championship play-offs before losing to Middlesbrough at the semi-final stage.**
• **The Bees paid out a club record £2.1 million when they signed FC Twente defender Andreas Bjelland in July 2015. The following month the west Londoners received a record £9 million when striker Andre Gray joined Burnley.**
• Singer Rod Stewart had trials at Brentford in 1961 before concentrating on his music career, while TV presenter and actor Bradley Walsh played for the club's reserve team in the late 1970s.
• **Defender Ken Coote played in a club record 514 league games for the Bees between 1949 and 1964.**

HONOURS

*Division 2 champions 1935*
*Division 3 (S) champions 1933*
*Division 4 champions 1963*
*Third Division champions 1999*
*League Two champions 2009*

# BRIGHTON AND HOVE ALBION

**Year founded:** 1900
**Ground:** AMEX Stadium (30,750)
**Previous name:** Brighton and Hove Rangers
**Nickname:** The Seagulls
**Biggest win:** 10-1 v Wisbech (1965)
**Heaviest defeat:** 0-9 v Middlesbrough (1958)

Founded originally as Brighton and Hove Rangers in 1900, the club changed to its present name the following year. In 1920 Brighton joined Division Three as founder members, but had to wait another 38 years before gaining promotion to a higher level.
• **The club reached the final of the FA Cup for the only time in their history in 1983, holding favourites Manchester United to a 2-2 draw at Wembley. The Seagulls were unable to repeat their heroics in the replay, however, and crashed to a 4-0 defeat. In the same year Brighton were relegated from the old First Division, ending a four-season stint in the top flight.**
• A decade earlier, the Seagulls were briefly managed by the legendary Brian Clough. His time in charge of the club, though, was not a successful one and included an 8-2 thrashing by Bristol Rovers – the worst home defeat in Brighton's history.

• Brighton's record scorer is 1920s striker Tommy Cook, with 114 league goals. Cult hero Peter Ward, though, enjoyed the most prolific season in front of goal for the club, notching 32 times as the Seagulls gained promotion from the old Third Division in 1976/77. Ernie 'Tug' Wilson made the most appearances for the south coast outfit, with 509 between 1922 and 1936.

• Argentinian striker Leonardo Ulloa is both Brighton's record buy and sale, joining the Seagulls from Almeria for £2 million in 2013 before moving on to Leicester City a year later for £8 million.

• The club's most-capped player is winger Steve Penney, who played 17 times for Northern Ireland in the 1980s.

> HONOURS
> *Division 3 (S) champions* 1958
> *Second Division champions* 2002
> *League One champions* 2011
> *Division 4 champions* 1965
> *Third Division champions* 2001

## BRISTOL CITY

**Year founded:** 1894
**Ground:** Ashton Gate (13,414)
**Previous name:** Bristol South End
**Nickname:** The Robins
**Biggest win:** 11-0 v Chichester City (1960)
**Heaviest defeat:** 0-9 v Coventry City (1934)

Founded as Bristol South End in 1894, the club took its present name when it turned professional three years later. In 1900 City merged with Bedminster, whose ground at Ashton Gate became the club's permanent home in 1904.

• **The Robins enjoyed a golden decade in the 1900s, winning promotion to the top flight for the first time in 1906 after a campaign in which they won a joint-record 14 consecutive games. The following season City finished second, and in 1909 they reached the FA Cup final for the first and only time in their history, losing 1-0 to Manchester United at Crystal Palace.**

• Since then the followers of Bristol's biggest club have had to endure more downs than ups. The Robins returned to the top flight after a 65-year absence

in 1976, but financial difficulties led to three consecutive relegations in the early 1980s (City being the first club ever to suffer this awful fate).

• **City's strikers were on fire in 1962/63 as the Robins scored 100 goals in Division Three. Sadly for their fans, City could only finish 14th in the league – the lowest place ever by a club hitting three figures.**

• With 315 goals in 597 league games for the club between 1951 and 1966, England international striker John Atyeo is both the Robins' top scorer and record appearance maker. In the history of league football only Dixie Dean (Everton) and George Camsell (Middlesbrough) scored more goals for the same club.

• **The Robins won the League One title in 2015 with a club record 99 points. For good measure they also won the Football League Trophy – after a 2-0 victory over Walsall in the final – to become the first club to win the competition three times.**

> HONOURS
> *League One champions* 2015
> *Division 2 champions* 1906
> *Division 3 (S) champions* 1923, 1927, 1955
> *Football League Trophy* 1986, 2003, 2015
> *Welsh Cup* 1934

## BRISTOL ROVERS

**Year founded:** 1893
**Ground:** Memorial Stadium (11,916)
**Previous name:** Black Arabs, Eastville Rovers, Bristol Eastville Rovers
**Nickname:** The Pirates
**Biggest win:** 15-1 v Weymouth (1900)
**Heaviest defeat:** 0-12 v Luton Town (1936)

Bristol Rovers can trace their history back to 1883 when the Black Arabs club was founded at the Eastville Restaurant in Bristol. The club was renamed Eastville Rovers the following year in an attempt to attract more support from the local area, later adding 'Bristol' to their name before finally settling on plain old 'Bristol Rovers' in 1898.

• **Rovers have lived up to their name by playing at no fewer than nine different**

grounds. Having spent much of their history at Eastville Stadium, they have been based at the Memorial Stadium since 1996.

• The only Rovers player to have appeared for England while with the Pirates, Geoff Bradford, is the club's record scorer, netting 242 times in the league between 1949 and 1964. The club's record appearance maker is central defender Stuart Taylor, who turned out in 546 league games between 1966 and 1980.

• **Rovers legend Ronnie Dix is the youngest player ever to score in the Football League, getting off the mark in a 3-0 win against Norwich City in 1928 when he was aged just 15 years and 180 days.**

• Relegated from League Two in 2014, Rovers regained their league status the following season after beating Grimsby Town on penalties in the Conference play-off final at Wembley to become the first club to bounce straight back to the Football League since Carlisle in 2005.

> HONOURS
> *Division 3 (S) champions* 1953
> *Division 3 champions* 1990

## KEVIN DE BRUYNE

> **Born:** Drongen, Belgium, 28th June 1991
> **Position:** Midfielder
> **Club career:**
> 2008-12 Genk 84 (14)
> 2012-14 Chelsea 3 (0)
> 2012 Genk (loan) 13 (2)
> 2012-13 Werder Bremen (loan) 33 (10)
> 2014-15 Wolfsburg 51 (13)
> 2015- Manchester City
> **International record:**
> 2010- Belgium 33 (8)

When Kevin De Bruyne moved from Wolfsburg to Manchester City for a club record £55 million in August 2015 he became the second most expensive player in British football history (after Angel Di Maria).

• **An attacking midfielder who passes the ball well and loves to strike from distance, De Bruyne enjoyed a great season in 2014/15, contributing a Bundesliga record 21 assists as Wolfsburg finished second in the league and scoring in his side's 3-1 German Cup final victory over Borussia Dortmund. After an outstanding** campaign, De Bruyne was named German Footballer of the Year in 2015, the first Belgian to win this award.

• First capped in a friendly against Finland in 2010, De Bruyne was part of the Belgian team that reached the quarter-finals of the 2014 World Cup in Brazil.

# BURNLEY

**Year founded:** 1882
**Ground:** Turf Moor (21,401)
**Nickname:** The Clarets
**Biggest win:** 9-0 v Darwen (1892), v New Brighton (1957) and v Penrith (1984)
**Heaviest defeat:** 0-11 v Darwen (1885)

One of England's most famous old clubs, Burnley were founded in 1882 when the Burnley Rovers rugby team decided to switch to the round ball game. The club was a founder member of the Football League in 1888 and has since won all four divisions of the league – a feat matched only by Preston and Wolves.

• **Burnley have twice won the league championship, in 1921 and 1960. The first of these triumphs saw the Clarets go on a 30-match unbeaten run, the longest in a single season until Arsenal went through the whole of 2003/04 undefeated. In its own way, Burnley's 1960 title win was just as remarkable, as the Clarets only ever topped the league on the last day of the season after a 2-1 win at Manchester City.**

• The club's only FA Cup triumph came in 1914 when they defeated Liverpool 1-0 in the last final at Crystal Palace. After the final whistle Burnley's captain Tommy Boyle became the first man to receive the cup from a reigning monarch, King George V.

• **On 16th April 2011 Burnley defender Graham Alexander became only the second outfield player in the history of English football to make 1,000 professional appearances when he came on as a sub in the Clarets' 2-1 win over Swansea City. Alexander is also the most successful penalty taker ever in the domestic game, with 78 goals in 86 attempts from the spot.**

• Burnley splashed out a club record £9 million on Brentford striker Andre Gray shortly after dropping out of the Premier League in 2015. Three years earlier the Clarets sold winger Jay Rodriguez to Southampton for a club record fee of £7 million.

• **Burnley are the last club to score a century of goals in consecutive top-flight seasons, hitting the back of the net 102 times in 1960/61 and 101 in 1961/62.**

> **HONOURS**
> *Division 1 champions 1921, 1960*
> *Division 2 champions 1898, 1973*
> *Division 3 champions 1982*
> *Division 4 champions 1992*
> *FA Cup 1914*

# BURTON ALBION

**Year founded:** 1950
**Ground:** Pirelli Stadium (6,912)
**Nickname:** The Brewers
**Biggest win:** 12-1 v Coalville Town (1954)
**Heaviest defeat:** 0-10 v Barnet (1970)

Burton Albion were founded at a public meeting at the Town Hall in 1950. The town had previously supported two Football League clubs, Burton Swifts and Burton Wanderers, who merged to form Burton United in 1901 before folding nine years later.

• **The Brewers gained promotion to the Football League for the first time in 2009, going up as Conference champions. Six years later, managed by former Chelsea striker Jimmy Floyd Hasselbaink, Burton gained promotion to the third tier for the first time after winning the League Two title.**

• DR Congo midfielder Jacques Maghoma played in a record 155 league games for Burton before joining Sheffield Wednesday in the summer of 2013. The club's leading scorer is striker Billy Kee, with 39 league goals between 2011 and 2014.

• **In 2006 Burton achieved the greatest result in their history when they held mighty Manchester United to a 0-0 draw at home in the third round of the FA Cup. A record visiting contingent at Old Trafford of 11,000 Brewers fans attended the replay, but they had little to cheer about as United strolled to an emphatic 5-0 victory.**

• In 2011 Burton's funds received a welcome boost to the tune of £200,000 when goalkeeper Adam Legzdins joined Derby County in a club record deal.

> **HONOURS**
> *League Two champions 2015*
> *Conference champions 2009*

# BURY

**Year founded:** 1885
**Ground:** Gigg Lane (11,840)
**Nickname:** The Shakers
**Biggest win:** 12-1 v Stockton (1897)
**Heaviest defeat:** 0-10 v Blackburn Rovers (1887) and West Ham (1982)

The club with the shortest name in the Football League, Bury were founded in 1885 at a meeting at the Old White Horse Hotel in Bury, as successors to two other teams in the town, the Bury Unitarians and the Bury Wesleyans. Bury were founder members of the Lancashire League in 1889, joining the Football League five years later.

• **Bury have won the FA Cup on two occasions, in 1900 and 1903. In the second of these triumphs, the Shakers thrashed Derby County 6-0 at Crystal Palace to record the biggest ever victory in an FA Cup final.**

• On 27th August 2005 Bury became the first club to score 1,000 goals in all four tiers of the Football League. The landmark was reached when Brian Barry-Murphy scored the first of the Shakers' goals in their 2-2 home draw with Wrexham in a League Two fixture.

• **The following year Bury set a less happy record, when they became the first club to be thrown out of the FA Cup for fielding an ineligible player – Stephen Turnbull, a loan signing from Hartlepool United.**

• Bury became the first Football League club to sign a player from the Indian sub-continent when striker Baichung Bhutia joined from East Bengal in 1999.

> **HONOURS**
> *Division 2 champions 1895*
> *Division 3 champions 1961*
> *Second Division champions 1997*
> *FA Cup 1900, 1903*

**B**

**BURY**

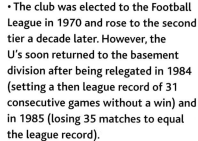

## GARY CAHILL

**Born:** Dronfield, 19th December 1985
**Position:** Defender
**Club career:**
2004-08 Aston Villa 28 (2)
2004-05 Burnley (loan) 27 (1)
2007-08 Sheffield United (loan) 16 (2)
2008-12 Bolton Wanderers 130 (13)
2012- Chelsea 100 (5)
**International record:**
2010- England 36 (3)

Along with his Chelsea team-mate Eden Hazard, Gary Cahill was one of just two players to be voted into the PFA Team of the Year in both 2014 and 2015.

• Signed from Bolton Wanderers for a bargain £7 million in January 2012, Cahill has since won all three domestic honours with the Blues – including the Premier League and League Cup double in 2015 – plus the Champions League (2012) and the Europa League (2013).

• Cahill started out with Aston Villa, before joining Bolton in 2008 in a £5 million deal. In 2010 he became only the second Bolton player – after striker Michael Ricketts – to be capped by England in 48 years. Then, the following season, he became the first Wanderers player for 52 years

to score for England when he netted in a 3-0 win over Bulgaria in a Euro 2012 qualifier in Sofia.

• At the 2014 World Cup in Brazil Cahill was the only England player to feature in all 270 minutes of the Three Lions' three group games. In the autumn of 2014 he was named England vice-captain by Three Lions boss Roy Hodgson.

## CAMBRIDGE UNITED

**Year founded:** 1912
**Ground:** Abbey Stadium (8,127)
**Previous name:** Abbey United
**Nickname:** The U's
**Biggest win:** 7-0 v Weymouth (2007) and v Forest Green (2009)
**Heaviest defeat:** 0-7 v Sunderland (2002)

Cambridge United were founded as Abbey United in 1912 before taking their current name two years after turning professional in 1949.

*Gary Cahill became the first Bolton player to score for England for 52 years before he signed for Chelsea*

• The club was elected to the Football League in 1970 and rose to the second tier a decade later. However, the U's soon returned to the basement division after being relegated in 1984 (setting a then league record of 31 consecutive games without a win) and in 1985 (losing 35 matches to equal the league record).

• More happily for their fans, Cambridge won the first ever play-off final at Wembley, beating Chesterfield 1-0 in 1990 to earn promotion to the old Third Division.

• England international winger Andy Sinton is the U's youngest ever player, making his debut against Wolves in 1982 aged 16 and 228 days.

HONOURS
*Division 3 champions 1991*
*Division 4 champions 1977*

## ERIC CANTONA

**Born:** Paris, France, 24th May 1966
**Position:** Striker
**Club career:**
1983-88 Auxerre 81 (23)
1985-86 Martigues (loan) 15 (4)
1988-91 Marseille 40 (13)
1988-89 Bordeaux (loan) 11 (6)
1989-90 Montpellier (loan) 33 (10)
1991-92 Nimes 17 (2)
1992 Leeds United 28 (9)
1992-97 Manchester United 144 (64)
**International record:**
1987-95 France 45 (20)

Maverick Frenchman Eric Cantona is the most successful foreign player in Premiership history, winning the league championship in five of his six seasons in English football and landing the Double twice.

• In 1993 Cantona became the first ever player to win back-to-back league titles with two different clubs when he fired Manchester United to the championship just 12 months after helping Leeds do the same. Amazingly for such an influential figure, Cantona's switch across the Pennines cost the Old Trafford side just £1.2 million in November 1992.

• The signing of the inspirational Cantona proved to be the catalyst

*'Ooh la la, zees eez not possible zat ze great Cantona's picture eez ere and not on ze cover!'*

won a record 145 caps for England since making her debut in 2001.

• **The first international caps were awarded by England in 1886, following a proposal put forward by the founder of the Corinthians, N.L. Jackson. To this day players actually receive a handmade 'cap' to mark the achievement of playing for their country. England caps are made by a Bedworth-based company called Toye, Kenning & Spencer, who also provide regalia for the Freemasons.**

• The most capped player in the history of the game is Egypt midfielder Ahmed Hassan, who played an astonishing 184 times for his country between 1995 and 2012. The women's record is held by Kristine Lilly, who made 352 appearances for the USA between 1987 and 2010.

• **England lined up with three centurions for the first time ever in September 2013 when Steven Gerrard, Frank Lampard and Ashley Cole all played in a World Cup qualifier away to Ukraine.**

## CARDIFF CITY

**Year founded:** 1899
**Ground:** Cardiff City Stadium (33,280)
**Previous name:** Riverside
**Nickname:** The Bluebirds
**Biggest win:** 16-0 v Knighton Town (1961)
**Heaviest defeat:** 2-11 v Sheffield United (1926)

Founded as the football branch of the Riverside Cricket Club, the club changed to its present name in 1908, three years after Cardiff was awarded city status.

• **Cardiff are the only non-English club to have won the FA Cup, lifting the trophy in 1927 after a 1-0 victory over Arsenal at Wembley. They came close to repeating that feat in 2008, but were beaten 1-0 by Portsmouth in only the second FA Cup final staged at the new Wembley.**

for a decade of dominance by United in the 1990s. In 1994 the former Marseille star was voted PFA Player of the Year as United won the Double for the first time in their history, Cantona coolly slotting home two penalties in his side's 4-0 thrashing of Chelsea in the FA Cup final to become the first Frenchman to win the trophy and the first continental European to score in the final. Two years later, United won the Double for a second time and again Cantona was their match-winner in the FA Cup final, scoring the only goal of the game against Liverpool. Another PFA Player of the Year award duly followed.

• **However, the period in between these triumphs saw Cantona serve a nine-month ban – the longest in Premier League history – after he launched a 'kung fu' kick at an abusive Crystal Palace fan in a match at Selhurst Park in January 1995. The hot-headed Frenchman was also fined £10,000 by the FA and ordered to complete 120 hours of community**

**service after being found guilty of assault.**

• Since his retirement from the game in 1997 when he was aged just 30, Cantona has pursued a successful career as an actor, starring as himself in the 2009 film, *Looking for Eric*.

## CAPS

Legendary goalkeeper Peter Shilton has won more international caps than any other British player. 'Shilts' played for England 125 times between 1970 and 1990 and would have won many more caps if he had not faced stiff competition for the No. 1 shirt from his great rival Ray Clemence, who won 61 caps during the same period. In women's football, midfielder Fara Williams has

### IS THAT A FACT?

England's team against the Republic of Ireland at the 1990 World Cup had a record 574 caps between them, an average of 52.2 caps per player.

*Cardiff City returned to their traditional blue strip in 2015*

until 1965, when they won promotion to the second tier for the first time.

• **The club's greatest moment came in 1974 when, in their one season in the top flight, they sat on top of the old First Division after the opening three games. The Cumbrians, though, were quickly knocked off their lofty perch and ended the campaign rock bottom.**

• Following a long period of decline Carlisle were facing relegation from the Football League in 1999. However, needing a win against Plymouth on the last day of the season to stay up, United were saved when on-loan goalkeeper Jimmy Glass went up for a corner and scored a never-to-be-forgotten winner.

• **Carlisle have appeared in the Football League Trophy final on a record six occasions, and in 1995 became the first and only team to lose an English trophy on the 'golden goal' rule when they conceded in extra-time in the final against Birmingham City.**

• Goalkeeper Alan Ross made a record 466 appearances for the Blues between 1963 and 1979.

• On 7th April 1947 a crowd of 51,621 squeezed into Cardiff's old Ninian Park Stadium for the club's match against Bristol City – an all-time record attendance for the third tier of English football.

• Cardiff have won the Welsh Cup 22 times, just one short of Wrexham's record. The Bluebirds' domination of the tournament in the 1960s and 1970s earned them regular qualification for the European Cup Winners' Cup and in 1968 they reached the semi-finals of the competition before losing 4-3 on aggregate to Hamburg.

• Cardiff's record appearance maker is defender Phil Dwyer, who turned out 476 times for the club between 1972 and 1985. The Bluebirds' record scorer is Len Davies, who banged in 128 league goals in the 1920s.

• **Chilean international midfielder Gary Medel, an £11 million recruit from Sevilla in August 2013, is the club's record signing. A year later Medel became the Bluebirds' record sale when he joined Inter Milan for £10 million.**

• Defender Alf Sherwood won a club record 39 caps for Wales while with Cardiff between 1946 and 1956.

HONOURS
***Championship champions*** *2013*
***Division 3 (S) champions*** *1947*
***Third Division champions*** *1993*
***FA Cup*** *1927*
***Welsh Cup*** *1912, 1920, 1922, 1923, 1927, 1928, 1930, 1956, 1959, 1964, 1965, 1967, 1968, 1969, 1970, 1971, 1973, 1974, 1976, 1988, 1992, 1993*

## CARLISLE UNITED

**Year founded:** 1903
**Ground:** Brunton Park (18,202)
**Nickname:** The Blues
**Biggest win:** 8-0 v Hartlepool (1928) and v Scunthorpe (1952)
**Heaviest defeat:** 1-11 v Hull City (1939)

Carlisle United were formed in 1903 following the merger of two local clubs, Shaddongate United and Carlisle Red Rose. The Blues joined the Third Division (North) in 1928 and were long-term residents of the bottom two divisions

HONOURS
***Division 3 champions*** *1965*
***Third Division champions*** **1995**
***League Two champions*** *2006*
***Football League Trophy*** *1997, 2011*

## MICHAEL CARRICK

**Born:** Wallsend, 28th July 1981
**Position:** Midfielder
**Club career:**
1998-2004 West Ham United 136 (6)
1999 Swindon Town (loan) 6 (2)
2000 Birmingham City (loan) 2 (0)
2004-06 Tottenham Hotspur 64 (2)
2006- Manchester United 263 (17)
**International record:**
2001- England 33 (0)

Manchester United vice-captain Michael Carrick has enjoyed huge success with the Red Devils since joining them from Tottenham in 2006 for £18 million. In over a decade at the club the midfielder has won five Premier League titles, the Champions League (2008) and the League Cup (2010).

• **A superb passer of the ball who can unpick a massed opposition defence with one through ball, Carrick began** his playing career at West Ham, scoring twice in the Hammers' record 9-0 aggregate FA Youth Cup final win over Coventry City in 1999. He went on to play for the East Enders until 2004 when he joined Spurs for £3.5 million.

• After a brilliant campaign in 2012/13, Carrick was nominated for the PFA Footballer of of the Year award, but missed out to Gareth Bale. However, Arsenal boss Arsene Wenger argued that the United star should have topped the poll, saying, "He is a quality passer. He could play for Barcelona, he would be perfectly suited to their game."

• **Carrick was first capped by England way back in 2001, but has often struggled to cement a regular place in the national side. After a disappointing season in 2013/14 he was left out of Roy Hodgson's squad for the World Cup in Brazil, but the following year he returned to the England team for the Euro 2016 qualifier at Wembley against Lithuania and impressed in a 4-0 win.**

*Michael Carrick – good enough to play for Barcelona!*

# IKER CASILLAS

**Born:** Madrid, Spain, 20th May 1981
**Position:** Goalkeeper
**Club career:**
1999-2015 Real Madrid 510
2015- Porto
**International record:**
2000- Spain 162

Iker Casillas is the only goalkeeper to have skippered his country to success in both the European Championships and the World Cup. The ex-Real Madrid star pulled off the first leg of this double when Spain beat Germany in the Euro 2008 final in Vienna, before landing the biggest prize of all two years later after his country's 1-0 defeat of the Netherlands in the 2010 World Cup final in Johannesburg. He then made it a hat-trick as Spain retained the European Championships in 2012.

• **In 2000 Casillas became the youngest goalkeeper to play in the Champions League final, appearing in Real's 3-0 victory over Valencia just four days after his 19th birthday. He won the competition again two years later, after coming on as a sub in Real's 2-1 defeat of Bayer Leverkusen in the final in Glasgow, and a third time in 2014. In the final against Atletico Madrid that year he played in his 430th victory for Real, a record for the club.**

• Casillas is the highest capped international player from a major European football nation, and is tenth in the list of the most-capped players ever. In 2012 he set a new record of 73 international clean sheets when Spain beat Serbia 2-0 in a friendly, extending his total to an incredible 92 games by the end of August 2015.

• **Thanks in part to Spain's huge success in recent years, Casillas now holds the record for playing in the most international victories. He passed Lilian Thuram's record of 94 wins when he came on as a sub in Spain's 3-1 friendly defeat of South Korea in May 2012 and became the first player ever to win 100 internationals when Spain thrashed Italy 4-0 in the final of Euro 2012.**

## EDINSON CAVANI

**Born:** Salto, Uruguay, 14th February 1987
**Position:** Striker
**Club career:**
2005-07 Danubio 25 (10)
2007-10 Palermo 109 (34)
2010-13 Napoli 104 (78)
2013- Paris St Germain 65 (34)
**International record:**
2008- Uruguay 76 (27)

Long-haired Uruguayan striker Edinson Cavani is the most expensive player in the history of French football, his £55 million move from Napoli to Paris St Germain in 2013 beating the previous record of Radamel Falcao when he joined Monaco from Atletico Madrid.

• In his two seasons with PSG Cavani has helped the club from the French capital win the league on both occasions, while forming a formidable partnership with his extrovert strike partner Zlatan Ibrahimovic. However, a goal he scored against Lens in October 2014 landed him in hot water after he celebrated by firing an imaginery gun.

*'Let me out!!!'*

Shown a yellow card for this action, Cavani protested and was promptly sent off for dissent.

• A powerfully-built centre-forward who finishes with aplomb on the ground and in the air, Cavani had to wait until 2012 before winning his first domestic silverware, the Coppa Italia with Napoli. The next season he was the top scorer in Serie A with 29 goals, sparking interest in his services all around Europe.

• **Cavani scored against Colombia on his international debut in 2008, and two years later his partnership with Luis Suarez was a key factor in Uruguay's progress to the World Cup semi-finals. In 2011 he was part of the Uruguayan side which beat Paraguay in the final of the Copa America.**

## SANTI CAZORLA

**Born:** Llanera, Spain, 13th December 1984
**Position:** Midfielder
**Club career:**
2003-04 Villarreal B 40 (4)
2003-06 Villarreal 40 (4)
2006-07 Recreativo de Huelva 54 (2)
2007-11 Villarreal 127 (23)
2011-12 Malaga 38 (9)
2012- Arsenal 106 (23)
**International record:**
2008- Spain 73 (11)

Arsenal playmaker Santi Cazorla became the first ever Spanish player to win the FA Cup twice in 2015 when he put in a 'Man of the Match' performance in the Gunners' 4-0 drubbing of Aston Villa. The previous year he entered the history books as the first Spanish player to score in the final when he curled in a delightful free kick against Hull City at

*With all his assists, Arsenal players are used to getting gifts from Santi*

Wembley in 2014, triggering Arsenal's comeback from 2-0 down to eventual 3-2 winners.

• **A skilful and perceptive midfielder, Cazorla began his career with Villarreal, before joining Recreativo de Huelva where his outstanding performances saw him voted Spanish Player of the Year in 2007. He returned to Villarreal that same year, then joined Malaga in 2011 for around £18 million. After helping Malaga qualify for the Champions League for the first time in their history, he moved on to Arsenal for £16 million in 2012.**

• Cazorla enjoyed his best season for Arsenal in 2014/15, scoring seven goals in the Premier League and making 11 assists — a total only beaten by Chelsea's Cesc Fabregas.

• **Cazorla first played for Spain in 2008, going on to appear in his country's 1-0 victory over Germany** later that year in the final of the European Championships. He missed out on the 2010 World Cup through injury, but returned to the national side to help Spain win Euro 2012.

**IS THAT A FACT?**
Edinson Cavani is the all-time leading Uruguayan scorer in the Champions League with 15 goals for Napoli and Paris St Germain.

## PETR CECH

**Born: Pilzen**, Czech Republic, 20th
May 1982
**Position:** Goalkeeper
**Club career:**
**1999**-2001 Chmel Blsany 27
2001-02 Sparta Prague 27
2002-04 Rennes 70
2004-15 Chelsea 333
2015- Arsenal
**International record:**
2002- Czech Republic 114

A brilliant shot-stopper
who dominates his
penalty area with his
imposing physique,
Petr Cech is the only
goalkeeper to have won
the FA Cup four times.
He has also won
the Premier

League four times with Chelsea and in
the first of these triumphs, in 2004/05,
set a record by keeping 24 clean sheets.
• **The giant goalkeeper also holds the
record for the most clean sheets, 166,
in the Premier League era for a single
club and is closing in on David James'
all-time record of 170 shut-outs.
His total of 228 clean sheets in all
competitions is a record for Chelsea.**
• Cech was a member of the Czech
Republic side which reached
the semi-finals of
Euro 2004 before
losing to eventual
winners Greece.
In March 2013
he became
only the
second Czech
player, after
Karel Poborsky, to
play 100 times for
his country.

• **In October 2006 Cech suffered
a depressed fracture of the skull
following a challenge by Reading's
Stephen Hunt.** He returned to action
after three months out of the game
wearing a rugby-style headguard
for protection, and went on to make
494 appearances in all competitions
for Chelsea – a club record for an
overseas player – until he joined local
rivals Arsenal for around £10 million
in July 2015.
• In 2012 Cech starred in the Blues'
Champions League final victory over
Bayern Munich, blocking a penalty from
former team-mate Arjen Robben in
extra-time and then saving two more
in the shoot-out. The following year he
added more silverware to his collection
when he helped Chelsea win the Europa
League after the Blues beat Benfica in
the final.

*Peter Cech still
can't quite believe
that Chelsea let
him go to Arsenal*

## CELTIC

**Year founded:** 1888
**Ground:** Celtic Park
(60,355)
**Nickname:** The Bhoys
**Biggest win:** 11-0 v
Dundee (1895)
**Heaviest defeat:** 0-8 v
Motherwell (1937)

The first British team to win
the European Cup, Celtic were
founded by an Irish priest in 1887
with the aim of raising funds
for poor children in Glasgow's
East End slums. The club were
founder members of the
Scottish League in 1890,
and have gone on to spend
a record 118 seasons in
the top flight.
• **Celtic have won the
Scottish Cup more
times than any other
club, with 36 victories
in the final. The Bhoys
first won the cup in
1892, beating Queen's
Park 5-1 in a replay.**
• Under legendary manager Jock
Stein Celtic won the Scottish league for
nine consecutive seasons in the 1960s
and 1970s, with a side featuring great
names like Billy McNeill, Jimmy Johnstone,

## CHARLTON ATHLETIC

**Year founded:** 1905
**Ground:** The Valley (27,111)
**Nickname:** The Addicks
**Biggest win:** 8-1 v Middlesbrough (1953)
**Heaviest defeat:** 1-11 v Aston Villa (1959)

Charlton Athletic were founded in 1905 when a number of youth clubs in the south-east London area, including East Street Mission and Blundell Mission, decided to merge. The club, whose nickname 'the Addicks' stemmed from the haddock served by a local chippy, graduated from minor leagues to join the Third Division (South) in 1921.

• Charlton's heyday was shortly before and just after the Second World War. After becoming the first club to win successive promotions from the Third to First Division in 1935/36, the Addicks finished runners-up, just three points behind league champions Manchester City, in 1937. After losing in the 1946 FA Cup final to Derby County, Charlton returned to Wembley the following year and this time lifted the cup thanks to a 1-0 victory over Burnley in the final.

• Charlton's home ground, The Valley, used to be one of the biggest in English football. In 1938 a then record crowd of 75,031 squeezed into the stadium to see the Addicks take on Aston Villa in a fifth-round FA Cup tie. In 1985, though, financial problems forced Charlton to leave the Valley and the Addicks spent seven years as tenants of West Ham and Crystal Palace before making an emotional return to their ancestral home in 1992.

• When the play-offs were introduced in the 1986/87 season, Charlton figured among the first finalists, beating Leeds to preserve their First Division status. In 1998, during the long managerial reign of Alan Curbishley, the Addicks triumphed in the highest scoring Wembley play-off final, beating Sunderland 7-6 on penalties after a 4-4 draw to earn promotion to the Premiership.

• Sam Bartram, who was known as 'the finest keeper England never had', played a record 623 games for the club between 1934 and 1956. Bearded striker Derek Hales is Charlton's record goalscorer, notching 168 in two spells at the club in the 1970s and 1980s.

• Prematurely bald midfielder Jonjo Shelvey became Charlton's youngest ever player when he made his debut against Barnsley in April 2008 aged 16 and 59 days.

### HONOURS

**First Division champions** 2000
**Division 3 (S) champions** 1929, 1935
**League One champions** 2012
**FA Cup** 1947

## SIR BOBBY CHARLTON

**Born:** Ashington, 11th October 1937
**Position:** Midfielder
**Club career:**
1956-73 Manchester United 606 (199)
1973-74 Preston North End 38 (8)
1975 Waterford 31 (18)
**International record:**
1958-70 England 106 (49)

One of English football's greatest ever players, Sir Bobby Charlton had a magnificent career with Manchester United and England. He is England's second highest scorer with 49 goals in 106 international appearances, and United's all-time leading scorer with 249 goals in all competitions

• Charlton broke into the United first team in 1956, scoring twice on his debut against Charlton Athletic. Two years later he was one of the few United players to survive the Munich air crash, after being hauled from the burning wreckage by goalkeeper Harry Gregg.

• During the 1960s Charlton won everything the game had to offer, winning the league title twice (1965 and 1967), the FA Cup (1963), the European Cup (scoring twice in the final against Benfica at Wembley in 1968) and the World Cup with England in 1966 (along with his brother, Jack). Probably his best performance for his country came in the semi-final against Portugal at Wembley, when he scored both goals (including a trademark piledriver) in a 2-1 victory.

• European Footballer of the Year in 1966, Charlton eventually left United in 1973 to become player-manager of Preston. He returned to Old Trafford as a director in 1984 and was knighted a decade later.

---

## CHEATING

The most famous instance of on-pitch cheating occurred at the 1986 World Cup in Mexico when Argentina's Diego Maradona punched the ball into the net to open the scoring in his side's quarter-final victory over England. Maradona was unrepentant afterwards, claiming the goal was scored by "the hand of God, and the head of Diego".

• In a similar incident in 2009 France captain Thierry Henry clearly handled the ball before crossing for William Gallas to score the decisive goal in a World Cup play-off against Ireland. "I will be honest, it was a handball – but I'm not the ref," a sheepish Henry admitted after the match.

• In October 2014 Santos striker Leandro Damiao was roundly condemned after TV cameras caught him brazenly pulling his own shirt in an effort to con the referee into awarding a penalty during his side's 3-0 defeat to Criciuma.

• In September 2009 IFK Gothenburg goalkeeper Kim Christensen was caught by TV cameras using his feet to push the bottom of his posts a few centimetres inwards before a match against Orebro. The referee eventually spotted that the posts had been moved and pushed them back into the correct position. Christensen later admitted that he had moved the goalposts in several earlier matches.

• During the 2012/13 season Tottenham's Gareth Bale was booked a record seven times in all competitions for 'simulation' – more commonly known simply as 'diving'.

**IS THAT A FACT?**
In a 2009 poll conducted by radio station talkSPORT, former Tottenham striker Jurgen Klinsmann was voted the worst diver in Premier League history.

# CHELSEA

**Year founded:** 1905
**Ground:** Stamford Bridge (41,837)
**Nickname:** The Blues
**Biggest win:** 13-0 v Jeunesse Hautcharage (1971)
**Heaviest defeat:** 1-8 v Wolves (1953)

Founded in 1905 by local businessmen Gus and Joseph Mears, Chelsea were elected to the Football League in that very same year. At the time of their election, the club had not played a single match – only Bradford City can claim a similarly swift ascent into league football.

• Thanks to the staggering wealth of their Russian owner, Roman Abramovich, Chelsea are now one of the richest clubs in the world. Since taking over the Londoners in 2003, Abramovich has pumped hundreds of millions into the club and has been rewarded with four Premier League titles – the most recent of which, under two-time boss Jose Mourinho in 2014/15, saw the Blues top the table for a record 268 days – three FA Cups and three League Cups. After watching his team come agonisingly close on numerous occasions, Abramovich finally saw Chelsea win the Champions League in 2012 when, led by caretaker manager Roberto di Matteo, the Blues beat Bayern Munich on penalties in the final.

• The following year Chelsea won the Europa League after defeating Benfica 2-1 in the final in Amsterdam. That victory meant the Blues became the first British club to win all three historic UEFA trophies, as they had previously won the European Cup Winners' Cup in both 1971 and 1998. It was in the Cup Winners' Cup that Chelsea thrashed Luxembourg minnows Jeunesse Hautcharage 21-0 in 1971 to set a European record aggregate score.

• The Blues' recent success is in marked contrast to their early history. For the first 50 years of their existence Chelsea won precisely nothing, finally breaking their duck by winning the league championship in 1955. After a succession of near misses, the club won the FA Cup for the first time in 1970, beating Leeds 2-1 at Old Trafford in the first post-war final to go to a replay. Flamboyant striker Peter Osgood scored in every round of the cup run and remains the last player to achieve this feat.

• The club's fortunes declined sharply in the late 1970s and 1980s, the Blues spending much of the period in the Second Division while saddled with large debts. However, an influx of veteran foreign stars in the mid-1990s, including Gianfranco Zola, Ruud Gullit and Gianluca Vialli, sparked an exciting revival capped when the Blues won the FA Cup in 1997, their first major trophy for 26 years.

• In the final against Middlesbrough, Italian midfielder Di Matteo scored with a long-range shot after just 43 seconds – at the time the fastest ever goal in a Wembley final.

• Chelsea's arrival as one of England's top clubs was finally confirmed when charismatic manager Jose Mourinho led the Blues to the Premiership title in 2005. The club's tally of 95 points and 29 wins set records for the competition, while goalkeeper Petr Cech went a then record 1,025 minutes during the season without conceding a goal. A second Premiership title followed in 2006, before Mourinho was sensationally sacked a year later. When the club first won the championship way back in 1955, they did so with a record low of just 52 points.

## IS THAT A FACT?

Chelsea have won a record four FA Cups at the new Wembley. Oddly, on each of these occasions, the Blues have had a different manager: Jose Mourinho (2007), Guus Hiddink (2009), Carlo Ancelotti (2010) and Roberto di Matteo (2012).

• In 2007 Chelsea won the first ever FA Cup final at the new Wembley, Ivorian striker Didier Drogba scoring the only goal against Manchester United. In the same year the Blues won the League Cup, making them just the third English team after Arsenal (1993) and Liverpool (2001) to claim a domestic cup double. The Blues also won the FA Cup in 2009 and 2010, making them the first team to retain the trophy at the new Wembley.

• Hardman defender Ron 'Chopper' Harris is Chelsea's record appearance maker, turning out an incredible 795 times for the club between 1962 and 1980. Midfielder Frank Lampard, a key figure in the club's recent successes,

*Jose Mourinho makes his Chelsea players feel ten feet tall!*

scored a record 211 goals in all competitions between 2001 and 2014. Legendary striker Jimmy Greaves scored the most goals in a single season, with 41 in 1960/61.

• Between 2004 and 2008 the Blues were unbeaten in 86 consecutive home league matches, a record for both the Premiership and the Football League. The impressive run was eventually ended by Liverpool, who won 1-0 at Stamford Bridge on 26th October 2008.

• Chelsea clinched the title in 2010 with an 8-0 thrashing of Wigan, a resounding victory that meant the Blues finished the season with a Premier League record 103 goals and a top-flight best ever goal difference of 71.

• The club's record signing is Fernando Torres, who cost a British record £50 million when he moved to west London from Liverpool in January 2011. Three years later the Blues sold Brazilian defender David Luiz to PSG for a club record £50 million.

### HONOURS
**Division 1 champions** *1955*
**Premier League champions** *2005, 2006, 2010, 2015*
**Division 2 champions** *1984, 1989*
**FA Cup** *1970, 1997, 2000, 2007, 2009, 2010, 2012*
**Double** *2010*
**League Cup** *1965, 1998, 2005, 2007, 2015*
**Champions League** *2012*
**European Cup Winners' Cup** *1971, 1998*
**Europa League** *2013*
**European Super Cup** *1998*

## CHESTERFIELD

**Year founded:** 1866
**Ground:** Proact Stadium (10,504)
**Previous name:** Chesterfield Town
**Nickname:** The Spireites
**Biggest win:** 10-0 v Glossop North End (1903)
**Heaviest defeat:** 0-10 v Gillingham (1987)

The fourth oldest club in the UK, Chesterfield were founded in 1866. The club was elected to the Second Division in 1899 as Chesterfield Town but lost its league status a decade later, only to return as plain Chesterfield when Division Three (North) was created in 1921.

• Chesterfield fans still complain about a refereeing decision in the 1997 FA Cup semi-final against Middlesbrough which they believe denied their team a place in the final at Wembley. TV replays showed that Jonathan Howard's shot had crossed the Boro line, but referee David Elleray thought otherwise. The game went to a replay in which the Spireites were eventually beaten.

• In the 1923/24 campaign Chesterfield goalkeeper Arthur Birch scored five goals for the club, all of them penalties – a record tally by a keeper in a single season.

• One-club man Dave Blakey played in a club record 617 league games between 1948 and 1967. Striker Ernie Moss is the Spireites' top scorer with 162 goals in three spells at the club between 1968 and 1986.

### HONOURS
**Division 3 (N) champions** *1931, 1936*
**Division 4 champions** *1970, 1985*
**League Two champions** *2011, 2014*
**Football League Trophy** *2012*

## CLEAN SHEETS

Former Manchester United goalkeeper Edwin van der Sar holds the British record for consecutive league clean sheets, keeping the ball out of his net for 14 Premier League games and a total of 1,311 minutes in the 2008/09 season. He was finally beaten on 4th March 2009 by Newcastle's Peter Lovenkrands in United's 2-1 victory at St James' Park.

• The world record for clean sheets is held by Brazilian goalkeeper Mazaropi of Vasco de Gama who went 1,816 minutes without conceding in 1977/78.

• Italy's long-serving goalkeeper Dino Zoff holds the international record, going 1,142 minutes without having to pick the ball out of his net between September 1972 and June 1974. Another Italian goalkeeper, Walter Zenga, holds the record for clean sheets at the World Cup, with a run of 518 minutes at the 1990 tournament. However, New Zealand's Richard Wilson did even better during the qualifying rounds for the 1982 tournament, going

921 minutes without conceding.

• England's overall clean sheet record is held by Peter Shilton, who shut out the opposition in 66 of his 125 international appearances between 1970 and 1990. The international record is held by Spain's Iker Casillas with 92 in 162 appearances.

• Former Liverpool and Aston Villa goalkeeper David James holds the Premier League record for clean sheets with 170, followed by Petr Cech with 166 for Chelsea – a record for a single club.

## CLUB WORLD CUP

A competition contested between the champion clubs of all six continental confederations of FIFA, the Club World Cup was first played in Brazil in 2000 but has only been an annual tournament since 2005 when it replaced the old Intercontinental Cup.

• Manchester United's participation in the first Club World Cup led to the Red Devils pulling out of the FA Cup in 2000, a tournament they had won the previous season. United's decision attracted a lot of criticism at the time, not least from many of their own fans.

• Barcelona have the best record in the competition, having won two finals – 2-1 against Estudiantes in 2009 and 4-0 against Santos in 2011 – as well as finishing as runners-up to Brazilian club Internacional in 2006.

• Manchester United became the first British winners of the tournament when a goal by Wayne Rooney saw off Ecuadorian side Quito in the 2008 final in Yokohama. Chelsea missed a chance to match United's feat when they lost 1-0 in the 2012 final to Brazilian side Corinthians.

• The 2014 champions were Real Madrid, who beat Argentinian side San Lorenzo 2-0 in Marrakesh.

## COLCHESTER UNITED

**Year founded:** 1937
**Ground:** The Colchester Community Stadium (10,105)
**Nickname:** The U's
**Biggest win:** 9-1 v Bradford City (1961) and v Leamington (2005)
**Heaviest defeat:** 0-8 v Leyton Orient (1989)

Founded as the successors to amateur club Colchester Town in 1937, Colchester United joined the Football League in 1950. The club lost its league status in 1990, but regained it just two years later after topping the Conference.

• **The U's reached the heady heights of the Championship for the first time in 2006, but only hung around for two seasons before dropping down into League One.**

• The first brothers to be sent off in the same match while playing for the same team were Colchester's Tom and Tony English against Crewe in 1986.

• **In 1971, the U's became the first English club to win a tournament in a penalty shoot-out after defeating West Brom 4-3 on penalties in the final of the Watney Cup at the Hawthorns.**

• Colchester's coffers received a record boost of £2.5 million in January 2007 when defender Greg Halford joined Reading.

HONOURS
*Conference champions 1992*

## CHRIS COLEMAN

**Born:** Swansea, 10th June 1970
**Managerial career:**
2003-07 Fulham
2007-08 Real Sociedad
2008-10 Coventry City
2011-12 Larissa
2012- Wales

Chris Coleman was appointed manager of Wales in January 2012 following the tragic death of his predecessor, Gary Speed. In September 2015 the Swansea-born boss led his country to their highest-ever FIFA ranking of 9th, after four wins and two draws in their first six Euro 2016 qualifying matches.

• **Coleman's first experience of management came at Fulham, where he was the youngest ever Premier League manager when he was put in charge of the Cottagers, aged 32 and 10 months, in April 2003.**

• After parting company with the west Londoners in 2007, Coleman managed Spanish side Real Sociedad and Coventry, where he was sacked after leading the Midlanders to their lowest position – 19th in the Championship – for 45 years in 2010.

• **A tough centre-back in his playing days with Swansea, Crystal Palace, Blackburn and Fulham, Coleman won 32 caps for Wales before his career was ended by a bad car crash in 2002.**

## COLOURS

In the 19th century, players originally wore different coloured caps, socks and armbands – but not shirts – to distinguish between the two sides. The first standardised kits were introduced in the 1870s, with many clubs opting for the colours of the schools or other sporting organisations from which they had emerged.

• **In 2012 Cardiff City decided to change the colour of their home shirt, when they switched from blue to red shirts at the instigation of club owner Vincent Tan – who believed that red was a 'luckier' colour. Many Cardiff fans, though, were outraged and after numerous protests the club reverted to blue shirts in January 2015.**

• Thanks largely to the longstanding success of Arsenal, Liverpool and Manchester United, teams wearing red have won more trophies in England than those sporting any other colour. Teams wearing stripes have fared less well, their last FA Cup success coming in 1987 (Coventry City) and their last league triumph way back in 1936 (Sunderland).

• **Until 1989 both teams regularly changed colours in FA Cup ties where there was a kit clash. The last final in which both teams wore change kits was in 1982 when Tottenham (yellow) beat QPR (red) 1-0 in a replay at Wembley.**

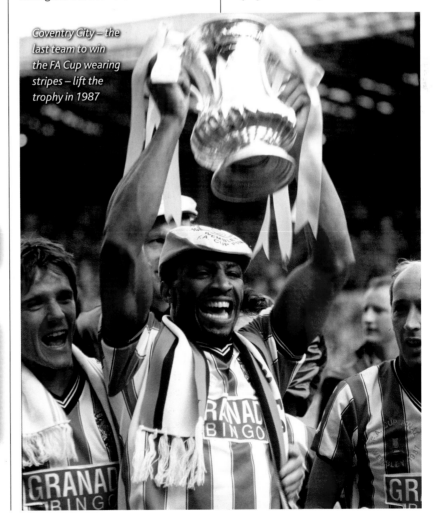

*Coventry City – the last team to win the FA Cup wearing stripes – lift the trophy in 1987*

## COMMUNITY SHIELD

The Community Shield was originally known as the Charity Shield and since 1928 has been an annual fixture usually played at the start of the season between the reigning league champions and the FA Cup winners. Founded in 1908 to provide funds for various charities, the Charity Shield was initially played between the league champions and the Southern League champions, developing into a game between select teams of amateurs and professionals in the early 1920s.

• Manchester United were the first club to win the Charity Shield, defeating QPR 4-0 in a replay at Stamford Bridge. With 16 outright wins and four shared, United are also the most successful side in the history of the competition.

• United were also involved in the highest scoring Charity Shield match, beating Swindon Town 8-4 in 1911, with the Red Devils' Harold Halse grabbing a record six of the goals.

• Brighton (in 1910) and Leicester City (in 1971) are the only clubs to have won the Shield, but never the league or the FA Cup.

• Manchester United's Ryan Giggs is the most successful player in the history of the Shield, with nine wins in 15 appearances (another record).

## COMPUTER GAMES

FIFA 13 sold more than 4.5 million copies worldwide in the first five days after its launch in 2012, leading publishers EA to claim it was the biggest selling sports video launch of all time. The FIFA series as a whole has sold over 100 million copies since it launched in 1993, making it the best selling football video game of all time.

• The first football video game was created in 1973 by Tomohiro Nishikado, who later designed Space Invaders. Called simply Soccer, the ball-and-paddle game allowed two players to each control a goalkeeper and a striker.

• Wayne Rooney appeared on a record consecutive seven covers of the FIFA series from 2006-12 until he was replaced by Lionel Messi as the face of the franchise from FIFA 13 onwards.

• In November 2012 Vugar Huseynzade was appointed manager of Azerbaijan side Baku FC after impressing club officials with his skills on Football Manager. The 21-year-old student landed the job ahead of a number of experienced coaches and ex-pros, including former France star Jean-Pierre Papin.

## CONFEDERATIONS CUP

The Confederations Cup is a competition held every four years contested by the holders of each of the six FIFA confederation championships – such as the European Championships and the Copa America – plus the World Cup holders and host nation.

• Since 2005 the Confederations Cup has been held in the country that will host the following year's World Cup, acting as a dress rehearsal for the larger and more prestigious tournament.

• Brazil have the best record in the tournament with four victories to their name: in 1997 (after a 6-0 win over Australia in the final), in 2005 (4-1 against Argentina), 2009 (3-2 against the USA) and 2013 (3-0 against Spain). The only other countries to win the Confederations Cup are France (in 2001 and 2003) and Mexico (in 1999).

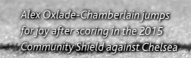

*Alex Oxlade-Chamberlain jumps for joy after scoring in the 2015 Community Shield against Chelsea*

• Spain recorded the biggest ever win at the Confederations Cup when they hammered minnows Tahiti 10-0 in 2013. Spanish striker Fernando Torres scored four of the goals to set a new individual record for the tournament – and if hadn't missed a penalty it would have been five.

## CONFERENCE

The pinnacle of the non-league system which feeds into the Football League, the Football Conference was renamed the National League in 2015 but is still better known by its previous name. The league was founded as the Alliance Premier League in 1979 and has been divided into three sections – National, North and South – since 2004.

• Promotion and relegation between the Football League and the Conference became automatic in 1987, when Scarborough United replaced Lincoln City.

• However, clubs have to satisfy the Football League's minimal ground requirements before their promotion can be confirmed and Kidderminster Harriers, Macclesfield Town and Stevenage Borough all failed on this count in the mid-1990s after topping the Conference table.

•The league is currently sponsored by Vanarama (since 2014), while it was previously sponsored by Gola (1984-86), Vauxhall (1986-98), Nationwide Building Society (1998-2007), Blue Square (2007-13) and Skrill (2013-14).

• The most goals scored by one player in a single Conference season is 41 by Nuneaton Borough's Paul Culpin in 1983/84 .

## COPA AMERICA

The oldest surviving international football tournament in the world, the Copa America was founded in 1916. The first championships were held in Argentina as part of the country's independence centenary commemorations, with Uruguay emerging as the winners from a four-team field. Originally known as the South American Championship, the tournament was renamed in 1975. Previously, the Copa America was held every two years, but in 2007 it was decided to stage future tournaments at four-year intervals.

• Uruguay have won the tournament a record 15 times, while Argentina are second in the winners' list, lifting the trophy on 14 occasions. The current holders are Chile, who won the competition for the first time as hosts in 2015 after beating Argentina on penalties in the final.

• Norberto Mendez of Argentina and Zizinho of Brazil share the tournament record of 17 goals. Three players have scored a record nine goals in a single tournament: Jair Pinto (Brazil, 1949), Humberto Maschio (Argentina, 1957) and Javier Ambrois (Uruguay, 1957).

## COPA LIBERTADORES

The Copa Libertadores is the South American equivalent of the Champions League, played annually between top clubs from all the countries in the continent (in recent years, leading clubs from Mexico have also participated). Argentine club Independiente have the best record in the competition, winning the trophy seven times, including four in a row between 1972 and 1975.

• Ecuadorian striker Albert Spencer is the leading scorer in the history of the competition with 54 goals (48 for Uruguayan club Penarol, helping them to win the first two tournaments in 1960 and 1961, and six for Ecuadorian outfit Barcelona de Guayaquil).

• In a first-round match in 1970, Penarol thrashed Venezuelan club Valencia 11-2 to record the biggest ever win in the competition.

• Argentinian clubs have won the trophy a record 23 times, seven more than those from Brazil. The most successful player in the Copa Libertadores is Argentinian defender Francisco Sa, who won the tournament six times in the 1970s with Independiente and Boca Juniors.

*Bristol Rovers players celebrate their return to this book thanks to their promotion from the Conference*

## IS THAT A FACT?

In a match against Malaysia on 4th May 2015 Vietnam women's winger Nguyen Thi Tuyet Dung became the first player ever to score two goals direct from a corner in the same match – what's more, she scored one with her right foot and one with her left!

## CORNERS

Corner kicks were first introduced in 1872, but goals direct from a corner were not allowed until 1924. The first player to score from a corner in league football was Billy Smith of Huddersfield in the 1924/25 season. On 2nd October 1924 Argentina's Cesareo Onzari scored direct from a corner against reigning Olympic champions Uruguay in Buenos Aires, the first goal of this sort in an international fixture.

• **The first Premier League match to feature no corners was between Wigan Athletic and Chelsea on 21st August 2010. Despite the lack of action on the wings, Chelsea still won 6-0.**

• A corner count has been proposed as an alternative to penalty shoot-outs as a way of deciding drawn cup ties. This method was used to determine the result of the 1965 All-African Games football tournament, with Congo beating Mali 7-2 on corners after a 0-0 draw.

• **Former Yugoslav international Dejan Petkovic holds the world record for the most goals scored direct from a corner with eight, his last effort coming for Brazilian side Flamengo in 2009.**

• The start of the 1974 World Cup final between West Germany and the Netherlands was delayed when English referee Jack Taylor spotted that the groundstaff had forgotten to put corner flags on the pitch.

## DIEGO COSTA

**Born:** Lagarto, Brazil, 7th October 1988
**Position:** Striker
**Club career:**
2006 Braga 0 (0)
2006 Penafiel (loan) 13 (5)
2007-09 Atletico Madrid 0 (0)
2007 Braga (loan) 7 (0)
2007-08 Celta (loan) 30 (5)
2008-09 Albacete (loan) 34 (9)
2009-10 Valladolid 34 (8)
2010-14 Atletico Madrid 94 (43)
2012 Rayo Vallecano (loan) 16 (10)
2014- Chelsea 26 (20)
**International record:**
2013 Brazil 2 (0)
2014- Spain 7 (1)

Diego Costa has the best goals/minutes ratio of any player in Premier League history, after banging in a goal every 103 minutes on average

during his first season with Chelsea in 2014/15. Costa's goals helped his new club win the title and the League Cup, and also saw him voted into the PFA Team of the Year.

• **After a fairly undistinguished start to his career, Costa gradually developed into one of Europe's deadliest forwards after rejoining Atletico Madrid from Valladolid in 2010. Three years later he scored a vital goal in the Copa del Rey final as Atleti beat Real Madrid 2-1 to record their first victory over their glitzy city rivals since 1999.**

• The following season Costa was third-top scorer in La Liga with 27 goals – only Cristiano Ronaldo and Lionel Messi were more prolific – as Atletico surprised everyone by lifting the title. Costa also helped Atleti reach the final of the Champions League for the first time, but had to limp out of the

*Diego Costa always holds his breath when he is running with the ball*

showpiece event against Real with a hamstring injury after just eight minutes. In the close season he joined Chelsea for £32 million.

• Costa won the first of two caps for Brazil in 2013, but later that year gained Spanish citizenship and declared his intention to play for his adopted nation. He made his debut for Spain in a 1-0 friendly win over Italy in March 2014.

## THIBAUT COURTOIS

**Born:** Bree, Belgium, 11th May 1992
**Position:** Goalkeeper
**Club career:**
2009-2011 Genk 41
2011- Chelsea 32
2011-14 Atletico Madrid (loan) 111
**International record:**
2011- Belgium 31

Widely rated as one of the best goalkeepers in the world, Thibaut Courtois was a key member of the Chelsea side that won both the Premier League and League Cup in 2015 during his first season at Stamford Bridge after a three-year loan at Atletico Madrid.

• Courtois came through the youth ranks at Genk to help the Belgian

outfit win the league title in 2011, a season in which he was voted Goalkeeper of the Year.

• A tall and muscular goalkeeper who specialises in confidently plucking high crosses from the skies, Courtois joined Chelsea for around £5 million in July 2011, but was swiftly moved out on loan to Spain. He enjoyed three magnificent years with Atletico, helping the Madrid side win the Europa League in 2012, the Copa del Rey in 2013 and the league title in 2014. In addition, he became the first Atletico goalkeeper ever to retain the Ricardo Zampora trophy – awarded to the goalkeeper with the best goals-to-games ratio – when he topped the poll in both 2013 and 2014.

• Courtois is the youngest ever goalkeeper to have played for Belgium

after making his debut as a 19-year-old in a 0-0 friendly draw with France in 2011. After keeping six clean sheets in the qualifying matches for the 2014 World Cup his good form continued at the tournament proper, where he helped Belgium reach the quarter-finals before a 1-0 defeat to Argentina ended their hopes of glory.

## PHILIPPE COUTINHO

**Born:** Rio de Janeiro, Brazil, 12th June 1992
**Position:** Midfielder
**Club career:**
2009-10 Vasco de Gama 19 (1)
2010-13 Inter Milan 28 (3)
2012 Espanyol (loan) 16 (5)
2013- Liverpool 81 (13)
**International record:**
2010- Brazil 11 (1)

A tricky midfielder who has been compared to South American superstars Lionel Messi and Ronaldinho, Philippe Coutinho was the only Liverpool player to be voted into the PFA Team of the Year in 2015.

• The previous season Coutinho was one of the Reds' stand-out players as they challenged for the league title in

*Oops! It's not too often you see the ball get past Chelsea goalkeeper Thibaut Courtois*

*Liverpool's Coutinho – a typically Brazilian number 10*

Coventry were founded in 1883 by workers from the local Singer's bicycle factory and were named after the company until 1898. The club was elected to the Second Division in 1919, but their league career started unpromisingly with a 5-0 home defeat to Tottenham Hotspur.

• A club with a history of ups and downs, Coventry were the first team to play in seven different divisions: Premier, Division One, Two, Three, Four, Three (North) and Three (South). They have also played in the Championship and, from 2012, League One.

• Coventry's greatest moment came in 1987 when the club won the FA Cup for the only time, beating Tottenham 3-2 in an exciting Wembley final. Two years later, though, the Sky Blues were dumped out of the cup by non-league Sutton United in one of the competition's biggest ever upsets.

• Promoted to the old First Division for the first time in 1967, Coventry remained there until 2001 – at the time only Arsenal, Everton and Liverpool could boast longer tenures in the top flight.

• Long-serving goalkeeper Steve Ogrizovic played in a club record 504 league games between 1984 and 2000.

• Sky Blues legend Clarrie Bourton scored a club record 173 league goals between 1931 and 1937, including a season's best 49 goals in 1931/32.

> **HONOURS**
> *Division 2 champions* 1967
> *Division 3 champions* 1964
> *Division 3 (S) champions* 1936
> *FA Cup* 1987

2013/14. Indeed, it was the Brazilian's well-taken winner in a 3-2 victory against Manchester City late on in the campaign which made the Reds the odds-on favourites for the trophy before they eventually had to be satisfied with second place.

• Coutinho moved to Italian giants Inter Milan from Vasco de Gama when he was just 18, but struggled to adapt to Serie A. However, a loan spell at Spanish outfit Espanyol in 2012 proved a turning point in his career and the following January he joined Liverpool in a £8.5 million deal.

• A typical Brazilian number 10 who combines vision, flair and creativity in equal measure, Coutinho made his debut for his country in a 3-0 friendly win against Iran in 2010 when he was aged just 18. He missed out on Brazil

boss Luis Felipe Scolari's squad for the 2014 World Cup, but was called up by new boss Dunga for the 2015 Copa America in Chile.

## COVENTRY CITY

**Year founded:** 1883
**Ground:** Ricoh Arena (32,609)
**Previous name:** Singers FC
**Nickname:** The Sky Blues
**Biggest win:** 9-0 v Bristol City (1934)
**Heaviest defeat:** 2-11 v Berwick Rangers (1901)

## CRAWLEY TOWN

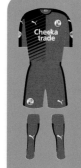

**Year founded:** 1896
**Ground:** Broadfield Stadium (6,134)
**Nickname:** The Red Devils
**Biggest win:** 8-0 v Droylsden (2008)
**Heaviest defeat:** 0-7 v Bath City (2000)

Founded in 1896, Crawley Town started out in the West Sussex League, eventually rising to the Conference in 2004. Dubbed 'the Manchester City of non-league', Crawley splashed out more than £500,000 on new players at the start of the 2010/11 season, an investment which paid off when the club won promotion to the Football League at the end of the campaign.

• **Runaway Conference champions, Crawley's haul of 105 points set a new record for the division, while they also equalled the records for fewest defeats (3), most wins (31) and best goal difference (63). The following season Crawley enjoyed a second successive promotion, after finishing third in League Two behind Swindon and Shrewsbury.**

• Crawley reached the fifth round of the FA Cup for the first time in their history in 2011 after knocking out Swindon, Derby and Torquay. To their fans' delight they were then paired with Manchester United, and their team did them proud, only losing 1-0 at Old Trafford.

• **The Red Devils received a club record £800,000 in January 2012 when striker Matt Tubbs joined Bournemouth.**

HONOURS
*Conference champions 2011*

## CREWE ALEXANDRA

**Year founded:** 1877
**Ground:** Gresty Road (10,153)
**Nickname:** The Railwaymen
**Biggest win:** 8-0 v Rotherham (1932)
**Heaviest defeat:** 2-13 v Tottenham Hotspur (1960)

Founded by railway workers in 1877, the Crewe Football Club added 'Alexandra' to their name in honour of Princess Alexandra, wife of the future king, Edward VII. The club were founder members of the Second Division in 1892, although they lost their league status four years later before rejoining the newly formed Third Division (North) in 1921.

• **Helped by a club record 19-match unbeaten run Crewe were League Two play-off winners in 2012, but they had to wait until the following year before landing their first piece**

of major silverware, the Football League Trophy. During Alex's 2-0 win over Southend United, 19-year-old sub George Ray became the first player ever to make his club debut at Wembley.

• Alex fans endured a miserable spell in the mid-1950s when their club failed to win away from home for a record 56 consecutive matches. The depressing run finally ended with a 1-0 win at Southport in April 1957.

• **Club legend Herbert Swindells scored a record 126 goals for Crewe between 1927 and 1937. Crewe's appearance record is held by Tommy Lowry who turned out in 475 games between 1966 and 1977.**

• Goalkeeper Clayton Ince is Crewe's most-capped player, making 31 appearances for Trinidad and Tobago while at Gresty Road between 1999 and 2005.

HONOURS
*Football League Trophy 2013*
*Welsh Cup 1936, 1937*

*In 2010 the International Astronomical Union named a minor planet '14282 Cruijff' in honour of Dutch football legend Johan Cruyff*

## JOHAN CRUYFF

**Born:** Amsterdam, Netherlands, 5th April 1947
**Position:** Midfielder/striker
**Club career:**
1964-73 Ajax 240 (190)
1973-78 Barcelona 142 (48)
1979-80 Los Angeles Aztecs 27 (16)
1980-81 Washington Diplomats 32 (12)
1981 Levante 10 (2)
1981-83 Ajax 36 (14)
1983-84 Feyenoord 33 (11)
**International record:**
1966-78 Netherlands 48 (33)

Arguably the greatest European player ever, Johan Cruyff was captain of the brilliant Netherlands side which reached the final of the 1974 World Cup and of the outstanding Ajax team which won the European Cup three times on the trot in the early 1970s.

• **Unquestionably the best player in the world at the time, Cruyff became the first man to win the European**

## CRYSTAL PALACE

Player of the Year award three times, topping the poll in 1971, 1973 and 1974.

• Fast, skilful, creative and a prolific scorer, Cruyff was also a superb organiser on the pitch. His talents prompted Barcelona to shell out a world record £922,000 fee to bring him to the Nou Camp in 1973 and the following year Cruyff helped the Catalans win their first title for 14 years.

• After his retirement, Cruyff coached both Ajax and Barcelona. He led the Spanish giants to four consecutive league titles between 1991 and 1994 and, in 1992, guided them to their first ever European Cup success, with a 1-0 victory over Sampdoria at Wembley.

• Cruyff's magnificent contribution to football in Holland was recognised in a 2004 poll when he was voted the sixth greatest Dutch person ever, ahead of two of the world's finest painters, Rembrandt and Vincent Van Gogh.

## CRYSTAL PALACE

Year founded: 1905
Ground: Selhurst Park (26,255)
Nickname: The Eagles
Biggest win: 9-0 v Barrow (1959)
Heaviest defeat: 0-9 v Burnley (1909) and v Liverpool (1989)

The club was founded in 1905 by workers at the then cup final venue at Crystal Palace, and was an entirely separate entity to the amateur club of the same name which was made up of groundkeepers at the Great Exhibition and reached the first ever semi-finals of the FA Cup in 1872.

• After spending their early years in the Southern League, Palace were founder members of the Third Division (South) in 1920. The club had a great start to their league career, going up to the Second Division as champions in their first season.

• Palace's greatest moment came in 1990 when they reached the FA Cup final. In the final at Wembley against Manchester United, Ian Wright came off the bench to score twice in a thrilling 3-3 draw before the Eagles went down 1-0 in the replay. The following season the Eagles finished a best-ever third in the top flight.

• Pre-war striker Peter Simpson is the club's all-time leading scorer with 153 league goals between 1930 and 1936. Rugged defender Jim Cannon holds the club appearance record, making 660 appearances between 1973 and 1988.

• Palace are the only club to have been promoted to the top flight four times via the play-offs, most recently in 2013. The Eagles are also the only club to have won play-off finals at four different venues: Selhurst Park (1989), old Wembley (1997), Millennium Stadium (2004) and new Wembley (2013).

• Less happily for their fans, Palace have been relegated a record four times from the Premier League, including a particularly unfortunate occasion in 1993 when they went down with a record 49 points (from 42 games). Two years later they became the only Premier League club to be relegated after finishing fourth

*Crystal Palace's new signing is great in the air!*

bottom, owing to the restructuring of the league from 22 down to 20 clubs.

• The club made their record signing in July 2015, when French midfielder Yohan Cabaye signed from PSG for around £10 million. The Eagles' record sale is pacy winger Wilfried Zaha, who joined Manchester United for £15 million in 2013.

• A record fourth-tier crowd of 37,774 watched Palace's home match with Millwall on 31st March 1961, but it proved to be a disappointing afternoon for the Selhurst faithful as the Eagles slumped to a 2-0 defeat.

• Palace's famous fans include comedians Eddie Izzard and Jo Brand, and rapper Dizzee Rascal.

### HONOURS
***Division 2 champions*** *1979*
***First Division champions*** *1994*
***Division 3 (S) champions*** *1921*

## CUP WINNERS' CUP

A competition for the domestic cup winners of all European countries, the European Cup Winners' Cup ran for 39 seasons from 1960/61 until 1998/99. Barcelona have the best record in the competition with four wins (in 1979, 1982, 1989 and 1997).

• In 1963 Tottenham Hotspur became the first British club to win the competition and the first to win a major European trophy, when they thrashed Atletico Madrid 5-1 in Rotterdam – a record score for a European final.

• English clubs won the cup eight times – a figure unmatched by any other country. England's successful teams were Tottenham (1963), West Ham (1965), Manchester City (1970), Chelsea (1971 and 1998), Everton (1985), Manchester United (1991) and Arsenal (1994).

• In 1963 Sporting Lisbon tonked APOEL Nicosia 16-1 in a second-round, first-leg tie to record the biggest ever win in any European fixture. Chelsea hold the competition record for the biggest aggregate win, smashing Luxembourg side Jeunesse Hautcharage 21-0 in 1971.

• Borussia Dortmund striker Lothar Emmerich scored a competition record 14 goals in the 1965/66 season.

## DAGENHAM & REDBRIDGE

**Year founded:** 1992
**Ground:** Victoria Road (6,078)
**Previous name:** Dagenham
**Nickname:** The Daggers
**Biggest win:** 8-1 v Woking (1994)
**Heaviest defeat:** 0-9 v Hereford United (2004)

The self-styled 'pub team from Essex' were formed in 1992 following the merger of local rivals Dagenham and Redbridge Forest, the latter having previously incorporated the once-famous amateur clubs Ilford, Leytonstone and Walthamstow Avenue.

• In 2007 Dagenham & Redbridge were promoted to the Football League for the first time in their history after winning the Conference.
Three years later, the Daggers recorded the biggest ever play-off win when they thrashed Morecambe 6-0 in the semi-final on their way up to League One.

• Dagenham's record appearance maker, Tony Roberts, is the only goalkeeper to have scored in the FA Cup from open play, netting in a fourth qualifying round tie against Basingstoke in 2001. Less impressively, the Welsh international is the only keeper to have been sent off in the competition while in the opposition penalty area. The bizarre incident happened late on in the Daggers' 5-2 loss to Southend in 2008 when Roberts went up for a corner and was red carded for headbutting a Shrimpers defender.

• The Daggers' coffers received a welcome boost in January 2013 when they sold striker Dwight Gayle to Peterborough United for a club record £700,000. The club made their record signing in 2010 when defender Damien McCrory joined the Daggers from Plymouth Argyle for £10,000.

• In August 2014 Dagenham were involved in the joint-record highest scoring League Cup tie ever when they drew 6-6 after extra-time at home to Brentford in the first round, before eventually losing on penalties.

## KENNY DALGLISH

**Born:** Glasgow, 4th March 1951
**Position:** Striker
**Club career:**
1968-77 Celtic 204 (112)
1977-90 Liverpool 354 (118)
**International record:**
1971-87 Scotland 102 (30)

The last player to score 100 league goals in both the Scottish and English leagues, Kenny Dalglish began his career at Celtic, winning nine major trophies before moving to Liverpool in 1977 for a then British record fee of £440,000. A true Anfield legend, Dalglish won nine championships, two FA Cups and four League Cups with the Reds, plus the European Cup in 1978, 1981 and 1984. He was voted Footballer of the Year in 1979 and 1983.

• A clever striker with a superb first touch, Dalglish won a record 102 caps for Scotland and scored 30 goals – a figure matched only by Denis Law. He represented his country at three World Cups in 1974, 1978 and 1982.

• In 1986 he became the first player-manager to lead a club to the title when he won the championship with Liverpool, and he secured two more titles in 1988 and 1990 before suddenly resigning in 1991.

• Eight months later he took over at Blackburn and in 1995 steered Rovers to the Premiership title, becoming only the third manager to win the title with two different clubs. In 1997 Dalglish became Newcastle manager, but was sacked after a poor start to the 1998/99 season.

• He was briefly manager of Celtic but was out of the game for nine years before going back to Liverpool in 2009, initially as youth academy coach. In January 2011 Dalglish replaced Roy Hodgson as manager but, despite winning the Carling Cup the following year and guiding the Reds to the 2012 FA Cup final, the Kop legend was sacked at the end of the 2011/12 season after a poor league campaign.

## DEATHS

The first recorded death as a direct result of a football match came in 1889 when William Cropper of Derbyshire side Staveley FC died of a ruptured bowel sustained in a collision with an opponent.

• In 1931 Celtic's brilliant young international goalkeeper John Thompson died in hospital after fracturing his skull in a collision with Rangers forward Sam English. Some 40,000 fans attended his funeral, many of them walking the 55 miles from Glasgow to Thompson's home village in Fife. In the same decade two other goalkeepers, Jimmy Utterson of Wolves and Sunderland's Jimmy Thorpe, also died from injuries sustained on the pitch. Their deaths led the Football Association to change the rules so that goalkeepers could not be tackled while they had the ball in their hands.

• In 1998 11 players were killed by a bolt of lightning which struck the pitch during a game in the Democratic Republic of Congo. Oddly, all those who died were members of the visiting team while the players from the home side, Busanga, survived unscathed.

• In May 2010 Goran Tunjic collapsed and died from a heart attack while playing for Croatian county level side Mladost FC. Unfortunately, the referee completely failed to comprehend the unfolding tragedy... and gave Tunjic a yellow card for diving.

• Argentinian league football was suspended in May 2015 as mark of respect after a fourth division player, Emanuel Ortega of San Martin de Burzaco, died after fracturing his skull when he fell against a perimeter wall while challenging for the ball. Ten days later, another Argentinian player, Cristian Gomez of second-tier Atletico Parana, died after collapsing on the pitch.

• In August 2014 Cameroonian player Albert Ebosse of Algerian side JS Kabylie was killed by a stone thrown from the stands at the end of his side's 2-1 defeat to USM Alger.

**IS THAT A FACT?**
In a tragic incident in October 2014 Indian player Peter Biaksangzuala died after injuring his spine when he fell awkwardly while performing a somersault to celebrate a goal he had scored for his club, Bethlehem Vengthlang.

# DEBUTS

Aston Villa striker Howard Vaughton enjoyed the best England debut ever, scoring five goals in a 13-0 rout of Ireland in 1882.

• **The worst ever international debut was by American Samoa goalkeeper Nicky Salapu against Fiji in 2001. He conceded 13 goals in that game, and then another 44 within a week in three matches against Samoa, Tonga and Australia.**

• Freddy Eastwood scored the fastest goal on debut, netting after just seven seconds for Southend against Swansea in 2004. Almost as impressively, goalkeeper Tony Coton was just 83 seconds into his debut with Birmingham City in 1980 when he saved a penalty with his first touch in top-flight football.

• **The fastest goal by an England player on debut was by future Tottenham boss Bill Nicholson after just 19 seconds against Portugal at Goodison Park in 1951. Strangely, it turned out to be his only international appearance.**

• The only player to score a hat-trick on his Premier League debut is Middlesbrough's Italian striker Fabrizio Ravenelli, who scored all of his team's goals in a 3-3 draw with Liverpool on the opening day of the 1996/97 season.

## FABIAN DELPH

**Born:** Bradford, 21st November 1991
**Position:** Midfielder
**Club career:**
2006-09 Leeds United 46 (6)
2009-15 Aston Villa 107 (3)
2012 Leeds United (loan) 5 (0)
2015- Manchester City
**International record:**
2014- England 6 (0)

Fabian Delph played a huge role in Aston Villa's run to the 2015 FA Cup final, scoring the opener in the Villans' 2-0 quarter-final victory over local rivals West Brom and then the winner in a surprise 2-1 defeat of Liverpool in the semi-final at Wembley. However, in July 2015, a week after declaring that he would remain as skipper at Villa Park, he stunned the club's fans by signing for Manchester City for a bargain £8 million.

• **Delph made his name at Leeds, where his impressive performances in midfield earned him the Football League Young Player of the Year** award in 2009. In the same year he joined Villa in a £6 million deal.

• An energetic midfielder who never seems to stop running, Delph took a while to adjust to Premier League football and was loaned back to Leeds in 2012. The following season, though, his form picked up to the extent that he was voted Aston Villa's 2014 Player of the Year by the fans.

• **Delph came through the England Under-19 and Under-21 system to make his debut for the senior team in a friendly against Norway in September 2014.**

*Fabian Delph is so good he doesn't even need to look at the ball!*

# MEMPHIS DEPAY

**Born:** Moordrecht, Netherlands, 13th February 1994
**Position:** Winger
**Club career:**
2011-15 PSV Eindhoven 90 (39)
2015- Manchester United
**International record**
2013- Netherlands 17 (3)

A fast and tricky winger who loves to run at defenders, Memphis Depay signed for Manchester United for £29 million in May 2015 after finishing top scorer in the Dutch league the previous season with 22 goals for champions PSV Eindhoven.

• At the World Cup in Brazil in 2014 Depay became the youngest ever Dutchman to score at the finals when he notched the winner in a 3-2 victory against Australia aged 20 and four months.

• He also scored in the Netherlands' 2-0 group stage win against Chile, and his outstanding performances in Brazil saw him nominated for the Best Young Player award along with Raphael Varane and the eventual winner Paul Pogba.

• Depay first enjoyed a taste of international success in 2011, when he helped the Netherlands win the Under-17 European Championships in Serbia, scoring in a 5-2 thrashing of Gemany in the final.

## DERBIES

So called because they matched the popularity of the Epsom Derby horserace, 'derby' matches between local sides provoke intense passions among fans and players alike.

• Probably the most intense derby match in Britain, and possibly the whole world, is between bitter Glasgow rivals Rangers and Celtic. In the 2010/11 season the two teams met a record seven times, the clashes provoking so many violent incidents in Glasgow that the chairman of the Scottish Police Federation called for future Old Firm matches to be banned. Although Rangers have since tumbled down the divisions, Celtic v Rangers remains the most played derby in world football – the two teams having met an incredible 400 times (Rangers hold the edge, with 159 wins to Celtic's 145) .

• Other famous derbies include Liverpool v Everton, Arsenal v Tottenham, Manchester City v Manchester United, Newcastle v Sunderland and, on mainland Europe, Inter v AC Milan, Sporting Lisbon v Benfica and Lazio v Roma. Strangely, the match often described as 'the world's greatest derby', the 'El Clasico' clash between Barcelona and Real Madrid, is not a derby in the strict sense.

• Manchester derbies have produced many dramatic moments, notably in 1974 when former United legend Denis Law scored for City with a cheeky backheel in the closing stages at Old Trafford. The goal doomed United to relegation from the First Division and prompted thousands of their fans to invade the pitch in an attempt to get the match abandoned. They succeeded in their aim, but the result (a 1-0 win for City) stood.

*Memphis Depay was the top scorer in the Dutch league in 2014/15 before signing for Manchester United*

• The biggest win in a derby match in England was Nottingham Forest's 12-0 thrashing of east Midland rivals Leicester City in the old First Division in 1909. In the Premier League era Chelsea recorded the most emphatic derby win when they smashed Arsenal 6-0 at Stamford Bridge in March 2014.

• **Arsenal have won a record 113 London derbies since the Premier League began in 1992.**

## DERBY COUNTY

**Year founded:** 1884
**Ground:** iPro Stadium (33,597)
**Nickname:** The Rams
**Biggest win:** 12-0 v Finn Harps (1976)
**Heaviest defeat:** 2-11 v Everton (1890)

Derby were formed in 1884 as an offshoot of Derbyshire Cricket Club and originally wore an amber, chocolate and blue strip based on the cricket club's colours. Perhaps wisely, they changed to their traditional black-and-white colours in the 1890s.

• **The club were founder members of the Football League in 1888 and seven years later moved from the ground they shared with the cricketers to the Baseball Ground (so named because baseball was regularly played there in the 1890s). Derby had to oust a band of gypsies before they could move in, one of whom is said to have laid a curse on the place as he left. No doubt, then, the club was pleased to leave the Baseball Ground for Pride Park in 1997... although when Derby's first game at the new stadium had to be abandoned due to floodlight failure, there were fears that the curse had followed them!**

• Runners-up in the FA Cup final in 1898, 1899 and 1903, Derby reached their last final in 1946. Before the match the club's captain, Jack Nicholas, visited a gypsy encampment and paid for the old curse to be lifted. It worked, as Derby beat Charlton 4-1 after extra-time.

• **Under charismatic manager Brian Clough, Derby took the top flight by storm after winning promotion to the First Division in 1969. Three years**

later they won the league in one of the closest title races ever. Having played all their fixtures ahead of their title contenders, Derby's players were actually sitting on a beach in Majorca when they heard news of their victory. The following season Derby reached the semi-finals of the European Cup and, in 1975 under the management of former skipper Dave Mackay, they won the championship again.

• Sadly, the club have failed to live up to those glory days in the decades since. By the early 1980s the Rams had sunk as low as the Third Division and were only saved from extinction when publisher Robert Maxwell bailed them out. The club enjoyed a reasonable spell in the Premiership in the late 1990s, but their most recent season in the top flight in 2007/08 was an utter disaster – the Rams managing just one win in the whole campaign, equalling a Football League record set by Loughborough in 1900.

• **Between September 2007 and September 2008 Derby went a record 36 league games without a win, including a record 32 games in the Premier League and another four in the Championship.**

• Derby's best ever goalscorer was one of the true greats of the game in the late 19th and early 20th centuries, Steve Bloomer. He netted an incredible 332 goals in two spells at the club between 1892 and 1914. Striker Kevin Hector, a two-time title winner with the club in the 1970s, played in a record 485 league games for the Rams during two spells at the Baseball Ground.

### HONOURS
***Division 1 champions** 1972, 1975*
***Division 2 champions** 1912, 1915, 1969, 1987*
***FA Cup** 1946*

## ANGEL DI MARIA

**Born:** Rosario, Argentina, 14th February 1988
**Position:** Winger
**Club career:**
2005-07 Rosario Central 35 (6)
2007-10 Benfica 76 (7)
2010-14 Real Madrid 122 (22)
2014-15 Manchester United 27 (3)
2015- Paris St Germain
**International record:**
2008- Argentina 66 (15)

Argentina winger Angel Di Maria became the most expensive footballer in British transfer history when he joined Manchester United from Real Madrid for an incredible £59.7 million in August 2014. His first season at Old Trafford, though, was something of a disappointment and in the summer of 2015 he was sold to Paris St Germain for a £15 million loss.

• **After beginning his career with his hometown club Rosario, Di Maria came to prominence during a three-year stay with Benfica where he was hailed as "Argentina's next superstar" by the legendary Diego Maradona.**

• He joined Real Madrid for around £20 million in 2010 and helped the Spanish titans win the Copa del Rey in 2011 and the league title the following year. In 2014 he scored the opening goal in the Copa del Rey final as Real beat arch rivals Barcelona 2-1 in Valencia.

• **A tricky player who loves to take on opposition defenders, Di Maria scored the winning goal in the final of the 2008 Olympic Games in Beijing as Argentina beat Nigeria 1-0 to claim the Gold medal. In 2014 he was part of the Argentina team that reached the World Cup final and the following year he scored twice in his country's 6-1 rout of Paraguay in the semi-final of the Copa America. However, he was injured in the final against hosts Chile and had to limp off in the first half.**

## DISCIPLINE

Yellow and red cards were introduced into English league football on 2nd October 1976, and on the same day Blackburn's David Wagstaffe received the first red card during his side's match with Leyton Orient. Five years later cards were withdrawn by the Football Association as referees were getting 'too flashy', but the system was re-introduced in 1987.

• **A stormy last 16 match between the Netherlands and Portugal in 2006 was the most ill-disciplined in the history of the World Cup. Russian referee Valentin Ivanov was the busiest man on the pitch as he pulled out his yellow card 16 times and his red one four times, with the match ending as a nine-a-side affair.**

• On Boxing Day 2014 Gareth Barry became the first player in Premier League history to be shown 100 yellow

*'You're off, son!' Chelsea's John Terry receives his marching orders from referee Mark Clattenburg*

## DONCASTER ROVERS

**Year founded:** 1879
**Ground:** Keepmoat Stadium (15,231)
**Nickname:** The Rovers
**Biggest win:** 10-0 v Darlington (1964)
**Heaviest defeat:** 0-12 v Small Heath (1903)

Founded in 1879 by Albert Jenkins, a fitter at Doncaster's Great Northern Railway works, Doncaster turned professional in 1885 and joined the Second Division of the Football League in 1901.

• Remarkably, Doncaster hold the record for the most wins in a league season (33 in 1946/47) and for the most defeats (34 in 1997/98).

• Doncaster's leading scorer is Tom Keetley, who banged in 180 league goals for Rovers, including a club record six in a single game against Ashington in 1929.

• In 1946 Doncaster were involved in the longest ever football match, a Third Division (North) cup tie against Stockport County at Edgeley Park which the referee ruled could extend beyond extra-time in an attempt to find a winner. Eventually, the game was abandoned after 203 minutes due to poor light.

• Rovers received a club record £2 million when defender Matt Mills joined Reading in 2009. The following year Doncaster broke their own transfer record, splashing out £1.15 million on Sheffield United striker Billy Sharp.

> **HONOURS**
> *League One champions* 2013
> *Division 3 (North) champions* 1935, 1947, 1950
> *Division 4 champions* 1966, 1969
> *Third Division champions* 2004
> *Football League Trophy* 2007

## DOUBLES

The first club to win the Double of league championship and FA Cup were Preston North End, in the very first season of the Football League in 1888/89. The Lancashire side achieved this feat in fine style, remaining undefeated in the league and keeping a clean sheet in all their matches in the FA Cup.

# TOP 10

## PREMIER LEAGUE YELLOW CARDS

| | | |
|---|---|---|
| 1. | Gareth Barry | 105 |
| 2. | Lee Bowyer | 99 |
| | Kevin Davies | 99 |
| | Paul Scholes | 99 |
| 5. | Scott Parker | 92 |
| 6. | Robbie Savage | 88 |
| 7. | George Boateng | 87 |
| 8. | Kevin Nolan | 86 |
| 9. | Phil Neville | 84 |
| | Wayne Rooney | 84 |

cards. By the end of the campaign the Everton midfielder had taken his record tally to 105.

• Roy McDonough, a journeyman striker for Walsall, Colchester, Southend and Exeter in the 1970s and 1980s, was sent off a record 21 times during his career, earning himself the nickname 'Red Card Roy'.

• Richard Dunne, Duncan Ferguson and Patrick Vieira share the record for receiving the most red cards in Premier League matches, with eight each.

• When a mass brawl erupted in the middle of the pitch during a match between Argentinian sides Victoriano Arenas and Claypole on 26th February 2011, referee Damian Rubino showed red cards to all 22 players and 14 substitutes as well as coaches and technical staff. The total of 36 players sent off set a new world record, smashing the previous 'best' of 20!

• The most yellow cards handed out to one player in a Premier League season is 14 – in 2014/15 Sunderland's Lee Cattermole became the sixth player to reach this figure. In the same season QPR midfielder Joey Barton became the first Premier League player to be shown a yellow card in seven consecutive games. The run came to end in Rangers' next game at Hull when Barton received a straight red!

• Arsenal and Manchester United have both won the Double a record three times. The Reds' trio of successes all came within a five-year period in the 1990s (1994, 1996 and 1999), with the last of their Doubles comprising two-thirds of a legendary Treble which also included the Champions League. Arsenal first won the Double in 1971 and since then the Gunners have twice repeated the feat under manager Arsène Wenger in 1998 and 2002.

• Perhaps, though, the most famous Double of all was achieved by Tottenham Hotspur in 1961 as it was the first such success in the 20th century. Under legendary manager Bill Nicholson, Spurs clinched the most prized honour in the domestic game with a 2-0 victory over Leicester City in the FA Cup final. The other English clubs to win the Double are Aston Villa (1897), Liverpool (1986) and Chelsea (2010).

• Northern Ireland side Linfield have won a world record 23 Doubles. Rangers, with 18 Doubles, lie in second place, while Greek outfit Olympiacos (17 Doubles) are in third place.

## DRAWS

Everton have drawn more matches in the top flight than any other club, having finished on level terms in 1,091 out of 4,366 matches. Even the Toffees, though, can't match Norwich City's record of 23 draws in a single season, set in the First Division in 1978/79.

• The highest scoring draw in the top division of English football was 6-6, in a match between Leicester City and Arsenal in 1930. That bizarre scoreline was matched in a Second Division encounter between Charlton and Middlesbrough at The Valley in 1960, with a certain Brian Clough grabbing a hat-trick for the visitors.

• The highest scoring draw in Premier League history came on the last day of the 2012/13 season at the Hawthorns when West Brom and Manchester United drew 5-5 in Sir Alex Ferguson's last game in charge of the Red Devils.

• The fourth qualifying round of the FA Cup between Alvechurch and Oxford United in 1971 went to five replays before Alvechurch finally won 1-0 in the sixth game between the clubs. The total playing time of 11 hours is a record for an FA Cup tie.

• Aston Villa have drawn a record 267 Premier League games. In the 2014/15 season Sunderland equalled the Premier League record for 0-0 draws – set by Sheffield United in 1993/94 – with nine, the last of which at Arsenal ensured their top-flight survival.

## DIDIER DROGBA

**Born:** Abidjan, Ivory Coast, 11th March 1978
**Position:** Striker
**Club career:**
1998-2002 Le Mans 63 (12)
2002-03 En Avant Guingamp 45 (20)
2003-04 Marseille 35 (18)
2004-12 Chelsea 226 (100)
2012-13 Shanghai Shenhua 11 (8)
2013-14 Galatasaray 37 (15)
2014-15 Chelsea 28 (4)
2015- Montreal Impact 1 (0)
**International record:**
2002-14 Ivory Coast 104 (65)

Chelsea legend Didier Drogba is the only player to have scored in four FA Cup finals, his goals helping the Blues win the trophy in 2007, 2009, 2010 and 2012. In the last of those years he also played a vital part in the Londoners' first ever Champions League success, heading the equaliser against Bayern Munich in the final and then calmly scoring in the penalty shoot-out to secure the Blues' historic triumph.

• After rising to prominence with Marseille, Drogba moved to Chelsea for a then club record fee of £24 million in the summer of 2004. In his first two seasons in west London Drogba helped the Blues win back-to-back Premier League titles, and the League Cup in 2005.

• In 2006/07 he won the Golden Boot and was a key figure in Chelsea's FA Cup and League Cup double, scoring the winning goals in both finals and becoming the first African player ever to get on the scoresheet in the FA Cup final when he slotted the vital goal against Manchester United in the first ever final at the new Wembley.

• Drogba enjoyed his best season with the Blues in 2009/10, scoring the winner in the FA Cup final against Portsmouth. He also fired in a career-best 29 league goals to win the Golden Boot for a second time. After leaving the Blues in 2012 he returned to Stamford Bridge two years later, helping his old club win the Premier League again in 2015.

*'I did it myyyyyy waaaaaayyy!'*

• The all-time leading goalscorer for the Ivory Coast by some distance, Drogba was voted African Footballer of the Year in 2006 and 2009.

# DUNDEE

**Year founded:** 1893
**Ground:** Dens Park (11,506)
**Nickname:** The Dee
**Biggest win:** 10-0 v Alloa (1947), v Dunfermline (1947) and v Queen of the South (1962)
**Heaviest defeat:** 0-11 v Celtic (1895)

Dundee were founded in 1893 after the merger of two local clubs, Dundee Our Boys and Dundee East End.

• **The club's greatest ever moment was in 1962 when The Dee won the Scottish title under the managership of Bob Shankly, brother of the legendary Bill. The following season Dundee reached the semi-finals of the European Cup, before bowing out to eventual winners AC Milan.**

• Dundee were the first club to retain the Scottish League Cup, following victories in the final over Rangers in 1952 and Kilmarnock in 1953.

• **Future Tottenham hero Alan Gilzean scored a club record 113 league**

goals for the Dee between 1957 and 1964, including a season's best 52 in 1963/64.

• On 9th November 2013 novice striker Craig Wighton became Dundee's youngest ever scorer when he netted in a 2-0 win against Raith Rovers, aged 16 years, three months and 19 days.

HONOURS
*Division 1 champions* 1962
*Division 2 champions* 1947
*First Division champions* 1979, 1992
*Championship champions* 2014
*Scottish Cup* 1910
*Scottish League Cup* 1952, 1953, 1974

# DUNDEE UNITED

**Year founded:** 1909
**Ground:** Tannadice Park (14,229)
**Previous name:** Dundee Hibernian
**Nickname:** The Terrors
**Biggest win:** 14-0 v Nithsdale Wanderers (1931)
**Heaviest defeat:** 1-12 v Motherwell (1954)

Originally founded as Dundee Hibernian by members of the city's Irish community in 1909, the club changed to its present name in 1923 to attract

support from a wider population.

• **The club emerged from relative obscurity to become one of the leading clubs in Scotland under long-serving manager Jim McLean in the 1970s and 1980s, winning the Scottish Premier Division in 1983. The club's success, allied to that of Aberdeen, led to talk of a 'New Firm' capable of challenging the 'Old Firm' of Rangers and Celtic for major honours.**

• United reached the semi-finals of the European Cup in 1984 and the final of the UEFA Cup in 1987, where they lost to Gothenburg. The club's European exploits also include four victories over Barcelona – a 100 per cent record against the Catalans which no other British team can match.

• **After being losing finalists on six previous occasions, Dundee United finally won the Scottish Cup in 1994 when they beat Rangers 1-0 in the final. They won the trophy for a second time in 2010, following a comfortable 3-0 win against shock finalists Ross County, but went down in the 2014 final to surprise winners St Johnstone.**

• The Terrors, so called because of the lion on their club badge, have a miserable record in the Scottish League Cup in recent decades. Since last winning the competition in 1981 they have appeared in five finals – most recently against Celtic in 2015 – and lost them all.

• **United's top scorer is Peter McKay, who knocked in 158 league goals between 1947 and 1954.**

• In a BBC poll in 2006 Dundee United fan Zippy from Rainbow was voted Britain's favourite celebrity football fan. The show's presenter, Geoffrey Hayes, a longstanding Terrors' fan, had previously insisted on the puppet's bright orange colour to reflect United's famous tangerine shirts.

• **Tannadice Park, Dundee United's home since their foundation, is situated just a few hundred yards from Dundee's Dens Park, making the two clubs the closest neighbours in British football.**

*Dundee United take on QPR in a pre-season friendly*

HONOURS
*Premier League champions* 1983
*Division 2 champions* 1925, 1929
*Scottish Cup* 1994, 2010
*Scottish League Cup* 1980, 1981

*England are always 'red-dy' for action*

## ENGLAND

**First international:** Scotland 0 England 0, 1872
**Most capped player:** Peter Shilton, 125 caps (1971-90)
**Leading goalscorer:** Bobby Charlton, 49 goals (1958-70)
**First World Cup appearance:** England 2 Chile 0, 1950
**Biggest win:** England 13 Ireland 0, 1882
**Heaviest defeat:** Hungary 7 England 1, 1954

England, along with their first opponents Scotland, are the oldest international team in world football. The two countries met in the first official international in Glasgow in 1872, with honours being shared after a 0-0 draw. The following year William Kenyon-Slaney of Wanderers FC scored England's first ever goal in a 4-2 victory over Scotland at the Kennington Oval.

• With a team entirely composed of players from England, Great Britain won the first Olympic Games football tournament in 1908 and repeated the feat in 1912.

• England did not lose a match on home soil against a team from outside the British Isles until 1953 when they were thrashed 6-3 by Hungary at Wembley. The following year England went down to their worst ever defeat to the same opposition, crashing 7-1 in Budapest.

• Although Walter Winterbottom was appointed as England's first full-time manager in 1946, the squad was picked by a committee until Alf Ramsey took over in 1963. Three years later England hosted and won the World Cup – the greatest moment in the country's football history by some considerable margin.

• There were many heroes in that 1966 team, including goalkeeper Gordon Banks, skipper Bobby Moore and striker Geoff Hurst, who scored a hat-trick in the 4-2 victory over West Germany in the final at Wembley. Ramsey, too, was hailed for his part in the success and was knighted soon afterwards.

• Since then, however, England fans have experienced more than their fair share of disappointment. A second appearance in the World Cup final was within the grasp of Bobby Robson's team in 1990 but, agonisingly, they lost on penalties in the semi-final to the eventual winners, West Germany.

• In 1996 England hosted the European Championships and were again knocked out on penalties by Germany at the semi-final stage. England have lost four more times on penalties at major tournaments, most recently going out of Euro 2012 on spot-kicks to Italy, to leave them with the worst shoot-out record (one win in seven) of any country in the world.

• With 50 goals for England, Wayne Rooney is the leading scorer for the Three Lions. 1960s striker Jimmy Greaves, meanwhile, scored a record six hat-tricks for England.

• Gary Lineker is the only England player to win the World Cup Golden Boot, with six goals at the 1986 tournament in Mexico.

• Billy Wright, the first player to appear 100 times for England, captained his

## TOP 10

### ENGLAND GOALSCORERS

| | | |
|---|---|---|
| 1. Wayne Rooney (2003- ) | 50 |
| 2. Bobby Charlton (1958-70) | 49 |
| 3. Gary Lineker (1984-92) | 48 |
| 4. Jimmy Greaves (1958-67) | 44 |
| 5. Michael Owen (1998-2008) | 40 |
| 6. Tom Finney (1946-58) | 30 |
| Nat Lofthouse (1950-58) | 30 |
| Alan Shearer (1992-2000) | 30 |
| 9. Vivian Woodward (1903-11) | 29 |
| Frank Lampard (1999-2014) | 29 |

country 90 times – a record equalled by Bobby Moore.

• Ashley Cole featured in 107 games for England without scoring once – a record for an outfield player.

• England's worst ever World Cup showing came at the 2014 tournament in Brazil when they failed to win a single one of their three group games against Italy, Uruguay and Costa Rica.

## HONOURS

**World Cup winners** *1966*
**World Cup Record**
*1930 Did not enter*
*1934 Did not enter*
*1938 Did not enter*
*1950 Round 1*
*1954 Quarter-finals*
*1958 Round 1*
*1962 Quarter-finals*
*1966 Winners*
*1970 Quarter-finals*
*1974 Did not qualify*
*1978 Did not qualify*
*1982 Round 1*
*1986 Quarter-finals*
*1990 Semi-finals*
*1994 Did not qualify*
*1998 Round 2*
*2002 Quarter-finals*
*2006 Quarter-finals*
*2010 Round 2*
*2014 Round 1*

# CHRISTIAN ERIKSEN

**Born:** Middelfart, Denmark, 14th February 1992
**Position:** Midfielder
**Club career:**
2010-13 Ajax 113 (25)
2013- Tottenham Hotspur 58 (17)
**International record:**
2010- Denmark 53 (6)

Danish Footballer of the Year in both 2014 and 2015, Christian Eriksen was a key figure in Tottenham's run to the 2015 League Cup final, scoring both goals in a 2-2 draw at Sheffield United in the second leg of the semi-final that secured Spurs a 3-2 aggregate win.

• As a youth player with OB Copenhagen Eriksen was a transfer target for numerous top European clubs, but after trials with Chelsea, Manchester United, Barcelona and Real Madrid, he decided to join Ajax as a 16-year-old in 2008. It proved to be a wise move, as the youngster soon cemented a place in the Dutch giants' side and went on to win three league titles before joining Spurs for £11 million in 2013.

• When he made his international debut in 2010 against Austria, aged 18, Eriksen became the fourth youngest Danish player ever to appear for the national team. He then became the youngest Danish player ever to score in a European championship qualifier when he netted in a 2-0 win against Iceland the following year.

• Aged just 18 and four months, Eriksen was the youngest player to appear at the 2010 World Cup in South Africa.

*Christian Eriksen scored more free kicks in the Premier League in 2014/2015 than any other player (three)*

*More than 100,000 people took part in an online vote to name the Euro 2016 mascot. And the winning name was... Super Victor!*

## EURO 2016

Euro 2016 in France will be the biggest European Championships ever, with 24 teams competing in the finals compared to the usual 16. The expanded format means that a record 51 games will be played at the finals.

• A record 16 countries will qualify for the knock-out stages, which for the first time will feature a round of 16 before the quarter-finals.

• A record-equalling 10 venues will host matches at the finals, with the final itself being played in the 81,000-capacity Stade de France on 10th July 2016.

• Among the countries likely to be appearing at their first European Championship finals at Euro 2016 are Iceland, Northern Ireland and Wales.

## EUROPA LEAGUE

The inaugural Europa League final was played between Atletico Madrid and Fulham in Hamburg in 2010, the Spanish side winning 2-1 thanks to a late winner by Uruguayan striker Diego Forlan. Two years later Atletico won the competition for a second time after beating Athletic Bilbao 3-0 in the final in Bucharest.

• In 2011 Porto beat Braga 1-0 in Dublin in the first ever all-Portuguese European final. Porto's match-winner was Colombian striker Radamel Falcao, whose goal in the final was his 17th in the competition that season – a record for the tournament.

• The competition is now in its third incarnation, having previously been known as the Fairs Cup (1955-71) and the UEFA Cup (1971-2009). The tournament was originally established in 1955 as a competition between cities, rather than clubs. The first winners were Barcelona, who beat London 8-2 on aggregate in a final which, bizarrely, did not take place until 1958! Sevilla have the best overall record in the competition with four wins, most recently in 2015 when they beat Ukrainian side Dnipro Dnipropetrovsk 3-2 in the final in Warsaw.

• The first team to win the newly named UEFA Cup were Tottenham Hotspur in 1972, who beat Wolves 3-2 on aggregate in the only all-English final. Following Chelsea's triumph in the 2013 Europa League, English clubs have won the competition 11 times... an impressive record, although Spanish teams lead the way with 15 victories.

• Swedish striker Henrik Larsson is the leading scorer in the history of the UEFA Cup with 40 goals for Feyenoord, Celtic and Helsingborg between 1993 and 2009. Inter Milan defender Giuseppe Bergomi made a record 96 appearances in the competition between 1980 and 1998.

*Sevilla celebrated their 2015 Europa League victory in low-key style*

CONGRATULATIONS!

# EUROPEAN CHAMPIONSHIPS

Originally called the European Nations Cup, the idea for the European Championships came from Henri Delaunay, the then secretary of the French FA. The first championships in 1960 featured just 17 countries (the four British nations, Italy and West Germany were among those who declined to take part). The first winners of the tournament were the Soviet Union, who beat Yugoslavia 2-1 in the final in Paris.

• **Germany have the best record in the tournament, having won the trophy three times (in 1972, 1980 and 1996) and been runners-up on a further three occasions. Spain have also won the championships three times (1964, 2008 and 2012) and are the only country to retain the trophy following a 4-0 demolition of Italy in the final at Euro 2012 – the biggest win in any European Championships or World Cup final.**

• Germany also hold a number of minor records, having played the most games in the finals (43), won the most matches (23) and scored the most goals (65).

• **French legend Michel Platini is the leading scorer in the finals of the European Championships with nine goals. England's Alan Shearer is in second place with a total of seven goals at the 1996 and 2000 tournaments.**

• Including qualifying matches, Portugal's Cristiano Ronaldo is the leading scorer in the competition with 26 goals.

• **In the qualifying tournament for the 2008 finals Germany recorded the biggest ever win in the history of the competition, thrashing minnows San Marino 13-0 on their home patch.**

• Holland's Edwin van der Sar and France's Lilian Thuram share the appearance record at the finals, having both played in 16 games. The pair are also among the eight players to have played in a record four tournaments, both featuring between 1996 and 2008.

> **European Championships Finals**
> *1960 USSR 2 Yugoslavia 1 (Paris)*
> *1964 Spain 2 USSR 1 (Madrid)*
> *1968 Italy 2 Yugoslavia 0• (Rome)*
> *1972 West Germany 3 USSR 0 (Brussels)*
> *1976 Czechoslovakia 2* West Germany 2 (Belgrade)*

> *1980 West Germany 2 Belgium 1 (Rome)*
> *1984 France 2 Spain 0 (Paris)*
> *1988 Netherlands 2 USSR 0 (Munich)*
> *1992 Denmark 2 Germany 0 (Gothenburg)*
> *1996 Germany 2 Czech Republic 1 (London)*
> *2000 France 2 Italy 1 (Rotterdam)*
> *2004 Greece 1 Portugal 0 (Lisbon)*
> *2008 Spain 1 Germany 0 (Vienna)*
> *2012 Spain 4 Italy 0 (Kiev)*
> *• After 1-1 draw      * Won on penalties*

## EUROPEAN GOLDEN BOOT

Now officially known as the European Golden Shoe, the European Golden Boot has been awarded since 1968 to the leading scorer in league matches in the top division of every European league. Since 1997 the award has been based on a points system which gives greater weight to goals scored in the leading European leagues.

• **Real Madrid superstar Cristiano Ronaldo is the only player to have the award four times, most recently in 2015 with an impressive total of 48 goals. However, his arch rival Lionel Messi holds the record for the most goals scored by a Golden Boot winner, with an incredible 50 in 2011/12.**

• The first British winner of the award was Liverpool's Ian Rush in 1984, and the most recent was Sunderland's Kevin Phillips in 2000. Since then, Thierry Henry (in 2004 and 2005), Cristiano Ronaldo (in 2008) and Luis Suarez (jointly with Cristiano Ronaldo in 2014) have won the Golden Shoe after topping both the Premiership and European goalscoring charts. When Ronaldo first won the Golden Shoe with Real Madrid in 2011, he become the first player to win the award in two different countries.

*2015 European Golden Boot winner Cristiano Ronaldo sends a not-very-subtle message to Lionel Messi*

• The most controversial winner of the award was Rumania's Rodion Camataru, who scored 20 of his 44 goals for Dynamo Bucharest in the last six games of the 1986/87 season. Suspicions that some of these matches had not been played in a wholly competitive spirit were confirmed by evidence that emerged in the post-Communist era and in 2007 the runner-up in the 1987 list, Austria Vienna striker Toni Polster, was also granted a Golden Boot.

## EUROPEAN SUPER CUP

Founded in 1972 as a two-legged final between the winners of the European Cup and the European Cup Winners' Cup, the European Super Cup trophy is now awarded to the winners of a one-off match between the Champions League and Europa League holders.

• AC Milan and current holders Barcelona have won the trophy a record five times each. Liverpool are the most successful English club in the competition with three victories (in 1977, 2001 and 2005). In the first of these triumphs the Reds hammered Hamburg 6-0 in the second leg at Anfield to equal the record winning score for the final – set four years earlier by Ajax against AC Milan.

• Liverpool's Terry McDermott (against Hamburg in 1977) and Atletico Madrid's Radamel Falcao (against Chelsea in 2012) are the only two players to have ever scored a hat-trick in the European Super Cup.

• Monaco's Stade Louis II has hosted the final a record 16 times, including for 15 consecutive years between 1998 and 2012.

## EVERTON

**Year founded:** 1878
**Ground:** Goodison Park (39,573)
**Previous name:** St Domingo
**Nickname:** The Toffees
**Biggest win:** 11-2 v Derby County (1890)
**Heaviest defeat:** 0-7 v Sunderland (1934), v Wolves (1939) and v Arsenal (2005)

The club was formed as the church team St Domingo in 1878, adopting the name Everton (after the surrounding area) the following year. In 1888 Everton joined the Football League as founder members, winning the first of nine league titles three years later.

• One of the most famous names

*Ross Barkley's audition for Strictly Come Dancing ended with a flourish*

in English football, Everton hold the proud record of spending more seasons, 113, in the top flight than any other club. Relegated only twice, in 1930 and 1951, they have spent just four seasons in total outside the top tier.

• The club's unusual nickname, the Toffees, stems from a local business called Ye Ancient Everton Toffee House which was situated near Goodison Park. In the early 1930s Everton's precise style of play earned the club the tag 'The School of Science', a nickname which lingers to this day.

• The club's record goalscorer is the legendary Dixie Dean, who notched an incredible total of 383 goals in all competitions between 1925 and 1937. Dean's best season for the club was in the Toffees' title-winning campaign in 1927/28 when his 60 league goals set a Football League record that is unlikely ever to be beaten. Then, in 1930/31, he scored in a Football League record 12 consecutive games. Dean's total of 349 league goals is a record for a player with the same club.

• Everton's most capped player is long-serving goalkeeper Neville Southall, who made 93 appearances for Wales in the 1980s and 1990s. He is also the club's record appearance maker, turning out in 578 league games.

• In 1931 Everton won the Second Division title, scoring 121 goals in the process. The following season the Toffees banged in 116 goals on their way to lifting the First Division title, becoming the first club to find the net 100 times in consecutive seasons.

• The club's most successful decade, though, was in the 1980s when, under manager Howard Kendall, they won the league championship (1985 and 1987), FA Cup (1984) and the European Cup

## IS THAT A FACT?

Everton were the first club ever to recover from 2-0 down in the final to win the FA Cup, mounting a famous comeback against Sheffield Wednesday in 1966.

Winners' Cup (in 1985, following a 3-1 win over Austria Vienna in the final). Since those glory days Everton have had to play second fiddle to city rivals Liverpool, although the Toffees did manage to win the FA Cup for a fifth time in 1995, beating Manchester United in the final thanks to a single goal by striker Paul Rideout.

• The club's record signing is Belgian striker Romelu Lukaku, who moved to Merseyside from Chelsea for £28 million in July 2014 after spending the previous season on loan at Goodison Park. The Toffees' previous most expensive player, afro-haired midfielder Marouane Fellaini, became the club's record sale when he joined Manchester United for £27.5 million in August 2013.

• In 1893 Everton's Jack Southworth became the first player in Football League history to score six goals in a match when he fired a double hat-trick in a 7-1 victory against West Bromwich Albion.

• Everton's Louis Saha scored the fastest ever goal in the FA Cup final, when he netted after just 25 seconds against Chelsea at Wembley in 2009. However, the Toffees were unable to hold onto their lead and were eventually beaten 2-1 – one of a record eight times Everton have lost in the final.

• The oldest ground in the Premier League, Goodison Park is the only stadium in the world to have a church, St Luke the Evangelist, inside its grounds. The stadium was the first club ground in England to host the FA Cup final (1894) and the only one in the UK to have staged a World Cup semi-final – the clash between West Germany and Russia in 1966.

• Everton were the first club to win a penalty shoot-out in the European Cup, beating German outfit Borussia Monchengladbach 4-3 at Goodison Park in 1970.

• Famous Everton fans include Labour politician Andy Burnham, snooker player John Parrott and 'Rocky' actor Sylvester Stallone.

HONOURS
**Division 1 champions** 1891, 1915, 1928, 1932, 1939, 1963, 1970, 1985, 1987
**Division 2 champions** 1931
**FA Cup** 1906, 1933, 1966, 1984, 1995
**European Cup Winners' Cup** 1985

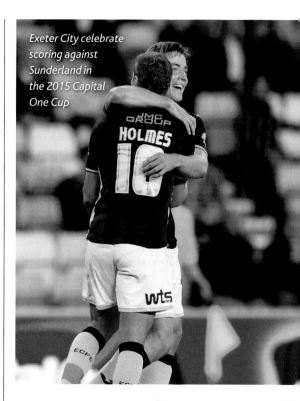

Exeter City celebrate scoring against Sunderland in the 2015 Capital One Cup

## EXETER CITY

**Year founded:** 1904
**Ground:** St James' Park (8,541)
**Nickname:** The Grecians
**Biggest win:** 14-0 v Weymouth (1908)
**Heaviest defeat:** 0-9 v Notts County (1948) and v Northampton Town (1958)

Exeter City were founded in 1904 following the amalgamation of two local sides, Exeter United and St Sidwell's United. The club were founder members of the Third Division (South) in 1920 and remained in the two lower divisions until they were relegated to the Conference in 2003. Now owned by the Exeter City Supporters' Trust, the club rejoined the Football League in 2008.

• The Grecians reached the FA Cup quarter-finals in 1931, before losing to Sunderland. Fifty years later they made it into the last eight again - after knocking out Leicester and Newcastle – but were beaten 2-0 by eventual winners Tottenham.

• Club legend Arnie Mitchell played a record 516 games for Exeter between 1952 and 1966. The Grecians' record scorer is Tony Kellow with 129 league goals in three spells at St James' between 1976 and 1988.

• On a tour of South America in 1914 Exeter became the first club side to play the Brazilian national team. The Grecians lost 2-0 but the occasion has gone into club folklore, with Exeter fans delighting in taunting their opponents by chanting, "Have you ever, have you ever, have you ever played Brazil?"

• Appointed in 2006, Exeter boss Paul Tisdale is the second longest-serving manager in English football behind Arsenal supremo Arsene Wenger.

> HONOURS
> **Division 4 champions** 1990

## EXTRA-TIME

Normally consisting of two halves of 15 minutes each, extra-time has been played to produce a winner in knock-out tournaments since the earliest days of football, although to begin with the playing of the additional time had to be agreed by the two captains. Extra-time was first played in an FA Cup final in 1875, Royal Engineers and the Old Etonians drawing 1-1 (Royal Engineers won the replay 2-0). In all, extra-time has been played in 19 finals, the most recent in 2014 when Arsenal eventually beat Hull City 3-2.

• The first World Cup final to go to extra-time was in 1934, when hosts Italy and Czechoslovakia were tied 1-1 at the end of 90 minutes. Seven minutes into the additional period, Angelo Schiavio scored the winner for Italy. Since then, six other finals have gone to extra-time, most recently in 2014 when Germany's Mario Gotze scored the winner against Argentina with just seven minutes to play.

• In an attempt to encourage attacking football and reduce the number of matches settled by penalty shoot-outs, FIFA ruled in 1993 that the first goal scored in extra-time would win the match. The first major tournament to be decided by the so-called 'golden goal' rule was the 1996 European Championships, Germany defeating the Czech Republic in the final thanks to a 94th-minute strike by Oliver Bierhoff. The 2000 final of the same competition was also decided in the same manner, David Trezeguet scoring a stunning winner for France against Italy in the 103rd minute.

• Concerns that the 'golden goal' put too much pressure on referees led UEFA to replace it with the 'silver goal' in 2002. Under this rule, which was used at Euro 2004 but scrapped afterwards, only the first half of extra-time was played if either team led at the interval.

• The first European Cup final to require extra-time was between Real Madrid and AC Milan in 1962, Real eventually winning 3-2. In all, 16 finals have gone to extra-time, but only five produced a winner inside the additional 30 minutes – the most recent in 2014, when Real Madrid beat city rivals Atletico 4-1 in Lisbon.

**IS THAT A FACT?**
The last League Cup final to be settled in extra-time was in 2008, when Jonathan Woodgate headed the winner in Tottenham's 2-1 defeat of London rivals Chelsea.

*Gareth Bale's extra-time goal sent Real Madrid on their way to victory in the 2014 Champions League final against city rivals Atletico*

## CESC FABREGAS

**Born:** Arenys de Mar, Spain,
4th May 1987
**Position:** Midfielder
**Club career:**
2003-11 Arsenal 212 (35)
2011-14 Barcelona 96 (28)
2014- Chelsea 34 (3)
**International record:**
2006- Spain 97 (14)

Cesc Fabregas became the third most expensive Spanish player in the Premier League (after Fernando Torres and Juan Mata) when he joined Chelsea from Barcelona in May 2014 for £30 million. He enjoyed a great first season with the west Londoners, helping them win the title and League Cup and topping the Premier League 'assists' table with 18 – just two short of Thierry Henry's record set in 2002/03.

• Fabregas came through the Barca youth system before signing for Arsenal in September 2003. A month later he became the Gunners' youngest ever player when he made his debut in a League Cup tie against Rotherham United, aged just 16 and 177 days. In 2008 he was named PFA Young Player of the Year and in the same year he was made Arsenal captain by boss Arsene Wenger.
• To the dismay of Gunners fans, Fabregas returned to Barcelona in 2011 for £25.4 million, making him the most expensive player ever to leave the Emirates. In three years at the Nou Camp, the midfielder helped the Catalans win both the Spanish Cup (in 2012) and La Liga (in 2013).
• **When Fabregas made his debut for Spain against Ivory Coast in 2006, he was the youngest player to represent his country for 70 years. A magnificent passer of the ball who** can unpick the tightest of defences, he has gone on to enjoy huge success with the Spanish national team, helping them to win the European Championships in 2008 and 2012, and the World Cup in 2010 when his clever pass set up Andres Iniesta for the winning goal in the final against the Netherlands.

*Cesc Fabregas shares an intimate moment with his 'trophy' girlfriend!*

## FA CUP

The oldest knock-out competition in the world, the FA Cup dates back to 1871 when it was established under the control of the Football Association. The first round of the first FA Cup was played on 11th November 1871, Clapham Rovers' Jarvis Kenrick scoring the very first goal in the competition in a 3-0 win over Upton Park.
• **The following year Wanderers beat Royal Engineers at Kennington Oval in the first ever FA Cup final. The only goal of the game was scored by Morton Peto Betts, who played under the pseudonym A.H. Chequer. Uniquely, Wanderers, as holders, were given a bye all the way through to the following year's final, and they took full advantage by beating Oxford University 2-1.**
• The FA Challenge Cup – the competition's full title – has always retained the same name despite being sponsored in recent years by Littlewoods (1994-98), AXA (1998-2002), E.ON (2006-11), Budweiser (2011-14) and Emirates (2015-).
• **There have, however, been five different trophies. The first trophy – known as the 'little tin idol' – was stolen from a Birmingham shop window in September 1895 where it was on display, having been won by Aston Villa a few months earlier. Sixty years later the thief revealed that the trophy was melted down and turned into counterfeit coins. A second trophy was used until 1910 when it was presented to the FA's long-serving President and former five-time cup winner, Lord Kinnaird. A new, larger trophy was commissioned by the FA from Fattorini and Sons Silversmiths in Bradford – and, by a remarkable coincidence, was won in its first year by Bradford City in 1911. This trophy was used until 1992, when it was replaced with an exact replica. In 2014 a new trophy, with an identical design to the 1911 one, was presented to that year's winners, Arsenal.**

*Theo Walcott was flying after opening the scoring for Arsenal in the 2015 FA Cup final*

• The only league team to have won the FA Cup in three consecutive years are Blackburn Rovers, who lifted the trophy in 1884, 1885 and 1886. The most successful club in the competition are Arsenal who, following their latest success in 2015, have won the FA Cup a record 12 times.

• **In 2000 Manchester United became the first holders not to defend their title when they failed to enter the FA Cup, opting instead to take part in the inaugural FIFA Club World Championship in Brazil.**

• Five years later United were involved in the first FA Cup final to be decided by penalties, losing 5-4 to Arsenal after a 0-0 draw at the Millennium Stadium, Cardiff. In 2007 the final returned to Wembley, Chelsea becoming the first club to lift the trophy at the new national stadium after a 1-0 victory over Manchester United.

• **Tottenham Hotspur are the only non-league side to win the competition, lifting the trophy for the first time in 1901 while members of the Southern League. West Ham were the last team from outside the top flight to win the cup, beating Arsenal 1-0 in the 1980 final.**

• Leicester City are the most unfortunate club in FA Cup history, losing all four of the finals they have appeared in.

• **In 1887 Preston North End recorded the biggest win in the history of the competition when they thrashed Hyde 26-0 in a first-round tie. In the same season, Preston's Jimmy Ross scored a record 19 goals in the competition.**

• Ashley Cole has won the FA Cup a record seven times. Three of his triumphs came with Arsenal (in 2002, 2003 and 2005), and he also enjoyed four successes with Chelsea (in 2007, 2009, 2010 and 2012).

## TOP 10

| FA CUP FINAL APPEARANCES | | |
|---|---|---|
| 1. Arsenal | 19 | (12 wins, 7 losses) |
| 2. Manchester United | 18 | (11 wins, 7 losses) |
| 3. Liverpool | 14 | (7 wins, 7 losses) |
| 4. Newcastle United | 13 | (6 wins, 7 losses) |
| Everton | 13 | (5 wins, 8 losses) |
| 6. Aston Villa | 11 | (7 wins, 4 losses) |
| Chelsea | 11 | (7 wins, 4 losses) |
| 8. Manchester City | 10 | (5 wins, 5 losses) |
| West Bromwich Albion | 10 | (5 wins, 5 losses) |
| 10. Tottenham Hotspur | 9 | (8 wins, 1 loss) |

• **The leading scorer in the FA Cup is Notts County's Henry Cursham, who banged in 49 goals between 1877 and 1888. Liverpool's Ian Rush scored a record five goals in three appearances in the final in 1986, 1989 and 1992, but Chelsea's Didier Drogba is the only player to have scored in four finals (2007, 2009, 2010 and 2012).**

• The only non-English club to win the FA Cup are Cardiff City, who beat Arsenal 1-0 in 1927. Previously, Scottish club Queen's Park reached the final in 1884 and 1885 but lost on both occasions.

## FAMILIES

The first brothers to win the World Cup together were West Germany's Fritz and Ottmar Walter in 1954. England's Bobby and Jack Charlton famously repeated the feat in 1966, when the Three Lions beat West Germany 4-2 in the final at Wembley.

• **The only time two sets of brothers have played in the FA Cup final was in 1876 when the victorious Wanderers side included Frank and Hubert Heron, while losers Old Etonians' line-up featured Alfred and Edward Lyttelton.**

• Between 1996 and 2007 brothers Gary and Phil Neville played in a record 31 games together for England.

• **The first time a father and son both**

played in the same international match was in 1996 when 17-year-old Eidur Gudjohnsen came on for his father Arnor, 34, in Iceland's 3-0 win over Estonia.

• A rare instance of a father and son scoring in the same match occurred in July 2015 when former Brazil star Rivaldo and his son Rivaldinho were both on target in Mogi Mirim's 3-1 win over Macae in the Brazilian second tier.

• **When Oldham boss Lee Johnson met his father's team, Yeovil Town, in April 2013 it was the first father-son managerial clash of this type since Fulham (managed by Bill Dodgin jnr) played Bristol Rovers (managed by Bill Dodgin snr) in 1971.**

## SIR ALEX FERGUSON

**Born:** Govan, 31st December 1942
**Managerial career:**
1974 East Stirling
1974-78 St Mirren
1978-86 Aberdeen
1985-86 Scotland (caretaker)
1986-2013 Manchester United

The legendary Sir Alex Ferguson is the most successful British manager in the history of the game. Over his long career he won 38 major trophies and is the only manager from these shores to win the Champions League on two occasions.

• **Ferguson's reputation was forged at Aberdeen between 1978 and 1986 where he transformed the Dons into Scotland's leading club, breaking the domination of the Glasgow Old Firm in the process. Under Fergie, Aberdeen won three Premier Division titles, four Scottish Cups, one League Cup and the European Cup Winners' Cup**

**IS THAT A FACT?**
In his 1,500 matches as Manchester United manager Sir Alex Ferguson celebrated 2,769 goals for his team at an average of 1.85 per game.

in 1983, making him easily the most successful boss in the club's history.

• He moved to Manchester United in 1986 and, after some difficult early years, established the Reds as the dominant force of the 1990s and the new millennium. With United Ferguson won a record 13 Premier League titles, five FA Cups, three League Cups, the European Cup Winners' Cup (in 1991) and the Champions League in both 1999 and 2008.

• **Fergie's 26-year and 1,500-game tenure at Old Trafford from November 1986 until his retirement in May 2013 included a record 625 top-flight wins and made him the Premier League's and Manchester United's longest serving manager, ahead of the 24-year stint of another Scot, Sir Matt Busby.**

• Ferguson is the only man to guide both Scottish and English clubs to success in all three domestic competitions and in Europe. He is also the only manager to win the English championship in three consecutive seasons with the same club twice, achieving this feat with United between 1999 and 2001 and 2007 and 2009. In the first of those years Fergie also won the FA Cup and Champions League to pull off an unprecedented Treble.

• **A committed but not especially skilful striker in his playing days in the 1960s and early 1970s, Ferguson scored over 150 goals for a number of Scottish clubs including Dunfermline, Rangers and Falkirk.**

• Knighted for services to football in 1999, Ferguson was named Premier League Manager of the Year on a record 11 occasions, claiming the award for the last time at the end of the 2012/13 season. Following the announcement of his retirement from the game, tributes flooded in from far and wide, with Prime Minister David Cameron describing Ferguson as "a remarkable man in British football".

## MAROUANE FELLAINI

**Born:** Etterbeek, Belgium, 22nd November 1987
**Position:** Midfielder
**Club career:**
2006-08 Standard Liege 64 (9)
2008-13 Everton 138 (25)
2013- Manchester United 43 (6)
**International record:**
2007- Belgium 63 (14)

*Fellaini in full flight*

After a disappointing first season at Old Trafford Marouane Fellaini enjoyed an excellent campaign in 2014/15, chipping in with six goals as Manchester United finished a creditable fourth in the Premier League.

• **The son of a Moroccan goalkeeper, Fellaini began his career with Standard Liege, with whom he won the Belgian title in 2008. He moved to Everton a few months later, and in his first season at Goodison Park helped his new club reach the FA Cup final, although he had to be content with a runners-up medal after Chelsea beat the Toffees 2-1 at Wembley.**

• A powerful midfielder who is a real threat in the air, Fellaini became the most expensive ever player to leave Everton when he joined United for £27.5 million in September 2013, teaming up once again with his old Goodison boss David Moyes. However, he endured a miserable first season with the Red Devils, starting just 15 Premier League games and failing to score a single goal.

• **Although he was also eligible to play for Morocco, Fellaini chose his birth country and made his debut for Belgium in 2007. At the 2014 World Cup in Brazil he scored Belgium's first goal at the tournament in a 2-1 victory over Algeria.**

*Under-fire FIFA President Sepp Blatter was not amused when a protester threw money at him*

## FIFA

FIFA, the Federation Internationale de Football Association, is the most important administrative body in world football. It is responsible for the organisation of major international tournaments, notably the World Cup, and enacts law changes in the game.

• **Founded in Paris in 1904, FIFA is now based in Zurich and has 209 members, 16 more than the United Nations. The President is Sepp Blatter (elected in 1998), while his predecessors include Jules Rimet (1921-54), Sir Stanley Rous (1961-74) and Joao Havelange (1974-98). On 29th May 2015 Blatter was re-elected as President for a fourth time, fending off a challenge from Prince Ali bin Hussein of Jordan. However, the election was completely overshadowed by the dramatic arrest by the FBI of 14 high-ranking FIFA officials on a variety of serious charges, including**

racketeering **and money laundering, and four days later Blatter announced that he would step down as President early in 2016.**

• Law changes that FIFA have introduced into the World Cup include the use of substitutes (1970), penalty shoot-outs to settle drawn games (1982) and three points for a group-stage win (1994).

• **The British football associations have twice pulled out of FIFA. First, in 1918 when they were opposed to playing matches against Germany after the end of the First World War, and in 1928 over the issue of payments to amateurs. This second dispute meant that none of the British teams were represented at the first World Cup in 1930.**

• In 1992 FIFA decided to introduce a ranking index for all its member countries. As of September 2015 the top-ranked nation was Argentina, followed by Belgium and Germany.

## ROBERTO FIRMINO

**Born:** Maceio, Brazil, 2nd October 1991
**Position:** Midfielder
**Club career:**
2009-10 Figueirense 38 (8)
2010-15 1899 Hoffenheim 140 (35)
2015- Liverpool
**International record:**
2014- Brazil 10 (4)

An attacking midfielder who possesses good vision, technical skills and an eye for goal, Roberto Firmino became Liverpool's third most expensive ever when he signed for the Reds from Hoffenheim in the summer of 2015 for a cool £29 million.

• **Firmino joined his first club, Figueirense, as a youngster after being spotted by a local football-loving dentist. He helped Figueirense** gain promotion from the Brazilian second tier in 2010, before moving to Germany in January 2011.

• After taking a while to settle with Hoffenheim, Firmino enjoyed a sensational campaign in 2013/14 when he was named the Bundesliga's 'Breakthrough Player' after scoring 16 league goals – a total only bettered by three other players.

• His fine form saw him earn a first cap for Brazil in November 2014 and later that month he scored his first international goal in a friendly against Austria. The following year he was in the Brazil squad that reached the semi-finals of the Copa America in Chile.

## FLEETWOOD TOWN

**Year founded:** 1997
**Ground:** Highbury Stadium (5,327)
**Previous names:** Fleetwood Wanderers, Fleetwood Freeport
**Nickname:** The Trawlermen
**Biggest win:** 13-0 v Oldham Town (1998)
**Heaviest defeat:** 0-7 v Billingham Town (2001)

Established in 1997 as the third incarnation of a club which dates back to 1908, Fleetwood Town have enjoyed a remarkable rise in recent years. In 2012 the Trawlermen were promoted to the Football League as Conference champions, and just two years later they went up to the third tier after beating Burton Albion 1-0 in the League Two play-off final.

• The Trawlermen's points tally of 103 in 2011/12 was just two short of Crawley Town's Conference record of 105, set in the previous season. Fleetwood's superb campaign also saw them reach the third round of the FA Cup for the first time in their history.

• In May 2012 Fleetwood sold striker Jamie Vardy to Leicester City for £1 million – a record fee for a non-league club.

• With a capacity of just 5,327 Fleetwood's Highbury Stadium is the smallest in League One.

HONOURS
*Conference champions* 2012

## FLOODLIGHTS

The first ever floodlit match was played at Bramall Lane between two representative Sheffield sides on 14th October 1876 in front of a crowd of 10,000 people (around 8,000 of whom used the cover of darkness to get in without paying). The pitch was illuminated by four lamps, powered by dynamos driven by engines located behind the goals.

• For many years the Football Association banned floodlight football, so the first league match played under lights did not take place until 1956, when Newcastle beat Portsmouth 2-0 at Fratton Park. It was hardly the most auspicious of occasions, though, as floodlight failure meant the kick-off was delayed for 30 minutes.

• Arsenal became the first top-flight club in England to install floodlights in 1951 – some 20 years after legendary Gunners manager Herbert Chapman had advocated their use. Chesterfield were the last Football League club to install floodlights, finally putting up a set in 1967.

• In the winter of 1997 two Premier League games, at West Ham and Wimbledon, were abandoned because of floodlight failure. What seemed to be an unfortunate coincidence was eventually revealed to be the work of a shadowy Far Eastern betting syndicate, four members of whom were eventually arrested and sentenced to three years each in prison.

• The first FA Cup tie to be played under floodlights was on 14th September 1955, when Kidderminster Harriers hosted Brierley Hill Alliance in a preliminary round replay.

*The floodlights at the well-known beauty-spot of Adams Park, Wycombe*

# FOOTBALL ASSOCIATION

Founded in 1863 at a meeting at the Freemasons' Tavern in central London, the Football Association is the oldest football organisation in the world and the only national association with no mention of the country in its name.

• The first secretary of the FA was Ebenezer Cobb Morley of Barnes FC, nicknamed 'The Father of Football', who went on to draft the first set of laws of the game. The most controversial of the 14 laws he suggested outlawed kicking an opponent, known as 'hacking'. The first match to be played under the new laws was between Barnes and Richmond in 1863.

• In 1871 the then secretary of the FA, Charles Alcock, suggested playing a national knock-out tournament similar to the competition he had enjoyed as a schoolboy at Harrow School. The idea was accepted by the FA and the competition, named the FA Challenge Cup, has been running ever since. The FA Cup, as it is usually called, has long been the most famous national club competition in world football.

• Since 1992, the FA has run the English game's top division, the Premier League, which was formed when the old First Division broke away from the then four-division Football League.

• The FA is also responsible for the appointment of the management of the England men's and women's football teams. The FA's main asset is the new Wembley Stadium, which it owns via its subsidiary, Wembley National Stadium Limited.

• Among the innovations the FA has fought against before finally accepting are the formation of an international tournament, the use of substitutes and the use of floodlights.

# FOOTBALL LEAGUE

The Football League was founded at a meeting at the Royal Hotel, Piccadilly, Manchester in April 1888. The prime mover behind the new body was Aston Villa director William McGregor, who became the league's first President.

• The 12 founder members were Accrington, Aston Villa, Blackburn Rovers, Bolton Wanderers, Burnley, Derby County, Everton, Notts County, Preston North End, Stoke City, West Bromwich Albion and Wolverhampton Wanderers. At the end of the inaugural 1888/89 season, Preston were crowned champions.

• In 1892 a new Second Division, absorbing clubs from the rival Football Alliance, was added to the League and by 1905 the two divisions were made up of a total of 40 clubs. After the First World War, the League was expanded again to include a Third Division (later split between North and South sections).

• A further expansion after 1945 took the number of clubs playing in the league to its long-time total of 92. The formation of the Premier League in 1992 reduced the Football League to three divisions – now known as the Championship, League One and League Two.

• As well as being the governing body for the three divisions, the Football League also organises two knock-out competitions: the League Cup (known as the Capital One Cup for sponsorship reasons) and the Football League Trophy (aka the Johnstone's Paint Trophy).

• Important changes introduced by the Football League include goal difference (as opposed to goal average) to separate clubs level on points (1976), three points for a win (1981) and the play-off promotion system (at the start of the 1986/87 season).

# FOOTBALL LEAGUE TROPHY

Known for sponsorship reasons as the Johnstone's Paint Trophy since 2006, the Football League Trophy is a knock-out competition for the 48 League One and League Two clubs which began in 1983.

• The most successful team in the competition are Bristol City with three victories in the final: against Bolton in 1986, Carlisle United in 2003 and Walsall in 2015.

• Southend United recorded the biggest ever win in the competition in 1990, with a remarkable 10-1 thrashing of Aldershot.

• A competition record crowd of 80,841 attended the 1988 final at Wembley between Wolves and Burnley. The Black Country fans went home happier after their side's 2-0 win over the Clarets.

# FOOTBALLER OF THE YEAR

Confusingly, there are two Footballer of the Year awards in England and Scotland. The Football Writers' Association award was inaugurated in 1948, and the first winner was England winger Stanley Matthews. In 1974 the Professional Footballers' Association (PFA) set up their own award, Leeds hard man Norman 'Bites Yer Legs' Hunter being the first to be honoured by his peers.

• Liverpool midfielder Terry McDermott was the first player to win both awards in the same season after helping Liverpool retain the title in 1980. A total of 17 different players have won both Footballer of the Year awards in the same season, most recently Chelsea midfielder Eden Hazard in 2015. Former Arsenal striker Thierry Henry won a record five awards, landing the 'double' in both 2003 and 2004, and also carrying off the Football Writers' award in 2006.

• In 1977 Aston Villa striker Andy Gray became the first player to win both the main PFA award and the Young Player of the Year trophy. Only Cristiano Ronaldo in 2007 and Gareth Bale in 2013 have since matched this achievement.

**Football Writers' Player of the Year (since 1990)**
*1990 John Barnes (Liverpool)*
*1991 Gordon Strachan (Leeds Utd)*
*1992 Gary Lineker (Tottenham)*
*1993 Chris Waddle (Sheffield Wednesday)*
*1994 Alan Shearer (Blackburn Rovers)*
*1995 Jurgen Klinsmann (Tottenham)*
*1996 Eric Cantona (Manchester Utd)*
*1997 Gianfranco Zola (Chelsea)*
*1998 Dennis Bergkamp (Arsenal)*
*1999 David Ginola (Tottenham)*
*2000 Roy Keane (Manchester Utd)*
*2001 Teddy Sheringham (Manchester Utd)*
*2002 Robert Pires (Arsenal)*
*2003 Thierry Henry (Arsenal)*
*2004 Thierry Henry (Arsenal)*
*2005 Frank Lampard (Chelsea)*
*2006 Thierry Henry (Arsenal)*
*2007 Cristiano Ronaldo (Manchester Utd)*
*2008 Cristiano Ronaldo (Manchester Utd)*
*2009 Steven Gerrard (Liverpool)*
*2010 Wayne Rooney (Manchester Utd)*
*2011 Scott Parker (West Ham Utd)*
*2012 Robin van Persie (Arsenal)*
*2013 Gareth Bale (Tottenham)*
*2014 Luis Suarez (Liverpool)*
*2015 Eden Hazard (Chelsea)*

*2015 Footballer of the Year, Eden Hazard*

## PFA Footballer of the Year (since 1990)

*1990 David Platt (Aston Villa)*
*1991 Mark Hughes (Manchester Utd)*
*1992 Gary Pallister (Manchester Utd)*
*1993 Paul McGrath (Aston Villa)*
*1994 Eric Cantona (Manchester Utd)*
*1995 Alan Shearer (Blackburn Rovers)*
*1996 Les Ferdinand (Newcastle Utd)*
*1997 Alan Shearer (Newcastle Utd)*
*1998 Dennis Bergkamp (Arsenal)*
*1999 David Ginola (Tottenham)*
*2000 Roy Keane (Manchester Utd)*
*2001 Teddy Sheringham (Manchester Utd)*
*2002 Ruud van Nistelrooy (Manchester Utd)*
*2003 Thierry Henry (Arsenal)*
*2004 Thierry Henry (Arsenal)*
*2005 John Terry (Chelsea)*
*2006 Steven Gerrard (Liverpool)*
*2007 Cristiano Ronaldo (Manchester Utd)*
*2008 Cristiano Ronaldo (Manchester Utd)*
*2009 Ryan Giggs (Manchester Utd)*
*2010 Wayne Rooney (Manchester Utd)*
*2011 Gareth Bale (Tottenham)*
*2012 Robin van Persie (Arsenal)*
*2013 Gareth Bale (Tottenham)*
*2014 Luis Suarez (Liverpool)*
*2015 Eden Hazard (Chelsea)*

# FRANCE

**First international:** Belgium 3 France 3, 1904
**Most capped player:** Lilian Thuram, 142 caps (1994-2008)
**Leading goalscorer:** Thierry Henry, 51 goals (1997-2010)
**First World Cup appearance:** France 4 Mexico 1, 1930
**Biggest win:** France 10 Azerbaijan 0, 1995
**Heaviest defeat:** France 1 Denmark 17, 1908

The fourth most successful European football nation ever, France won the World Cup for the first and only time on home soil in 1998 with a stunning 3-0 victory over Brazil in the final in Paris. Midfield genius Zinedine Zidane was the star of the show, scoring two goals.

• Two years later France became the first World Cup holders to go on to win the European Championships when they overcame Italy in the final in Rotterdam. This, though, was a much closer affair with the French requiring a 'golden goal' by striker David Trezeguet in extra-time to claim the trophy.

• France had won the European Championships once before, in 1984. Inspired by the legendary Michel Platini, who scored a record nine goals in the tournament, Les Bleus beat Spain 2-0 in the final in Paris.

• French striker Just Fontaine scored an all-time record 13 goals at the 1958 World Cup finals in Sweden.

## IS THAT A FACT?

The only six players to win 100 caps for France – Marcel Desailly, Didier Deschamps, Thierry Henry, Lilian Thuram, Patrick Vieira and Zinedine Zidane – were all part of Les Bleus' victorious 1998 World Cup squad.

His remarkable strike rate helped his country finish third in the tournament.

• When World Cup holders France were beaten 1-0 by Senegal in the 2002 World Cup, it was one of the biggest shocks in the history of the tournament. Les Bleus slumped out of the competition in the first round on that occasion, but bounced back to reach the final again in 2006... only to suffer the agony of a penalty shoot-out defeat at the hands of Italy. In 2010, though, the French endured another nightmare campaign, internal disputes between leading players and coach Raymond Domenech contributing to a humiliating first-round exit in South Africa.

• In 1908 France suffered one of the biggest ever defeats in international football when they were hammered 17-1 by Denmark in the semi-finals of the Olympic Games tournament in London. The French team were so depressed afterwards that they declined to play for the bronze medal against Holland.

• Current France manager Didier Deschamps, who will be hoping to lead his country to victory on home soil at Euro 2016, captained Les Bleus a record 51 times between 1994 and 2000.

## HONOURS

***World Cup winners*** *1998*
***European Championships winners*** *1984, 2000*
***Confederations Cup winners*** *2001, 2003*

**World Cup Record**
*1930 Round 1*
*1934 Round 1*
*1938 Round 2*
*1950 Did not qualify*
*1954 Round 1*
*1958 Third place*
*1962 Did not qualify*
*1966 Round 1*
*1970 Did not qualify*
*1974 Did not qualify*
*1978 Round 1*
*1982 Fourth place*
*1986 Third place*
*1990 Did not qualify*
*1994 Did not qualify*
*1998 Winners*
*2002 Round 1*
*2006 Runners-up*
*2010 Round 1*
*2014 Quarter-finals*

Celtic defend an Inter Milan free-kick during the 2015 Europa League

## FREE KICKS

A method for restarting the game after an infringement, free kicks may either be direct (meaning a goal may be scored directly) or indirect (in which case a second player must touch the ball before a goal may be scored).

• **In 2000 a new rule was introduced which allowed the referee to punish dissent by moving a free kick 10 yards nearer the defenders' goal. The rule change, though, was deemed not to be a success and was unceremoniously scrapped five years later.**

• Maynor Figueroa scored the longest-range free kick in Premier League history when he walloped one in from an incredible 88 metres for Wigan against Stoke City on 12th December 2009.

• **Brazilian midfielder Juninho Pernambucano holds the world record for the most goals scored direct from a free kick with 76, most of them coming during his time at French club Lyon between 2001 and 2009. Incredibly, the record for the most free kicks scored by a player for just one club is held by a goalkeeper,**

Rogerio Ceni of Sao Paulo with 60. **Meanwhile, David Beckham is the leading scorer from free kicks in the Premier League with 15, and also has a record seven for England.**

• Vanishing spray from an aerosol can to mark the 10 yards defenders must retreat from an attacking free kick was introduced to the Premier League at the start of the 2014/15 season. The spray was first used at an international tournament in the 2011 Copa America and made its debut at the World Cup in Brazil in 2014.

## FRIENDLIES

The first official international friendly took place on 30th November 1872 between Scotland and England at the West of Scotland Cricket Ground, Partick, Glasgow. The Scottish side for the match, which ended in a 0-0 draw, was made up entirely of players from the country's leading club, Queen's Park.

• **England's first ever friendly against continental opposition was on 6th**

June 1908 against Austria in Vienna. England won that match 6-1 and two days later they did even better against the same opposition, winning 11-1.

• On 6th February 2007 London played host to a record four international friendlies on the same night – and England weren't even one of the eight teams in action! At the Emirates Stadium Portugal beat Brazil 2-0, Ghana

### IS THAT A FACT?
The longest ever friendly was played between two teams from a children's charity in Southampton at St Mary's Stadium in May 2015. The game lasted a world record 102 hours and the final score was Reds 910 Whites 725.

thrashed Nigeria 4-1 at Brentford's Griffin Park, South Korea beat European champions Greece 1-0 at Craven Cottage, while at Loftus Road Denmark were 3-1 winners over Australia.

• **England have got the better of the World Cup holders in friendlies on 10 occasions, most recently beating Spain 1-0 at Wembley in November 2011.**

• Then England manager Sven-Goran Eriksson became the first Three Lions boss to substitute all 11 starters in a 2-1 friendly defeat to Italy in 2002. However, two years later FIFA ruled that the maximum number of substitutes that could be used in an international friendly would be limited to six per team.

## FULHAM

**Year founded:** 1879
**Ground:** Craven Cottage (25,700)
**Previous name:** Fulham St Andrew's
**Nickname:** The Cottagers
**Biggest win:** 10-1 v Ipswich Town (1963)
**Heaviest defeat:** 0-10 v Liverpool (1986)

London's oldest club, Fulham were founded in 1879 by two clergymen. Originally known as Fulham St Andrew's, the club adopted its present name nine years later. After winning the Southern League in two consecutive seasons Fulham were elected to the Football League in 1907.

• **Before moving to Craven Cottage in 1896, Fulham had played at no fewer than 11 different grounds. Including a stay at Loftus Road from 2002-04 while the Cottage was being redeveloped, Fulham have played at 13 venues, a total only exceeded by QPR.**

• The proudest moment in the club's history came as recently as May 2010 when Fulham met Atletico Madrid in Hamburg in the first Europa League final. Sadly for their fans and their inspirational manager Roy Hodgson, the Cottagers lost 2-1 in extra-time despite putting up a spirited fight.

• **In 1975 Fulham reached the FA Cup final for the first (and so far only) time, losing 2-0 to West Ham. The Cottagers have appeared in the semi-final six times, including a forgettable occasion in 1908 when they were hammered 6-0 by Newcastle, to this day the biggest ever winning margin at that stage of the competition.**

• Midfield legend Johnny Haynes holds the club's appearance record, turning out in 594 league games between 1952 and 1970. 'The Maestro', as he was known to Fulham fans, is also the club's most honoured player at international level, with 56 England caps. Welsh international striker Gordon Davies is Fulham's top scorer with 159 league goals in two spells at the club between 1978 and 1991.

• **In January 2014 Fulham made their record signing when they bought striker Konstantinos Mitroglou from Olympiakos for £12.4 million. Two years earlier midfielder Mousa Dembele left Craven Cottage for** Tottenham for a club record £12 million.

• Bankrolled by then owner Mohamed Al-Fayed, Fulham climbed from the basement division to the Premiership in just four years between 1997 and 2001 – a year less than the then Harrods boss had predicted. Only Swansea City have made a quicker rise through the divisions, taking just three years between 1978 and 1981. However, Fulham's 13-year stay in the top flight ended in 2014 after a season in which they used 39 different players – a record for a Premier League campaign.

• **Fulham's biggest ever win, 10-1 against Ipswich on Boxing Day 1963, was the last time a team scored double figures in the English top flight.**

### HONOURS

*Division 2 champions 1949*
*First Division champions 2001*
*Division 3 (S) champions 1932*
*Second Division champions 1999*

*Fulham are London's oldest club*

## PAUL GASCOIGNE

**Born:** Gateshead, 25th May 1967
**Position:** Midfielder
**Club career:**
1985-88 Newcastle United 92 (21)
1988-92 Tottenham Hotspur 92 (19)
1992-95 Lazio 43 (6)
1995-98 Rangers 74 (30)
1998-2000 Middlesbrough 41 (4)
2000-02 Everton 32 (1)
2002 Burnley 6 (0)
2003 Gansu Tianma 4 (2)
2004 Boston United 5 (0)
**International record:**
1988-98 England 57 (10)

The most talented English midfielder of his generation, Paul Gascoigne could unlock the tightest of defences with a clever pass or a trademark dribble past a couple of opponents. His prodigious skills prompted Tottenham to sign him for £2 million from Newcastle in 1988, making him the most expensive British player at the time.

• **Troubled by injuries throughout his career, Gascoigne was at his peak at the 1990 World Cup in Italy when his brilliant performances powered England to the last four. 'Gazzamania' completely swept the country after his tears during the England-Germany semi-final (after he picked up a yellow card which meant he would miss the final) perfectly summed up the mood of disappointment that swept the nation as England went on to lose a penalty shoot-out. A few months later he was voted BBC Sports Personality of the Year – only the second footballer, after Bobby Moore in 1966, to receive the award.**

• Gazza also starred at Euro '96, scoring a superb solo goal in the local derby with Scotland at Wembley that many rate as the best England goal ever. However, he was controversially left out of England's 1998 World Cup squad after a series of drunken incidents and never added to his 57 caps.

• **At club level, Gascoigne is one of a select band of players to have won both the FA Cup (with Spurs in 1991) and the Scottish Cup (with Rangers in 1996). While at Ibrox he also won two league titles and the League Cup.**

• A fun-loving character who was once described as being "as daft as a brush" by then England manager Bobby Robson, Gazza has sadly struggled with alcohol addiction and mental health problems since quitting the game in 2004.

## DAVID DE GEA

**Born:** Madrid, 7th November 1990
**Position:** Goalkeeper
**Club career:**
2008-09 Atletico Madrid B 35
2009-11 Atletico Madrid 57
2011- Manchester United 131
**International record:**
2014- Spain 5

David De Gea is the most expensive goalkeeper in the history of the British game, costing Manchester United around £18 million when he moved from Atletico Madrid in June 2011.

• **After coming through the youth ranks at Atletico, De Gea enjoyed a great first season with the Madrid club, helping them win the Europa League** following a 2-1 victory against Fulham in the final in Hamburg. At the start of the following campaign he starred in Atletico's UEFA Super Cup victory over Champions League holders Inter Milan, saving a late penalty from Uruguayan striker Diego Milito.

• Following some unconvincing early performances for United De Gea was dropped by then manager Sir Alex Ferguson, but after winning his place back his form soon improved. In 2013 he helped United win the Premier League title and his individual contribution to that success was recognised when he was voted into the PFA Team of the Year.

• **He enjoyed an even better campaign in 2014/15, again being voted into the PFA Team of the Year and winning the Match of the Day 'Save of the Season' award for a second time thanks to a stunning tip-over against Everton.**

• De Gea's girlfriend Edurne Garcia represented Spain at the 2015 Eurovision Song Contest, but she only managed to finish a disappointing 21st.

*David de Gea looks delighted that his transfer to Real Madrid has fallen through!*

*German players Mario Gotze and Jerome Boateng 'celebrate' winning the World Cup*

## GERMANY

**First international:** Switzerland 5 Germany 3, 1908
**Most capped player:** Lothar Matthaus, 150 caps (1980-2000)
**Leading goalscorer:** Miroslav Klose, 71 goals (2001-14)
**First World Cup appearance:** Germany 5 Belgium 2, 1934
**Biggest win:** Germany 16 Russia 0, 1912
**Heaviest defeat:** Austria 6 Germany 0, 1931

Germany (formerly West Germany) have the joint second best record in the World Cup behind Brazil, having won the tournament four times and reached the final on a record eight occasions. They have also won the European Championships a joint-record three times and been losing finalists on another three occasions.

• The Germans recorded their fourth World Cup triumph in Brazil in 2014, when they beat Argentina 1-0 in the final thanks to Mario Gotze's extra-time goal. Perhaps more remarkable, though, was their performance in the semi-final when they massacred

## TOP 10

### GERMANY CAPS

| | | |
|---|---|---|
| 1. | Lothar Matthaus (1980-2000) | 150 |
| 2. | Miroslav Klose (2001-14) | 137 |
| 3. | Lukas Podolski (2004- ) | 123 |
| 4. | Philipp Lahm (2004-14) | 113 |
| 5. | Bastian Schweinsteiger (2004- ) | 109 |
| 6. | Jurgen Klinsmann (1987-98) | 108 |
| 7. | Jurgen Kohler (1986-98) | 105 |
| 8. | Per Mertesacker (2004-14) | 104 |
| 9. | Franz Beckenbauer (1965-77) | 103 |
| 10. | Thomas Hasler (1988-2000) | 101 |

the hosts 7-1 – the biggest ever win at that late stage of the competition. Germany's other victories came in 1954 (against Hungary), on home soil in 1974 (against the Netherlands) and at Italia '90 (against Argentina).

• Lothar Matthaus, a powerhouse in the German midfield for two decades, played in a record 25 matches at the World Cup in five tournaments between 1982 and 1998. His total of 150 caps for Germany is also a national record.

• Germany striker Miroslav Klose is the all-time leading scorer at the World Cup with a total of 16 goals, one ahead of Brazil's Ronaldo and two better than Gerd 'the Bomber' Muller.

• Between 10th July 2010 and 22nd June 2012 Germany won a world record 15 competitive matches on the trot – a run which ended when they lost 2-1 to Italy in the semi-final of Euro 2012.

• Germany have played in a record 106 games at the World Cup and scored a tournament best 224 goals.

### HONOURS
*World Cup winners* 1954, 1974, 1990, 2014
*European Championships winners* 1972, 1980, 1996
**World Cup Record**
*1930 Did not enter*
*1934 Third place*
*1938 Round 1*
*1950 Did not enter*
*1954 Winners*
*1958 Fourth place*
*1962 Quarter-finals*
*1966 Runners-up*
*1970 Third place*
*1974 Winners*
*1978 Round 1*
*1982 Runners-up*
*1986 Runners-up*
*1990 Winners*
*1994 Quarter-finals*
*1998 Quarter-finals*
*2002 Runners-up*
*2006 Third place*
*2010 Third place*
*2014 Winners*

## GERRARD

## STEVEN GERRARD

**Born:** Whiston, 30th May 1980
**Position:** Midfielder
**Club career:**
1998-2015 Liverpool 504 (120)
2015- LA Galaxy 7 (1)
**International record:**
2000-14 England 114 (21)

Liverpool legend Steven Gerrard is the only player to have scored in the FA Cup final, the League Cup final, the UEFA Cup final and the Champions League final. He achieved this feat between 2001 and 2006 while winning all four competitions with the Reds (and, indeed, earning winners' medals in the FA Cup and League Cup on two occasions).

• Famed for his surging runs and thunderous shooting, Gerrard broke into the Liverpool team in 1998 and, five years later, then Anfield boss Gerard Houllier made the Kop idol his skipper – and he retained the armband until he decided to move on to LA Galaxy in 2015. By then he had made more than 500 Premier League appearances for the Reds, one of just three players (along with Ryan Giggs and former team-mate Jamie Carragher) to reach that milestone with one club.

• In the 2006 FA Cup final Gerrard scored two stunning goals against West Ham, including a last-minute

*Steven Gerrard seems to be enjoying the LA sunshine*

equaliser which many rate as the best ever goal in the final. Liverpool went on to win the match on penalties and Gerrard's heroics were rewarded with the 2006 PFA Player of the Year award. Three years later he was voted Footballer of the Year by the football writers. Then, in 2014, he was voted into the PFA Team of the Year for a record eighth time.

• Gerrard made his international debut for England against Ukraine in 2000 and scored his first goal for his country with a superb 20-yarder in the famous 5-1 thrashing of Germany in Berlin in 2001. In the absence of regular skipper Rio Ferdinand, he captained England at the 2010 World Cup and, after being appointed the permanent captain by new boss Roy Hodgson, he led his country at the 2012 European Championships and the 2014 World Cup.

### IS THAT A FACT?

With a total of 40 goals in the Champions League and Europa League Steven Gerrard is Liverpool's highest ever scorer in European competition.

• With 114 caps to his name before he announced his retirement from international football in July 2014, Gerrard is third on the list of England's all-time appearance makers behind Peter Shilton and David Beckham.

## GIANT-KILLING

Many of the most remarkable instances of giant-killing have occurred in the FA Cup, with a number of non-league clubs claiming the scalps of top-flight opposition. One of the biggest such shocks came in 1989 when Coventry City, who had won the FA Cup just two years earlier, were knocked out of the competition by non-league Sutton United in the third round.

• In 2013 Luton Town became the first non-league side to knock a Premier League team out of the FA Cup when they sensationally beat Norwich City 1-0 at Carrow Road in the fourth round.

• In their non-league days Yeovil Town beat a record 20 league teams in the FA Cup. The Glovers' most famous win came in the fourth round in 1949 against First Division Sunderland, who they defeated 2-1 on their notorious sloping pitch at Huish Park.

• Other famous FA Cup giant-killings include non-league Hereford United beating Newcastle 2-1 in 1972, Wrexham knocking out reigning league champions Arsenal 2-1 in 1992 and Bradford City coming from 2-0 down to beat Chelsea 4-2 at Stamford Bridge in 2015.

• Giant-killings also happen occasionally at international level. At the 1950 World Cup in Brazil, for instance, England sensationally lost 1-0 to an unheralded United States team. The result was so unexpected that many people assumed it was a misprint when they saw it in the newspapers and that the true score was 10-1 to England! Other major World Cup shocks include Cameroon's 1-0 defeat of holders Argentina in 1990, Senegal's 1-0 win over holders France in 2002 and Costa Rica's surprise 1-0 win over Italy in 2014.

# RYAN GIGGS

**Born:** Cardiff, 29th November 1973
**Position:** Winger/midfielder
**Club career:**
1991-2014 Manchester United 672 (114)
**International record:**
1991-2007 Wales 64 (12)

In a glorious career with Manchester United, Ryan Giggs became the most decorated player in English football history. Between 1991 and 2014, when he announced his retirement from the game, he won 22 major honours: a record 13 Premier League titles, four FA Cups, three League Cups and two Champions League trophies. In 2009 he was voted PFA Player of the Year by his fellow professionals.

• Now Manchester United's assistant manager after a brief spell as the club's caretaker manager in 2014, Giggs scored at least one goal in a record 21 Premier League seasons before drawing a blank in the 2013/14 campaign. He also holds the Premier League appearance record, 632 games, and has also played more games in the top flight for the same club, 672, than any other player.

• A one-club man throughout his stellar career, Giggs made a record 963 appearances for United in all competitions – 205 more than the previous record holder, Bobby Charlton.

• Giggs enjoyed his best ever year in 1999 when he won the Premiership, FA Cup and Champions League with United. His goal against Arsenal in that season's FA Cup semi-final, when he dribbled past four defenders before smashing the ball into the roof of the net from a tight angle, was voted the best of the past 50 years by 'Match of the Day' viewers in 2015.

• A tremendous crosser of the ball, Giggs made a record 162 'assists' in the Premier League era. He is also the only one of the 25 players to have scored more than 100 Premier League goals to have notched more on away grounds (60) than at home (49) – testimony, perhaps, to his outstanding ability on the counter-attack.

• Once Wales' youngest ever player, Giggs previously played for England Schoolboys under the name Ryan Wilson (the surname being that of his father, a former Welsh rugby league player). However, having no English grandparents, Giggs was ineligible to play for the England national team and was proud to represent Wales on 64 occasions before retiring from international football in 2007.

# GILLINGHAM

**Year founded:** 1893
**Ground:** Priestfield Stadium (11,582)
**Previous name:** New Brompton
**Nickname:** The Gills
**Biggest win:** 12-1 v Gloucester City (1946)
**Heaviest defeat:** 2-9 v Nottingham Forest (1950)

Founded by a group of local businessmen as New Brompton in 1893, the club changed to its present name in 1913. Seven years later Gillingham joined the new Third Division but in 1938 were voted out of the league in favour of Ipswich Town. They eventually returned in 1950.

• Goalkeeper John Simpson played in a record 571 league games for the Gills between 1957 and 1972, while his team-mate Brian Yeo scored a club record 136 goals.

• In 1952 the Gills' Jimmy Scarth notched three goals in just two minutes and 30 seconds against Leyton Orient to set a record for the fastest Football League hat-trick which stood until 2004.

• In their 1995/96 promotion campaign Gillingham only conceded 20 goals – a record for a 46-game season in the Football League.

• Winger Luke Freeman became the youngest ever player in the FA Cup proper when he came on as a sub for Gillingham against Barnet in 2007 when aged just 15 years and 233 days.

HONOURS
*Division 4 champions* 1964
*League Two champions* 2013

# OLIVIER GIROUD

**Born:** Chambery, France, 30th September 1986
**Position:** Striker
**Club career:**
2005-08 Grenoble 23 (2)
2007-08 Istres (loan) 33 (14)
2008-10 Tours 44 (24)
2010-12 Montpellier 73 (33)
2010 Tours (loan) 17 (6)
2012- Arsenal 97 (41)
**International record:**
2011- France 38 (10)

When Arsenal striker Olivier Giroud flicked in a late goal for the Gunners in their 4-0 demolition of Aston Villa in the 2015 FA Cup final it was the first time in the history of the competition that players of four different nationalities had scored for the same team in the final, the Frenchman's strike following goals by Theo Walcott (England), Alexis Sanchez (Chile) and Per Mertesacker (Germany).

*Arsenal's Olivier Giroud*

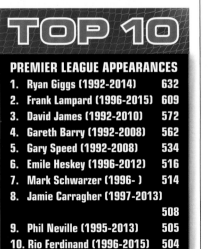

## TOP 10

### PREMIER LEAGUE APPEARANCES

| | | |
|---|---|---|
| 1. | Ryan Giggs (1992-2014) | 632 |
| 2. | Frank Lampard (1996-2015) | 609 |
| 3. | David James (1992-2010) | 572 |
| 4. | Gareth Barry (1992-2008) | 562 |
| 5. | Gary Speed (1992-2008) | 534 |
| 6. | Emile Heskey (1996-2012) | 516 |
| 7. | Mark Schwarzer (1996- ) | 514 |
| 8. | Jamie Carragher (1997-2013) | 508 |
| 9. | Phil Neville (1995-2013) | 505 |
| 10. | Rio Ferdinand (1996-2015) | 504 |
| | Steven Gerrard (1998-2015) | 504 |

• A tall, powerful striker who finishes well on the ground and in the air, Giroud first came to the fore when he was top scorer in the French second division with Tours in 2009/10, his goalscoring feats also earning him the Ligue 2 Player of the Year award.

• A move to Montpellier followed, and in only his second season with the club Giroud helped the southern French side win the league for the first time in their history. The striker's 21 goals during the campaign made him the league's joint-top scorer and were instrumental in Montpellier's surprise success. Later that summer he joined Arsenal for £9.6 million and two years later he won his first trophy with the Gunners, the FA Cup in 2014.

• Giroud won his first cap for France in a 1-0 friendly win over the USA in 2011. He represented his country at the 2014 World Cup, scoring France's 100th goal at the tournament in a 5-2 thrashing of Switzerland.

• In a poll of 250 American women in February 2015 Giroud was voted "the hottest player in the Premier League".

*Swansea City star Bafetimbi Gomis has purrrfected his panther celebration*

## GOAL CELEBRATIONS

Elaborate and sometimes spectacular goal celebrations have been a feature of English football since the mid-1990s when the Premier League started opening its doors to large numbers of overseas players. Middlesbrough striker Fabrizio Ravanelli, for instance, was famed for pulling his shirt over his head after scoring, and soon players were removing their shirts altogether, sometimes to reveal personal, political or religious messages written on a t-shirt.

• In 2003 FIFA decided that things had got out of hand and ruled that any player removing his shirt would be booked. The first player to be sent off after falling foul of this new law was Everton's Tim Cahill, who was shown a second yellow against Manchester City in 2004.

• In 2013 West Brom striker Nicolas Anelka was fined a record £80,000 by the FA and banned for five matches after celebrating a goal at West Ham by placing his arm across his chest in a gesture known as the 'quenelle' which, especially in Anelka's native France, carries anti-semitic connotations. The former France star was subsequently sacked by his club for gross misconduct.

• In one of the most bizarre goal celebrations ever, Manchester United star Carlos Tevez produced a baby's dummy from his shorts and sucked on it after scoring against Birmingham at Old Trafford in 2008. He later explained that the routine was a tribute to his young daughter, Florencia. Earlier in his career, Tevez was sent off while playing for Boca Juniors against arch-rivals River Plate when he celebrated a goal in front of the opposition fans by imitating a chicken.

• In September 2014 Cameroonian striker Joel of Brazilian side Coritiba celebrated a goal against Sao Paulo by jumping over an advertising hoarding – only to fall down a hole leading to an underground stairwell. "I've made a fool of myself," he reflected afterwards.

• A craze for players to don masks while celebrating a goal reached its zenith in February 2015 when Borussia Dortmund's Marco Reus and Pierre-Emerick Aubameyang pulled on Batman and Robin masks after their side's opener in a 3-0 win over Schalke.

## GOAL OF THE SEASON

The Goal of the Season award has been awarded by BBC TV's flagship football programme Match of the Day since 1971 (apart from the years 2001-04 when, for broadcasting rights reasons, the award was given by ITV). The first winner was Coventry City's Ernie Hunt, whose spectacular volley against Everton at Highfield Road topped the poll.

• Manchester United striker Wayne Rooney is the only player to win the award three times, most recently in 2011 for an acrobatic overhead kick against local rivals Manchester City. Liverpool's John Aldridge (in 1988 and 1989) and Arsenal's Jack Wilshere (in 2014 and 2015) are the only two players to have won the award in consecutive seasons.

• Only two players have won the award for goals scored for their countries rather than their clubs: Scotland's Kenny Dalglish in 1983 and England's Bryan Robson in 1986.

• Liverpool players have won the Goal of the Season award a record six times, most recently in 2006 when Steven Gerrard's 30-yarder in the FA Cup final against West Ham topped the list.

**IS THAT A FACT?**

In a Premier League online poll to celebrate the league's 20th anniversary in 2012, Eric Cantona's balletic pirouette and nonchalent pose after he scored against Sunderland in December 1996 was voted the best ever goal celebration.

## GOALKEEPERS

• On 27th March 2011 Sao Paulo's Rogerio Ceni became the first goalkeeper in the history of football to score 100 career goals when he netted with a free kick in a 2-1 win against Corinthians. His unlikely century was made up of 56 free kicks and 44 penalties. He has since added a further 28 goals to his tally to become one of Sao Paulo's top 10 all-time leading scorers.

**• Just five goalkeepers have scored in the Premier League: Peter Schmeichel (Aston Villa), Brad Friedel (Blackburn Rovers), Paul Robinson (Tottenham), Tim Howard (Everton) and Asmir Begovic (Stoke City). Begovic's goal after just 13 seconds against Southampton in November 2013 is the fastest ever by a goalkeeper in English football history and was scored at a greater distance (91.9 metres) than any goal ever.**

• The most-travelled English goalkeeper is John 'Budgie' Burridge who, in a career lasting from 1969 to 1997, played for no fewer than 29 different clubs, including Aston Villa, Blackpool, Crystal Palace and Sheffield United.

**• Gianluigi Buffon is the world's most expensive goalkeeper after moving to Juventus from Parma in 2001 for a cool £32.6 million.**

• David James holds the record for both Premier League appearances by a goalkeeper (573) and for clean sheets (170).

*Sao Paulo's record-breaking goalkeeper Rogerio Ceni celebrates scoring another goal*

## GOAL-LINE TECHNOLOGY

Goal-line technology was introduced to the Premier League for the first time for the 2013/14 season after the league agreed to adopt the Hawk-Eye system, which uses seven cameras per goal and notifies the match officials whether or not the ball has crossed the line via a vibration and optical signal sent to the officials' watches within one second of the incident.

**• In July 2012 FIFA's International Football Association Board, which determines the laws of the game, agreed to the principle of using goal-line technology at future FIFA tournaments. The following year Goal Control, a similar system to Hawk-Eye, was used at the 2013 Confederations Cup and again at the 2014 World Cup in Brazil.**

• For many years then FIFA President Sepp Blatter was opposed to the introduction of goal-line technology, believing that it would undermine the authority of the match officials. However, he changed his mind after the 2010 World Cup, during which a number of questionable goal-line decisions were made, most notably the denying of a goal to England when Frank Lampard's shot clearly crossed the line in his country's last 16 match with Germany. "I was so shocked that the goal was not allowed," Blatter said later. "The next day, when I gathered myself, I made the declaration that we should start to consider the technology and look for a simple way to implement it."

**• The first Premier League goal to be decisively awarded using goal-line technology was scored by Edin Dzeko for Manchester City against Cardiff City on 18th January 2014.**

## GOALS

Manchester United have scored more league goals than any other English club. Up to the start of the 2015/16 season, the Red Devils had managed 7,709 goals. Liverpool, though, have scored the most goals at home (4,626), while Notts County have conceded the most in total (6,998).

**• Peterborough United hold the record for the most league goals in a season, banging in 134 in 1960/61 on their way to claiming the Fourth Division title. Less impressively, Darwen conceded a record 141 goals in the Second Division in 1898/99 and promptly resigned from the Football League.**

• Aston Villa hold the top-flight record, with 128 goals in 1930/31. Despite their prolific attack, the Villans were pipped to the First Division title by Arsenal (amazingly, the Gunners managed 127

goals themselves). Title-winners Chelsea became the first team to score a century of goals in the Premier League era in 2009/10, the Blues taking their tally to 103 with an 8-0 thrashing of Wigan on the final day of the season. Premier League winners Manchester City (102) and runners-up Liverpool (101) both notched a century of league goals in 2013/14 – the first time since 1961 that two teams had hit three figures in the top flight – while City set a new record by hitting an incredible 156 goals in all competitions.

• Arthur Rowley scored a record 434 Football League goals between 1946 and 1965, notching four for West Brom, 27 for Fulham, 251 for Leicester City and 152 for Shrewsbury. Former Republic of Ireland international John Aldridge is the overall leading scorer in post-war English football, with an impressive total of 476 goals in all competitions for Newport County, Oxford United, Liverpool and Tranmere between 1979 and 1998.

• Joe Payne set an English Football League record for goals in a game by scoring 10 times for Luton against Bristol Rovers on 13th April 1936.

• The most goals scored in a Football League match is 17 on Boxing Day 1935 when Tranmere hammered Oldham 13-4 in Division Three (North). The Premier League record is a mere 11, when Portsmouth beat Reading 7-4 at Fratton Park in 2007. Neither of these games, though, was anything like as goal-filled as the 1887 FA Cup first round clash between Preston and Hyde which contained 26 goals – all scored by Preston!

• A record 66 goals were scored in the top flight on Boxing Day 1963, an average of 6.6 per match. The highest

score was at Craven Cottage where Fulham demolished Ipswich 10-1. Much less entertainment was on offer in the old First Division on 28th April 1923 when just 10 goals were scored in 10 games, and not a single away side managed to find the net.

• Iranian striker Ali Daei is the leading scorer in international football with an incredible 109 goals between 1993 and 2006.

## JIMMY GREAVES

**Born:** East Ham, 20th February 1940
**Position:** Striker
**Club career:**
1957-61 Chelsea 157 (124)
1961-62 AC Milan 14 (9)
1962-70 Tottenham 321 (220)
1970-71 West Ham United 38 (13)
**International record:**
1959-67 England 57 (44)

With 44 goals for England, Jimmy Greaves is his country's fourth highest ever goalscorer behind Bobby Charlton, Gary Lineker and Wayne Rooney. He scored on his international debut in 1959 in a 4-1 defeat by Peru, and went on to bag a record six hat-tricks for his country. Famously, Greaves also scored on his debut for all the clubs he played for.

• A quicksilver striker who always carefully picked his spot when shooting, Greaves began his career at Chelsea. In the 1960/61 season he hit an incredible 41 league goals for the Blues – a post-war record for the top flight – and also scored a record 13 goals for England.

• After a brief spell with AC Milan, Greaves moved to Tottenham where he helped the club claim two major trophies, the European Cup Winners' Cup in 1963 and the FA Cup in 1967. His haul of 220 league goals for Spurs remains a club record.

• At 21, Greaves was the youngest player to score 100 league goals. He netted his 200th aged 23 years and 290 days, coincidentally exactly the same age at which Dixie Dean reached the same landmark with Everton.

• Arguably English football's most consistent ever striker, Greaves was top scorer in the First Division six times and notched a total of 357 league goals – both top-flight records that are unlikely to be broken.

• He experienced the lowest point of his career in 1966 when, after starting in England's opening matches at the World Cup, he was left out of the team for the triumphant final against West Germany. Bitterly disappointed, he was the only member of the squad not to attend the victory bash in a London hotel.

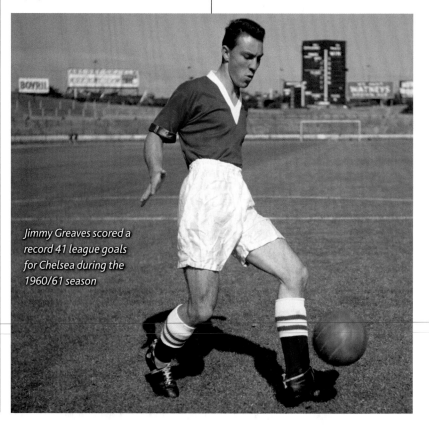

Jimmy Greaves scored a record 41 league goals for Chelsea during the 1960/61 season

## IS THAT A FACT?

Aston Villa have scored a record 841 goals in the FA Cup, but have also conceded more goals (534) in the competition than any other club.

• After hanging up his boots Greaves overcame alcoholism to launch a new career as a TV personality, his double act with former Liverpool star Ian St John being especially popular with viewers.

## PEP GUARDIOLA

**Born:** Santpedor, Spain, 18th January 1971
**Managerial career:**
2007-08 Barcelona B
2008-12 Barcelona
2013- Bayern Munich

Bayern Munich manager Pep Guardiola is the only coach to lead a club to six trophies in a calendar year, claiming an amazing sextuple in 2009 when his former charges Barcelona won the Spanish title, the Copa del Rey, the Champions League, the Spanish Super Cup, the UEFA Super Cup and, finally, the FIFA Club World Cup.

**• When Barcelona won the Champions League in 2009, following a 2-0 win over Manchester United in the final in Rome, the 38-year-old Guardiola became the youngest coach ever to win the trophy.**

• After winning 14 trophies in four years – an impressive haul unmatched by any other Barcelona manager – Guardiola quit the Catalan club in 2012, citing "tiredness" as the main reason for his decision. A year later he took over the reins at Bayern Munich and in his first season with the German giants in 2013/14 won the league and cup Double, the FIFA Club World Cup and the European Super Cup. However, Bayern fans were disappointed to see their side lose their grip on the Champions League following a 5-0 aggregate trouncing by Real Madrid in the semi-finals and the following year he suffered defeat at the same stage of the competition by his old Barca team.

**• A defensive midfielder in his playing days, Guardiola was a key member of Johan Cruyff's attack-minded 'Dream Team' which won Barcelona's first European Cup in 1992 and four La Liga titles in the early 1990s.**

• In 1992 Guardiola captained Spain to Gold at the 1992 Olympics in Barcelona. He made his debut for the senior team later that year and went on to represent his country 47 times.

*'And that's magic!' Is there no end to Pep Guardiola's talents?*

• After signing for Chelsea for £32 million in May 2012, Hazard's eye-catching performances in his first season at Stamford Bridge saw him voted into the PFA Team of the Year. However, his temperament was questioned by some pundits after he was stupidly sent off in the League Cup semi-final against Swansea for kicking the ball from underneath the body of a time-wasting ball boy. The following year, though, saw him up his game a notch and he was voted PFA Young Player of the Year and second behind Liverpool's Luis Suarez in the main poll.

• Hazard was first capped by Belgium, aged 17, against Luxembourg in 2008 and has gone on to win more than 50 caps.

## HEADERS

In 2011 Ryujiro Ueda, a defender with Fagiano Okayama, scored with a header from 58.6 metres in a J-League match against Yokohama to set a record for the longest distance headed goal. He was helped, though, by some dodgy goalkeeping, the Yokohama keeper allowing the ball to bounce over his head and dribble into the net.

• Huddersfield striker Jordan Rhodes scored the fastest headed hat-trick in Football League history in 2009, nodding in three goals against Exeter City in eight minutes and 23 seconds to smash a record previously held by Everton legend Dixie Dean.

• Stoke's giraffe-like striker Peter Crouch holds the record for the most headed goals in Premier League history, with 47. The former England international passed Alan Shearer's old record when he nodded in on the final day of the 2014/15 season in a crushing 6-1 defeat of Liverpool.

### IS THAT A FACT?

Malcolm Macdonald is the only player to have scored four headers in the same match for England – against Cyprus at Wembley in April 1975. He also grabbed another goal in a 5-0 win with a left-foot shot.

• A record 26 out of a total 76 goals were scored from headers at the 2012 European Championships in Poland and Ukraine.

## HEART OF MIDLOTHIAN

**Year founded:** 1874
**Ground:** Tynecastle (17,529)
**Nickname:** Hearts
**Biggest win:** 21-0 v Anchor (1880)
**Heaviest defeat:** 1-8 v Vale of Leven (1883)

Hearts were founded in 1874, taking their unusual and romantic-sounding name from a popular local dance hall which, in turn, was named after the famous novel *The Heart of the Midlothian* by Sir Walter Scott. The club were founder members of the Scottish league in 1890, winning their first title just five years later.

• The club enjoyed a golden era in the late 1950s and early 1960s, when they won two league championships and five cups. In the first of those title triumphs in 1958 Hearts scored 132 goals, many of them coming from the so-called 'Terrible Trio' of Alfie Conn, Willie Bauld and Jimmy Wardhaugh. The total is still a record for the top flight in Scotland. In the same year Hearts conceded just 29 goals, giving them the best ever goal difference in British football, an incredible 103.

• In 1965 Hearts came agonisingly close to winning the championship again when they were pipped by Kilmarnock on goal average after losing 2-0 at home to their title rivals on the last day of the season. Twenty-one years later they suffered a similar fate, losing the title on goal difference to Celtic after a surprise last-day defeat against Dundee. Annoyingly for their fans, on both occasions Hearts would have won the title if the alternative method for separating teams level on points had been in use.

• The club's record goalscorer is John Robertson with 214 goals between 1983 and 1998. Midfielder Gary Mackay made a record 640 appearances for Hearts between 1980 and 1997.

• Hearts won the Scottish Cup in 2012, thrashing local rivals Hibs 5-1 in the final at Hampden Park – the biggest victory in the final since Hearts themselves were tonked by the same score by Rangers in 1996. It was the eighth time that Hearts had won the Scottish Cup, making them the fourth most successful club in the competition after Celtic, Rangers and Queen's Park.

• Hearts' Scott Robinson is the youngest player ever to appear in the SPL, making his debut as a sub against Inverness Caledonian Thistle on 26th April 2008 when aged just 16 and 45 days.

• Relegated from the Premiership in 2014, Hearts bounced back by winning the Championship in fine style the following season with a second-tier record 91 points. Along the way Hearts thrashed Cowdenbeath 10-0, the biggest win north or south of the border during the 2014/15 season.

### HONOURS

*Division 1 champions* 1895, 1897, 1958, 1960
*First Division champions* 1980
*Championship champions* 2015
*Scottish Cup* 1891, 1896, 1901, 1906, 1956, 1998, 2006, 2012
*League Cup* 1955, 1959, 1960, 1963

## JORDAN HENDERSON

**Born:** Sunderland, 17th June 1990
**Position:** Midfielder
**Club career:**
2008-11 Sunderland 71 (4)
2009 Coventry City (loan) 10 (1)
2011- Liverpool 139 (17)
**International record:**
2010- England 22 (0)

A dynamic and hardworking midfielder who can also score the occasional spectacular goal from the edge of the box, Jordan Henderson joined Liverpool for around £20 million from Sunderland in 2011.

• A product of the Back Cats' academy, Henderson was twice voted Sunderland Young Player of the Year after making his debut for his hometown club in a forgettable 5-0 defeat at Chelsea in November 2008.

• He helped Liverpool win the League Cup in 2012, although he was substituted before the Reds' penalty

Liverpool captain Jordan Henderson

'What you talkin' about, Gary?'

shoot-out victory over Cardiff City in the final, and later that year played in Liverpool's 2-1 defeat by Chelsea in the FA Cup final. Henderson was made Liverpool vice-captain in 2014, and in his first 14 matches wearing the skipper's armband never once finished on the losing side. In the summer of 2015 he was appointed the Reds' captain by boss Brendan Rodgers.

• **First capped by England in 2010, Henderson was named his country's Under-21 Player of the Year in 2012. In the same year he was called up as a late replacement to the senior squad for Euro 2012, and he also figured at the 2014 World Cup in Brazil.**

## THIERRY HENRY

**Born:** Paris, 17th August 1977
**Position:** Striker
**Club career:**
1994-98 Monaco 105 (20)
1999 Juventus 16 (3)
1999-2007 Arsenal 254 (174)
2007-10 Barcelona 80 (35)
2010-2014 New York Red Bulls 122 (51)
2012 Arsenal (loan) 4 (2)
**International record:**
1997-2010 France 123 (51)

Arguably Arsenal's greatest ever player, Thierry Henry is the Gunners' all-time

top goalscorer. During an eight-year stay in north London after signing from Juventus for a bargain £10.5 million in 1999 he scored 224 goals, many of them memorable ones. He briefly returned to Arsenal on loan from New York Red Bulls in 2012, adding two more goals to his Gunners account.

• **Frighteningly quick and a reliably clinical finisher, Henry started out with Monaco and helped the club win the French title in 1997. He was even more successful at Arsenal, winning two league titles and three FA Cups, and in 2006 become the first ever player to win the Footballer of the Year award three times. The following year he joined Barcelona, with whom he won the Spanish league title and the Champions League in 2009.**

• A two-time winner of the European Golden Boot, Henry's total of 175 league goals for Arsenal puts him fifth in the list of all-time Premier League scorers. The Frenchman was also a great provider of goals, creating a Premier League record of 20 'assists' in 2002/03.

• **A member of the French squad that won the World Cup in 1998, Henry collected a European Championships winners' medal two years later. In 2006 he had to settle for a runners-up medal in the World Cup final.**

• With 51 international goals to his name, Henry is easily France's record scorer. Capped 123 times, he stands second behind Lilian Thuram in France's all-time top appearance makers.

# HIBERNIAN

**Year founded:** 1875
**Ground:** Easter Road (20,421)
**Previous name:** Hibernians
**Nickname:** Hibs
**Biggest win:** 22-1 v 42nd Highlanders (1881)
**Heaviest defeat:** 0-10 v Rangers (1898)

Founded in 1875 by Irish immigrants, the club took its name from the Roman word for Ireland, Hibernia. After losing many players to Celtic the club disbanded in 1891, but reformed and joined the Scottish League two years later.

• Hibs won the Scottish Cup for the first time in 1887 and lifted the same trophy again in 1902. Since then, however, the club have reached the final on a further 10 occasions, most recently in 2013 when they lost to Celtic, but failed to win once.

• The club enjoyed a golden era after the Second World War, winning the league championship in three out of five seasons between 1948 and 1952 with a side managed by Hugh Shaw that included the 'Famous Five' forward line of Bobby Johnstone, Willie Ormond, Lawrie Reilly, Gordon Smith and Willie Turnbull. All of the Famous Five went on to score 100 league goals for Hibs, a feat only achieved for the club since by Joe Baker.

• In 1955 Hibs became the first British side to enter the European Cup, having been invited to participate in the new competition partly because their Easter Road ground had floodlights. They did Scotland proud, reaching the semi-finals of the competition before falling 3-0 on aggregate to French side Reims.

• Hibs hold the British record for the biggest away win, thrashing Airdrie 11-1 on their own patch on 24th October 1959. As if to prove that astonishing result was no fluke, they also hit double figures at Partick later that season, winning 10-2.

• When Joe Baker made his international debut against Northern Ireland in 1959 he became the first man to represent England while playing for a Scottish club. In the same season Baker scored an incredible 42 goals in just 33 league games to set a club record.

• In 2001 Hibs splashed out a club record £700,000 to buy Ecuadorian defender Ulises de la Cruz from LDU Quito. Six years later the Easter Road outfit received a record £4.4 million when midfielder Scott Brown joined Celtic.

### HONOURS

*Division 1 champions* 1903, 1948, 1951, 1952
*Division 2 champions* 1894, 1895, 1933
*First Division champions* 1981, 1999
*Scottish Cup* 1887, 1902
*League Cup* 1972, 1991, 2007

# GLENN HODDLE

**Born:** Hayes, 27th October 1957
**Position:** Midfielder
**Club career:**
1975-87 Tottenham Hotspur 377 (88)
1987-90 Monaco 69 (27)
1991-93 Swindon Town 64 (1)
1993-95 Chelsea 31 (1)
**International record:**
1979-88 England 53 (8)

An extravagantly gifted midfielder, Glenn Hoddle gained 53 caps for England and might have won many more but for doubts about his work-rate and tackling ability.

• During a 12-year playing career with Tottenham Hotspur, Hoddle won the FA Cup twice (in 1981 and 1982) and the UEFA Cup (in 1984). He joined Monaco in 1987, where he played under Arsène Wenger, and the following year became the first Englishman to be part of a championship-winning side in France. "I couldn't understand why he hadn't been appreciated in England," Wenger said of him. "Perhaps he was a star in the wrong period, years ahead of his time."

• As player-manager of Swindon, Hoddle led the Wiltshire club into the top flight for the first time in their history in 1993. In the same role at Chelsea the following year he guided the Blues to their first FA Cup final for nearly a quarter of a century.

• In May 1996 Hoddle was appointed England manager, succeeding Terry Venables after Euro '96. Aged 38, he was the youngest man to fill the position since Walter Winterbottom.

*Hibernian's Dylan McGeouch pushes forward*

• Hoddle led England to the 1998 World Cup in France, where they were unlucky to lose to Argentina in a penalty shoot-out. The following year, though, he was dismissed from the job after suggesting in a newspaper interview that disabled people were somehow paying for sins committed in a previous life. He has subsequently managed Southampton, Tottenham and Wolves.

## ROY HODGSON

**Born:** Croydon, 9th August 1947
**Managerial career:**
1976-80 Halmstads
1982 Bristol City
1983-85 Orebro
1985-90 Malmo
1990-92 Neuchatel Xamax
1992-95 Switzerland
1995-97 Inter Milan
1997-98 Blackburn Rovers
1999 Inter Milan
1999-2000 Grasshoppers
2000-01 Copenhagen
2001 Udinese
2002-04 United Arab Emirates
2004-05 Viking
2006-07 Finland
2007-2010 Fulham
2010-11 Liverpool
2011-12 West Bromwich Albion
2012- England

After a disappointing showing at the 2014 World Cup, Roy Hodgson guided England to 11 consecutive matches unbeaten in 2014/15 – the Three Lions' best such run since they clocked up 13 undefeated games between 1995 and 1997.

• **Hodgson is the oldest man to be appointed England manager, taking charge in May 2012 at the age of 64 and then leading them to the quarter-finals of the European Championships. He is also the first England boss to have international experience, having previously managed Switzerland, United Arab Emirates and Finland.**

• After failing to make the grade as a player at Crystal Palace, Hodgson spent much of his early managerial career in Sweden. He won the title with Halmstads in 1979 before leading Malmo to a Swedish record five consecutive championships between 1985 and 1989.

• **Hodgson has enjoyed mixed fortunes with Premier League clubs, being sacked by both Blackburn and Liverpool after brief spells at the helm of those clubs, but doing much better with Fulham and West Brom. His time at Liverpool in the 2010/11 season was particularly forgettable, as he led the Reds to their worst start in 82 years and was eventually shown the door after just 31 games in charge, making his the shortest managerial reign in the history of the Anfield club.**

• His three-year stint at his previous club, Fulham, on the other hand, was much happier. In his first season at Craven Cottage Hodgson guided his team to an unlikely escape from relegation after the west Londoners won their final three Premier League fixtures. Two years later, in 2010, he easily topped that achievement by taking Fulham to the Europa League final. Although the Cottagers lost out to Atletico Madrid, Hodgson picked up the League Managers' Association Manager of the Year award for his efforts.

• **His other great success came with** Switzerland, who he took to the last 16 of the World Cup in 1994 – the country's best performance for 40 years. Hodgson also earned plaudits during two spells with Inter Milan, taking the Italian giants to the UEFA Cup final in 1997, where they were beaten on penalties by Schalke.

## HOME AND AWAY

Brentford hold the all-time record for home wins in a season. In 1929/30 the Bees won all 21 of their home games at Griffin Park in Division Three (South). However, their away form was so poor they missed out on promotion to champions Plymouth.

• **Chelsea hold the record for the longest unbeaten home run in the league, remaining undefeated at Stamford Bridge between February 2004 and October 2008. Ironically, the Blues' 86-game run was eventually broken by Liverpool, the previous holders of the same record.**

• Arsenal hold the record for the most consecutive away wins, with 12 in the Premier League in 2013. The highest number of straight home wins is 25, a record set by Bradford Park Avenue in the Third Division (North) in 1926/27.

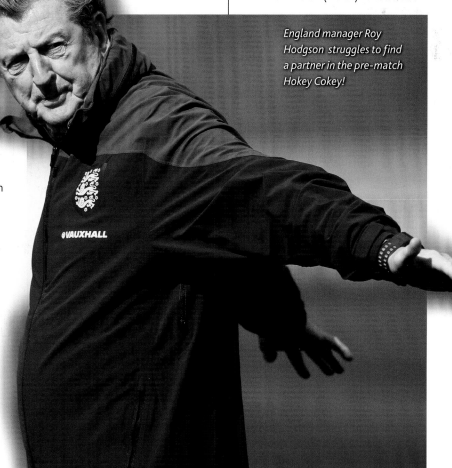

*England manager Roy Hodgson struggles to find a partner in the pre-match Hokey Cokey!*

• Stockport's 13-0 win over Halifax in 1934 is the biggest home win in Football League history (equalled by Newcastle against Newport in 1946). Sheffield United hold the record for the most emphatic away win, thrashing Port Vale 10-0 way back in 1892.

• Millwall scored a record 87 goals at home in 1927/28, a total which helped the London club top the Third Division (South) table that season. The away record is held by Arsenal, who scored 60 goals on their travels in their 1930/31 championship-winning campaign.

• Chelsea scored a Premier League record 68 goals at home in their 2009/10 Double season, while Liverpool hold the away record with 48 in 2013/14.

## HUDDERSFIELD TOWN

**Year founded:** 1908
**Ground:** John Smith's Stadium (24,500)
**Nickname:** The Terriers
**Biggest win:** 11-0 v Heckmondwike (1909)
**Heaviest defeat:** 1-10 v Manchester City (1987)

Huddersfield Town were founded in 1908 following a meeting held at the local Imperial Hotel some two years earlier – it took the club that long to find a ground to play at! The club were elected to the Second Division of the Football League two years later.

• **The Terriers enjoyed a golden era in the 1920s when, under the shrewd management of the legendary Herbert Chapman, they won three consecutive league titles between 1924 and 1926 – no other club had matched this feat at the time and only three have done so since. The Terriers also won the FA Cup in 1922.**

• Huddersfield won the first of their league titles in 1924 by pipping Cardiff City on goal average, the first time the champions had been decided by this method.

• **The early 1970s were a desperate time for Huddersfield, who slumped from the First to the Fourth Division in just four seasons, becoming the first league champions to be relegated to the bottom tier.**

*Huddersfield and Hull battle it out*

• In 1932 prolific striker Dave Mangnall scored in 11 consecutive games for Huddersfield – just one game short of the record set by Everton legend Dixie Dean the previous season.

• **Outside left Billy Smith made a record 521 appearances, scoring 114 goals, for Huddersfield between 1913 and 1934. Smith and his son, Conway, who started out with the Terriers before playing for QPR and Halifax, were the first father and son to both** hit a century of goals in league football.

• The Terriers smashed their transfer record in January 2014 when they forked out £5 million for Bradford City's Bermudan international striker Nahki Wells. The club's coffers were boosted by a record £8 million in 2012 when prolific striker Jordan Rhodes joined Blackburn.

| HONOURS | |
| --- | --- |
| **Division 1 champions** | *1924, 1925, 1926* |
| **Division 2 champions** | *1970* |
| **Division 4 champions** | *1980* |
| **FA Cup** | *1922* |

## HULL CITY

**Year founded:** 1904
**Ground:** KC Stadium (24,450)
**Nickname:** The Tigers
**Biggest win:** 11-1 v Carlisle United (1939)
**Heaviest defeat:** 0-8 v Wolves (1911)

Hull City were formed in 1904, originally sharing a ground with the local rugby league club. The club joined the Football League in 1905 but failed to achieve promotion to the top flight until 2008.

• Hull enjoyed their best ever moment when they reached their first ever FA Cup final in 2014. The Tigers roared into a shock 2-0 lead against favourites Arsenal at Wembley, but eventually went down 3-2 after extra-time. Nonetheless, Hull's cup exploits meant they competed in European competition for the first time in their history in 2014 but their stay in Europa League was a brief one as they were knocked out by Belgian side Lokeren before the group stage. Even worse, at the end of the campaign Hull were relegated from the Premier League.

• The Tigers first made it into the top flight in 2008 thanks to a play-off final victory over Bristol City, with local boy Dean Windass scoring the vital goal. The triumph meant that Hull had climbed from the bottom tier to the top in just five seasons – a meteoric rise only bettered in the past by Fulham, Swansea City and Wimbledon.

• The club's record goalscorer is Chris Chilton, who banged in 193 league goals in the 1960s and 1970s. His sometime team-mate Andy Davidson has pulled on a Hull shirt more than any other player, making 520 league appearances between 1952 and 1968.

• In his first spell at Hull between 1991 and 1996, goalkeeper Alan Fettis played a number of games as a striker during an injury crisis. He did pretty well too, scoring two goals!

• In September 2014 Hull splashed a club record £10 million on Palermo striker Abel Hernandez. A month earlier the Tigers received a club record £12 million when striker Shane Long moved to Southampton.

*Geoff Hurst celebrates scoring for England against Argentina in the 1966 World Cup quarter-final*

• Hull were the first team in the world to lose in a penalty shoot-out, Manchester United beating them 4-3 on spot-kicks in the semi-final of the Watney Cup in 1970.

HONOURS
**Division 3 (North) champions** *1933, 1949*
**Division 3 champions** *1966*

## SIR GEOFF HURST

**Born:** Ashton-under-Lyme, 8th December 1941
**Position:** Striker
**Club career:**
1959-72 West Ham United 410 (180)
1972-75 Stoke City 108 (30)
1975-76 West Bromwich Albion 10 (2)
1976 Seattle Sounders 24 (9)
**International record:**
1966-72 England 49 (24)

Geoff Hurst is the only player to have scored a hat-trick in the World Cup final. His famous treble against West Germany at Wembley helped England to a legendary 4-2 triumph in 1966, although his second goal remains one of the most controversial of all time as the Germans claimed the ball didn't cross the line after Hurst's shot bounced down off the underside of the crossbar.

• Along with Ian Rush, Hurst is the leading scorer in the history of the League Cup with an impressive total of 49 goals. He is also the last player to hit six goals in a top-flight league match, netting a double hat-trick in West Ham's 8-0 thrashing of Sunderland at Upton Park in 1968.

• A well-built centre-forward who was strong in the air and possessed a powerful shot, Hurst won an FA Cup winners' medal with West Ham in 1964 and, the following year, helped the Hammers win the European Cup Winners' Cup.

• In 1979 he was appointed manager of Second Division side Chelsea, but was sacked two years later after a dismal run of results. However, Hurst's great achievements on the pitch remain part of English folklore and earned him a knighthood in 1998.

**IBRAHIMOVIC**

*'What you looking at, ball?'*

## ZLATAN IBRAHIMOVIC

**Born:** Malmo, Sweden, 3rd October 1981
**Position:** Striker
**Club career:**
1999-2001 Malmo 40 (16)
2001-04 Ajax 74 (35)
2004-06 Juventus 70 (23)
2006-09 Inter Milan 88 (57)
2009-11 Barcelona 29 (16)
2010-11 AC Milan (loan) 29 (14)
2011-12 AC Milan 32 (28)
2012- Paris St Germain 91 (75)
**International record:**
2001- Sweden 105 (56)

An exceptionally gifted striker with an individualistic style of play, Sweden captain Zlatan Ibrahimovic is the only player to have won league titles with six different European clubs.

• His incredible run began with Ajax, who he had joined from his first club Malmo in 2001, when the Amsterdam giants won the Dutch league in 2004.

Ibrahomivic's golden touch continued with his next club, Juventus, where he won back-to-back Serie A titles, although these were later scrubbed from the record books following Juve's involvement in a match-fixing scandal.

• At his next club, Inter Milan, Ibrahimovic fared even better, helping the Nerazzurri win a hat-trick of titles in 2007, 2008 and 2009. He then moved to Barcelona, with Samuel Eto'o joining Inter as part of the deal, and, despite failing to see eye-to-eye with Barca boss Pep Guardiola, won a La Liga title medal in 2010. Returning to Italy, his astonishing run of success continued with AC Milan, who were crowned Serie A champions in 2011.

• **In the summer of 2012 Ibrahimovic was transferred to newly moneyed Paris St Germain for £31 million, taking his combined transfer fee up to a world record £150 million. In a tremendous first season with PSG he won the league title and was voted Ligue 1 Player of the Year. He repeated**

these feats in 2013/14, scoring 40 goals in all competitions to set a new club record. A third title duly arrived in 2015 and he also scored a hat-trick in the French Cup final against Saint-Etienne.

• With 56 international goals to his name, Ibrahimovic is Sweden's all-time top scorer.

## ANDRES INIESTA

**Born:** Albacete, Spain, 11th May 1984
**Position:** Midfielder
**Club career:**
2001-03 Barcelona B 54 (5)
2002- Barcelona 361 (33)
**International record:**
2006- Spain 104 (12)

Attacking midfielder Andres Iniesta is the joint-third highest appearance maker in Barcelona's illustrious history, playing in 549 matches in all competitions for the Catalan giants.

*Barcelona captain Andres Iniesta must have one heck of a trophy cabinet*

Serie A. The dominant force in Italian football in the last decade, Inter have 18 title wins to their name – a total only bettered by Juventus.

• Inter were the first Italian club to win the European Cup twice, beating the mighty Real Madrid 3-1 in the 1964 final before recording a 1-0 defeat of Benfica the following year. They had to wait 45 years, though, before making it a hat-trick with a 2-0 defeat of Bayern Munich in Madrid in 2010 – a victory that, with the domestic league and cup already in the bag, secured Inter their first ever Treble.

• Under legendary manager Helenio Herrera, Inter introduced the 'catenaccio' defensive system to world football in the 1960s. Playing with a sweeper behind two man-markers, Inter conceded very few goals as they powered to three league titles between 1963 and 1966.

• The club endured a barren period domestically until they were awarded their first Serie A title for 17 years in 2006 after Juventus and AC Milan, who had both finished above them in the league table, had points deducted for their roles in a match-fixing scandal. Inter went on to win the championship in more conventional style in the following four years – the last two of these triumphs coming under Jose Mourinho – to equal Juventus' record of five consecutive triumphs in the 1930s.

• Inter's ground, commonly known as the San Siro, is officially called the Stadio Giuseppe Meazza, named after the club's leading scorer who banged in an incredible 242 goals for the Nerazzurri in the 1930s.

• A product of the Barcelona youth system, La Masia, Iniesta is now revered as one of the great Spanish players of his generation. He has won seven league titles with Barca, plus four Champions League titles in 2006, 2009, 2011 and 2015, captaining the side in the last of these triumphs against Juventus.

• Nicknamed 'El Cerebro' ('The Brain') for his brilliant reading of the game, Iniesta made his debut for Spain in 2006 and scored his first goal for his country the following year in a 1-0 friendly win against England at Old Trafford. Then, in 2008, he helped Spain win the European Championships in Switzerland and Austria.

• In 2010 he became a cult figure for the whole Spanish nation when he scored the winning goal in the World Cup final against the Netherlands at Soccer City Stadium in Johannesburg. To cap a memorable day for the Barcelona star, he also picked up the Man of the Match award and was

shortlisted for the Golden Ball. Two years later he picked up the Player of the Tournament award as Spain retained the European Championships in Poland and the Ukraine.

## INTER MILAN

**Year founded:** 1908
**Ground:** San Siro (80,018)
**Nickname:** Nerazzurri (The black and blues)
**League titles:** 18
**Domestic cups:** 7
**European cups:** 6
**International cups:** 3

Founded in 1908 as a breakaway club from AC Milan, Internazionale (as they are known locally) are the only Italian team never to have been relegated from

**HONOURS**
*Italian champions* 1910, 1920, 1930, 1938, 1940, 1953, 1954, 1963, 1965, 1966, 1971, 1980, 1989, 2006, 2007, 2008, 2009, 2010
*Italian Cup* 1939, 1978, 1982, 2005, 2006, 2010, 2011
*European Cup/Champions League* 1964, 1965, 2010
*UEFA Cup* 1991, 1994, 1998
*Intercontinental Cup/Club World Cup* 1964, 1965, 2010

## INVERNESS CALEDONIAN THISTLE

**Year founded:** 1994
**Ground:** Caledonian Stadium (7,800)
**Previous name:** Caledonian Thistle
**Nickname:** Caley Thistle
**Biggest win:** 8-1 v Annan Athletic (1998)
**Heaviest defeat:** 0-6 v Airdrie (2001), v Celtic (2010 and 2014)

Founded as Caledonian Thistle in 1994 following the amalgamation of Highland league sides Caledonian and Inverness Thistle, the club was elected to the Scottish Third Division in the same year. In 1996, at the request of Inverness District Council, the club added 'Inverness' to its name.

• The club enjoyed the greatest day in their history in 2015 when they won the Scottish Cup after beating Championship side Falkirk 2-1 in the final. To cap a great season for Caley they also finished a best-ever third in the Premiership behind champions Celtic and runners-up Aberdeen.

• In February 2000 Thistle pulled off one of the biggest ever shocks in the Scottish Cup when they beat Celtic 3-1 in the third round at Parkhead. The Sun newspaper reported this famous giant-killing under the witty headline "Super Caley go ballistic, Celtic are atrocious".

• Incredibly, Caley went 'ballistic' again in 2003 when they knocked Celtic out of the cup for a second time, winning 1-0 at their tiny Caledonian Stadium. The club went on to reach the semi-final of the Scottish Cup for the first time in their history, before losing to Dundee. The following season they got to the semi-finals again, only to be beaten by Dunfermline in a replay.

• Defender Ross Tokely played in a record 456 games for Caley between 1996 and 2012. Dennis Wyness holds the club's goalscoring record with 101 goals in two spells in the Highlands between 1999 and 2008.

HONOURS
*First Division champions 2004, 2010*
*Third Division champions 1997*
*Scottish Cup 2015*

## IPSWICH TOWN

**Year founded:** 1878
**Ground:** Portman Road (30,311)
**Nickname:** The Blues
**Biggest win:** 10-0 v Floriana (1962)
**Heaviest defeat:** 1-10 v Fulham (1963)

The club was founded at a meeting at the town hall in 1878 but did not join the Football League until 1938, two years after turning professional.

• Ipswich were the last of just four clubs to win the old Second and First Division titles in consecutive seasons, pulling off this remarkable feat in 1962 under future England manager Alf Ramsey. The team's success owed much to the strike partnership of Ray Crawford and Ted Phillips, who together scored 61 of the club's 93 goals during the title-winning campaign.

• Two years after that title win, though, Ipswich were relegated after conceding 121 goals – only Blackpool in 1930/31 (125 goals against) have had a worse defensive record in the top flight. The Blues' worst defeat in a season to forget was a 10-1 hammering at Fulham, the last time a team has conceded double figures in a top-flight match.

• However, the club enjoyed more success under their longest-serving boss Bobby Robson, another man who went on to manage England, in the following two decades. In 1978 Ipswich won the FA Cup, beating favourites Arsenal 1-0 in the final at Wembley, and three years later they won the UEFA Cup with attacking midfielder John Wark contributing a then record 14 goals during the club's continental campaign.

• Ipswich have the best home record in European competition of any club, remaining undefeated at Portman Road in 31 games since making their debut in the European Cup in 1962 with a 10-0 hammering of Maltese side Floriana – the Blues' biggest win in their history.

• With 203 goals for the Tractor Boys between 1958 and 1969, Ray Crawford is the club's record goalscorer. Mick Mills is the club's record appearance maker, turning out 591 times between 1966 and 1982.

• Ipswich forked out a club record £4.75 million on Sampdoria goalkeeper Matteo Sereni in 2001. Striker Conor Wickham became the club's record sale when he joined Sunderland for £12 million in 2011.

HONOURS
*Division 1 champions 1962*
*Division 2 champions 1961*
*Division 3 (S) champions 1954, 1957*
*FA Cup 1978*
*UEFA Cup 1981*

## ITALY

**First international:** Italy 6 France 2, 1910
**Most capped player:** Gianluigi Buffon, 148 caps (1997– )
**Leading goalscorer:** Luigi Riva, 35 goals (1965-74)
**First World Cup appearance:** Italy 7 USA 1, 1934
**Biggest win:** Italy 11 Egypt 3, 1928
**Heaviest defeat:** Hungary 7 Italy 1, 1924

Italy have the joint best record of any European nation at the World Cup, having won the tournament four times (in 1934, 1938, 1982 and 2006). Only Brazil, with five wins, have done better in the competition.

• The Azzurri, as they are known to their passionate fans, are the only country to have been involved in two World Cup final penalty shoot-outs. In 1994 they lost out to Brazil, but in 2006 they beat France on penalties after a 1-1 draw in the final in Berlin.

• Italy's Vittorio Pozo is the only coach to win the World Cup twice, guiding

**IS THAT A FACT?**
Ipswich have remained in the top two flights of English football since gaining promotion to the old Second Division in 1957 – the longest continuous run of any current Championship club.

*Italian team line-ups can always be relied upon to provide a great set of beards and moustaches*

the Azzurri to victory on home soil in 1934 and again in France four years later.

• **The most humiliating moment in Italy's sporting history came in 1966 when they lost 1-0 to minnows North Korea at the World Cup in England. The Italians had a remarkably similar embarrassment at the 2002 tournament when they were knocked out by hosts South Korea after a 2-1 defeat. Fortunately for the Azzurri, neither 'East Korea' or 'West Korea' exist as independent countries!**

• In a bid to improve the performance of the national team, the Italian FA banned foreign players from signing for clubs in Serie A in 1964. Ironically, two years after the ban was lifted in 1980 Italy won the World Cup for a third time.

• **Italy have won the European Championships just once, beating Yugoslavia 2-0 in the final in Rome in 1968. They reached the final again in 2000 but lost to France, and endured more disappointment in 2012 when they were hammered 4-0 by Spain in the final in Kiev.**

HONOURS
***World Cup winners*** *1934, 1938, 1982, 2006*
***European Championships winners*** *1968*
**World Cup Record**
*1930 Did not enter*

*1934 Winners*
*1938 Winners*
*1950 Round 1*
*1954 Round 1*
*1958 Did not qualify*
*1962 Round 1*
*1966 Round 1*
*1970 Runners-up*
*1974 Round 1*
*1978 Fourth place*
*1982 Winners*
*1986 Round 2*
*1990 Third place*
*1994 Runners-up*
*1998 Quarter-finals*
*2002 Round 2*
*2006 Winners*
*2010 Round 1*
*2014 Round 1*

## BRANISLAV IVANOVIC

**Born:** Sremska Mitrovica, Serbia, 22nd February 1984
**Position:** Defender
**Club career:**
2001-02 Remont 13 (0)
2002-03 Srem 19 (2)
2003-06 OFK Belgrade 55 (5)
2006-08 Lokomotiv Moscow 54 (5)
2008- Chelsea 215 (20)
**International record:**
2005- Serbia 77 (10)

A rugged defender once described by Raheem Sterling as "the scariest player to play against", Branislav Ivanovic has made a huge contribution to Chelsea's recent successes, helping the Blues win the Double in 2010 and the Premier League and League Cup in 2015. In both of those seasons the tough-tackling Serb was voted into the PFA Team of the Year.

• **In 2013 Ivanovic cemented his cult status at Stamford Bridge by heading a stoppage-time winner against Benfica in the final of the Europa League. The previous year, though, he was forced to watch Chelsea's Champions League victory over Bayern Munich from the sidelines after being suspended for the final.**

• After starting out in his native Serbia, Ivanovic left OFK Belgrade for Lokomotiv Moscow in 2006. He won the Russian Cup with Lokomotiv in 2007 before joining Chelsea the following year for £9 million – a record fee for a Russian-based player.

• **Serbian Player of the Year in both 2012 and 2013, Ivanovic made his international debut in 2005. He played for his country at the 2010 World Cup in South Africa, Serbia's first as an independent nation.**

• In 2012 Ivanovic was made captain of his country and he is now third on the list of most-capped Serbians with 77 caps.

## JUVENTUS

JUVENTUS

**Year founded:** 1897
**Ground:** Juventus Stadium (41,254)
**Nickname:** The Zebras
**League titles:** 31
**Domestic cups:** 10
**European cups:** 8
**International cups:** 2

The most famous and the most successful club in Italy, Juventus were founded in 1897 by pupils at a school in Turin – hence the team's name, which means 'youth' in Latin. Six years later the club binned their original pink shirts and adopted their distinctive black-and-white-striped kit after an English member of the team had a set of Notts County shirts shipped out to Italy.

• **Juventus emerged as the dominant** force in Italian football in the 1930s when they won a best-ever five titles in a row. They have a record 31 titles to their name and are the only team in Italy allowed to wear two gold stars on their shirts, signifying 20 Serie A victories. In 2014/15 Juve won the league for a fourth year running and also reached the Champions League final, losing 3-1 to Barcelona in Berlin.

• When, thanks to a single goal by their star player Michel Platini, Juventus beat Liverpool in the European Cup final in 1985 they became the first ever club to win all three European trophies. However, their triumph at the Heysel Stadium in Brussels was overshadowed by the death of 39 of their fans, who were crushed to death as they tried to flee from crowd trouble before the kick-off.

• **When Juventus beat Lazio 2-1 in the final of the 2015 Coppa Italia it meant that the Zebras had won the cup for a record tenth time.**

• Juventus have won more Serie A matches (1,434) and scored more goals (4,649) than any other club.

• Juventus striker Enrique Omar Sivori holds the record for the most goals by a player in a Serie A match, with six in an incredible 9-1 thrashing of Inter Milan in 1961.

### HONOURS

*Italian champions* 1905, 1926, 1931, 1932, 1933, 1934, 1935, 1950, 1952, 1958, 1960, 1961, 1967, 1972, 1973, 1975, 1977, 1978, 1981, 1982, 1984, 1986, 1995, 1997, 1998, 2002, 2003, 2012, 2013, 2014, 2015
*Italian Cup* 1938, 1942, 1959, 1960, 1965, 1979, 1983, 1990, 1995, 2015
*European Cup/Champions League* 1985, 1996
*European Cup Winners' Cup* 1984
*UEFA Cup* 1977, 1990, 1993
*European Super Cup* 1984, 1996
*Club World Cup* 1985, 1996

*The annual post-Champions League final game of 'It' descended into farce in 2015*

## HARRY KANE

**Born:** Chingford, 28th July 1993
**Position:** Striker
**Club career:**
2011- Tottenham Hotspur 45 (24)
2011 Leyton Orient (loan) 18 (5)
2012 Millwall (loan) 22 (7)
2012-13 Norwich City (loan) 3 (0)
2013 Leicester City (loan) 13 (2)
**International record:**
2015- England 2 (1)

Following a stunning season with Tottenham in 2014/15, Harry Kane was voted PFA Young Player of the Year and named in the PFA Team of the Year.

• Kane's total of 31 goals in all competitions over the course of the campaign was the best haul by a Tottenham player since Gary Lineker banged in 35 in 1991/92. The young striker's excellent form also saw him named Premier League Player of the Month in both January and February 2015 – only the fourth player ever to win the award in consecutive months.

• A clever player who can create as well as score goals, Kane came through the Tottenham youth system and spent time on loan with Orient, Millwall, Norwich and Leicester before finally establishing himself in the Spurs first team in 2014. The following year he helped the north Londoners reach the League Cup final, but had to settle for a loser's medal after a 2-0 defeat to Chelsea at Wembley.

• An England international at Under-17, Under-19, Under-20 and Under-21 level, Kane made his senior debut against Lithuania in a Euro 2016 qualifier at Wembley in March 2015.

His international career got off to a dream start, too, as he came off the bench to score with a header after just 78 seconds – the third fastest goal by an England player on debut.

*Harry Kane is the new hero of White Hart Lane*

## TOP 10

### HIGHEST CAPPED REPUBLIC OF IRELAND PLAYERS

| | | |
|---|---|---|
| 1. Robbie Keane (1998- ) | | 140 |
| 2. Shay Given (1996- ) | | 130 |
| 3. Kevin Kilbane (1997-2011) | | 110 |
| 4. John O'Shea (2001- ) | | 104 |
| 5. Steve Staunton (1988-2002) | | 102 |
| 6. Niall Quinn (1986-2002) | | 91 |
| 7. Tony Cascarino (1985-2000) | | 88 |
| 8. Paul McGrath (1985-97) | | 83 |
| 9. Packie Bonner (1981-96) | | 80 |
| Richard Dunne (2000-14) | | 80 |

## ROBBIE KEANE

**Born:** Dublin, 8th July 1980
**Position:** Striker
**Club career:**
1997-99 Wolves 74 (24)
1999-2000 Coventry City 31 (12)
2000-01 Inter Milan 6 (0)
2001 Leeds United (loan) 18 (9)
2001-02 Leeds United 28 (4)
2002-08 Tottenham Hotspur 197 (80)
2008-09 Liverpool 19 (5)
2009-11 Tottenham Hotspur 41 (11)
2010 Celtic (loan) 16 (12)
2011 West Ham United (loan) 9 (2)
2011- LA Galaxy 101 (68)
2012 Aston Villa (loan) 6 (3)
**International record:**
1998- Republic of Ireland 140 (65)

Republic of Ireland captain Robbie Keane is his country's all-time top scorer and highest appearance maker. His total of 65 goals for the Irish since making his debut in 1998 puts him in fifth place in the all-time list of European international goalscorers, and is higher than any other still active striker. Keane also holds the record for the most goals in European Championship qualifiers with 21.

• Keane began his club career with Wolves, for whom he scored twice on his debut against Norwich in 1997.

*Robbie Keane is Ireland's top scorer and highest appearance maker*

Two years later, aged 19, he joined Coventry City for £6 million – then a record fee for a teenager.

• After brief spells with Inter Milan and Leeds, Keane moved to Tottenham in 2002. While at White Hart Lane he finally won the first trophy of his career, the Carling Cup in 2007/08 – a season in which he hit a personal best 23 goals in all competitions.

• His goals record prompted Liverpool to pay £20 million for him in the summer of 2008. It was a dream move for Keane, a childhood fan of the Reds, but he was used irregularly by then Liverpool boss Rafa Benitez and, in the January 2009 transfer window, he returned to Tottenham for £15 million. However, he soon found himself surplus to requirements at White Hart Lane and, after loan spells at Celtic and West Ham, Keane signed for LA Galaxy in a £3.5 million deal in the summer of 2011. In 2014 he

scored Galaxy's winning goal against New England Revolution as they won the MLS Cup for a record fifth time.

## ROY KEANE

**Born:** Cork, 10th August 1971
**Position:** Midfielder
**Club career:**
1989-90 Cobh Ramblers 12 (1)
1990-93 Nottingham Forest 114 (22)
1993-2005 Manchester United 323 (33)
2005-06 Celtic 10 (1)
**International record:**
1991-2005 Republic of Ireland 66 (9)

Manchester United legend Roy Keane is the club's most successful captain ever, leading the Reds to nine major trophies (including four Premier League titles) while wearing the armband between

1997 and 2005.

• The driving force in United's midfield for over a decade after arriving from Nottingham Forest for a then British record fee of £3.75 million in 1993, Keane won seven league titles and four FA Cups while at Old Trafford but he missed out on the Reds' 1999 Champions League triumph through suspension.

• A fiery, volatile character, Keane was sent off 13 times during his career – a record for the top flight. He set another unwanted record in 2002 when he was fined £150,000 by the FA for bringing the game into disrepute when he admitted in his autobiography that he had intended to hurt an opponent, Manchester City's Alf-Inge Haaland.

• Keane starred for the Republic of Ireland at the 1994 World Cup, being named his country's best player. However, before the 2002 tournament in Japan and Korea he stormed out of Ireland's training camp on the Pacific island of Saipan after a furious row with manager Mick McCarthy. Despite the intervention of Irish Prime Minister Bertie Ahern, Keane refused to return, although he later played for his country again under new boss Brian Kerr.

• After retiring in 2006 he moved into management with Sunderland and then Ipswich. In 2013 he became assistant manager of the Republic of Ireland, and the following year he briefly took up a similar role at Aston Villa.

## KEVIN KEEGAN

**Born:** Doncaster, 14th February 1951
**Position:** Striker
**Club career:**
1968-71 Scunthorpe United 124 (18)
1971-77 Liverpool 230 (68)
1977-80 Hamburg 90 (32)
1980-82 Southampton 68 (37)
1982-84 Newcastle United 78 (48)
**International record:**
1972-82 England 63 (21)

A busy, all-action striker with a sharp eye for goal, Kevin Keegan is the only British player to have twice been voted European Footballer of the Year and he was only the second player – after the great Johan Cruyff – to win the award in consecutive seasons (1978 and 1979).

• Keegan was also the first English player to appear in the European Cup final with two different clubs. In 1977 he was a winner with Liverpool against Borussia Monchengladbach, but three years later he had to settle for a runners-up medal after Hamburg were beaten by Nottingham Forest.

• Uniquely, Keegan's first three England appearances were all against the same opposition, Wales. He went on to win 63 caps, 31 of them as captain.

• Nicknamed 'Mighty Mouse' during his spell with Hamburg, Keegan had a top 10 hit in Germany with *Head Over Heels* in 1979. The single fared less well in the UK, stalling at number 31.

• Keegan finished his playing days at Newcastle in the early 1980s, returning to St James' Park a decade later as manager. But, after five years in charge, he dramatically quit the club a few months after his entertaining Toon team had narrowly missed out on the Premiership title. A brief second spell in charge of the Geordies ended in similar fashion in 2008 following a long-running disagreement with owner Mike Ashley about the club's management structure.

• Keegan also walked out on the England job in October 2000 just a few minutes after his team had lost a vital World Cup qualifier to Germany in the last ever match played at the old Wembley. He had only been in charge for 18 months, but had increasingly come under fire after a poor England showing at Euro 2000.

## KICK-OFF

Scottish club Queen's Park claim to have been the first to adopt the traditional kick-off time of 3pm on a Saturday, which allowed those people who worked in the morning time to get to the match.

• The fastest ever goal from a kick-off was scored in just two seconds by Nawaf Al Abed, a 21-year-old striker for Saudi Arabian side Al Hilal in a cup match against Al Shoalah in 2009. After a team-mate tapped the ball to him, Al Abed struck a fierce left-foot shot from the halfway line which sailed over the opposition keeper and into the net.

• Ledley King scored the fastest goal in Premier League history, striking just 9.9 seconds after the kick-off for Tottenham against Bradford City on 9th December 2000.

• The fastest goal in Football League history was scored after just four

*Kilmarnock's youth policy is really starting to pay off!*

seconds by Jim Fryatt for Bradford Park Avenue against Tranmere Rovers on 25th April 1964.

• The earliest kick-off for a Premier League match was at 11.15am on 2nd October 2005 when Manchester City entertained Everton. The early start, which was dictated by pay-per-view TV, seemed to suit City better as they won 2-0.

## KILMARNOCK

**Year founded:** 1869
**Ground:** Rugby Park (18,128)
**Nickname:** Killie
**Biggest win:** 13-2 v Saltcoats Victoria (1896)
**Heaviest defeat:** 1-9 v Celtic (1938)

The oldest professional club in Scotland, Kilmarnock were founded in 1869 by a group of local cricketers who were keen to play another sport during the winter months. Originally, the club played rugby (hence the name of Kilmarnock's stadium, Rugby Park) before switching to football in 1873.

• That same year Kilmarnock entered the inaugural Scottish Cup and on

18th October 1873 the club took part in the first ever match in the competition, losing 2-0 in the first round to Renton.

• Kilmarnock's greatest moment was back in 1965 when they travelled to championship rivals Hearts on the last day of the season requiring a two-goal win to pip the Edinburgh side to the title on goal average. To the joy of their travelling fans, Killie won 2-0 to claim the title by 0.04 of a goal.

• Kilmarnock have won the Scottish Cup three times, and claimed their first ever League Cup in 2012 when they beat Celtic 1-0 in the final at Hampden Park, Belgian striker Dieter van Tornhout scoring the winning goal six minutes from time.

• During a disappointing 2014/15 Premiership season Kilmarnock lost a club record seven consecutive league matches, despite finding the net at least once in all of those games.

• With a total of 167 goals for Kilmarnock and Rangers, former Killie striker Kris Boyd is the leading goalscorer in the history of the SPL.

### HONOURS
*Division 1 champions* 1965
*Division 2 champions* 1898, 1899
*Scottish Cup* 1920, 1929, 1997
*Scottish League Cup* 2012

# TOP 10

## KIT DEALS

1. Manchester United (Adidas)
   £75 million/year
2. Bayern Munich (Adidas)
   £43 million/year
3. Chelsea (Adidas) £30 million/year
4. Arsenal (Puma) £30 million/year
5. Real Madrid (Adidas)
   £27 million/year
6. Liverpool (New Balance)
   £25 million/year
7. Barcelona (Nike) £23 million/year
8. Juventus (Adidas) £17 million/year
9. AC Milan (Adidas) £14 million/year
   Paris St Germain (Nike)
   £14 million/year

## KIT DEALS

In July 2014 Manchester United signed the biggest ever kit deal in football history with German company Adidas. The deal, which starts at the beginning of the 2015/16 campaign, will see United paid £750 million over 10 seasons in return for wearing Adidas supplied training and playing kit.

• Outside the Premier League, Bayern Munich have the most lucrative kit deal in Europe, pulling in £43 million per year from Adidas after signing a new deal with the German manufacturers in 2015.

• Adidas are the biggest spending kit supliers, paying out a colossal £175 million per year for the privilege of providing kit for just four leading European clubs: Manchester United, Bayern Munich, Chelsea and Real Madrid.

## VINCENT KOMPANY

**Born:** Brussels, Belgium, 10th April 1986
**Position:** Defender
**Club career:**
2003-06 Anderlecht 73 (6)
2006-08 Hamburg 29 (1)
2008- Manchester City 204 (11)
**International record:**
2004- Belgium 60 (4)

In 2012 Vincent Kompany became the first Manchester City captain to lift the Premier League title when his team pipped local rivals Manchester United to top spot on the last day of the season.

Two years later he repeated the feat, scoring in his side's 2-0 defeat of West Ham which secured the 2014 title on the final day of the season. In the same campaign, he also skippered City to their first triumph in the League Cup for 38 years when they beat Sunderland 3-1 in the final at Wembley.

• In 2011 Kompany became the first City captain since Tony Book in 1969 to raise the FA Cup, when City beat Stoke City 1-0 in the final at Wembley. His consistent performances in both campaigns earned him a place in the PFA Premier League Team of the Season.

• Kompany began his career with Anderlecht, with whom he won the Belgian league in both 2004 and 2006. He moved on to Hamburg after that second triumph, before joining City for around £6 million in 2008. In July 2012 City awarded him a six-year contract, the longest in the club's history.

• Kompany was just 17 when he made his debut for Belgium against France in 2004, one of the youngest ever players to represent his country. He was appointed captain in 2011 and led his country to the last eight at the 2014 World Cup.

*Manchester United's new kit did seem to make some of its players very aggressive!*

## PHILIPP LAHM

**Born:** Munich, Germany, 11th November 1983
**Position:** Defender/midfielder
**Club career:**
2001-03 Bayern Munich II 63 (3)
2002- Bayern Munich 280 (10)
2003-05 Stuttgart (loan) 53 (2)
**International record:**
2004-14 Germany 113 (5)

In 2014 Philipp Lahm became the first ever European to lead his country to World Cup glory on South American soil when he skippered Germany in their 1-0 victory over Argentina in the final in Rio de Janeiro, Brazil. It turned out to be his last match for Germany, as he announced his retirement from international football soon afterwards.

• Equally at home playing at full-back or in a defensive midfield role, Lahm became Germany's youngest ever captain at the World Cup when he led the side at the 2010 tournament in South Africa, aged 26. On that occasion, he had to settle for third place.

• In 2013 Lahm became the first German player to lead his club to the Treble, when he helped Bayern win the Bundesliga, the German Cup and the Champions League, the latter trophy after a narrow 2-1 victory over Borussia Dortmund in the final at Wembley.

• 'The Magic Dwarf', as the pint-sized Lahm has been dubbed by fans, has won an impressive total of seven Bundesliga titles – just one short of the record held by former Bayern players Mehmet Scholl and Oliver Kahn – since making his debut for the German giants back in 2002.

## ADAM LALLANA

**Born:** St Albans, 10th May 1988
**Position:** Midfielder
**Club career:**
2006-14 Southampton 235 (48)
2007 Bournemouth (loan) 3 (0)
2014- Liverpool 27 (5)
**International record:**
2013- England 15 (0)

Liverpool midfielder Adam Lallana is the only player to have been voted into the PFA Team of the Year for the three current top divisions: League One, the

*Stylish Liverpool midfielder, Adam Lallana*

Championship and the Premier League.

• An intelligent player who can spot a killer pass while also carrying a goal threat himself, Lallana came through the ranks at Southampton to make his debut as an 18 year old in a 5-2 defeat of Yeovil Town in the League Cup in August 2006. He became a regular for the Saints in the 2009/10 season, during which he became the first Southampton midfielder since club legend Matt Le Tissier in 1994/95 to score 20 goals in a season in all competitions.

• After enjoying successive promotions with Southampton in 2011 and 2012, and being made captain in 2012, Lallana quickly demonstrated that he was more than comfortable playing at the highest level, with his dynamic displays earning him a nomination for the PFA Player of the Year in 2014. That summer he moved on to Liverpool for £25 million, Southampton's record sale at the time. Along with some other of Brendan Rodgers' new signings he took a while to find his feet at Anfield, but began to show improved form in the second part of the 2014/15 season.

• Lallana won his first England cap in November 2013, gaining rave reviews for his vibrant performance in a friendly against Chile at Wembley. He went on to be selected for Roy Hodgson's 2014 World Cup squad, featuring in all three group games.

## FRANK LAMPARD

**Born:** Romford, 20th June 1978
**Position:** Midfielder
**Club career:**
1996-2001 West Ham United 148 (24)
1995-96 Swansea City (loan) 9 (1)
2001-14 Chelsea 429 (147)
2014- New York City 3 (0)
2014-15 Manchester City (loan) 32 (6)
**International record:**
1999-2014 England 106 (29)

With 177 goals to his name, Frank Lampard is the highest scoring midfielder in Premier League history and, along with Wayne Rooney, one of just two players to hit double figures in the league in 10 consecutive seasons (2004-13). A model of consistency, his total of 609 Premier League appaearances is only bettered by Ryan Giggs.

• Lampard, who joined Chelsea from his first club West Ham for £11 million in 2001, is the highest goalscorer in the Blues' history with an impressive total of 211 goals in all competitions for the club, who he served for 13 highly successful years. In June 2014 he joined New York City, before spending the following season on loan at Chelsea's main title rivals, Manchester City.

• Lampard won the league three times and the FA Cup four times during his time with the Blues, including the Double in 2010. After numerous near misses, he finally won the Champions League with Chelsea in 2012, scoring one of his team's penalties in the shoot-out victory over Bayern Munich in the final. The following year he skippered the Blues to success in the Europa League after the Londoners beat Benfica in the final.

• Lampard played in a then record 164 consecutive Premier League games until illness forced him out of Chelsea's visit to Manchester City in December 2005. Goalkeepers David James and Brad Friedel have since passed his total, but Lampard still holds the Premier League record for an outfield player.

• The son of former England and West Ham defender Frank senior, Lampard made his international debut in 1999. He starred at the European Championships in 2004, scoring in three of his country's four games, but fared less well at the 2006 World Cup where he was one of three England players to miss a penalty in the quarter-final shoot-out defeat at the hands of Portugal. His luck was also out at the 2010 tournament in South Africa, when the officials failed to spot that his shot in England's second-round defeat by Germany had clearly crossed the line after bouncing down off the crossbar. His total of 29 goals for his country is a record for an England midfielder, while his total of nine converted penalties is also a Three Lions record.

## DENIS LAW

**Born:** Aberdeen, 24th February 1940
**Position:** Striker
**Club career:**
1956-60 Huddersfield Town 81 (16)
1960-61 Manchester City 44 (21)
1961-62 Torino 27 (10)
1962-73 Manchester United 309 (171)
1973-74 Manchester City 24 (9)
**International record:**
1958-74 Scotland 55 (30)

Along with Kenny Dalglish, Denis Law is Scotland's leading scorer with 30 international goals. Law, though, scored his goals in roughly half the number of games as 'King Kenny'.

• Law made his international debut in 1958, scoring in a 3-0 win against Wales. Aged 18, he was the youngest player to appear for Scotland since before the war. He went on to represent Scotland for 16 years, taking his bow at the 1974 World Cup in Germany.

• On two occasions Law was sold for fees that broke the existing British transfer record. In 1960 he moved from Huddersfield to Manchester City for a record £55,000, and two years later his £115,000 transfer from Torino to Manchester United set a new benchmark figure.

• With United, Law won two league titles and the FA Cup in 1963, but he missed out on the club's European Cup triumph in 1968 through a knee injury. He remains the only Scottish player to have been voted European Footballer of the Year, an award he won in 1964.

• The last goal Law scored, a clever backheel for Manchester City against United at Old Trafford in 1974, gave him no pleasure at all as it condemned his old club to relegation to the Second Division. "I have seldom felt so depressed as I did that weekend," he remarked later.

• In 2002 a statue of Law was unveiled at Old Trafford, scene of many of his greatest triumphs. The following year the Scottish Football Association marked UEFA's Jubilee by naming him as Scotland's 'Golden Player' of the previous 50 years.

## LAWS

Thirteen original laws of association football were adopted at a meeting of the Football Association in 1863, although these had their roots in the 'Cambridge Rules' established at Cambridge University as far back as 1848.

• No copy of those 1848 rules now exists, but they are thought to have included laws relating to throw-ins, goal-kicks, fouls and offside. They even allowed for a length of string to be used as a crossbar.

• Perhaps the most significant rule change occurred in 1925 when the offside law was altered so that an attacking player receiving the ball would need to be behind two opponents, rather than three. The effect of this rule change was dramatic, with the average number of goals per game in the Football League rising from 2.55 in 1924/25 to 3.44 in 1925/26.

• The laws of the game are governed by the International Football Association Board, which was founded in 1886 by the four football associations of the United Kingdom. Each of these associations still has one vote on the IFAB, with FIFA having four

**IS THAT A FACT?**
When Frank Lampard volleyed in for Manchester City in a 1-1 draw against his old team Chelsea in September 2014 it was the 39th Premier League club he had scored against – a record for the league.

votes. Any changes to the laws of the game require a minimum of six votes.

• In recent years the most important change to the laws of the game was the introduction of the 'back pass' rule in 1992, which prevented goalkeepers from handling passes from their own team-mates. The rule was introduced to discourage time-wasting and overly defensive play, following criticisms of widespread negative tactics at the 1990 World Cup.

## LEAGUE CUP

With eight wins to their name, most recently in the 2012 final against Cardiff, Liverpool have won the League Cup more often than any other club. The Reds have also appeared in the most finals, 11.

• **The competition has been known by more names than any other in British football. Originally called the Football League Cup (1960-81), it has subsequently been rebranded through sponsorship deals as the Milk Cup (1981-86), Littlewoods Cup (1986-90), Rumbelows Cup (1990-92), Coca-Cola Cup (1992-98), Worthington Cup (1998-2003), Carling Cup (2003-12) and, since 2012, the Capital One Cup.**

• Ian Rush won a record five winners' medals in the competition with Liverpool (1981-84 and 1995) and, along with Geoff Hurst, is also the leading scorer in the history of the League Cup with 49 goals. In the 1986/87 season Tottenham's Clive Allen scored a record 12 goals in the competition.

• **Oldham's Frankie Bunn scored a record six goals in a League Cup match when Oldham thrashed Scarborough 7-0 on 25th October 1989.**

• Liverpool won the competition a record four times in a row between 1981 and 1984, going undefeated for an

'Keep smiling JT, the cameras are on us!'

unprecedented 25 League Cup matches.

• **In 1983 West Ham walloped Bury 10-0 to record the biggest ever victory in the history of the League Cup. Three years later Liverpool equalled the Hammers' tally with an identical thrashing of Fulham.**

• Norman Whiteside, the youngest player ever to score in an FA Cup final (for Manchester United v Brighton in 1983), is also the youngest man ever to score in the League Cup final (for Manchester United v Liverpool, also in 1983), aged 17 years and 324 days.

• **Liverpool's John Arne Riise scored the fastest goal in the League Cup final, after just 45 seconds against Chelsea in 2005.**

• The first League Cup final to be played at Wembley was between West Brom and QPR in 1967. QPR were then a Third Division side and pulled off a major shock by winning 3-2. Prior to 1967, the final was played on a home and away basis over two legs.

• **On two occasions a League Cup match has featured a record 12 goals: Arsenal's 7-5 win at Reading in 2012, and Dagenham's 6-6 draw with**

**Brentford two years later.**

• Chelsea striker Didier Drogba scored a record four goals in League Cup finals, finding the target against Liverpool in 2005, Arsenal in 2007 (two goals) and Tottenham in 2008.

## LEEDS UNITED

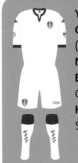

**Year founded:** 1919
**Ground:** Elland Road (37,890)
**Nickname:** United
**Biggest win:** 10-0 v Lyn Oslo (1969)
**Heaviest defeat:** 1-8 v Stoke City (1934)

Leeds United were formed in 1919 as successors to Leeds City, who had been expelled from the Football League after making illegal payments to their players. United initially joined the Midland League before being elected to the Second Division in 1920.

## TOP 10

### LEAGUE CUP MATCHES WON

| | | |
|---|---|---|
| 1. | Aston Villa | 135 |
| 2. | Liverpool | 127 |
| 3. | Tottenham Hotspur | 122 |
| 4. | Arsenal | 120 |
| 5. | West Ham United | 108 |
| 6. | Manchester City | 105 |
| | Manchester United | 105 |
| 8. | Norwich City | 103 |
| 9. | Nottingham Forest | 98 |
| 10. | Chelsea | 97 |

• Leeds' greatest years were in the 1960s and early 1970s under legendary manager Don Revie. The club were struggling in the Second Division when he arrived at Elland Road in 1961 but, building his side around the likes of Jack Charlton, Billy Bremner and Johnny Giles, Revie soon turned Leeds into a formidable force.

• During the Revie years Leeds won two league titles in 1969 and 1974, the FA Cup in 1972, the League Cup in 1968, and two Fairs Cup in 1968 and 1971. In the last of those triumphs Leeds became the first club to win a European trophy on the away goals rule after they drew 2-2 on aggregate with Italian giants Juventus.

• Leeds also reached the final of the European Cup in 1975, losing 2-0 to Bayern Munich. Sadly, rioting by the club's fans resulted in Leeds becoming the first English club to be suspended from European competition. The ban lasted three years.

• Peter Lorimer, another Revie-era stalwart, is the club's leading scorer, hitting 168 league goals in two spells at Elland Road: 1962-79 and 1983-86. Jack Charlton holds the club appearance record, turning out in 773 games in total between 1952 and 1973. Significantly, the next six players on the list behind 'Big Jack' are all his old team-mates from the 1960s and 1970s.

• Leeds and Wales legend John Charles scored a club record 42 league goals in 1953/54.

• In 1992 Leeds pipped Manchester United to the title to make history as the last club to win the old First Division before it became the Premiership. Ironically, Leeds' star player at the time, Eric Cantona, joined the Red Devils the following season. The club remained a force over the next decade, even reaching the Champions League semi-final in 2001, but financial mismanagement saw them plummet to League One in 2007 before they climbed back into the Championship three years later.

• Incredibly, Leeds failed to win a single FA Cup tie between 1952 and 1963 – the worst ever run by a league club in the post-war era.

• Former England captain Rio Ferdinand is both Leeds' record buy and record sale, joining the club from West Ham for £18 million in 2000 before leaving for Manchester United for a then British record £29.1 million two years later.

HONOURS

***Division 1 champions*** *1969, 1974, 1992*
***Division 2 champions*** *1924, 1964, 1990*
***FA Cup*** *1972*
***League Cup*** *1968*
***Fairs Cup*** *1968, 1971*

## LEICESTER CITY

**Year founded:** 1884
**Ground:** King Power Stadium (32,262)
**Previous name:** Leicester Fosse
**Nickname:** The Foxes
**Biggest win:** 13-0 v Notts Olympic (1894)
**Heaviest defeat:** 0-12 v Nottingham Forest (1909)

Founded in 1884 as Leicester Fosse by old boys from Wyggeston School, the club were elected to the Second Division a decade later. In 1919 they changed their name to Leicester City, shortly after Leicester was given city status.

• The Foxes have enjoyed great success in the League Cup, winning the trophy three times. Their first victory came against Stoke in 1964 and more recently they won the trophy twice under then manager Martin O'Neill, against Middlesbrough in 1997 and Tranmere Rovers in 2000.

• Leicester have won the second-tier championship seven times – a record only matched by Manchester City. On the last of these occasions in 2013/14 the Foxes set a number of significant club records, including highest number of points (102) and most league games won (33).

• In 1909, while still known as Leicester Fosse, the club suffered their worst ever defeat, losing 12-0 to East Midlands neighbours

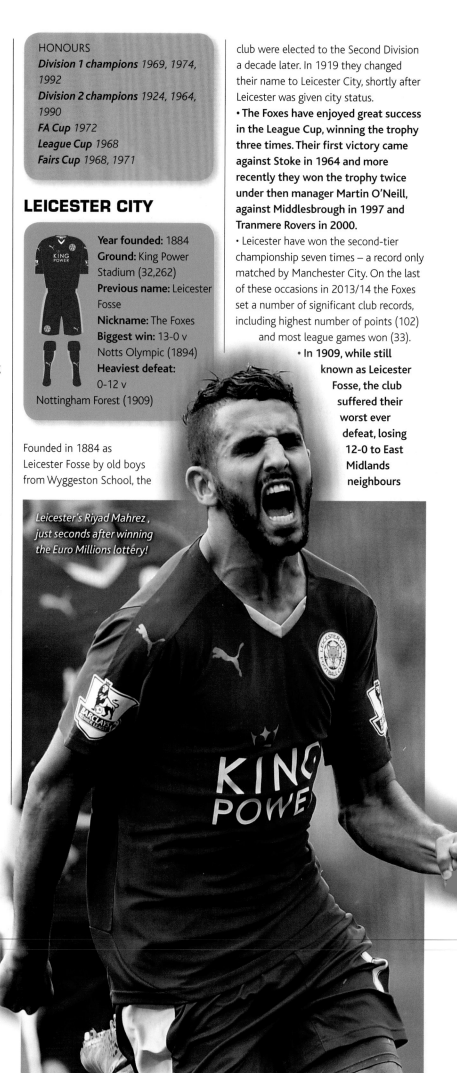

*Leicester's Riyad Mahrez, just seconds after winning the Euro Millions lottery!*

*Prolific Bayern Munich striker, Robert Lewandowski*

Nottingham Forest – still a record score for a top-flight match. It later emerged that the Leicester players had been celebrating the wedding of a team-mate for two full days before the game, which might have contributed to their pitiful performance!

• Leicester City are the only club to have played in four FA Cup finals and lost them all. Beaten in 1949, 1961 and 1963, they were defeated again by Manchester City in 1969 – the same season in which they were relegated from the top flight. Previously, only Manchester City (in 1926) had suffered this bitter double blow.

• **Leicester made their record sale in 2000, when England striker Emile Heskey moved to Liverpool for £11 million. In January 2015 the Foxes made their record signing, bringing Croatian striker Andrej Kramaric to the King Power from HNK Rijeka for £9 million.**

• Arthur Chandler holds the club goalscoring record, netting 259 times between 1923 and 1935. The club's appearance record is held by defender and ex-Leicestershire county cricketer Graham Cross, who turned out 599 times in all competitions for the Foxes between 1960 and 1976.

• **In 2014/15 Leicester became only the second club (after West Brom in 2004/05) to escape relegation from the Premier League after being rock bottom at Christmas. To the amazement of their fans, the**

previously struggling Foxes grabbed an impressive 22 points from their last nine games to pull clear of the dreaded drop zone.

• Leicester's most famous fan is *Match of the Day* presenter Gary Lineker, who scored over 100 goals for the club between 1978 and 1985.

> ### HONOURS
> ***Division 2 champions*** *1925, 1937, 1954, 1957, 1971, 1980*
> ***Championship champions*** *2014*
> ***League One champions*** *2009*
> ***League Cup*** *1964, 1997, 2000*

## ROBERT LEWANDOWSKI

**Born:** Warsaw, Poland, 21st August 1983
**Position:** Striker
**Club career:**
2005 Delta Warsaw 10 (4)
2005-06 Legia Warsaw II 5 (2)
2006-08 Znicz Pruszków 59 (36)
2008-10 Lech Poznan 58 (32)
2010-14 Borussia Dortmund 131 (74)
2014- Bayern Munich 30 (17)
**International record:**
2008- Poland 68 (26)

Pacy Polish striker Robert Lewandowski is the only player to have scored four goals in a Champions League semi-

final, achieving this record in Borussia Dortmund's 4-1 defeat of Real Madrid in 2013. His sensational performance powered Borussia into the final, where they lost 2-1 at Wembley to German rivals Bayern Munich.

• **After starting out in the Polish lower leagues, Lewandowski made his name at Lech Poznan. In only his second season in the top flight, in 2009/10, he led the scoring charts with 18 goals as Poznan won the title.**

• In the summer of 2010 Lewandowski moved on to Dortmund for around £4 million. The fee proved to be a bargain as Lewandowski's goals helped his club win two league titles and the German Cup in 2012, the Pole scoring a hat-trick in Borussia's 5-2 demolition of Bayern in the final. The following season Lewandowski set a new club record when he scored in 12 consecutive league games. After topping the Bundesliga scoring charts in 2013/14 he moved on to Bayern Munich, with whom he won the title in his first season in Bavaria.

• **Lewandowski first played for Poland aged 20 in 2008, coming off the bench to score in a World Cup qualifier against San Marino to become his country's second ever youngest goalscorer on his debut. In June 2015 he scored a four-minute hat-trick in a Euro 2016 qualifier against Georgia – the second fastest treble in the history of the European Championships.**

## LEYTON ORIENT

**Year founded:** 1881
**Ground:** The Matchroom Stadium (9,271)
**Previous name:** Eagle FC, Clapton Road, Orient
**Nickname:** The O's
**Biggest win:** 9-2 v Aldershot (1934) and v Chester (1962)
**Heaviest defeat:** 0-8 v Aston Villa (1929)

Originally founded by members of a local cricket team, the club chose the name 'Orient' in 1888 following a suggestion by one of the players who worked for the Orient Shipping Company.

• Over 40 Orient players and staff fought in the First World War, three of them dying in the conflict. In recognition of this sacrifice, the Prince of Wales (later King Edward VIII) watched an Orient match in 1921 – the first time a member of the Royal Family had attended a Football League fixture.

• Orient are the only club to have played league matches at the old Wembley Stadium. During the 1931/32 season, while still named Clapton Orient, the club played matches against Brentford and Southend at 'the home of football' after their own Lea Bridge ground was temporarily closed for failing to meet official standards.

• In the Third Division play-off final in 2001, Orient's Chris Tate scored against Blackpool after just 27 seconds – the fastest ever goal at the Millennium Stadium. Sadly for the O's, they lost the game 4-2.

• Orient's record scorer is Tommy Johnston, who banged in 121 goals in two spells at the club between 1956 and 1961. In 2009 the South Stand at Brisbane Road was named after the prolific striker.

HONOURS
*Division 3 (S) champions* 1956
*Division 3 champions* 1970

## GARY LINEKER

**Born:** Leicester, 30th November 1960
**Position:** Striker
**Club career:**
1978-85 Leicester City 194 (95)
1985-86 Everton 41 (30)
1986-89 Barcelona 103 (43)
1989-92 Tottenham Hotspur 105 (67)
1992-94 Nagoya Grampus 8 23 (9)
**International record:**
1984-92 England 80 (48)

Now a popular television presenter, Gary Lineker is England's third highest scorer with 48 goals, just one behind the legendary Bobby Charlton and two behind Wayne Rooney. He had a great chance to beat the record, but failed to score in any of his final six matches and even missed a penalty against Brazil in 1992 that would have equalled Charlton's tally.

• He is, though, England's leading scorer at the finals of the World Cup with 10 goals. At the 1986 tournament in Mexico Lineker scored six goals to win the Golden Boot, and he added another four at Italia '90.

• Lineker is the only player to have twice scored all four England goals in a match, grabbing all his side's goals in 4-2 away wins over Spain in 1987 and Malaysia in 1991. In all, he hit five hat-tricks for the Three Lions – just one behind Jimmy Greaves' record.

• At club level Lineker won the European Cup Winners' Cup with Barcelona in 1989 and the FA Cup with Spurs two years later. He was also voted PFA Player of the Year in 1986 after a single goal-filled season with Everton.

• In his last international, against Sweden at the 1992 European Championships, Lineker was controversially substituted by England boss Graham Taylor. The move backfired as England lost the match and were eliminated.

• A revered figure in his hometown, Lineker has a stand named after him at Leicester's King Power Stadium.

## LIVERPOOL

**Year founded:** 1892
**Ground:** Anfield (45,276)
**Nickname:** The Reds
**Biggest win:** 11-0 v Stromsgodset (1974)
**Heaviest defeat:** 1-9 v Birmingham City (1954)

Liverpool were founded as a splinter club from local rivals Everton following a dispute between the Toffees and the landlord of their original ground at Anfield, John Houlding. When the majority of Evertonians decided to decamp to Goodison Park in 1892, Houlding set up Liverpool FC after his attempts to retain the name 'Everton' had failed.

*Liverpool's Nathaniel Clyne stretches for the ball*

- With 18 league titles to their name, Liverpool are the second most successful club in the history of English football behind deadly rivals Manchester United. However, the Reds have failed to lift the championship trophy for over two decades, their last title coming way back in 1990.

- Liverpool dominated English football in the 1970s and 1980s after the foundations of the club's success were laid by legendary manager Bill Shankly in the previous decade. Under Shankly's successor, Bob Paisley, the Reds won 13 major trophies – a haul only surpassed by Sir Alex Ferguson.

- **As their fans love to remind their rivals Liverpool are the most successful English side in Europe, having won the European Cup/ Champions League on five occasions. The Reds first won the trophy in 1977, beating Borussia Monchengladbach 3-1 in Rome, and the following year became the first British team to retain the cup (after a 1-0 win in the final against Bruges at Wembley, club legend Kenny Dalglish grabbing the all-important goal).**

- In 1984 Liverpool became the first club to win the European Cup on penalties when they beat Roma by this method after a 1-1 draw. In 2005 the Reds won the trophy on spot-kicks again, this time against AC Milan, and remain the only club to have twice triumphed in the competition after a penalty shoot-out.

- **Liverpool have won the League Cup a record eight times, including four times in a row between 1981 and 1984, and are the only club to win the trophy twice on penalties (in 2001 and 2012). Reds striker Ian Rush is the joint-leading scorer in the history of the competition with 49 goals, hitting all but one of these for Liverpool in**

two spells at the club in the 1980s and 1990s.

- Rush also scored a record five goals in three FA Cup finals for Liverpool in 1986, 1989 and 1992 – all of which were won by the Reds. In all, the Merseysiders have won the trophy seven times, most recently in 2006 when they became only the second team (after Arsenal the previous year) to claim the cup on penalties.

- **When the Reds recorded their biggest ever victory, 11-0 against Norwegian no-hopers Stromsgodset in the Cup Winners' Cup in 1974, no fewer than nine different Liverpool players got on the scoresheet to set a British record for the most scoring players in a competitive match.**

- In 1986 Liverpool became only the third English side in the 20th century to win the Double, pipping rivals Everton to the league title and then beating the Toffees 3-1 in the FA Cup final at Wembley with a line-up that featured not a single English player – a first for the final.

- **England international striker Roger Hunt is the club's leading scorer in league games, with 245 goals between 1958 and 1969. His team-mate Ian Callaghan holds the Liverpool appearance record, turning out in 640 league games between 1960 and 1978.**

- Pony-tailed striker Andy Carroll is the club's record signing, joining the Reds from Newcastle for £35 million in January 2011. In the summer of 2014 Uruguayan striker Luis Suarez left Anfield for Barcelona for a club record £75 million.

- **Between 1976 and 1983 Liverpool full-back Phil Neal played in 365 consecutive league games – a record for the top flight of English football.**

- Liverpool's youngest player is Jerome Sinclair, who made his debut aged 16 and six days as a sub against West Brom in September 2012.

- **Famous Liverpool fans include comedian John Bishop and EastEnders actor Adam Woodyatt (aka Ian Beale).**

**IS THAT A FACT?** Liverpool's famous Champions League triumph against AC Milan in Istanbul in 2005 is the only time that a team has won the trophy after being 3-0 down in the final.

### HONOURS

**Division 1 champions** 1901, 1906, 1922, 1923, 1947, 1964, 1966, 1973, 1976, 1977, 1979, 1980, 1982, 1983, 1984, 1986, 1988, 1990
**Division 2 champions** 1894, 1896, 1905, 1962

**FA Cup** 1965, 1974, 1986, 1989, 1992, 2001, 2006
**League Cup** 1981, 1982, 1983, 1984, 1995, 2001, 2003, 2012
**Double** 1986
**European Cup/Champions League** 1977, 1978, 1981, 1984, 2005
**UEFA Cup** 1973, 1976, 2001
**European Super Cup** 1977, 2001, 2005

## HUGO LLORIS

**Born:** Nice, France, 26th December 1986
**Position:** Goalkeeper
**Club career:**
2004-06 Nice B 20
2005-08 Nice 72
2008-12 Lyon 146
2012- Tottenham Hotspur 99
**International record:**
2008- France 67

When Hugo Lloris made his Premier League debut in the Tottenham goal against Aston Villa on 7th October 2012, he brought to an end his team-mate Brad Friedel's record run of 310 consecutive appearances in the league stretching back eight years. Now rated as one of the best keepers in the country, Lloris helped Spurs reach the League Cup final in 2015 but finished on the losing side after a 2-0 defeat to Chelsea.

- **After starting out with his hometown club Nice, Lloris made his name with Lyon. During a four-year stint with the French giants, Lloris was voted Ligue 1**

*Spurs 'keeper Hugo Lloris*

Goalkeeper of the Year three times, but only managed to win one piece of silverware – the French Cup in 2012, following a 1-0 victory in the final over third-tier Quevilly.

• Famed for his superb reflexes and his ability to rush out to the edge of his box to snuff out dangerous opposition attacks, Lloris won the European Under-19 championship with France in 2005. He was awarded his first senior cap in 2008, keeping a clean sheet in a 0-0 draw with Uruguay, and he skippered his country for the first time in a 2-1 friendly win against England at Wembley in November 2010.

• At the 2014 World Cup in Brazil Lloris was in fine form, keeping three clean sheets in five games as France reached the quarter-final stage before losing to eventual winners Germany.

## DAVID LUIZ

**Born:** Diadema, Brazil, 22nd April 1987
**Position:** Defender
**Club career:**
2006-07 Vitoria 26 (1)
2007 Benfica (loan) 10 (0)
2007-11 Benfica 72 (4)
2011-14 Chelsea 81 (6)
2014- Paris St Germain 26 (2)
**International record:**
2010- Brazil 51 (3)

Flamboyant centre-back David Luiz joined Paris St Germain from Chelsea in June 2014 for £50 million, making him the world's most expensive ever defensive purchase. In his first season in the French capital he helped PSG win the domestic double and scored against Chelsea in the Champions League last 16 as his old employers were dumped out of the competition.

• The frizzy-haired Brazilian's skills on the ball made him a cult figure at Stamford Bridge, with stallholders outside the stadium doing a roaring trade in 'David Luiz wigs'. However, his occasionally erratic approach to the basics of defending led to some criticism, notably from *Sky Sports* pundit Gary Neville who, after one haphazard display by Luiz, said that he played as though "controlled by a 10 year old on a PlayStation".

• Luiz answered his critics in the best possible manner by playing a starring role in Chelsea's run to the 2012 Champions League final and then bravely stepping up to score one of his team's penalties in the shoot-out victory over Bayern Munich which brought the trophy to London for the first time. The following year he helped the Blues become the first British side to win the Europa League, after victory over his former club Benfica in the final.

• In 2010 Luiz made his debut for Brazil in a 2-0 friendly win over the USA, and two years later he captained his country for the first time in a 1-0 win against South Africa. He had mixed fortunes at the World Cup in 2014, scoring a thunderous free kick in the quarter-final against Colombia, but he ended the tournament in tears after Brazil were hammered 7-1 by Germany in the semi-final.

## LUTON TOWN

**Year founded:** 1885
**Ground:** Kenilworth Road (10,356)
**Nickname:** The Hatters
**Biggest win:** 15-0 v Great Yarmouth Town (1914)
**Heaviest defeat:** 0-9 v Small Heath (1898)

Founded in 1885 following the merger of two local sides, Luton Town Wanderers and Excelsior, Luton Town became the first professional club in the south of England five years later.

• The club's greatest moment came in 1988 when they beat Arsenal 3-2 in the League Cup final. The Hatters returned to Wembley for the final the following year, but lost to Nottingham Forest – the same club which beat them in their only FA Cup final appearance in 1959.

• In 1936 Luton striker Joe Payne scored a Football League record 10 goals in a Third Division (South) fixture against Bristol Rovers. The Hatters won the match 12-0 to record their biggest ever league victory

• Midfielder Bob Morton made a record 495 league appearances for the Hatters between 1946 and 1964, while his team-mate Gordon Turner scored a record 243 goals for the club.

• In 2013, a year before they returned to the Football League as Conference champions, the Hatters became the first non-league club to beat a Premier League side in the FA Cup when they won 1-0 at Norwich in the fourth round.

HONOURS
*Division 2 champions* 1982
*Division 3 (South) champions* 1937
*League One champions* 2005
*Division 4 champions* 1968
*Conference champions* 2014
*League Cup* 1988
*Football League Trophy* 2009

*The final of the silly hair wrestling championships was very closely contested*

## ALLY McCOIST

**Born:** Bellshill, 24th September 1962
**Position:** Striker
**Club career:**
1979-81 St Johnstone 57 (22)
1981-83 Sunderland 56 (8)
1983-98 Rangers 418 (251)
1998-2001 Kilmarnock 59 (12)
**International record:**
1986-98 Scotland 61 (19)

Rangers legend Ally McCoist is the highest scorer in the Gers' history with an incredible 355 goals for the Ibrox outfit in all competitions. His tally of 251 league goals is also a club record.

• During a 15-year career with Rangers, McCoist won no fewer than 10 league titles (including nine in a row between 1989 and 1997), nine Scottish League Cups and one Scottish Cup. His haul of medals is unmatched by any other Scottish player in the last quarter of a century.

• In 1992 McCoist hit a personal best 34 goals and won the European Golden Boot. In the same year he was voted Scottish Player of the Year. A Scotland international for over a decade, his total of 19 goals for his country is only bettered by four players.

• In 2007 McCoist became assistant manager of Rangers and was promoted to the top job in 2011 following Walter Smith's retirement. Although his time as manager was overshadowed by the financial meltdown which saw Rangers relegated to the bottom tier of Scottish football, McCoist led the club to two successive promotions before resigning in December 2014.

## MANAGER OF THE YEAR

Former Manchester United boss Sir Alex Ferguson won the FA Premier League Manager of the Year award a record 11 times, the same as all the other winning managers put together. He also won the old Manager of the Year award in 1993, giving him a total of 12 triumphs.

• Arsène Wenger (in 1998, 2002 and 2004) and Jose Mourinho (2005, 2006 and 2015) are the only other managers to win the award more than once since it was introduced in the 1993/94 season.

• The first manager to win the award despite not guiding his team to the title was George Burley, who was honoured in 2001 after leading Ipswich to fifth place in the Premiership a year after winning promotion.

• Tony Pulis topped the poll in 2014 despite his club, Crystal Palace, finishing only 11th in the Premier League – the lowest ever placing for a manager collecting the award.

## MANCHESTER CITY

**Year founded:** 1887
**Ground:** Etihad Stadium (47,405)
**Previous name:** Ardwick
**Nickname:** The Citizens
**Biggest win:** 12-0 v Liverpool Stanley (1890)
**Heaviest defeat:** 2-10 v Small Heath (1894)

City have their roots in a church team which was renamed Ardwick in 1887 and became founder members of the Second Division five years later. In 1894, after suffering financial difficulties, the club was reformed under its present name.

• Now owned by Sheikh Mansour of the Abu Dhabi Royal Family, City are one of the richest clubs in the world. Following a massive spending spree on the likes of Edin Dzeko, David Silva and Yaya Toure, the Sheikh received the first return on his huge investment in 2011 when City won the FA Cup, their first trophy for 35 years, after beating Stoke City 1-0 in the final at Wembley. More silverware followed the next season as City won the Premier League, their first league title since 1968, after pipping arch rivals Manchester United on goal difference. In 2014 City won the Premier League for a second time, banging in an impressive 102 goals in the process – just one behind Chelsea's record haul. For good measure, City also won the League Cup after beating Sunderland 3-1 in the final.

• Prior to the modern era, the late 1960s were the most successful period in City's history, a side featuring the likes of Colin Bell, Francis Lee and Mike Summerbee winning the league title (1968), the FA Cup (1969), the League Cup (1970) and the European Cup Winners' Cup (also in 1970) and for a short time usurping Manchester United as the city's premier club.

*Raheem Sterling must know that Manchester City were started as a church team*

• City also won the league title in 1937. Incredibly, the following season they were relegated to the Second Division despite scoring more goals than any other side in the division. To this day they remain the only league champions to suffer the drop in the following campaign.

• Eric Brook, an ever-present in that initial title-winning season, is City's joint leading scorer (along with 1920s marksman Tommy Johnson) with 158 league goals between 1928 and 1940. The club's record appearance maker is Alan Oakes, who turned out 564 times in the sky blue shirt between 1958 and 1976.

• In all, City have won the FA Cup five times and, in 1926, were the first club to reach the final and be relegated in the same season. A 1-0 defeat by Bolton at Wembley ensured a grim season ended on a depressing note.

• The 1957/58 season was more enjoyable, especially for fans who like goals, as City scored 104 times while conceding 100 – the first and only time this 'double century' has been achieved. City finished fifth in the old First Division that season, the highest ever position by a team conceding 100 or more goals.

• City have won the title for the second tier of English football a joint-record seven times, most recently in 2002 when they returned to the Premiership under then manager Kevin Keegan. Four years earlier the club experienced their lowest ever moment when they dropped into the third tier for the first and only time in their history – the first European trophy winners to sink this low.

• The highest attendance ever at an English club ground, 84,569, saw City beat Stoke 1-0 at their old Maine Road Stadium in the sixth round of the FA Cup in 1934.

• The club's most expensive purchase is Belgian midfielder Kevin De Bruyne, who signed from Wolfsburg for £55 million in August 2015. Striker Alvaro Negredo boosted City's coffers by a record £24 million when he joined Valencia in the summer of 2015 following a season's loan with the Spanish club.

• Mercurial midfielder David Silva is the club's highest capped international, having played 49 times for Spain since he joined the Citizens in 2010.

• Famous City fans include musicians Liam and Noel Gallagher, comedian Jason Manford and Princess Beatrice, who ran the 2010 London Marathon in the club's black away kit.

HONOURS

***Division 1 champions*** *1937, 1968*
***Premier League champions*** *2012, 2014*
***Division 2 champions*** *1899, 1903, 1910, 1928, 1947, 1966*
***First Division champions*** *2002*
***FA Cup*** *1904, 1934, 1956, 1969, 2011*
***League Cup*** *1970, 1976, 2014*
***European Cup Winners' Cup*** *1970*

# MANCHESTER UNITED

**Year founded:** 1878
**Ground:** Old Trafford (75,635)
**Previous name:** Newton Heath
**Nickname:** Red Devils
**Biggest win:** 10-0 v Anderlecht (1956)
**Heaviest defeat:** 0-7 v Blackburn (1926), v Aston Villa (1930) and v Wolverhampton Wanderers (1931)

The club was founded in 1878 as Newton Heath, a works team for employees of the Lancashire and Yorkshire Railway. In 1892 Newton Heath (who played in yellow-and-green-halved shirts) were elected to the Football League but a decade later went bankrupt, only to be immediately reformed as Manchester United with the help of a local brewer, John Davies.

• **United are the most successful club in the history of English football,**

*No, we're not sure what Marouane Fellaini is doing here either!!!*

## TOP 10

### PREMIER LEAGUE VICTORIES

| | | |
|---|---|---|
| 1. | Manchester United | 567 |
| 2. | Arsenal | 482 |
| 3. | Chelsea | 474 |
| 4. | Liverpool | 440 |
| 5. | Tottenham Hotspur | 355 |
| 6. | Everton | 321 |
| 7. | Aston Villa | 313 |
| | Newcastle United | 313 |
| 9. | Manchester City | 285 |
| 10. | Blackburn Rovers | 262 |

having won the league title a record 20 times. The Red Devils have been the dominant force of the Premier League era, winning the title a record 13 times under former manager Sir Alex Ferguson.

• United were the first English club to win the Double on three separate occasions, in 1994, 1996 and 1999. The last of these triumphs was particularly memorable as the club also went on to win the Champions League, beating Bayern Munich 2-1 in the final in Barcelona thanks to two late goals by Teddy Sheringham and Ole Gunner Solskjaer, to record English football's first ever Treble.

• **Under legendary manager Sir Matt Busby United became the first ever English club to win the European Cup in 1968, when they beat Benfica 4-1 in the final at Wembley. Victory was especially sweet for Sir Matt who, a decade earlier, had narrowly survived the Munich air crash which claimed the lives of eight of his players as the team returned from a European Cup fixture in Belgrade. United also won European football's top club prize in 2008, beating Chelsea in the Champions League final on penalties in Moscow.**

• United won the FA Cup for the first time in 1909, beating Bristol City 1-0 in the final. The club's total of 11 wins is only second to Arsenal, who have 12. In 2000 the Red Devils became the first holders not to defend the cup when they played in the first FIFA World Cup Championship instead.

• **The club's history, though, has not always been glorious. The 1930s were a particularly grim decade for United, who were threatened with relegation to the old Third Division on the final day of the 1933/34 season. In a bid to change their luck, United swapped**

their red shirts for cherry and white hoops for the first and only time, and beat Millwall 2-0 away to stay in the Second Division.

• Old Trafford has the highest capacity of any club ground in Britain but, strangely, when United set an all-time Football League attendance record of 83,260 for their home game against Arsenal on 17th January 1948 they were playing at Maine Road, home of local rivals Manchester City. This was because Old Trafford was badly damaged by German bombs during the Second World War, forcing United to use their neighbours' ground in the immediate post-war period.

• **United's leading appearance maker is Ryan Giggs, who played in an incredible 963 games in all competitions for the club between 1991 and 2014. Winger Steve Coppell played in a club record 206 consecutive league games between 1977 and 1981.**

• The club's highest goalscorer is Sir Bobby Charlton, who banged in 199 league goals for the club between 1956 and 1973. Charlton is also United's most capped international, playing 106 times for England in an illustrious career. Denis Law, another 1960s United legend, scored a record 18 hat-tricks for the club.

• **United recorded the biggest ever victory in Premier League history on 4th March 1995 when they thrashed Ipswich 9-0 at Old Trafford, with striker Andy Cole scoring five of the goals to set another record.**

• In 1999/2000 United won the Premier League with a record 18-point margin over runners-up Arsenal. Three years later striker Ruud van Nistelrooy scored in a record 10 consecutive Premier League games as United swept to yet another title.

• **Known for many years as a big-spending club, United's record signing is Argentinian Angel Di Maria, who cost £59.7 million when he moved from Real Madrid in August 2014. The club's most expensive sale is former Old Trafford hero Cristiano Ronaldo, who joined Real Madrid for a then world record £80 million in 2009.**

• Manchester United have more fans than any other club in the world. A 2012 survey across 39 different countries by market research firm Kantar discovered that the Red Devils have a staggering 659 million fans worldwide – equivalent to around 10% of the planet's population.

## MANSFIELD TOWN

**Year founded:** 1897
**Ground:** Field Mill (8,186)
**Previous names:** Mansfield Wesleyans, Mansfield Wesley
**Nickname:** The Stags
**Biggest win:** 9-2 v Rotherham United (1932)
**Heaviest defeat:** 1-7 v Reading (1932), v Peterborough United (1966) and v QPR (1966)

The club was founded as Mansfield Wesleyans, a boys brigade team, in 1897, before becoming Mansfield Town in 1910. The Stags eventually joined the Football League in 1931, remaining there until relegation to the Conference in 2008. Five years later the club bounced back to League Two as Conference champions.

• **In the 1950/51 season Mansfield were the first club ever to remain unbeaten at home in a 23-game fixture schedule, but just missed out on promotion to the old Second Division. The Stags finally reached the second tier in 1977, but were relegated at the end of the campaign.**

• Club legend Ted Harston scored an amazing 55 goals in the 1936/37 season – a record for the Third Division (North) – including a Stags' record seven goals in a game in an 8-2 drubbing of Hartlepool United.

• The Stags enjoyed the greatest day in their history in 1987 when they beat Bristol City on penalties at Wembley to win the Football League Trophy.

HONOURS
*Division 3 champions* 1977
*Division 4 champions* 1975
*Conference champions* 2013
*Football League Trophy* 1987

## DIEGO MARADONA

**Born:** Buenos Aires, Argentina, 30th October 1960
**Position:** Striker/midfielder
**Club career:**
1976-80 Argentinos Juniors 167 (115)
1980-82 Boca Juniors 40 (28)
1982-84 Barcelona 36 (22)
1984-91 Napoli 186 (83)
1992-93 Sevilla 25 (4)
1995-97 Boca Juniors 29 (7)
**International record:**
1977-94 Argentina 91 (34)

The best player in the world in the 1980s, Diego Maradona is considered by many to be the greatest footballer ever.
• During his career in his native Argentina, then in Spain and Italy, he smashed three transfer records. First, his £1 million move from Argentinos Juniors to Boca Juniors in 1980 was a world record for a teenager. Then he broke the world transfer record when he joined Barcelona from Boca for £4.2 million in 1982, and again when he signed for Napoli for £6.9 million in 1984.
• A superb dribbler who used his low centre of gravity to great effect, Maradona was almost impossible to mark. He was idolised at Napoli, who he led to a first ever Italian title in 1987 and a first European trophy two years later, when they won the UEFA Cup.
• He made his international debut aged 16 in 1977 and went on to play at four World Cups, captaining his country in a record 16 games at the finals. His greatest triumph came in 1986 when, after scoring the goals that beat England (including the infamous 'Hand of God' goal which he punched into the net) and Belgium in the quarter and semi-finals, he skippered Argentina to victory in the

final against West Germany. He also led his side to the 1990 final against the same opponents.
• However, Maradona's international career ended in disgrace when he was thrown out of the 1994 World Cup in the USA after failing a drugs test. He had previously been hit with a worldwide 15-month ban from football in 1991 after testing positive for cocaine.
• Despite these blots on his reputation, Maradona was voted 'The Player of the Century' by more than half of those who took part in a worldwide FIFA internet poll in 2000. In 2008 he became head coach of Argentina, but resigned two years later after his side were thrashed 4-0 by Germany in the World Cup quarter-finals.

## MASCOTS

In 2013 Lenny Berry, who had played the role of Bradford City's mascot 'City Gent' for 20 years, was forced to stand down from his role as he was no longer tubby enough to fill the costume.

• Swansea mascot Cyril the Swan was fined a record £1,000 in 1999 for celebrating a goal against Millwall in the FA Cup by running onto the pitch and pushing the referee. Two years later Cyril was in trouble again when he pulled off the head of Millwall's Zampa the Lion mascot and drop-kicked it into the crowd.
• In one of the most bizarre football sights ever, Wolves mascot Wolfie traded punches with his Bristol City counterpart City Cat during a half-time penalty shoot-out competition at Ashton Gate in 2002. City Cat, who was backed up by three little piggies representing a local company, got the better of the fracas which had to be broken up by stewards.
• The Mascot Grand National, an annual race over hurdles between football and other sporting mascots, has been held at Huntingdon Racecourse since 1999. The first winner was Birmingham's Beau Brummie Bulldog, while Oldham's Chaddy the Owl was the first mascot to retain the title.
• In October 2014 Torquay mascot Gilbert the Gull was criticised after apparently challenging his own fans to a fight during a 3-2 Conference defeat to Grimsby Town. "We've got the worst mascot in football," one fan complained afterwards.
• In June 2015 Partick Thistle unveiled possibly the most terrifying football mascot ever, Kingsley. Designed by Jags fan

*You wouldn't want to meet Partick Thistle mascot Kingsley down a dark alley!*

and Turner Prize-nominated artist David Shrigley with the deliberate aim of intimidating the opposition, the mascot was described by one Partick supporter as "a scary version of cartoon character Lisa Simpson".

## JUAN MATA

**Born:** Burgos, Spain, 28th April 1988
**Position:** Midfielder
**Club career:**
2006-07 Real Madrid B 34 (10)
2007-11 Valencia 130 (33)
2011-14 Chelsea 82 (18)
2014- Manchester United 48 (15)
**International record:**
2009- Spain 34 (10)

Along with his Spain and former Chelsea team-mate Fernando Torres, Juan Mata is the first player in football history to hold the World Cup, the European Championships, the Champions League and the Europa League simultaneously (if only briefly).

• After starting out with the Real Madrid B team, Mata made his name with Valencia, with whom he won the Copa del Rey in 2008. He moved to Chelsea in August 2011 for £23.5 million, scoring on his Blues debut as a sub against Norwich at Stamford Bridge. In January 2014 he moved on to Manchester United for £37 million – at the time a record fee for the Old Trafford outfit. Despite not always holding down a regular berth, he has averaged an impressive goal every three games with the Red Devils.

• A skilful midfielder with an eye for the killer pass, Mata enjoyed huge success in west London, winning the Champions League and FA Cup in 2012 and the Europa League the following year, after his corner set up Branislav Ivanovic for the winner in the final against Benfica. Mata's consistent performances saw him voted Chelsea Player of the Year in both 2012 and 2013 – only the fourth player to win the award in consecutive seasons – and he was also nominated for the PFA Player of the Year award.

• Mata made his debut for Spain in a 1-0 win over Turkey in 2009. The following year he was in the Spain squad that won the World Cup and in 2012 he scored in his country's 4-0 thrashing of Italy in the European Championships final in Kiev.

## MATCH-FIXING

The first recorded incidence of match-fixing occurred in 1900 when Jack Hillman, goalkeeper with relegation-threatened Burnley, was alleged to have offered a bribe to the Nottingham Forest captain. Hillman was found guilty of the charges by a joint Football Association and Football League commission and banned for one year.

• Nine players received bans after Manchester United beat Liverpool at Old Trafford in April 1915. A Liverpool player later admitted the result had been fixed in a Manchester pub before the match. For his part in the scandal, United's Enoch West was banned for life – although the punishment was later waived... when West was 62!

• In the mid-1960s English football was rocked by a match-fixing scandal when former Everton player Jimmy Gauld revealed in a newspaper interview that a number of games had been rigged as part of a betting coup. Gauld implicated three Sheffield Wednesday players in the scam, including England internationals Tony Kay and Peter Swan. The trio were later sentenced to four months in prison and banned for life from football. Ringleader Gauld received a four-year prison term.

*Manchester United's Juan Mata is also a keen flamenco dancer*

• In 2015 former Bolton, West Brom and Hull player Delroy Facey was jailed for two-and-a-half years after being found guilty of match-fixing allegations relating to non-league games.

• Brazilan referee Edilson Pereira de Carvalho was banned for life from the game in 2005 after being found to have taken bribes to fix a number of games in Brazil's top league. For years afterwards fans would shout 'Edilson!' at referees who they believed had made a bad decision against their club.

• In 2012 Bari defender Andrea Masiello was banned from playing for 26 months after admitting that he had been paid 50,000 euros to score an own goal against Lecce the previous year in his side's 2-0 defeat.

## SIR STANLEY MATTHEWS

**Born:** Stoke, 1st February 1915
**Died:** 23rd February 2000
**Position:** Winger
**Club career:**
1932-47 Stoke City 259 (51)
1947-61 Blackpool 379 (17)
1961-65 Stoke City 59 (3)
**International record:**
1934-57 England 54 (11)

Nicknamed 'the Wizard of the Dribble' for his magnificent skills on the ball, Stanley Matthews was one of the greatest footballers of all time. His club career spanned a record 33 years and, incredibly, he played his last game in the First Division for Stoke City five days after his 50th birthday. He remains the oldest player to appear in the top flight.

• **Matthews' England career was almost as lengthy, his 54 appearances for his country spanning 23 years between 1934 and 1957. He made his last appearance for the Three Lions at the age of 42, setting another record.**

• A brilliant winger who possessed superb close control, Matthews inspired Blackpool to victory in the 1953 FA Cup final after the Seasiders came back from 3-1 down to beat Bolton 4-3. Despite a hat-trick by his team-mate Stan Mortensen, the match is remembered as 'the Matthews final'. He had never won an FA Cup winners' medal before and the whole country (outside of Bolton) was willing Matthews to succeed.

• **The first player to be voted Footballer of the Year (in 1948) and European Footballer of the Year (in 1956), Matthews was knighted in 1965 – the only footballer to be so honoured while still playing. When he died in 2000 more than 100,000 people lined the streets of Stoke to pay tribute to one of the true legends of world football.**

## LIONEL MESSI

**Born:** Rosario, Argentina, 24th June 1987
**Position:** Striker/winger
**Club career:**
2004- Barcelona 315 (286)
**International record:**
2005- Argentina 103 (46)

Rated by many as the best player in the world, Lionel Messi is Barcelona's all-time leading scorer with 412 goals in all competitions. No fewer than 286 of those came in La Liga, making the diminutive Argentinian the competition's leading all-time scorer.

• **Life, though, could have been very different for Messi, who suffered from a growth hormone deficiency as a child in Argentina. However, his outrageous talent was such that Barcelona were prepared to move him and his family to Europe when he was aged just 13 and pay for his medical treatment.**

• Putting these problems behind him, he has flourished to the extent that in 2009 he was named both World Player of

*Surprise!!!! It's the one and only Lionel Messi...*

the Year and European Player of the Year, and in 2010 he was the inaugural winner of the FIFA Ballon d'Or – an award he retained in the following two years, making a remarkable hat-trick. A brilliant dribbler who possesses mesmeric ball skills, in 2012 Messi became the first player to be top scorer in four consecutive Champions League campaigns (2009-12) and he also set another record for the competition when he hit five goals in a single game against Bayer Leverkusen. In 2015 he hit a Spanish record 32nd hat-trick, and later that year helped Barcelona become the first European club to win the Treble of league, cup and Champions League twice, scoring twice in the Copa del Rey final against Athletic Bilbao.

• **Messi scored a world record 91 goals in the calendar year of 2012 for club and country, and the following year became the first player to score against every other La Liga club in consecutive matches.**

• Messi made his international debut in 2005 but it was a forgettable occasion – he was sent off after just 40 seconds for elbowing a Hungarian defender who was pulling his shirt. Happier times followed in 2007 when he was voted Player of the Tournament at the Copa America and in 2008 when he won a gold medal with the Argentine football team at the Beijing Olympics.

• **At the 2014 World Cup he won the Golden Ball as the tournament's outstanding player, but had to be satisfied with a runners-up medal after Argentina's defeat by Germany in the final. The following year he turned down the Player of the Tournament award at the Copa America following Argentina's defeat to hosts Chile in the final.**

## MIDDLESBROUGH

**Year founded:** 1876
**Ground:** Riverside Stadium (34,742)
**Nickname:** Boro
**Biggest win:** 11-0 v Scarborough (1890)
**Heaviest defeat:** 0-9 v Blackburn Rovers (1954)

Founded by members of the Middlesbrough Cricket Club at the Albert Park Hotel in 1876, the club turned professional in 1889 before reverting to amateur status three years later. Winners of the FA Amateur Cup in both 1895 and 1898, the club turned pro for a second time in 1899 and was elected to the Football League in the same year.

• **In 1905 Middlesbrough became the first club to sign a player for a four-figure transfer fee when they forked out £1,000 for Sunderland and England striker Alf Common. On his Boro debut Common paid back some of the fee by scoring the winner at Sheffield United... the Teesiders' first away win for two years!**

• The club had to wait over a century before winning a major trophy, but finally broke their duck in 2004 with a 2-1 victory over Bolton in the League Cup final at the Millennium Stadium, Cardiff.

• **Two years later Middlesbrough reached the UEFA Cup final, after twice overturning three-goal deficits earlier in the competition. There was no happy ending, though, as Boro were thrashed 4-0 by Sevilla in the final in Eindhoven.**

• In 1997 the club were deducted three points by the FA for calling off a Premier League fixture at Blackburn at short notice after illness and injury ravaged their squad. The penalty resulted in Boro being relegated from the Premier League at the end of the season. To add to their supporters' disappointment the club was also beaten in the finals of the League Cup and FA Cup in the same campaign.

• **Former goalkeeper Mark Schwarzer is Boro's highest capped international, playing 51 times for Australia while at the Riverside between 1997 and 2008.**

• In 1926/27 striker George Camsell hit an astonishing 59 league goals, including a record nine hat-tricks, for Boro as the club won the Second Division championship. His tally set

a new Football League record and, although it was beaten by Everton's Dixie Dean the following season, Camsell still holds the divisional record. An ex-miner, Camsell went on to score a club record 325 league goals for Boro – a tally only surpassed by Dean's 349 goals for Everton.

• **In November 2013 Middlesbrough appointed their first ever non-British manager, Aitor Karanka. The Spanish boss guided Boro to the Championship play-off final in 2015, but they lost 2-0 to Norwich City.**

**HONOURS**
*Division 2 champions* 1927, 1929, 1974
*First Division champions* 1995
*League Cup* 2006
*FA Amateur Cup* 1895, 1898

## MILLWALL

**Year founded:** 1885
**Ground:** The New Den (20,146)
**Previous name:** Millwall Rovers
**Nickname:** The Lions
**Biggest win:** 9-1 v Torquay (1927) and v Coventry (1927)
**Heaviest defeat:** 1-9 v Aston Villa (1946)

The club was founded as Millwall Rovers in 1885 by workers at local jam and marmalade factory, Morton and Co. In 1920 they joined the Third Division, gaining a reputation as a club with some of the most fiercely partisan fans in the country.

• **In 1988 Millwall won the Second Division title to gain promotion to the top flight for the first time in their history. The Lions enjoyed a few brief weeks at the top of the league pyramid in the autumn of 1988 but were relegated two years later.**

• The club's greatest moment, though, came in 2004 when they reached their first FA Cup final. Despite losing 3-0 to Manchester United, the Lions made history by becoming the first club from outside the top flight to contest the final in the Premier League era, while substitute Curtis Weston set a new record for the youngest player to appear in the final (17 years and 119 days).

• Current boss Neil Harris is the club's all-time leading scorer with 125 goals in two spells at the Den between 1998 and 2011. Hardman defender Barry Kitchener has made more appearances for Millwall than any other player, turning out in 602 games in all competitions between 1967 and 1982.

• On their way to winning the Division Three (South) championship in 1928 Millwall scored 87 goals at home, an all-time Football League record.

• In 1974 Millwall hosted the first league match to be played on a Sunday. To get around the law at the time, admission for the Lions' game with Fulham was by 'programme only' – the cost of the programme being the same as a match ticket.

### HONOURS
**Division 2 champions** *1988*
**Division 3 (S) champions** *1928, 1938*
**Second Division champions** *2001*
**Division 4 champions** *1962*

# MILTON KEYNES DONS

**Year founded:** 2004
**Ground:** stadium:mk (30,500)
**Nickname:** The Dons
**Biggest win:** 7-0 v Oldham (2014)
**Heaviest defeat:** 0-5 v Hartlepool (2005), v Huddersfield (2006), v Tottenham (2006) and v Rochdale (2007)

The club was effectively formed in 2004 when Wimbledon FC were controversially allowed to re-locate to Milton Keynes on the ruling of a three-man FA commission despite the opposition of the club's supporters, the Football League and the FA.

• Despite pledging to Wimbledon fans that they would not change their name, badge or colours, within a few seasons all three of these things had happened, reinforcing the impression amongst many in the game that the MK Dons are English football's first 'franchise'.

• The MK Dons have since handed back to Merton Council all the honours and trophies won by Wimbledon FC and claimed by AFC Wimbledon, the club started up by angry Wimbledon supporters which was promoted to the Football League in 2011 despite the claim by the FA Commission that the creation of such a team would "not be in the wider interests of football".

• The MK Dons won their first trophy in 2008 when they beat Grimsby Town 2-0 in the Football League Trophy final. The greatest day in the club's short history, however, came in 2015 when they were promoted to the Championship after thrashing Yeovil Town 5-1 on the last day of the season. In the same campaign MK Dons recorded their most stunning victory ever, beating Manchester United 4-0 in the League Cup second round.

*In 2014 AFC Wimbledon beat the MK Dons for the first time*

• MK Dons captain Dean Lewington has made a record 469 appearances for the club since 2004.

# LUKA MODRIC

**Born:** Zagreb, Croatia, 9th September 1985
**Position:** Midfielder
**Club career:**
2003-08 Dinamo Zagreb 112 (31)
2003 Zrinjski Mostar (loan) 22 (8)
2004 Inter Zapresic (loan) 18 (4)
2008-12 Tottenham Hotspur 127 (13)
2012- Real Madrid 83 (5)
**International record:**
2006- Croatia 84 (10)

After helping Real Madrid win the Champions League and Copa del Rey in 2014, floppy-haired midfielder Luka Modric was sidelined by

*Crafty Croation Luka Modric is an unsung hero amongst the 'Galacticos' of Real Madrid*

injury for the latter half of the 2014/15 season and could only watch on in frustration as his team fell short on both the domestic and European fronts.
• Modric started out with Croatian side Dinamo Zagreb, winning three league titles and the national Player of the Year award with his hometown club before joining Tottenham in 2008. He recovered from a broken leg to help Spurs qualify for the Champions League for the first time in 2010, but the following

summer he agitated for a move to Chelsea until being forced to honour his contract by Tottenham chairman Daniel Levy. He finally left White Hart Lane in 2012, joining Real for around £33 million.
• A gifted playmaker who is known as 'the Croatian Cruyff' in his home country, Modric made his international debut in 2006 and two years later starred at Euro 2008, where he was voted into the Team of the Tournament after some magnificent displays – only the second Croatian player ever to achieve this honour.
• Modric was one of Croatia's best players at the World Cup in 2014, but couldn't prevent his country going out of the tournament at the group stage after defeats to Brazil and Mexico.

# MONACO

**Year founded:** 1924
**Ground:** Stade Louis II (18,523)
**Nickname:** Les rouge et blanc (The red and whites)
**League titles:** 7
**Domestic cups:** 5

AS Monaco were founded in 1924, following the merger of a number of small clubs in the principality and the surrounding region. In 2011 the club was bought by an investment group led by Russian billionaire Dmitry Rybolovlev and they have since splashed the cash on some big-name players including a then French record £51 million on Colombian striker Radamel Falcao from Atletico Madrid in 2013.
• The club enjoyed a golden period in the early 1960s, winning two league titles under iconic manager Lucien Leduc. More recently, they were managed by a young Arsène Wenger between 1987 and 1994, a team including former Tottenham midfielder Glenn Hoddle claiming the French title in thrilling style in 1988.
• Monaco have never won a European trophy, but they came close in 2004 when they reached the Champions League final, only to lose 3-0 to José

Mourinho's Porto. The red and whites also reached the Cup Winners' Cup final in 1992, but went down 2-0 to German outfit Werder Bremen.

• **Despite being one of the most successful clubs in France in recent years, Monaco have struggled to attract the super-rich residents of the principality to the Stade Louis 11. In 2014/15 their average attendance was the second lowest in Ligue 1 (9,357), and the pitiful crowd of 5,488 that turned up to watch Monaco's home match against Reims was the lowest in the league all season.**

> HONOURS
> *French League champions* 1961, 1963, 1978, 1982, 1988, 1997, 2000
> *French Cup* 1960, 1963, 1980, 1985, 1991

## MONEY

The Premier League is easily the richest league in world football. In the 2013/14 season the league's revenues hit a record £3.26 billion, with domestic and worldwide TV rights accounting for more than half of that money. The Bundesliga followed some way behind, with revenues of around £1 billion less than the Premier League.

• **Real Madrid and Portugal star Cristiano Ronaldo is the world's richest footballer with an estimated wealth of around £152 million, taking into account all streams of revenue, including club wages, image rights, and income from endorsements and advertising. He is followed in the rich list by Lionel Messi (£145 million), Neymar (£97 million), Zlatan Ibrahimovic (£76 million) and Wayne Rooney (£74 million).**

• According to Forbes, Real Madrid are the

## TOP 10

| CLUB REVENUES IN 2013/14 | |
|---|---|
| 1. Real Madrid | 549m euros |
| 2. Manchester United | 518m euros |
| 3. Bayern Munich | 487m euros |
| 4. Barcelona | 484m euros |
| 5. Paris St Germain | 474m euros |
| 6. Manchester City | 414m euros |
| 7. Chelsea | 388m euros |
| 8. Arsenal | 359m euros |
| 9. Liverpool | 306m euros |
| 10. Juventus | 279m euros |

richest club in the world with revenues in 2013/14 of 549 million euros. And, despite missing out on Champions League qualification in 2013/14, Manchester United remain the richest club in Britain with revenues of 518 million euros.

• **Bayern Munich's Pep Guardiola is the highest paid manager in world football, pocketing a staggering £14.8 million every year – £6 million more than the Premier League's best-paid boss, Chelsea's Jose Mourinho.**

## BOBBY MOORE

> **Born:** Barking, 12th April 1941
> **Died:** 24th February 1993
> **Position:** Defender
> **Club career:**
> 1958-74 West Ham United 544 (22)
> 1974-77 Fulham 124 (1)
> 1976 San Antonio Thunder 24 (1)
> 1978 Seattle Sounders 7 (0)
> **International record:**
> 1962-73 England 108 (2)

The first and only Englishman to lift the World Cup, Bobby Moore captained England on 90 occasions – a record shared with Billy Wright. When he skippered the team for the first time against Czechoslovakia in 1963 he was aged just 22 and 47 days, making him England's youngest ever captain.

• **Moore's total of 108 caps was a record until it was surpassed by Peter Shilton in 1989, but he was England's most capped outfield player until David Beckham passed him in 2009.**

• At club level, Moore won the FA Cup with West Ham in 1964 and the European Cup Winners' Cup the following year. Then, in 1966, he made

*Cristiano Ronaldo is so rich he can afford a fleet of robots to do his personal appearances for him*

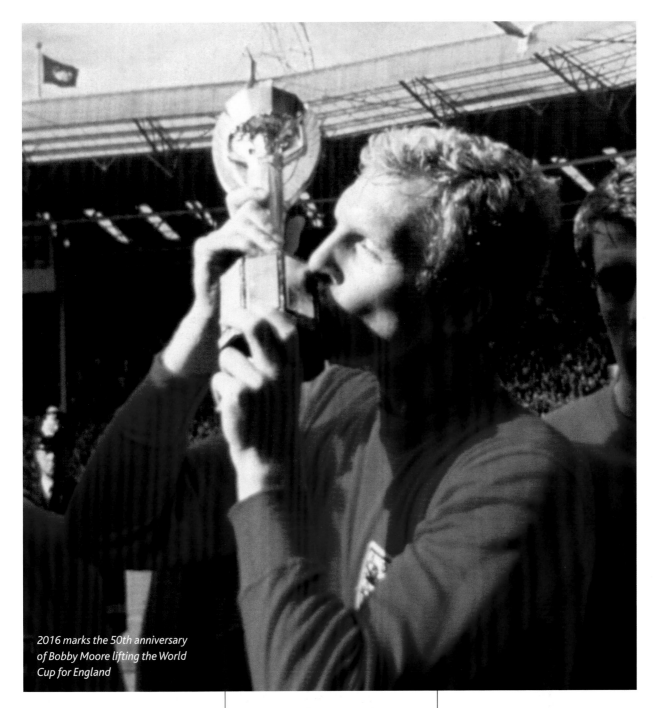

*2016 marks the 50th anniversary of Bobby Moore lifting the World Cup for England*

it a Wembley treble when England beat West Germany in the World Cup final. England boss Sir Alf Ramsey later paid tribute to his skipper and most reliable defender, saying, "He was the supreme professional. Without him England would never have won the World Cup."

• **In the same year Moore was voted the BBC Sports Personality of the Year – the first footballer to win the honour.**

• The world of football mourned Moore's death when he died of cancer in 1993, but he has not been forgotten. A decade later he was selected by the FA as England's 'Golden Player' of the previous 50 years and, in 2007, a huge bronze statue of England's greatest captain was unveiled outside the new Wembley.

## MORECAMBE

**Year founded:** 1920
**Ground:** Globe Arena (6,476)
**Nickname:** The Shrimps
**Biggest win:** 8-0 v Fleetwood Town (1993)
**Heaviest defeat:** 0-7 v Leek Town (1998)

Founded in 1920 after a meeting at the local West View Hotel, Morecambe joined the Lancashire Combination League that same year and subsequently spent the next 87 years in non-league football.

• **The greatest moment in the club's history came in 2007 when The Shrimps beat Exeter 2-1 in the Conference play-off final at Wembley to win promotion to the Football League.**

• Veteran midfielder Stewart Drummond made a club record 280 appearances for the Shrimps before retiring in 2015. In a previous spell with the club in their non-league days he made another 188 appearances.

• **In 2010 Morecambe reached the League Two play-offs, but a 6-0 hammering by Dagenham and Redbridge – the biggest ever play-off defeat – in the first leg of the semi-final ended their promotion hopes in emphatic fashion.**

# MOTHERWELL

**Year founded:** 1886
**Ground:** Fir Park (13,677)
**Nickname:** The Well
**Biggest win:** 12-1 v Dundee United (1954)
**Heaviest defeat:** 0-8 v Aberdeen (1979)

Motherwell were founded in 1886 following the merger of two local factory-based sides, Alpha and Glencairn. The club turned pro in 1893 and, in the same year, joined the newly formed Scottish Second Division.

• The club enjoyed its heyday in the 1930s, winning the league title for the first and only time in 1932 and finishing as runners-up in the Scottish Cup three times in the same decade.

• Striker Willie McFadyen scored a remarkable 52 league goals for The Well when they won the title in 1931/32, a Scottish top-flight record that still stands today. His team-mate Bob Ferrier played in a Scottish record 626 league games between 1917 and 1937.

• Motherwell had to wait until 1952 before they won the Scottish Cup for the first time, and they did it in some style by thrashing Dundee 4-0 in the final. Another success followed in 1991, The Well beating Dundee United 4-3 in an exciting final.

• After finishing second in the top flight in both 2013 and 2014, a slump in form in 2014/15 saw Motherwell forced to take part in the relegation/promotion play-offs. However, the Well ensured their survival with a 6-1 aggregate thrashing of Rangers in the final – the biggest win to date at any level in the Scottish play-offs.

• In May 2010 Motherwell were involved in the highest scoring game ever in the SPL, coming from 6-2 down to draw 6-6 with Hibs.

## HONOURS
*Division 1 champions* 1932
*First Division champions* 1982, 1985
*Division 2 champions* 1954, 1969
*Scottish Cup* 1952, 1991
*League Cup* 1951

# JOSE MOURINHO

**Born:** Setubal, Portugal, 26th January 1963
**Managerial career:**
2000 Benfica
2001-02 Uniao Leiria
2002-04 Porto
2004-07 Chelsea
2008-10 Inter Milan
2010-13 Real Madrid
2013- Chelsea

Chelsea manager Jose Mourinho is one of just four coaches to have won the domestic title in four different countries and the only one to have claimed the championship in England, Italy and Spain.

• Mourinho started out as Bobby Robson's assistant at Sporting Lisbon, Porto and Barcelona before briefly managing Benfica in 2000. Two years later he returned to Porto, where he won two Portuguese league titles and the UEFA Cup before becoming Europe's most sought-after young manager when his well-drilled side claimed the Champions League trophy in 2004.

• Shortly after this triumph, Mourinho replaced Claudio Ranieri as Chelsea manager, styling himself as a "Special One" in his first press conference. He certainly lived up to his billing, as his expensively assembled Blues team won back-to-back Premier League titles in 2005 and 2006, the FA Cup in 2007 and the League Cup in both 2005 and 2007.

• After falling out with owner Roman Abramovich, Mourinho left Stamford Bridge in September 2007. He made a sensational return to west London in 2013 and in his second season back with the Blues guided them to both the Premier League and the League Cup, picking up a third Manager of the Year award in the process.

• In between his stints at Chelsea, Mourinho took charge of Italian giants Inter Milan and led them to the Serie A title in 2009. The following year he did even better, guiding Inter to a Treble which included the Champions League, before leaving the San Siro to take over the reins at Real Madrid. He had to be satisfied with the Spanish Cup in his first season at the Bernabeu, but in 2012 his Real team raced to the title in some style, racking up a record 100 points tally while also scoring a record number of goals, 121. After a disappointing final season in the Spanish capital, he left Real in the summer of 2013.

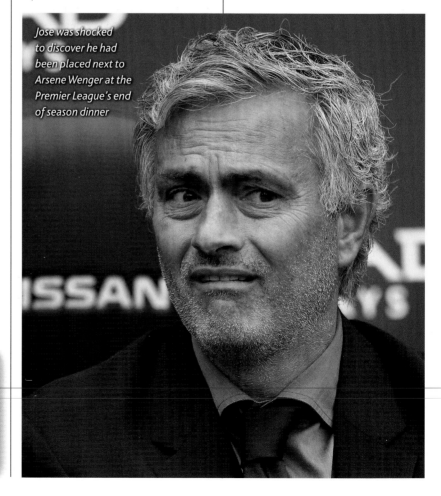

*Jose was shocked to discover he had been placed next to Arsene Wenger at the Premier League's end of season dinner*

*The Dutch fans are crazy, for sure!*

## THE NETHERLANDS

**First international:**
Belgium 1 Netherlands
4, 1905
**Most capped player:**
Edwin van der Sar, 130
caps (1995-2008)
**Leading goalscorer:**
Robin van Persie, 49
goals (2005- )
**First World Cup**
**appearance:** Netherlands 2
Switzerland 1, 1934
**Biggest win:** Netherlands 11 San
Marino 0, 2011
**Heaviest defeat:** England amateurs 9
Netherlands 1, 1909

Long associated with an entertaining style of attacking football, the Netherlands have only won one major tournament, the European Championships in 1988. In the final that year the Dutch beat Russia with goals from their two biggest stars of the time, Ruud Gullit and Marco van Basten.

• The Netherlands are the only country to have lost all three World Cup finals they have played in. On the first two of these occasions they had the misfortune to meet the hosts in the final, losing to West Germany in 1974 and Argentina in 1978. Then, in the 2010 final, they went down 1-0 in extra-time to Spain in Johannesburg following a negative, at times brutal, Dutch performance which was totally at odds with the country's best footballing traditions.

• A professional league wasn't formed in the Netherlands until 1956, and it took some years after that before the country was taken seriously as a football power. Their lowest ebb was reached in 1963 when the Dutch were humiliatingly eliminated from the European Championships by minnows Luxembourg.

• However, the following decade saw a renaissance in Dutch football. With exciting players like Johan Cruyff, Johan Neeskens and Ruud Krol in their side, the Netherlands were considered the best team in Europe. Pivotal to their success was the revolutionary 'Total Football' system devised by manager Rinus Michels which allowed the outfield players constantly to switch positions during the game.

• In qualifying for the 2006 World Cup the Netherlands racked up a European record 32 points from their 12 games (10 wins and two draws).

• At the 2014 World Cup in Brazil the Netherlands used all 23 players in their squad, the first time this had happened at the tournament. Manager Louis van Gaal's 'mix and match' approach worked well, as his team finished in third place.

• The Netherlands' all-time leading scorer is former Arsenal and Manchester United striker Robin Van Persie, with 49 goals since making his debut in 2005.

## TOP 10

### PREMIER LEAGUE APPEARANCES BY DUTCH PLAYERS

1. **George Boateng** (Coventry, Aston Villa, Middlesbrough, Hull,1998-2010)  **382**
2. **Dennis Bergkamp** (Arsenal, 1995-2006)  **315**
3. **Edwin van der Sar** (Fulham, Manchester United, 2001-11)  **313**
4. **Jimmy Floyd Hasselbaink** (Leeds, Chelsea, Middlesbrough, Charlton,1997-2007)  **288**
5. **Mario Melchiot** (Chelsea, Birmingham, Wigan, 1999-2010)  **283**
6. **Robin van Persie** (Arsenal, Manchester United, 2004- )  **280**
7. **Dirk Kuyt** (Liverpool, 2006-12)  **208**
8. **Ken Monkou** (Southampton, 1992-99)  **198**
9. **Boudewijn Zenden** (Chelsea, Middlesbrough, Liverpool, Sunderland, 2001-11)  **180**
10. **Ruud van Nistelrooy** (Manchester United, 2001-06)  **150**

### HONOURS
***European Championships winners***
*1988*
**World Cup Record**
*1930 Did not enter*
*1934 Round 1*
*1938 Round 1*
*1950 Did not enter*
*1954 Did not enter*
*1958 Did not qualify*
*1962 Did not qualify*
*1966 Did not qualify*
*1970 Did not qualify*
*1974 Runners-up*
*1978 Runners-up*
*1982 Did not qualify*
*1986 Did not qualify*
*1990 Round 2*
*1994 Quarter-finals*
*1998 Fourth place*
*2002 Did not qualify*
*2006 Round 2*
*2010 Runners-up*
*2014 Third place*

## MANUEL NEUER

**Born:** Gelsenkirchen, Germany, 27th March 1986
**Position:** Goalkeeper
**Club career:**
2004-08 Schalke II 26
2006-11 Schalke 156
2011- Bayern Munich 127
**International record:**
2009- Germany 58

World Goalkeeper of the Year in 2013 and 2014, Bayern Munich's Manuel Neuer became the first goalkeeper to figure in the top three of the FIFA Ballon D'or when he came third behind Cristiano Ronaldo and Lionel Messi in 2014.

• A magnificent shot-stopper with excellent reflexes and a good distributor of the ball, Neuer signed for Bayern from Schalke for £19 million in 2011, at the time the second biggest transfer fee ever for a goalkeeper. In 2013 he helped Bayern Munich claim the Treble, collecting a first winner's medal in the Champions League when the Bavarians defeated fellow Germans Borussia Dortmund 2-1 in the final at Wembley.

• The previous year Neuer's penalty saves from Cristiano Ronaldo and Kaka in the semi-final shoot-out against Real Madrid enabled Bayern to reach the Champions League final, where they faced Chelsea at their home ground, the Allianz Arena. In the subsequent shoot-out that settled the match, Neuer became the first ever goalkeeper to score in a Champions League final, although he still finished on the losing side.

• Neuer impressed at the 2010 World Cup, helping Germany come third in South Africa. Four years later he was instrumental in Germany's success in Brazil, keeping four clean sheets and collecting the Golden Glove award.

*Manuel Neuer has as safe a pair of hands as you will find in football*

## GARY NEVILLE

**Born:** Bury, 18th February 1975
**Position:** Defender
**Club career:**
1992-2011 Manchester United 400 (5)
**International record:**
1995-2007 England 85 (0)

England's highest capped right-back, Gary Neville is one of the most decorated players in the modern game, winning eight Premier League titles, three FA Cups, two League Cups and the Champions League in an illustrious career with his one and only club, Manchester United.

• A fixture in his country's defence for over a decade, Neville played in more games in the finals of the European Championships, 11, than any other England player. Along with his younger brother Phil, Neville also holds the record for the most England games played by a pair of brothers, 144 – three more than the Charltons of 1966 World Cup fame managed in total. In addition, the Nevilles played in 31 England games together, to set another record.

• After retiring from the game during the 2010/11 season, Neville became a pundit for *Sky Sports*, earning rave reviews for his thought-provoking insights into the game and surprising those who feared he would be biased towards Manchester United with his impartial viewpoint in his new role.

• In 2012 Neville joined Roy Hodgson's backroom staff on a four-year contract, and was part of the coaching team that assisted the Three Lions boss at the European Championships in Poland and the Ukraine, and then at the 2014 World Cup in Brazil.

## NEWCASTLE UNITED

**Year founded:** 1892
**Ground:** St James' Park (52,405)
**Nickname:** The Magpies
**Biggest win:** 13-0 v Newport County (1946)
**Heaviest defeat:** 0-9 v Burton Wanderers (1895)

*Newcastle United's Chancel Mbemba gets airborne*

£15 million move from Blackburn Rovers in 1996. Shearer's predecessor Andy Cole scored 41 goals in all competitions in 1993/94 to set another club record.

• **The club's leading appearance maker is goalkeeper Jimmy Lawrence, who featured in 432 league games between 1904 and 1921. Another goalkeeper, Shay Given, is easily Newcastle's most honoured international with 83 caps for the Republic of Ireland between 1997 and 2009.**

• Newcastle supporters have not had much to cheer about in recent years, their team having failed to win a major trophy since 1969. That was the Fairs Cup, the Magpies beating Hungarian side Ujpest Dozsa 6-2 on aggregate in a two-legged final.

• **The mid-1990s, though, promised much. A swashbuckling side managed by Toon legend Kevin Keegan swept to the new First Division title in 1993 before emerging as Premiership title contenders in the 1995/96 season. At one stage during that campaign Newcastle held a 12-point lead over eventual winners Manchester United, but they were unable to hold their advantage and ultimately finished in second place.**

• In January 2011 Newcastle sold striker Andy Carroll to Liverpool for a staggering £35 million, the highest fee at the time for a British player moving from one Premier League club to another. Michael Owen is Newcastle's most expensive player, joining the club from Real Madrid for £16 million in 2005.

• **Toon legend Alan Shearer scored the fastest ever goal for Newcastle, after just 10.4 seconds against Manchester City in 2003. Shearer's quickfire effort was the second fastest Premier League goal ever, behind Tottenham's Ledley King who scored after just 9.9 seconds against Bradford City three years earlier.**

The club was founded in 1892 following the merger of local sides Newcastle East End and Newcastle West End, gaining election to the Football League just a year later.

• **In 1895 Newcastle suffered their worst ever defeat, going down 9-0 to Burton Wanderers in a Second Division match. However, their most embarrassing loss was a 9-1 home hammering by Sunderland in December 1908. The Toon recovered, though, to win the title that season, making that defeat by their local rivals the heaviest ever suffered by the eventual league champions. The Magpies recorded their best ever win in 1946, thrashing Newport County 13-0 to equal Stockport County's record for the biggest ever victory in a Football League match. Star of the show at St James' Park was Len Shackleton, who scored six of the goals on his Newcastle debut to set a club record.**

• Newcastle have a proud tradition in the FA Cup, having won the competition on six occasions. In 1908 the Magpies reached the final after smashing Fulham 6-0, the biggest ever win in the semi-final. Then, in 1924, 41-year-old defender Billy Hampson became the oldest player ever to appear in the cup final, when he turned out for the Toon in their 2-0 defeat of Aston Villa at Wembley.

• **The club's best cup era was in the 1950s when they won the trophy three times, boss Stan Seymour becoming the first man to lift the cup as a player and a manager. Legendary centre-forward Jackie Milburn was instrumental to Newcastle's success, scoring in every round in 1951 and then notching after just 45 seconds in the 1955 final against Manchester City... the fastest Wembley cup final goal ever until Roberto di Matteo scored for Chelsea after 43 seconds in 1997.**

• Milburn is the club's leading goalscorer in league matches with 178 strikes between 1946 and 1957. However, Alan Shearer holds the overall club goalscoring record, finding the net 206 times in all competitions after his then world record

**HONOURS**

***Division 1 champions*** 1905, 1907, 1909, 1927

***Division 2 champions*** 1965

***First Division champions*** 1993

***Championship champions*** 2010

***FA Cup*** 1910, 1924, 1932, 1951, 1952, 1955

***Fairs Cup*** 1969

# NORWICH CITY

**Year founded:** 1902
**Ground:** Carrow Road (27,244)
**Nickname:** The Canaries
**Biggest win:** 10-2 v Coventry City (1930)
**Heaviest defeat:** 2-10 v Swindon Town (1908)

Founded in 1902 by two schoolteachers, Norwich City soon found themselves in hot water with the FA and were expelled from the FA Amateur Cup in 1904 for being 'professional'. The club joined the Football League as founder members of the Third Division in 1920.

• Norwich were originally known as the Citizens, but adopted the nickname Canaries in 1907 as a nod to the longstanding popularity of canary-keeping in the city – a result of 15th-century trade links with Flemish weavers who had brought the birds over to Europe from Dutch colonies in the Caribbean. Soon afterwards, the club changed their colours from blue and white to yellow and green.

• City fans enjoyed the greatest day in their history when Norwich beat Sunderland 1-0 at Wembley in 1985 to win the League Cup. However, joy soon turned to despair when the Canaries were relegated from the top flight at the end of the season, the first club to experience this particular mix of sweet and sour.

• Ron Ashman is the club's leading appearance maker, turning out in 592 league matches between 1947 and 1964. The Canaries' leading scorer is Ashman's team-mate John Gavin, who notched 122 league goals between 1948 and 1958.

• Norwich's most capped player is Mark Bowen, who played 35 times for Wales during his Carrow Road career.

• In 2013 the Canaries splashed out a club record £8.5 million to bring Dutch striker Ricky van Wolfswinkel to Carrow Road from Sporting Lisbon. The following year Norwich received a club record £9 million when they sold midfielder Leroy Fer to QPR.

• Promoted via the play-offs to the Premier League in 2015, Norwich have reached the semi-finals of the FA Cup three times without ever making it to Wembley. The most notable occasion was in 1959 when, as a third-tier club, Norwich beat both Manchester United and Tottenham before losing 1-0 in a replay to Luton Town.

• Norwich City's anthem, *On the Ball City*, is a music hall song that has been associated with the club throughout their history and is believed to be the oldest fans' song anywhere in the world that is still regularly heard at matches. Among the celebrity fans sometimes seen belting out the song are TV presenter Stephen Fry and Prince Andrew.

• Now under the ownership of cook and recipe book author Delia Smith, Norwich came a best ever third in the inaugural Premiership season in 1992/93 – albeit with a goal difference of -4, the worst ever by a team finishing in the top three in the top flight. The club enjoyed a spirited run in the UEFA Cup in the following campaign, defeating Vitesse Arnhem and German giants Bayern Munich before going out to Inter Milan.

HONOURS
**Division 2 champions** 1972, 1986
**First Division champions** 2004
**Division 3 (S) champions** 1934
**League One champions** 2010
**League Cup** 1985

*Things are looking bright at Norwich these days!*

# NOTTINGHAM FOREST

**Year founded:** 1865
**Ground:** The City Ground (30,576)
**Nickname:** The Reds
**Biggest win:** 14-0 v Clapton (1891)
**Heaviest defeat:** 1-9 v Blackburn Rovers (1937)

One of the oldest clubs in the world, Nottingham Forest were founded in 1865 at a meeting at the Clinton Arms in Nottingham by a group of former players of 'shinty' (a form of hockey), who decided to switch sports to football.

• Over the following years the club was at the forefront of important innovations in the game. For instance, shinguards were invented by Forest player Sam Widdowson in 1874, while four years later a referee's whistle was first used in a match between Forest and Sheffield Norfolk. In 1890, a match between Forest and Bolton Wanderers was the first to feature goal nets.

• Forest adopted their famous red tops in tribute to the Italian patriot Giuseppe Garibaldi, whose followers were known as the 'redshirts'. Legend also has it that the club donated a spare kit to newly formed Arsenal in 1886 and the Londoners have worn red ever since.

• Forest enjoyed a golden era under legendary manager Brian Clough, who sat in the City Ground hotseat from 1975 until his retirement in 1993. After winning promotion to the top flight in 1977, the club won the league championship the following season – a feat that no promoted team has achieved since. Forest also won the League Cup to become the first side to win this particular double. Even more incredibly, the Reds went on to win the European Cup in 1979 with a 1-0 victory over Malmo in the final. The next year Forest retained the trophy, beating Hamburg 1-0 in the final in Madrid, to become the first and only team to win the European Cup more times than their domestic league.

• Hardman defender Stuart 'Psycho' Pearce is Forest's most capped international, playing 76 times for England while at the City Ground between 1987 and 1997.

• In 1959, in the days before subs, Forest won the FA Cup despite being

*Michael Mancienne of Nottingham Forest – European Cup winners in 1979 and '80*

reduced to 10 men when Roy Dwight, an uncle of pop star Elton John, was carried off with a broken leg after 33 minutes of the final against Luton Town. It was the first time that a club had won the cup with fewer than 11 players.

• Defender Bobby McKinlay, a member of that 1959 team, is Forest's longest serving player, turning out in 614 league games in 19 seasons at the club. The Reds' record scorer is Grenville Morris, who fell just one short of a double century of league goals for the club in the years before the First World War.

• Nottingham Forest's City Ground is just 330 yards from Notts County's Meadow Lane, making the two clubs the nearest neighbours in the Football League.

### HONOURS

**Division 1 champions** 1978
**Division 2 champions** 1907, 1922
**First Division champions** 1998
**Division 3 (S) champions** 1951
**FA Cup** 1898, 1959
**League Cup** 1978, 1979, 1989, 1990
**European Cup** 1979, 1980
**European Super Cup** 1979

# NOTTS COUNTY

**Year founded:** 1862
**Ground:** Meadow Lane (20,229)
**Nickname:** The Magpies
**Biggest win:** 15-0 v Rotherham (1885)
**Heaviest defeat:** 1-9 v Aston Villa (1888), v Blackburn (1889) and v Portsmouth (1927)

Notts County are the oldest professional football club in the world. Founded in 1862, the club were founder members of the Football League in 1888 and have since played a record 4,802 matches in the competition (losing a record 1,848 games).

• In their long history County have swapped divisions more often than any other league club, winning 13 promotions and suffering the agony of relegation 16 times, most recently dropping into League Two in 2015.

• The club's greatest ever day was way back in 1894 when, as a Second Division outfit, they won the FA Cup – the first time a team from outside the top flight

had lifted the trophy. In the final at Goodison Park, County beat Bolton 4-1, with Jimmy Logan scoring the first ever hat-trick in the FA Cup final.

• Striker Henry Cursham scored a competition record 48 goals for Notts County in the FA Cup between 1880 and 1887, playing alongside his two brothers in the same County team.

• Giant goalkeeper Albert Iremonger played in a club record 564 games for County between 1905 and 1926, the last occasion when he was 42, making him the club's oldest ever player. A temperamental character, Iremonger was known for running out of his goal to argue with the ref.

• In their long and distinguished history Notts County have had 60 different managers, a record for an English club.

**HONOURS**
*Division 2 champions* 1897, 1914, 1923
*Division 3 (S) champions* 1931, 1950
*Division 4 champions* 1971
*Third Division champions* 1998
*League Two champions* 2010
*FA Cup* 1894

## NUMBERS

Shirt numbers were first used in a First Division match by Arsenal against Sheffield Wednesday at Hillsborough on 25th August 1928. On the same day Chelsea also wore numbers for their Second Division fixture against Swansea at Stamford Bridge.

• In 1933 teams wore numbers in the FA Cup final for the first time. Everton's players were numbered 1-11 while Manchester City's wore 12-22. Six years later, in 1939, the Football League made the use of shirt numbers obligatory for all teams.

• England and Scotland first wore numbered shirts on 17th April 1937 for the countries' Home International fixture at Hampden Park. Scotland won 3-1. The following year numbers were introduced for the World Cup tournament in France.

• Celtic were the last club in Scotland to wear numbers, only sporting them for the first time in 1960.

• Squad numbers were adopted by Premier League clubs at the start of the 1993/94 season. The highest number worn to date by a Premier League player is 62 by Manchester City's Abdul

### TOP 10
**HIGHEST SHIRT NUMBERS WORN IN AN FA CUP FINAL**
1. Mario Balotelli (Manchester City, 2011) — 45
2. Yaya Toure (Manchester City, 2011 & 2013) — 42
3. Andreas Andersson (Newcastle United, 1998) — 40
   Jack Grealish (Aston Villa, 2015) — 40
5. Nicolas Anelka (Chelsea, 2009 & 2010) — 39
   Hector Bellerin (Arsenal, 2015) — 39
   Nadir Belhadj (Portsmouth, 2010) — 39
   Craig Bellamy (Liverpool, 2012) — 39
9. Andy Griffin (Newcastle United, 1999) — 38
10. Martin Skrtel (Liverpool, 2012) — 37

Razak when he came on as a sub against West Brom in 2011. However, Arsenal defender Nico Yennaris went two higher in October 2011, when he wore the number 64 shirt in a League Cup tie against Bolton.

• Squad numbers were first worn in the FA Cup final in 1993 between Arsenal and Sheffield Wednesday. Gunners substitute David O'Leary sported the highest number, 22.

• In 2005 Sao Paulo goalkeeper Rogerio Ceni wore the highest ever shirt number in football history, 618, to commemorate his record-breaking 618th appearance for the Brazilian club.

• In 2010 Australia's Thomas Oar set a world record for a high shirt number in an international match when he sported '121' on his back for an Asian Cup qualifier against Indonesia.

## OLDHAM ATHLETIC

**Year founded:** 1895
**Ground:** Boundary Park (10,638)
**Previous name:** Pine Villa
**Nickname:** The Latics
**Biggest win:** 11-0 v Southport (1962)
**Heaviest defeat:** 4-13 v Tranmere Rovers (1935)

Originally known as Pine Villa, the club was founded by the landlord of the Featherstone and Junction Hotel in 1895.

Four years later the club changed to its present name and in 1907 Oldham joined the Second Division, winning promotion to the top flight after three seasons.

• The Latics enjoyed a golden era in the early 1990s under manager Joe Royle, reaching the League Cup final (in 1990), two FA Cup semi-finals (1990 and 1994) and earning promotion to the top flight (1991). The club were founder members of the Premier League in 1992 but were relegated two years later. In 1997 Oldham dropped into the third tier, and they are now the longest serving members of League One.

• In 1915 Oldham looked almost certain to win the First Division championship, but they blew the opportunity by losing their last two games, at home to Burnley and Liverpool. Everton took full advantage of Oldham's loss of nerve by claiming the title by a single point.

• In 1989 Oldham striker Frankie Bunn scored six of his side's goals in a 7-0 hammering of Scarborough in the third round of the League Cup. He remains the only player to have notched a double hat-trick in the competition.

• Defender Ian Wood made a club record 525 appearances for Oldham between 1965 and 1979. Cult hero Roger Palmer is the Latics' top scorer with 141 goals between 1980 and 1994.

**HONOURS**
*Division 2 champions* 1991
*Division 3 (N) champions* 1953
*Division 3 champions* 1974

## MARTIN O'NEILL

**Born:** Kilrea, 1st March 1952
**Managerial career:**
1990-95 Wycombe Wanderers
1995 Norwich City
1995-2000 Leicester City
2000-05 Celtic
2006-10 Aston Villa
2011-13 Sunderland
2013- Republic of Ireland

Appointed manager of the Republic of Ireland in November 2013 following the departure of Giovanni Trapattoni, Martin O'Neill was unfortunate to see his side drawn in a tough Euro 2016 qualifying group which included three strong opponents in Germany, Poland and Scotland.

• One of the most articulate managers in the game, O'Neill started out at Wycombe Wanderers in 1990, taking the Chairboys out of the Conference and into the Football League before spending a short period at Norwich. He left Carrow Road in 1995 to move to Leicester, who he guided into the Premier League the following year. He then led the Foxes to the League Cup in 1997, and won the competition again three years later.

• In 2000 O'Neill joined Celtic, with whom he won the Treble in his first season. Dubbed 'Martin the Magnificent' by the fans, O'Neill led the Glasgow giants to two more league titles, four more cups and to the final of the UEFA Cup in 2003 before leaving the club to look after his sick wife in 2005. He returned to management the following year with Aston Villa, making the Villans a regular top six side during his four-year tenure. In December 2011 he was appointed manager of Sunderland, the club he had supported as a boy, but a poor run of results saw him sacked after just 16 months.

• A one-time law student at Queen's University in Belfast, O'Neill spent most of his playing career with Nottingham Forest, with whom he won the league championship and two European Cups. A hard-working midfielder, O'Neill also played for Norwich, Manchester City and Notts County, and captained Northern Ireland at the 1982 World Cup in Spain.

## MICHAEL O'NEILL

**Born:** Portadown, 5th July 1969
**Managerial career:**
2006-08 Brechin City
2009-11 Shamrock Rovers
2011- Northern Ireland

A surprise choice as his country's manager in December 2011, Michael O'Neill led Northern Ireland to their best ever start to a qualifying campaign with four wins out of six in their bid to make it to Euro 2016.

• After a spell in charge of Brechin City, O'Neill rose to prominence as manager of Shamrock Rovers, who he led to the League of Ireland title in 2010 and the Setanta Sports Cup the following year. In 2011 he became

*Michael O'Neill was a surprise choice as Northern Ireland manager in 2011*

the first manager to lead a League of Ireland side into the group stage of a European competition when Rovers beat Partizan Belgrade in the final qualifying round of the Europa League.

• In his playing days O'Neill turned out for a number of clubs, including Dundee United, Hibs and Newcastle, for whom he was the club's leading scorer in the old First Division in 1987/88.

## MICHAEL OWEN

**Born:** Chester, 14th December 1979
**Position:** Striker
**Club career:**
1997-2004 Liverpool 216 (118)
2004-05 Real Madrid 35 (13)
2005-09 Newcastle United 71 (26)
2009-12 Manchester United 31 (5)
2012-13 Stoke City 8 (1)
**International record:**
1998-2008 England 89 (40)

Former Liverpool, Newcastle and Manchester United striker Michael Owen is England's fifth highest scorer of all time. He once seemed certain to become his country's record scorer, but his international career came to a juddering halt when he was 28.

• Frighteningly quick in his heyday with Liverpool, Owen enjoyed a golden year in 2001 when he won the FA Cup, League Cup and UEFA Cup in the same season with the Merseysiders, scoring both the Reds' goals in their 2-1 FA Cup final defeat of Arsenal at

the Millennium Stadium. In the same year he was voted European Footballer of the Year, the last English player to achieve that distinction.

• Owen joined Real Madrid for £8 million in 2004, but the following year moved back to England when he signed for Newcastle for a club record £16 million. His unveiling at St James' Park was attended by 20,000 excited Toon fans, but after failing to set Tyneside alight he made a surprise move to Manchester United in 2009. In his first season at Old Trafford he helped United win the Carling Cup, scoring in the final against Aston Villa before limping off injured, and in 2011 he picked up his first Premier League winners' medal with the Red Devils. He moved on to Stoke in 2012, before announcing his retirement a year later.

• Owen is the only England player to have scored at four international tournaments, notching at two World Cups and two European Championships. His strike against Argentina at the 1998 World Cup, when he sped past two defenders before slamming the ball high into the net, is one of the most famous England goals of all time. In the same year he was voted BBC Sports Personality of the Year, becoming only the third footballer to win the award.

• Of Owen's 40 goals for England, 26 of them came in competitive matches – a figure only bettered by Wayne Rooney. He is also the only England player to have scored for his country at both the old and new Wembleys.

*Oops! Swansea goalkeeper Lukasz Fabianski looks on helplessly as Federico Fernandez (not pictured) puts the ball into his own net*

## OWN GOALS

The first ever own goal in the Football League was scored on the opening day of the inaugural 1888/89 season, the unfortunate George Cox of Aston Villa putting through his own net in his team's 1-1 draw with Wolves.

• **The record number of own goals in a single match is, incredibly, 149. In 2002 Madagascan team Stade Olympique l'Emyrne staged a predetermined protest against alleged refereeing bias by constantly whacking the ball into their own net, their match against AS Adema finishing in a 149-0 win for their opponents. The Madagascan FA** took a dim view of the incident and promptly handed out long suspensions to four SOE players.

• On the last day of the 1976/77 season Millwall's John Moore scored an own goal which proved to be the winner for Nottingham Forest, securing their promotion to the old First Division. Forest fans were so grateful to the luckless Moore they voted him their club's 'Player of the Year'!

• **During the 1934/35 season Middlesbrough's Bobby Stuart scored five own goals – a record for a single campaign.**

• A record 47 own goals were scored in the 2012/13 Premier League season. The unfortunate Richard Dunne, formerly of QPR, holds the individual Premier League own goal record, with an amazing 10 strikes at the wrong end.

• **A record six own goals were scored in the 1998 World Cup in France – an average of one every 10.67 matches.**

• In a match at Stamford Bridge in 1954 Chelsea benefitted from a bizarre incident when Leicester defenders Jack Froggatt and Stan Milburn connected with the ball at the same time and then watched in horror as it flew past the Foxes' goalkeeper for a unique 'shared own goal'.

### IS THAT A FACT?

Sunderland are the only club to have twice conceded three own goals in the same Premier League match: in a 3-1 home defeat by Charlton in 2003 and in a humiliating 8-0 thrashing at Southampton in 2014.

## OXFORD UNITED

**Year founded:** 1893
**Ground:** Kassam Stadium (12,500)
**Previous name:** Headington, Headington United
**Nickname:** The U's
**Biggest win:** 9-1 v Dorchester Town, 1995
**Heaviest defeat:** 0-7 v Sunderland, 1998

The club was founded by a local vicar and doctor in 1893 as Headington, primarily as a way of allowing the cricketers of Headington CC to keep fit during the winter months. The name Oxford United was adopted in 1960, six years before Oxford were elected to the Football League.

• **In 1964 Oxford became the first Fourth Division side to reach the quarter-finals of the FA Cup. However, despite being backed by a record crowd of 22,750 at their old Manor Ground, the U's went down 2-1 to eventual finalists Preston.**

• The club enjoyed a golden era under controversial owner Robert Maxwell in the

1980s, although the decade began badly when the newspaper proprietor proposed that Oxford and Reading should merge as the 'Thames Valley Royals'. The fans' well-organised campaign against the idea was successful, and their loyalty was rewarded when Oxford became the first club to win consecutive third and second-tier titles to reach the top flight in 1985.

• **The greatest day in the club's history, though, came in 1986 when Oxford defeated QPR 3-0 at Wembley to win the League Cup. The following two decades saw a period of decline, however, and by 2006 Oxford had become the first major trophy winners to sink down into the Conference.**

• Prolific striker John Aldridge, who later went on to star for Liverpool, scored a club record 30 league goals in the 1984/85 season.

> HONOURS
> *Division 2 champions* 1985
> *Division 3 champions* 1968, 1984
> *League Cup* 1986

# ALEX OXLADE-CHAMBERLAIN

> **Born:** Portsmouth, 15th August 1993
> **Position:** Winger
> **Club career:**
> 20010-11 Southampton 36 (9)
> 2011- Arsenal 78 (6)
> **International record:**
> 2012- England 20 (4)

One of the most exciting attacking talents to emerge in the Premier League for many years, Alex Oxlade-Chamberlain became the youngest English scorer in the Champions League when he netted for Arsenal against Olympiacos at the start of the 2011/12 campaign.

• **'The Ox', as he has been dubbed by fans for his powerful, direct style of play, began his career at Southampton where he became the club's second youngest player (behind Theo Walcott) when he made his debut as a substitute against Huddersfield on 2nd March 2010, aged 16.**

• The following season he helped the Saints gain promotion to the Championship, his thrilling displays earning him a place in the League One Team of the Year. A transfer target for numerous Premier League clubs, he moved to Arsenal for an initial fee of £12

million in August 2011. He collected his first medal with the Gunners when he came on as a sub in their 4-0 demolition of Aston Villa in the 2015 FA Cup final, setting up the final goal himself for Olivier Giroud.

• **After a number of outstanding performances for the Under-21s, Oxlade-Chamberlain made his first appearance for the full England side as a sub against Norway in May 2012. New England boss Roy Hodgson clearly liked what he saw, taking the youngster to the Euros and giving him a first competitive start in the 1-1 draw with France, where he became his country's second youngest player (behind Wayne Rooney in 2004) at the tournament. Later that year he scored his first England goal in a 5-0 thrashing of San Marino.**

• Oxlade-Chamberlain is one of just four England players to have a father who also represented the Three Lions, his dad Mark earning eight caps on the wing during the early 1980s.

# MESUT OZIL

> **Born:** Gelsenkirchen, Germany, 15th October 1988
> **Position:** Midfielder
> **Club career:**
> 2006-08 Schalke 30 (0)
> 2008-10 Werder Bremen 71 (13)
> 2010-13 Real Madrid 102 (19)
> 2013- Arsenal 42 (9)
> **International record:**
> 2009- Germany 66 (18)

An attacking midfielder with skill and creativity in abundance, Mesut Ozil became Arsenal's record signing when he joined the Gunners for £42.4 million from Real Madrid in September 2013. He has since gone on to win the FA Cup in consecutive years in 2014 and 2015 – a feat only previously achieved by one other German player, Michael Ballack (with Chelsea in 2009 and 2010).

• **Ozil originally captured Real's attention after some impressive performances at the 2010 World Cup for Germany, starring in his side's four-goal thrashings of England and**

Argentina in the knock-out rounds before a semi-final defeat by eventual winners Spain. **Immediately after the tournament Ozil moved to Spain from Werder Bremen, for whom he had scored the winning goal in the 2009 German Cup final and helped reach the UEFA Cup final in the same year.**

• In the summer of 2009 Ozil was named as Man of the Match after the German Under-21 side smashed their English counterparts 4-0 in the European Championships final, prompting the manager of the team to hail him as 'the German Messi'.

• **Ozil was Germany's top scorer with eight goals during qualification for the 2014 World Cup and he played a full part in his country's success in Brazil, notably scoring the decisive second goal in a last 16 victory over Algeria.**

*Arsenal's record signing, Mesut Ozil*

PSG'S MVP!

## PARIS ST GERMAIN

**Year founded:** 1970
**Ground:** Parc des Princes (48,712)
**Nickname:** PSG
**League titles:** 5
**Domestic cups:** 9
**European cups:** 1

Founded as recently as 1970 following a merger between Paris FC and Stade Saint-Germain, Paris St Germain are now one of the richest clubs in the world after being bought by the Qatar Investment Authority in 2011.

• Since then PSG have splashed out millions on star players like Zlatan Ibrahimovic, Edinson Cavani and David Luiz, and the club's free-spending policy was rewarded when they won the French league in 2013. The club from the French capital repeated the feat in 2014 to claim their first back-to-back titles and in 2015 they made it three on the trot.

• In 1996 PSG became only the second French club to win a European trophy when they beat Rapid Vienna 1-0 in the final of the Cup Winners' Cup. The Paris outfit had a good chance to become the only club to retain the trophy the

following year, but lost in the final to Barcelona.

• PSG claimed their first ever French double in 2015, thanks in part to a Zlatan Ibrahimovic hat-trick in their 4-1 thrashing of Saint-Etienne in the French Cup final.

HONOURS
*French league champions* 1986, 1994, 2013, 2014, 2015
*French Cup* 1982, 1983, 1993, 1995, 1998, 2004, 2006, 2010, 2015
*European Cup Winners' Cup* 1996

## PARTICK THISTLE

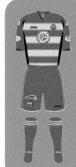

**Year founded:** 1876
**Ground:** Firhill (10,102)
**Nickname:** The Jags
**Biggest win:** 16-0 v Royal Albert (1931)
**Heaviest defeat:** 1-10 v Dunfermline (1959)

Founded in 1876, the club adopted the name Partick Thistle to distinguish themselves from local rivals Partick FC.

• The club emerged from the shadows of giant Glasgow neighbours Celtic and Rangers to win the Scottish Cup in 1921, and in 1972 Partick enjoyed the greatest day in their history when they thrashed Celtic 4-1 in the League

Cup final at Hampden Park.

• The club's longest serving player is goalkeeper Alan Rough, who made 410 league appearances between 1969 and 1982. Rough is also the club's most decorated international, winning 51 caps.

• Partick's record sale was made as far back as 1982 when top marksman Mo Johnston joined Watford in a £200,000 deal.

HONOURS
*Division 2 champions* 1897, 1900, 1971
*First Division champions* 1976, 2002, 2013
*Second Division champions* 2001
*Scottish Cup* 1921
*League Cup* 1972

## PELE

**Born:** Tres Coracoes, Brazil, 23rd October 1940
**Position:** Striker
**Club career:**
1956-74 Santos 412 (470)
1975-77 New York Cosmos 56 (31)
**International record:**
1957-71 Brazil 92 (77)

Born Edson Arantes do Nascimento, but known throughout the world by his nickname, Pelé is generally recognised as the greatest footballer ever to play the game.

The great Pele – arguably the best footballer of all time

• In 1957, aged just 16 years and nine months, he scored on his debut for Brazil against Argentina to become the youngest international goalscorer ever. The following year he made headlines around the globe when he scored twice in Brazil's 5-2 World Cup final defeat of hosts Sweden, in the process making history as the youngest ever World Cup winner.

• Four years later he missed most of Brazil's successful defence of their trophy through injury but was later awarded a winners' medal by FIFA. After being kicked out of the 1966 World Cup, he was back to his best at the 1970 tournament in Mexico, opening the scoring in the final against Italy and inspiring a magnificent Brazilian side to a comprehensive 4-1 victory. He remains the only player in the world with three World Cup winners' medals.

• Fast, strong, tremendously skilful and powerful in the air, Pelé was the complete footballer. He was also a phenomenal goalscorer who remains Brazil's top scorer of all time with an incredible 77 goals (in just 92 games), a record only surpassed in international football by three players. Twelve of those goals came at the World Cup, making him the fifth highest scorer in the history of the tournament.

• Pelé's career total of 1,281 goals in 1,365 top-class matches is officially recognised by FIFA as a world record, although many of his goals came in friendlies for his club Santos. The Brazilian ace's most prolific patch saw him score in 14 consecutive games, to set another world record.

## MANUEL PELLEGRINI

**Born:** Santiago, Chile, 16th September 1953
**Managerial career:**
1987-90 Universidad Chile
1990 Palestino
1991-92 Palestino
1992-93 O'Higgins
1993-95 Universidad Catolica
1998 Palestino
1998-2001 Universitaria Quito
2001-02 San Lorenzo
2002-03 River Plate
2004-09 Villarreal
2009-10 Real Madrid
2010-13 Malaga
2013- Manchester City

Manuel Pellegrini is the first non-European manager to win the Premier League, the Chilean having guided

*Manuel Pellegrini decided to dress like a teenager to help him relate to his younger players...*

Manchester City to the title in 2014, just a year after replacing Roberto Mancini in the Etihad hotseat. He achieved the feat in fine style, too, as his City side banged in 102 league goals – just one short of Chelsea's Premier League record.

• After a lengthy apprenticeship in Chile, Ecuador and Argentina, Pellegrini moved to Europe to take over the reins at Villarreal in 2004. During five years with the Spanish club he led them to the semi-finals of the Champions League in 2006, and a best ever second place in La Liga in 2008.

• The following year Pellegrini took charge at Real Madrid, overseeing the signing of £200 million worth of talent in Cristiano Ronaldo, Kaka, Karim Benzema and Xabi Alonso. His expensively assembled 'Galacticos' proceeded to rack up a then club record 96 points, but they were still pipped to the title by arch-rivals Barcelona, and Pellegrini was unceremoniously dismissed.

• Pellegrini moved on to Malaga, guiding 'Los Boquerones' to a creditable fourth place in 2012 and the quarter-finals of the Champions League a year later despite the club suffering a financial crisis which saw it banned from European competition in 2013/14.

## PENALTIES

Penalty kicks were first proposed by goalkeeper William McCrum of the Irish FA in 1890 and adopted the following year. Wolves' John Heath was the first player to take and score a penalty in a Football League match, in a 5-0 win against Accrington at Molineux on 14th September 1891.

• Francis Lee holds the British record for the most penalties in a league season, scoring 15 for Manchester City in Division One in 1971/72. He earned many of the penalties himself, leading fans to dub him 'Lee Won Pen'. In the Premier League era, Andy Johnson scored a record 11 penalties for Crystal Palace in 2004/05, but to no avail as the Eagles were still relegated.

• The first penalty awarded in a World Cup final was scored by Holland's Johan Neeskens after just one minute of the 1974 final against

*Another Lionel Messi penalty hits the back of the net*

West Germany. Only one player has missed a spot-kick in a World Cup final in normal play, Italy's Antonio Cabrini in 1982.

• Alan Shearer is the most prolific penalty-taker in the Premier League era, scoring 56 times from the spot. Liverpool have scored a record 102 penalties in the Premier League – one more than Chelsea.

• The most penalties ever awarded in a British match is five in the game between Crystal Palace and Brighton at Selhurst Park in 1989. Palace were awarded four penalties (one scored, three missed) while Brighton's consolation goal in a 2-1 defeat also came from the spot.

• Argentina's Martin Palermo missed a record three penalties in a Copa America match against Colombia in 1999. His first effort struck the crossbar, his second penalty sailed over, but remarkably Palermo still insisted on taking his side's third spot-kick of the match. Perhaps he shouldn't have bothered, as his shot was saved by the goalkeeper.

• Four players – Craig Burley (Derby), Darren Bent (Sunderland), Steven Gerrard (Liverpool) and Sergio Aguero (Manchester City) – have all taken a record three penalties in a Premier League match. None of them, however,

## TOP 10

| PREMIER LEAGUE PENALTIES SCORED | |
|---|---|
| 1. Liverpool | 102 |
| 2. Chelsea | 101 |
| 3. Arsenal | 94 |
| 4. Manchester United | 89 |
| Newcastle United | 89 |
| 6. Everton | 80 |
| 7. Tottenham Hotspur | 71 |
| 8. Manchester City | 66 |
| 9. Aston Villa | 64 |
| 10. Blackburn Rovers | 58 |

managed to score a hat-trick from the spot.

• The first goalkeeper to save a penalty in the FA Cup final at Wembley was Wimbledon's Dave Beasant, who palmed away John Aldridge's spot-kick in 1988 to help the Dons record a shock 1-0 win over hot favourites Liverpool.

## PENALTY SHOOT-OUTS

Penalty shoot-outs were first used in England as a way to settle drawn matches in the Watney Cup in 1970. In the first ever shoot-out Manchester United beat Hull City in the semi-final of

the competition, United legend George Best being the first player to take a penalty while his team-mate Denis Law was the first to miss.

• The third/fourth place play-off between Birmingham and Stoke in 1972 was the first FA Cup match to be decided by penalties, Birmingham winning 4-3 after a 0-0 draw. However, spot-kicks weren't used to settle normal FA Cup ties until the 1991/92 season, Rotherham United becoming the first team to progress by this method when they beat Scunthorpe United 7-6 in the shoot-out after their first-round replay finished 3-3. In 2005 Arsenal became the first team to win the final on penalties, defeating Manchester United 5-4 after a 0-0 draw.

• The first World Cup match to be settled by penalties was the 1982 semi-final between France and West Germany. The Germans won 5-4 in the shoot-out after an exciting 3-3 draw with France's Jean-Luc Ettori becoming the first goalkeeper to save a spot-kick in the new-style decider. In 1994 the final was settled by penalties for the first time, Brazil defeating Italy 3-2 on spot-kicks after a dull 0-0 draw. The 2006 final also went to penalties, Italy beating France 5-3.

• Remarkably, Steaua Bucharest goalkeeper Helmuth Duckadem saved

132

all four Barcelona penalties he faced in the shoot-out to decide the 1986 European Cup final. His heroics ensured that Steaua won the game, one of 10 European Cup/Champions League finals to be decided by spot-kicks.

• The longest FA Cup shoot-out saw Scunthorpe defeat Worcester City 14-13 after 32 penalties had been taken to settle their second round tie in December 2014. Three months earlier Liverpool beat Middlesbrough by the same score in the longest League Cup shoot-out.

• The longest ever penalty shoot-out was between KK Palace and Civics in the first round of the 2005 Namibian Cup. After an incredible total of 48 kicks, KK Palace emerged victorious 17-16. At junior level, Under-10 sides Mickleover Lightning Blue Sox and Chellaston required an extraordinary 66 penalties to settle their Derby County Cup match in 1998, before Blue Sox narrowly won 2-1.

• When Bradford City beat Arsenal in the 2012/13 League Cup quarter-final, they did so in their ninth straight penalty shoot-out win – a record for English football.

## PETERBOROUGH UNITED

**Year founded:** 1934
**Ground:** London Road (15,314)
**Nickname:** The Posh
**Biggest win:** 9-1 v Barnet (1998)
**Heaviest defeat:** 1-8 v Northampton Town (1946)

Peterborough were founded in 1934 at a meeting at the Angel Hotel to fill the void left by the collapse of local club Peterborough and Fletton United two years earlier.

• The club's unusual nickname, The Posh, stemmed from Peterborough and Fletton manager Pat Tirrel's remark in 1921 that the club wanted "Posh players for a Posh team". When the new club played its first game against Gainsborough Trinity in 1934 there were shouts of "Up the Posh!" and the nickname stuck.

• Peterborough were finally elected to the Football League in 1960 after

numerous failed attempts. The fans' long wait was rewarded when Peterborough stormed to the Fourth Division title in their first season, scoring a league record 134 goals. Striker Terry Bly notched an amazing 52 of the goals to set a hard-to-beat club record.

• In 1968 the club became the first since the Second World War to be relegated for non-football reasons, dropping from the Third to the Fourth Division after making illegal payments to players and collecting a 19-point deduction as a punishment.

• Peterborough reached the quater-finals of the FA Cup for the first and only time in 1965, going down 5-1 to Chelsea at Stamford Bridge.

HONOURS
*Division 4 champions* 1961, 1974
*Football League Trophy* 2014

## PITCHES

According to FIFA rules, a football pitch must measure between 100 and 130 yards in length and 50 and 100 yards in breadth. It's no surprise, then, that different pitches vary hugely in size.

• Of Premier League clubs, Manchester City have the largest pitch, their surface at the Etihad Stadium measuring 115 yards by 74 yards to give a total playing area of 8,710 square yards.

• At the opposite end of the scale, Stoke City have the smallest pitch in the top flight. The playing surface at the Britannia Stadium is just 7,630 square yards (109 x 70yds).

• The first portable natural grass pitch was used for the 1993 America Cup clash between America and England at the Detroit Silverdome. The grass was grown in hexagonal segments in the stadium car park and then reassembled in the covered stadium.

• At the start of the 1981/82 season QPR became the first English club to install an artificial pitch, with Oldham, Luton Town and Preston soon following suit. By

1994, however, Preston were the last club still playing on 'plastic' and at the start of the 1994/95 season the Football League banned all artificial surfaces on the grounds that they gave home clubs an unfair advantage. In Scotland, Premiership clubs Kilmarnock and Motherwell both currently play on 3G artificial pitches.

• In 2014 Maidstone entertained Stevenage in the first FA Cup tie played on a 3G pitch. Home side Maidstone made use of their greater experience on the artificial surface to win 2-1.

## MICHEL PLATINI

**Born:** Joeuf, France, 21st June 1955
**Position:** Midfielder
**Club career:**
1972-79 Nancy 181 (98)
1979-82 St Etienne 104 (58)
1982-87 Juventus 147 (68)
**International record:**
1976-87 France 72 (41)

The only man to be voted European Footballer of the Year in three consecutive years (1983, 1984 and 1985), Platini is a legendary figure in world football.

• An elegant attacking midfielder with a striker's scoring instinct, Platini starred in the French team that reached the World Cup semi-final in 1982 and 1986, only to lose on both occasions to West Germany.

• In between those disappointments, however, Platini captained France to their first ever trophy when, as the host nation, they won the 1984 European Championships. Again, Platini was the main inspiration, scoring a record nine goals in the tournament, including one from a free kick in his side's 2-0 defeat of Spain in the final.

• After playing for Nancy and St Etienne, Platini joined Juventus for £1.2 million in 1982. Three-times top scorer in Serie A, he hit the winning goal for the

**IS THAT A FACT?**
In June 2015 a giant swastika was marked on the pitch ahead of Croatia's Euro 2016 qualifier against Italy. An angry Croatian FA spokesman denounced the action as "sabotage" after the 1-1 draw, but UEFA still docked Croatia one point as a punishment for the incident.

Italian giants in the 1985 European Cup final against Liverpool, although Juventus' victory was completely overshadowed by the deaths of 39 fans in the Heysel tragedy.

• After managing France for four years between 1988 and 1992, Platini was elected President of UEFA in 2007. In July 2015 Platini announced that he would stand as a candidate for FIFA President in 2016 following Sepp Blatter's resignation.

## PLAY-OFFS

The play-off system was introduced by the Football League in the 1986/87 season. Initially, one club from the higher division competed with three from the lower division at the semi-final stage but this was changed to four teams from the same division in the 1988/89 season. The following season a one-off final at Wembley replaced the original two-legged final.

• **Crystal Palace and Blackpool have been promoted from the play-offs a record four times each, while the Seasiders are the only club to have gone up from three different divisions via the play-offs.**

• Preston have appeared in the play-offs on a record 10 occasions, but have only once been promoted – beating Swindon Town 4-0 in the League One final in 2015.

• **The Championship play-off final is the most financially rewarding sporting event in the world, its worth to the winners in prize money, TV and advertising revenue, and increased gate receipts, being estimated at around £120 million.**

• In 2015 Swindon Town and Sheffield United drew 5-5 in the League One play-off semi-final second leg, the highest ever score in a play-off match.

## PLYMOUTH ARGYLE

**Year founded:** 1886
**Ground:** Home Park (17,150)
**Previous name:** Argyle FC
**Nickname:** The Pilgrims
**Biggest win:** 8-1 v Millwall (1932) and v Hartlepool (1994)
**Heaviest defeat:** 0-9 v Stoke City (1960)

The club was founded as Argyle FC in 1886 in a Plymouth coffee house, the name deriving from the Argyll and Sutherland Highlanders who were stationed in the city at the time. The current name was adopted in 1903, when the club became fully professional and entered the Southern League.

• **After joining the Football League in 1920, Plymouth just missed out on promotion from the Third Division (South) between 1922 and 1927, finishing in second place in six consecutive seasons... a record of misfortune no other club can match.**

• Sammy Black, a prolific marksman during the 1920s and 1930s, is the club's leading goalscorer with 185 league goals. The Pilgrims' longest serving player is Kevin Hodges, with 530 appearances between 1978 and 1992.

• **The largest city in England never to have hosted top-flight football, Plymouth have won the third tier of English football a record four times, most recently topping the Second Division in 2004.**

• In one of the most bizarre incidents ever in the history of football, Plymouth conceded a goal scored by the referee in a Division Three fixture against Barrow in 1968. A shot from a Barrow player was heading wide until it deflected off the boot of referee Ivan Robinson and into the Pilgrims' net for the only goal of the match.

**HONOURS**
*Division 3 (S) champions 1930, 1952*
*Division 3 champions 1959*
*Second Division champions 2004*
*Third Division champions 2002*

## MAURICIO POCHETTINO

**Born:** Murphy, Argentina, 2nd March 1972
**Managerial career:**
2009-12 Espanyol
2013-14 Southampton
2014- Tottenham Hotspur

Appointed boss of Tottenham in May 2014, Mauricio Pochettino is only the second Argentinian to manage in the Premier League – after Ossie Ardiles, who also enjoyed a spell in the White Hart Lane hotseat in the 1990s. His first season at the north London club was

reasonably successful, but he failed to bring the Champions League qualification craved by the fans.

• **Pochettino began his managerial career with Spanish side Espanyol in 2009, but was sacked three years later when the Barcelona-based club slipped to the bottom of La Liga.**

• Later that season, however, he was a surprise choice to replace Nigel Adkins at Southampton. Despite never speaking to the press in English, Pochettino soon won over the Saints fans by introducing a vibrant and entertaining attacking style of play. In his only full season at St Mary's in 2013/14, Pochettino led Southampton to a then best ever eighth place finish in the Premier League.

• **A central defender in his playing days, Pochettino twice won the Copa del Rey with Espanyol. He also represented Argentina at the 2002 World Cup, famously fouling Michael Owen in the penalty area to allow England captain David Beckham to score the only goal of the group game between the sides from the spot.**

## PAUL POGBA

**Born:** Lagny-sur-Marne, France, 15th March 1993
**Position:** Midfielder
**Club career:**
2011-12 Manchester United 3 (0)
2012- Juventus 89 (20)
**International record:**
2013- France 23 (5)

Named Best Young Player at the 2014 World Cup, France midfielder Paul Pogba

*Paul Pogba – one of the world's most exciting young players*

is one of the hottest properties in the global game.

• With his club side Juventus Pogba has won three successive Scudetto titles after joining the Turin giants from Manchester United in 2012. He also helped Juve reach the Champions League final in 2015 after a surprise semi-final victory over holders Real Madrid. His outstanding performances for club and country saw him win the 2013 Golden Boy award for the best young player in Europe.

• Pogba started out with Le Havre before moving to England in 2009 aged just 16. However, he only made a handful of appearances for United and frustrated with his lack of progress at Old Trafford decided to move to Italy.

• A combative midfielder whose tentacle-like long legs have earned him the nickname 'Paul the Octopus', Pogba made his debut for France in 2013 and the following year was his country's most impressive performer as 'Les Bleus' reached the quarter-finals of the World Cup in Brazil.

## PORT VALE

**Year founded:** 1876
**Ground:** Vale Park (19,052)
**Previous name:** Burslem Port Vale
**Nickname:** The Valiants
**Biggest win:** 9-1 v Chesterfield (1932)
**Heaviest defeat:** 0-10 v Sheffield United (1892) and v Notts County (1895)

Port Vale's name derives from the house where the club was founded in 1876. Initially, the club was known as Burslem Port Vale – Burslem being the Stoke-on-Trent town where the Valiants are based – but the prefix was dropped in 1911.

• In their first season as a league club, in 1892/93, Port Vale suffered the worst ever home defeat in Football League history when Sheffield United hammered them 10-0. However, Vale's defence was in much better

nick in 1953/54 when they kept a league record 30 clean sheets on their way to the Third Division (North) championship.

• Midfielder Gareth Ainsworth is both Vale's record purchase and sale, arriving from Lincoln for £500,000 in 1997 before moving on the next year to Wimbledon for £2 million.

• After a 12-year gap Port Vale returned to the Football League in October 1919, replacing the disbanded Leeds City. Bizarrely, the Valiants inherited the Yorkshiremen's playing record (won four, lost two, drawn two) and went on to finish in a respectable 13th position.

• Loyal defender Roy Sproson is Port Vale's longest serving player, appearing in a phenomenal 761 league games between 1950 and 1972. Only two other players in the history of league football have made more appearances for the same club. With 154 league goals in two spells at the club between 1923 and 1933 Wilf Kirkham is the Valiants' record goalscorer.

> HONOURS
> *Division 3 (N) champions* 1930, 1954
> *Division 4 champions* 1959
> *Football League Trophy* 1993, 2001

## FC PORTO

**Year founded:** 1893
**Ground:** Estadio do Dragao (50,092)
**Nickname:** The Dragons
**League titles:** 27
**Domestic cups:** 19
**European cups:** 5
**International cups:** 2

Easily the most successful Portuguese side of recent years, Porto were founded in 1893 by a local wine salesman who had been introduced to football on his regular business trips to England.

• Seven league title wins in the last 10 seasons have taken Porto's total of domestic championships to 27, seven behind arch-rivals Benfica. In the three seasons between 2011 and 2013 Porto lost just one league game (to Gil Vicente)... the best run of form of any team in Europe during that period.

• Porto have the best record in Europe of any Portuguese side, with two victories in the European Cup/Champions League (in 1987 and 2004) and two in the UEFA Cup (in 2003 and 2011), the latter of these triumphs coming under Andre Villas-Boas – at 33, the youngest coach ever to win a European competition.

• Porto are the only Portuguese club to have been crowned world champions, claiming the Intercontinental Cup in both 1987 and 2004.

HONOURS
*Portuguese League champions* 1935, 1939, 1940, 1956, 1959, 1978, 1979, 1985, 1986, 1988, 1990, 1992, 1993, 1995, 1996, 1997, 1998, 1999, 2003, 2004, 2006, 2007, 2008, 2009, 2011, 2012, 2013
*Portuguese Cup* 1922, 1925, 1932, 1937, 1956, 1958, 1968, 1977, 1984, 1988, 1991, 1994, 1998, 2000, 2001, 2003, 2006, 2009, 2011
*European Cup/Champions League* 1987, 2004
*UEFA Cup/Europa League* 2003, 2011
*European Super Cup* 1987
*Intercontinental Cup* 1987, 2004

## PORTSMOUTH

**Year founded:** 1898
**Ground:** Fratton Park (21,178)
**Nickname:** Pompey
**Biggest win:** 9-1 v Notts County (1927)
**Heaviest defeat:** 0-10 v Leicester City (1928)

Portsmouth were founded in 1898 by a group of sportsmen and businessmen at a meeting in the city's High Street. After starting out in the Southern League the club joined the Third Division in 1920.

• In 1949 the club became the first team to rise from the third tier to claim the league championship, and the following year became the first of just five clubs to retain the title since the end of the Second World War.

• The most influential player in that team was half-back Jimmy Dickinson, who went on to play a record 764 times for Pompey, the second highest number of Football League appearances with any single club. Dickinson is also Portsmouth's most decorated international, winning 48 caps for England.

• Another legendary figure from that period, right-winger Peter Harris is the club's leading marksman, with 193 goals between 1946 and 1960.

• The club won the FA Cup for the first time in 1939, when Pompey thrashed favourites Wolves 4-1 in the final at Wembley. In 2008 they lifted the cup for a second time when a single goal from Nigerian striker Kanu was enough to beat Cardiff City in only the second final at the new Wembley.

• In the same year Portsmouth splashed out a record £11 million on lanky Liverpool striker Peter Crouch. Midfielder Lassana Diarra is Pompey's record sale, joining Real Madrid for £18 million in 2008.

• Since those heady days Portsmouth's financial problems have seen the club slide all the way down to League Two, but there was some good news for their long-suffering followers in April 2013 when Pompey were bought by the Portsmouth Supporters' Trust to become the largest fan-owned club in England.

HONOURS
*Division 1 champions* 1949, 1950
*First Division champions* 2003
*Division 3 (South) champions* 1924
*Division 3 champions* 1962, 1983
*FA Cup* 1939, 2008

## PORTUGAL

**First international:** Spain 3 Portugal 1, 1921
**Most capped player:** Luis Figo, 127 caps (1991-2006)
**Leading goalscorer:** Cristiano Ronaldo, 55 goals (2003- )
**First World Cup appearance:** Portugal 3 Hungary 1, 1966
**Biggest win:** Portugal 8 Liechtenstein 0, 1994 and 1999
**Heaviest defeat:** Portugal 0 England 10, 1947

Portugal have never won a major trophy, although they reached the final of the European Championships in 2004. Playing on home soil they were hot

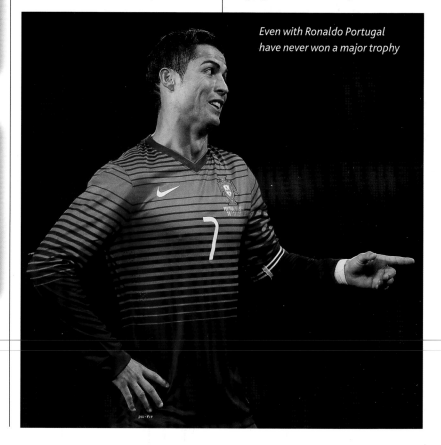

*Even with Ronaldo Portugal have never won a major trophy*

favourites to beat Greece, but went down to a surprise 1-0 defeat. Eight years later they missed out on a chance to appear in another final when they lost a Euro 2012 semi-final shoot-out to Spain.

• **Portugal's best showing at the World Cup was in 1966 when they finished third after going out to hosts England in the semi-finals. Much of their success was down to legendary striker Eusebio, who topped the goalscoring charts with nine goals.**

• The southern Europeans also reached the semi-finals of the World Cup in 2006, after beating Holland in 'The Battle of Nuremburg' in the last 16 and England on penalties in the quarter-finals. A 1-0 defeat to France, though, ended their hopes of appearing in the final.

• **Luiz Felipe Scolari has the best record of any Portugal manager with 42 wins between 2003 and 2008. The Brazilian is also the only man to oversee victory against England in two penalty shoot-outs, at Euro 2004 and the 2006 World Cup in Germany.**

**World Cup Record**
*1930-38 Did not enter*
*1950-62 Did not qualify*
*1966 Third place*
*1970-82 Did not qualify*
*1986 Round 1*
*1990-98 Did not qualify*
*2002 Round 1*
*2006 Fourth place*
*2010 Round 2*
*2014 Round 1*

## PREMIER LEAGUE

The Premier League was founded in 1992 and is now the most watched and most lucrative sporting league in the world, boasting record revenues of £3.26 billion in the 2013/14 season.

• **Initially composed of 22 clubs, the Premier League was reduced to 20 teams in 1995. A total of 47 clubs have played in the league but just five – Manchester United, Blackburn Rovers, Arsenal, Chelsea and Manchester City – have won the title. Of this group, United are easily the most successful, having won the league 13 times.**

• Manchester United recorded the biggest win in Premier League history in 1995 when they hammered Ipswich Town 9-0. In the same match Andy Cole hit a record five goals, a feat since

matched by Alan Shearer (Newcastle United), Jermain Defoe (Tottenham) and Dimitar Berbatov (Manchester United).

• **Only seven clubs have appeared in the league in every season since its inception: Arsenal, Aston Villa, Chelsea, Everton, Liverpool, Manchester United and Tottenham Hotspur. United lead the all-time table with 1,886 points (including a record 567 wins in 886 games), while Everton have lost more games (312) than any other club.**

• Alan Shearer is the leading scorer in the history of the Premier League with a total of 260 goals for Blackburn Rovers and Newcastle between 1992 and 2006.

• **Ryan Giggs holds the Premier League appearance record, turning out in 632 games for Manchester United between 1992 and 2014.**

## PRESTON NORTH END

**Year founded:** 1879
**Ground:** Deepdale (23,404)
**Nickname:** The Lilywhites
**Biggest win:** 26-0 v Hyde (1887)
**Heaviest defeat:** 0-7 v Blackpool (1948)

Preston were founded in 1879 as a branch of the North End Cricket and Rugby Club, playing football exclusively from 1881.

• **Founder members of the Football League in 1888, Preston won the inaugural league title the following year, going through the entire 22-game season undefeated and conceding just 15 goals (a league record). For good measure the club also won the FA Cup, beating Wolves 3-0 in the final, to become the first club to win the Double. During their cup run, Preston demolished Hyde 26-0 to record the biggest ever win in any English competition, striker Jimmy Ross scoring seven of the goals to set a club record that has never been matched. Ross went on to score a record 20 goals in the cup that season.**

• Of the 12 founder members of the league, Preston are the only club still playing at the same ground, making Deepdale the oldest league football

stadium anywhere in the world.

• **The legendary Tom Finney is Preston's most capped international, turning out for England in 76 games. The flying winger is also the club's highest scorer, with 187 strikes between 1946 and 1960. North End's leading appearance maker is Alan Kelly, who played in goal for the club in 447 league games between 1958 and 1973.**

• Along with Wolves and Burnley, Preston are one of just three clubs to have won all four divisions of English football, achieving this feat in 1996 when they topped the Third Division (now League Two).

• **Preston have participated in the play-offs a record 10 times, but have only once managed to go on to win promotion. Mind you, the Lilywhites did so in fine style, thrashing Swindon 4-0 in the League One final in 2015, thanks partly to Jermaine Beckford's hat-trick – only the third ever in a play-off final.**

HONOURS
*Division 1 champions 1889, 1890*
*Division 2 champions 1904, 1913, 1951*
*Division 3 champions 1971*
*Second Division champions 2000*
*Third Division champions 1996*
*FA Cup 1889, 1938*
*Double 1889*

## PROMOTION

Automatic promotion from the Second to First Division was introduced in the 1898/99 season, replacing the 'test match' play-off-style system. The first two clubs to go up automatically were Glossop North End and Manchester City.

• **Birmingham City, Leicester City and Notts County have gained a record 13 promotions, while the Foxes have gone up to the top flight on a record 12 occasions – most recently in 2014, after winning the Championship.**

• Not all clubs who have been promoted have done so through playing merit. The most notorious case involved Arsenal in 1919 who were elected to the First Division at the expense of local rivals Tottenham, allegedly thanks to the underhand tactics employed by the Gunners' then chairman, Sir Henry Norris.

• **Swansea City enjoyed the fastest rise from the bottom tier to the top flight, winning promotion in three seasons out of four between 1977/78 and 1980/81.**

## QUEEN'S PARK

**Year founded:** 1867
**Ground:** Hampden Park (51,866)
**Nickname:** The Spiders
**Biggest win:** 16-0 v St Peters (1885)
**Heaviest defeat:** 0-9 v Motherwell (1930)

Founded in 1867 at a meeting at a house in south Glasgow, Queen's Park are Scotland's oldest club and a genuine sporting institution.

• **The dominant force in the game north of the border in the 19th century, Queen's Park won the first ever Scottish Cup in 1874 and held the trophy for the next two years as well. In all, they have won the competition 10 times... a cup record only bettered by Old Firm giants Celtic and Rangers.**

• Queen's Park's star player of the Victorian era was Charles Campbell, who won a record eight Scottish Cup winners' medals.

• **Queen's Park are the only Scottish side to have played in the final of the FA Cup, losing to Blackburn Rovers in both 1884 and 1885 before the Scottish FA banned its clubs from entering the competition two years later.**

• Queen's Park, who play their home games at the near 52,000-capacity Hampden Park, became the first Scottish side to appear on TV when their friendly with famous London amateur club Walthamstow Avenue was broadcast in 1951, the Spiders wining 2-0.

### HONOURS

**Division 2 champions** 1923, 1956
**Second Division champions** 1981
**Third Division champions** 2000
**Scottish Cup** 1874, 1875, 1876, 1880, 1881, 1882, 1884, 1886, 1890, 1893

## QUEENS PARK RANGERS

**Year founded:** 1882
**Ground:** Loftus Road (18,489)
**Nickname:** The R's
**Biggest win:** 9-2 v Tranmere Rovers (1960)
**Heaviest defeat:** 1-8 v Mansfield Town (1965) and v Manchester United (1969)

Founded in 1882 following the merger of St Jude's and Christchurch Rangers, the club was called Queens Park Rangers because most of the players came from the Queens Park area of north London.

• **A nomadic outfit in their early days, QPR have staged home matches at no fewer than 19 different venues, a record for a Football League club.**

• The club enjoyed its finest moment in 1967 when Rangers came from two goals down to defeat West Bromwich Albion 3-2 in the first ever League Cup final to be played at Wembley. In the same season the R's won the Third Division title to pull off a unique double.

• **Loftus Road favourite Rodney Marsh hit a club record 44 goals that season, 11 of them coming in the League Cup. George Goddard, though, holds the club record for league goals with 37 in 1929/30. Goddard is also the club's leading scorer, notching 174 league goals between 1926 and 1934.**

• In 1976 QPR finished second in the old First Division, being pipped to the league championship by Liverpool. Six years later Rangers reached the FA Cup final for the only time in their history but went down 1-0 to Tottenham in a replay after the original match finished 1-1.

• **No other player has pulled on Rangers' famous hoops more often than Tony Ingham, who made 519 league appearances over 13 years after signing from Leeds in 1950.**

• Something of a yo-yo club in recent seasons, QPR endured the worst ever start to a Premier League season in 2012/13 when they went 16 games without a win. Relegated at the end of that campaign, they bounced back via the play-offs the following year. The 2014/15 season, though, was another miserable one for the R's, and after they lost a record 11 consecutive Premier League away games at the start of the campaign they were relegated back to the Championship.

• **The Hoops' most capped international is defender Alan McDonald, who played 52 times for Northern Ireland between 1986 and 1996.**

*QPR shocked the world when they signed the Karate Kid!*

### HONOURS

**Division 2 champions** 1983
**Championship champions** 2011
**Division 3 (S) champions** 1948
**Division Three champions** 1967
**League Cup** 1967

# SERGIO RAMOS

**Born:** Camas, Spain, 30th March 1986
**Position:** Defender
**Club career:**
2003-04 Sevilla B 26 (2)
2004-05 Sevilla 39 (2)
2005- Real Madrid 314 (40)
**International record:**
2005- Spain 128 (10)

Real Madrid defender Sergio Ramos is the youngest European player ever to win 100 caps for his country, reaching three figures a week before his 27th birthday when Spain played Finland in a World Cup qualifier in March 2013. Ramos marked the occasion in style, scoring his side's goal in a 1-1 draw.

He has gone on to become Spain's third-highest capped player behind Iker Casillas and Xavi.

• **A strong tackler who can play either in central defence or at right-back, Ramos started out at Sevilla before joining Real for around £20 million in 2005 – aged 19 at the time, he was the most expensive teenager in Spanish football history.**

• Ramos has won three La Liga titles and the Champions League with Real. The defender played a vital role in his club's triumph in Lisbon against city rivals Atletico Madrid in 2014, heading a last-minute equaliser which enabled Real to go on and win the game in extra-time. He also scored in the semi-final and final of the 2014 FIFA Club World Cup, and was voted Player of the Tournament. Less impressively, Ramos has been sent off a club record 19 times for the Spanish giants.

• **Ramos has enjoyed huge success at international level, winning two European Championships (2008 and 2012) and the World Cup in South Africa in 2010.**

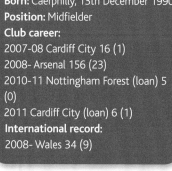

# AARON RAMSEY

**Born:** Caerphilly, 13th December 1990
**Position:** Midfielder
**Club career:**
2007-08 Cardiff City 16 (1)
2008- Arsenal 156 (23)
2010-11 Nottingham Forest (loan) 5 (0)
2011 Cardiff City (loan) 6 (1)
**International record:**
2008- Wales 34 (9)

Box-to-box midfielder Aaron Ramsey is the youngest player ever to captain Wales, skippering his country for the first time in a Euro 2012 qualifier against England on 26th March 2011 when he was aged just 20 and 90 days.

• **Ramsey is a product of the Cardiff City youth system, and became the club's youngest ever player when he made his debut as a sub against Hull City on the last day of the 2006/07 campaign aged 16 and 124 days. The following season he cemented his place in the Bluebirds' team and played in the 2008 FA Cup final against Portsmouth – aged 17, he was the second youngest player ever to appear in the final after Millwall's Curtis Weston in 2004.**

• In June 2008 Ramsey signed for Arsenal for £4.8 million. When he notched his first goal for the Gunners against Fenerbahce in October 2008, he became only the second player born in the 1990s to score in the Champions League.

• **Ramsey's career stalled after he suffered a double fracture of his right leg in February 2010, but he recovered to enjoy his best season yet for the Gunners in 2013/14. The Welshman's stunning displays saw him nominated for the PFA Young Player of the Year award, and he finished the season in glorious fashion by scoring the winner in the Gunners' 3-2 victory over Hull City in the FA Cup final. The following year he won the cup again, playing all 90 minutes of the Gunners' 4-0 rout of Aston Villa.**

*Sergio Ramos has been sent off more times than any other Real Madrid player*

# RANGERS

**Year founded:** 1873
**Ground:** Ibrox Stadium (50,947)
**Nickname:** The Gers
**Biggest win:** 14-2 v Blairgowrie (1934)
**Heaviest defeat:** 2-10 v Airdrieonians (1886)

The most decorated club in the history of world football, Rangers were founded by a group of rowing enthusiasts in 1873. The club were founder members of the Scottish League in 1890, sharing the inaugural title with Dumbarton.

• Rangers have won the league title 54 times, a record of domestic success which is unmatched by any club on the planet. Between 1989 and 1997 the Gers topped the league in nine consecutive seasons, initially under Graeme Souness then under Walter Smith, to equal a record previously set by arch rivals Celtic.

• In 2000 Rangers became the first club in the world to win 100 major trophies. The Glasgow giants have since extended their tally to 115, most recently adding the League Cup and SPL title in 2011. The club's tally of seven domestic Trebles is also unequalled anywhere in the world.

*Kenny Miller of Rangers and Celtic's Mikael Lustig discuss the history of the Old Firm*

• Way back in 1898/99 Rangers enjoyed their best ever league season, winning all 18 of their matches to establish yet another world record.

• The club's record goalscorer is Rangers manager Ally McCoist. In a 15-year Ibrox career between 1983 and 1998 McCoist banged in an incredible 251 goals (355 in all competitions), including a record 28 hat-tricks. McCoist is also the club's most capped international, winning 59 of his 61 Scotland caps while with the Gers.

• Rangers also hold two important records in the Scottish League Cup, with more wins (27) and more appearances in the final (34) than any other club. The Gers' first win in the competition came in its inaugural year when they thrashed Aberdeen 4-0 in the final in 1947.

• The club's record in the Scottish Cup is not quite as impressive, the Gers' 33 triumphs in the competition being bettered by Celtic's 36. However, it was in the Scottish Cup that Rangers recorded their biggest ever victory, thrashing Blairgowrie 14-2 in 1934. Striker Jimmy Fleming scored nine of the goals on the day to set a club record.

• Despite all their domestic success, Rangers have only won a single European trophy. That was the Cup Winners' Cup, which they claimed in 1972 after beating Dynamo Moscow 3-2 in the final in Barcelona. The club, though, did reach the final of the same competition in both 1961 and 1967 and were also runners-up in the UEFA Cup in 2008, when an estimated 150,000 (mostly ticketless) Rangers fans followed their team to the final in Manchester.

• No player has turned out in the royal blue shirt of Rangers more often than former captain John Greig, who made 755 appearances in all competitions between 1961 and 1978. The league record, though, is held by Sandy Archibald (513 games between 1917 and 1934).

• A Scottish League record crowd of 118,567 saw Rangers play Celtic at Ibrox on 2nd January 1939. The home fans went home happy after the Gers beat their city rivals 2-1. In 2013, a year after being forced into liquidation and made to start from scratch in the bottom tier, Rangers attracted a crowd of 50,082 for their final Scottish Third Division match of the season against Berwick – a world record for a fourth-tier fixture.

• In the summer of 2015 Rangers appointed their first ever English manager, former Brentford boss Mark Warburton.

HONOURS
*Division 1 champions* 1891 (shared), 1899, 1900, 1901, 1902, 1911, 1912, 1913, 1918, 1920, 1921, 1923, 1924, 1925, 1927, 1928, 1929, 1930, 1931, 1933, 1934, 1935, 1937, 1939, 1947, 1949, 1950, 1953, 1956, 1957, 1959, 1961, 1963, 1964, 1975
*Premier League champions* 1976, 1978, 1987, 1989, 1990, 1991, 1992, 1993, 1994, 1995, 1996, 1997
*SPL champions* 1999, 2000, 2003, 2005, 2009, 2010, 2011
*League One champions* 2014
*Third Division champions* 2013
*Scottish Cup* 1894, 1897, 1898, 1903, 1928, 1930, 1932, 1934, 1935, 1936, 1948, 1949, 1950, 1953, 1960, 1962, 1963, 1964, 1966, 1973, 1976, 1978, 1979, 1981, 1992, 1993, 1996, 1999, 2000, 2002, 2003, 2008, 2009
*Scottish League Cup 1*947, 1949, 1961, 1962, 1964, 1965, 1971, 1976, 1978, 1979, 1982, 1984, 1985, 1987, 1988, 1989, 1991, 1993, 1994, 1997, 1999, 2002, 2003, 2005, 2008, 2010, 2011
*European Cup Winners' Cup* 1972

# READING

**Year founded:** 1871
**Ground:** Madejski Stadium (24,161)
**Nickname:** The Royals
**Biggest win:** 10-2 v Crystal Palace (1946)
**Heaviest defeat:** 0-18 v Preston (1894)

Reading were founded in 1871, making them the oldest Football League club south of Nottingham. After amalgamating with local clubs Reading Hornets (in 1877) and Earley FC (in 1889), the club was eventually elected to the new Third Division in 1920.

• The oldest club still competing in the FA Cup never to have won the trophy, Reading have got as far as the semi-finals just twice, losing to Cardiff City in 1927 and Arsenal in 2015.

*Real Madrid – ten times winners of the European Cup/ Champions League*

• In the 1985/86 season Reading set a Football League record by winning their opening 13 matches, an outstanding start which provided the launch pad for the Royals to go on to top the old Third Division at the end of the campaign.

• **Reading's greatest moment, though, came in 2006 when, under manager Steve Coppell, they won promotion to the top flight for the first time in their history. They went up in fine style, too, claiming the Championship title with a Football League record 106 points and going 33 matches unbeaten (a record for the second tier) between 9th August 2005 and 17th February 2006.**

• Prolific marksman Ronnie Blackman holds two scoring records for the club, with a total of 158 goals between 1947 and 1954 and a seasonal best of 39 goals in the 1951/52 campaign.

• **During the 1978/79 season Reading goalkeeper Steve Death went 1,074 minutes without conceding a goal – a Football League record until 2009,**

when Manchester United's Edwin van der Sar beat it.

• Reading smashed their transfer record in 2007 when they bought Emerse Fae from Nantes for £2.5 million. Unfortunately, the Ivory Coast international contracted malaria while away on Africa Cup of Nations duty and started just six games for the Royals.

• **In 2007 Reading were involved in the Premier League's highest scoring match, losing 7-4 away to Portsmouth. Five years later they were on the losing side again in the joint-highest scoring League Cup match, going down 7-5 at home to Arsenal.**

HONOURS

*Championship champions* 2006, 2012

*Division 3 (S) champions* 1926

*Division 3 champions* 1986

*Second Division champions* 1994

*Division 4 champions* 1979

## REAL MADRID

**Year founded:** 1902
**Ground:** Estadio Bernabeu (81,044)
**Previous name:** Madrid
**Nickname:** Los Meringues
**League titles:** 32
**Domestic cups:** 18
**European cups:** 14
**International cups:** 4

Founded by students as Madrid FC in 1902, the title 'Real' (meaning 'Royal') was bestowed on the club by King Alfonso XIII in 1920.

• **One of the most famous names in world football, Real Madrid won the first ever European Cup in 1956 and went on to a claim a record five consecutive victories in the competition with a side featuring greats such as Alfredo di Stefano,**

Ferenc Puskas and Francisco Gento. Real's total of 10 victories in the European Cup/Champions League – their last success coming in 2014 after they beat city rivals Atletico Madrid in the final in Lisbon – is also a record.

• The club have dominated Spanish football over the years, winning a record 32 league titles (nine more than nearest rivals Barcelona) including a record five on the trot on two occasions (1961-65 and 1986-90).

• Real Madrid have broken the world transfer record on the last five occasions, splashing out eye-watering sums on Portuguese star Luis Figo (£37 million from Barcelona in 2000), French midfielder Zinedine Zidane (£46 million from Juventus in 2001), Brazilian playmaker Kaka (£56 million from AC Milan in 2009), Cristiano Ronaldo (£80 million from Manchester United in 2009) and Gareth Bale (£86 million from Tottenham in 2013).

• During the 2014/15 season Real won a Spanish record 22 consecutive matches in all competitions.

> HONOURS
> *Spanish League* 1932, 1933, 1954, 1955, 1957, 1958, 1961, 1962, 1963, 1964, 1965, 1967, 1968, 1969, 1972, 1975, 1976, 1978, 1979, 1980, 1986, 1987, 1988, 1989, 1990, 1995, 1997, 2001, 2003, 2007, 2008, 2012
> *Spanish Cup* 1905, 1906, 1907, 1908, 1917, 1934, 1936, 1946, 1947, 1962, 1970, 1974, 1975, 1980, 1982, 1989, 1993, 2011
> *European Cup/Champions League* 1956, 1957, 1958, 1959, 1960, 1966, 1998, 2000, 2002, 2014
> *UEFA Cup* 1985, 1986
> *European Super Cup* 2002, 2014
> *Intercontinental Cup/Club World Cup* 1960, 1998, 2002, 2014

## REFEREES

In the 19th century Colonel Francis Marinden was the referee at a record nine FA Cup finals, including eight on the trot between 1883 and 1990. His record will never be beaten as the FA now appoints a different referee for the FA Cup final every year.

• The first referee to send off a player in the FA Cup final was Peter Willis, who dismissed Manchester United defender Kevin Moran in the 1985 final for a foul on Everton's Peter Reid. Video replays showed that it was a harsh decision.

• Michael Oliver became the youngest Premier League referee ever when he took charge of the Birmingham City-Blackburn Rovers fixture on 21st August 2010, aged 25 and 182 days.

• **On 9th February 2010 Amy Fearn became the first woman to referee a Football League match when she took charge of the last 20 minutes of Coventry's home game with Nottingham Forest after the original ref, Tony Bates, limped off with a calf injury.**

• English referees have taken charge of the World Cup final on a record four occasions: George Reader (1950), William Ling (1954), Jack Taylor (1974) and Howard Webb (2010).

• **In a Premier League career which began in 2000 Mike Dean has issued a record 1,338 yellow cards.**

## RELEGATION

Birmingham City boast the unwanted record of having been relegated from the top flight more often than any other club, having taken the drop 12 times – most recently in 2010/11. However, the Blues have not experienced that sinking feeling as often as Notts County, who have suffered 16 relegations in total. Meanwhile, Bristol City were the first club to suffer three consecutive relegations, dropping from Division One to Division Four between 1979/80 and 1981/82.

• **In the Premier League era Crystal Palace have been the most unfortunate club, dropping out of the top flight on no fewer than four occasions. In 1993 they were desperately unlucky to go down with a record 49 points, a tally matched by Norwich in 1985 in the old First Division. Southend in 1988/89 and Peterborough in 2012/13 were even more unfortunate, being relegated from the old Third Division and the Championship respectively despite amassing 54 points.**

• Nathan Blake and Hermann Hreidarsson share the unwanted record of having each been relegated from the Premier League an incredible five times during their careers.

• **When Derby County went down from the Premier League in 2008, they did so with the lowest points total of any club in the history of the English league football. The Rams accumulated only 11 points in a miserable campaign, during which they managed to win just one match out of 38.**

*'Now go and stand in the corner... you've been a very naughty boy!'*

142

• Dave Bassett is the only manager to have been relegated three times from the Premier League, suffering the drop with Sheffield United (1994), Nottingham Forest (1997) and Leicester City (2001).

## REPLAYS

In the days before penalty shoot-outs, the FA Cup fourth qualifying round tie between Alvechurch and Oxford City went to a record five replays before Alvechurch reached the first round proper with a 1-0 win in the sixth match between the two clubs.

**• The first FA Cup final to go to a replay was the 1875 match between Royal Engineers and Old Etonians, Engineers winning 2-0 in the second match. The last FA Cup final to require a replay was the 1993 match between Arsenal and Sheffield Wednesday, the Gunners triumphing 2-1 in the second game. In 1999 the FA scrapped final replays, ruling that any drawn match would be settled on the day by penalties.**

• In 1912 Barnsley required a record six replays in total before getting their hands on the FA Cup. Fulham also played six replays in their run to the FA Cup final in 1975, but the extra games appeared to have taken their toll as they lost limply 2-0 to West Ham at Wembley.

**• The only European Cup final to be replayed was in 1974 between Bayern Munich and Atletico Madrid. After a 1-1 draw in Brussels, the Germans easily won the replay 4-0.**

*Ireland and Scotland battle it out in a Euro 2016 qualifier*

## REPUBLIC OF IRELAND

**First international:** Republic of Ireland 1 Bulgaria 0, 1924
**Most capped player:** Robbie Keane, 140 caps (1998- )
**Leading goalscorer:** Robbie Keane, 65 goals (1998- )
**First WorldCup appearance:** Republic of Ireland 1 England 1, 1990
**Biggest win:** 8-0 v Malta (1983)
**Heaviest defeat:** 0-7 v Brazil (1982)

The Republic of Ireland enjoyed their most successful period under English manager Jack Charlton in the late 1980s and early 1990s. 'Big Jack' became a legend on the Emerald Isle after guiding the Republic to their first ever World Cup in 1990, taking the team to the quarter-finals of the tournament – despite not winning a single match – before they were eliminated by hosts Italy.

**• Ireland have a tremendous recent record against England, and following a 0-0 draw in Dublin with Roy Hodgson's men in June 2015 are undefeated in six of these derbies dating back to their last defeat in 1985. Indeed, the Republic were the first country from outside the United Kingdom to beat England on home soil, winning 2-0 at Goodison Park in 1949.**

• The Republic have qualified for the European Championships on two occasions, but failed to advance from their group in both 1988 and 2012.

**• In 2009, in a World Cup play-off against France, the Republic were on the wrong end of one of the worst refereeing decisions of all time when Thierry Henry's blatant handball went unpunished before he crossed for William Gallas to score the goal that ended Ireland's hopes of reaching the 2010 finals in South Africa.**

• Republic of Ireland striker Robbie Keane has won more caps (140) and scored more international goals (65) than any other player from the British Isles.

| World Cup Record | |
| --- | --- |
| 1930 | Did not enter |
| 1934 | Did not qualify |
| 1938 | Did not qualify |
| 1950 | Did not enter |
| 1954-86 | Did not qualify |
| 1990 | Quarter-finals |
| 1994 | Round 2 |
| 1998 | Did not qualify |
| 2002 | Round 2 |
| 2006 | Did not qualify |
| 2010 | Did not qualify |
| 2014 | Did not qualify |

# FRANCK RIBERY

**Born:** Boulogne-sur-Mer, France, 7th April 1983
**Position:** Winger
**Club career:**
2000-02 Boulogne 28 (6)
2002-03 Ales 19 (1)
2003-04 Stade Brestois 35 (3)
2004-05 Metz 20 (1)
2005 Galatasaray 14 (0)
2005-07 Marseille 60 (11)
2007- Bayern Munich 193 (68)
**International record:**
2006-14 France 81 (16)

Tricky Bayern Munich winger Franck Ribery is the only player to have been voted French Player of the Year and German Footballer of the Year in the same season, winning both awards in 2008.

• After playing for a number of lesser French clubs and Galatasaray, with whom he won the Turkish cup in 2005, Ribery rose to prominence with Marseille. Following a fine season in 2006/07, when he was voted French Player of the Year for the first time, he moved on to Bayern in a £20 million deal.

• Ribery, whose scarred face is the result of a serious car accident when he was just two years old, enjoyed his best season with the German giants in 2012/13 when he helped Bayern win the domestic double and the Champions League, after a 2-1 defeat of Borussia Dortmund in the final at Wembley.

• Once described by the legendary Zinedine Zidane as "the jewel of French football", Ribery made his debut for France just before the 2006 World Cup. He played exceptionally well at the tournament, helping Les Bleus reach the final where they lost on penalties to Italy. However, he fared less well at the 2010 World Cup, being one of five players suspended by the French FA after boycotting a training session in support of expelled team-mate Nicolas Anelka, and after missing the 2014 tournament through injury he retired from international football.

# ARJEN ROBBEN

**Born:** Bedum, Netherlands, 23rd June 1984
**Position:** Winger
**Club career:**
2000-02 Groningen 50 (8)
2002-04- PSV 56 (17)
2004-07 Chelsea 67 (15)
2007-09 Real Madrid 50 (11)
2009- Bayern Munich 127 (73)
**International record:**
2003- Netherlands 86 (28)

Flying winger Arjen Robben is one of a handful of players to have won the domestic league title with four clubs in four different countries, having finished top of the pile with PSV (2003), Chelsea (2005 and 2006), Real Madrid (2008) and Bayern Munich (2010, 2013, 2014 and 2015).

• After starting out with Groningen, Robben made his name with PSV, with whom he was named Dutch Young Player of the Year in 2003. The following year he joined Chelsea where, despite suffering a number of injuries and a testicular cancer scare during his three years in London, he enjoyed huge success, collecting five winners' medals before departing for Real Madrid in 2007 for £24 million.

• After two years he was on the move

## IS THAT A FACT?

When Arjen Robben banged in two goals against Paderborn in a 6-0 Bayern Munich victory in February 2015 it meant the Dutchman had scored against every Bundesliga club he had faced.

'Badman' and Robben – superheroes of the Bundesliga!

again, to Bayern Munich, where he won the domestic double in his first season and was also voted Player of the Year in Germany – the first Dutchman to receive the honour. Robben, though, was denied a treble when Bayern were beaten in the final of the Champions League by Inter Milan. Two years later, in 2012, he suffered more heartbreak in the same tournament when Bayern were beaten by Chelsea in the final in Munich, but the following year he finally got his hands on the trophy when he scored a last-minute winner against Borussia Dortmund in the final at Wembley.

• The pacy wideman has also experienced much disappointment at international level, being part of the Netherlands team that lost in the 2010 World Cup final to Spain. Four years later he starred in his country's 5-1 hammering of world champions Spain at the World Cup in Brazil, but he was denied another chance to win the trophy when Argentina beat the Netherlands in the semi-final.

## ROCHDALE

**Year founded:** 1907
**Ground:** Spotland Stadium (10,249)
**Nickname:** The Dale
**Biggest win:** 8-1 v Chesterfield (1926)
**Heaviest defeat:** 1-9 v Tranmere Rovers (1931)

Founded at a meeting at the town's Central Council Office in 1907, Rochdale were elected to the Third Division (North) as founder members in 1921.

• In their long history, Rochdale have gained promotion just three times, most recently to League One in 2014. Long years spent in the bottom tier mean that the Dale have the lowest average position, 76th, of any club since the expansion of the Football League to four divisions in 1921.

• The proudest day in the club's history came in 1962 when they reached the League Cup final. Rochdale lost 4-0 on aggregate to Norwich City, then in the Second Division, but took pride in becoming the first team from the

bottom tier to reach a major cup final. The Dale's manager at the time was Tony Collins, the first ever black boss of a league club.

• Rochdale failed to win a single game in the FA Cup for 18 years from 1927 – the longest period of time any club has gone without victory in the competition. The appalling run finally came to an end in 1945 when the Dale beat Stockport 2-1 in a first-round replay.

• The Dale's coffers received a record £900,000 when midfielder Bobby Grant moved on to Blackpool in 2013.

## BRENDAN RODGERS

**Born:** Carnlough, 26th January 1973
**Managerial career:**
2008-09 Watford
2009 Reading
2010-12 Swansea City
2012- Liverpool

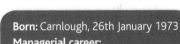

Appointed manager of Liverpool in June 2012 after just one season in the Premier League with Swansea City, Brendan Rodgers enjoyed a superb campaign with the Reds in 2013/14, leading them to second place in the league and qualification for the Champions League for the first time in five years. His achievements saw him awarded the LMA Manager of the Year award, the first Liverpool boss to win this honour. However, after a disappointing season in 2014/15 doubts were raised about his long-term future at Anfield.

• After injury forced him to retire aged just 20, Rodgers began his coaching career at Reading, where he was youth team manager. He moved to Chelsea to take a similar role at Stamford Bridge in 2006.

• He became Watford manager in 2008 but left after a season to return to Reading. However, after a disappointing run of results, he was sacked by chairman John Madejski in December 2009.

• Rodgers' fortunes turned around at Swansea, who he joined in 2010 and led into the Premier League the following year after a play-off final victory against Reading.

'Tea, tea... will someone please make me a cup of tea!'

## JAMES RODRIGUEZ

**Born:** Cucuta, Colombia, 12th July 1991
**Position:** Midfielder
**Club career:**
2007-08 Envigado 30 (9)
2008-10 Banfield 42 (5)
2010-13 Porto 63 (25)
2013-14 Monaco 34 (9)
2014- Real Madrid 29 (13)
**International record:**
2011- Colombia 37 (12)

A talented playmaker who is also a prolific goalscorer, James Rodriguez became the fourth most expensive footballer in the world when he moved from Monaco to Real Madrid for £63 million in July 2014.

• **Rodriguez was rated one of the hottest properties in the global game after he enjoyed a sensational 2014 World Cup in Brazil. Not only did he win the Golden Boot with six goals for Colombia, but he also picked up three FIFA Man of the Match awards and was voted into the tournament Dream Team by members of FIFA.com. His briliant left-footed volley against Uruguay in the first knock-out round was voted the goal of the tournament and also won the 2014 Puskas award for the best goal of the entire year.**

• After starting his career with Envigado in Colombia, Rodriguez soon moved on to Banfield where he became the youngest ever overseas player to score in the Argentinian league. His huge potential attracted the attention of Porto, who signed him in 2010. In just three years with the Portuguese giants Rodriguez won three league titles, the Europa League and the Portuguese Cup. In the last of these competitions, Rodriguez became the first player for 30 years to score a hat-trick in the final when he notched a treble in Porto's 6-2 hammering of Vitoria Guimaraes in 2011. The following year he was voted Portuguese Player of the Season.

• **In 2013 Rodriguez moved on to Monaco for around £37 million, making him the second most expensive player ever (behind former Porto team-mate Hulk) in Portuguese football. In his one season in France**

Rodriguez topped the assists list and was voted into the Ligue 1 XI.
• Despite an injury-hit first season in Madrid, Rodriguez still chipped in with 13 league goals as Real finished second behind Barcelona.

## CRISTIANO RONALDO

**Born:** Madeira, Portugal, 5th February 1985
**Position:** Winger/Striker
**Club career:**
2001-03 Sporting Lisbon 25 (3)
2003-09 Manchester United 196 (84)
2009- Real Madrid 200 (225)
**International record:**
2003- Portugal 120 (55)

Cristiano Ronaldo is the all-time leading scorer in the Champions League with a total of 78 goals for Manchester United and Real Madrid. In 2013/14 he hit a record 17 goals in the competition, including one in the final as Real won a record tenth title with victory over Atletico Madrid in Lisbon.

• **Born on the Portuguese island of Madeira, Ronaldo began his career with Sporting Lisbon before joining Manchester United in a £12.25 million deal in 2003. The following year he won his first trophy with the Red Devils, opening the scoring as United beat Millwall 3-0 in the FA Cup final. He later helped United win a host of major honours, including three Premiership titles and the Champions League in 2008 before signing for Real for a then world record £80 million in 2009.**

• In 2007 Ronaldo was voted PFA Player of the Year and Young Player of the Year, the first man to achieve this double since Andy Gray in 1977. The following

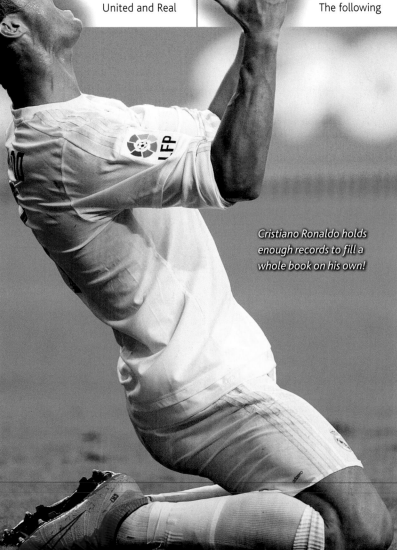

*Cristiano Ronaldo holds enough records to fill a whole book on his own!*

season he scored a remarkable 42 goals for United in all competitions, and won the European Golden Boot. Three years later, in his second season with Real, he became the first player ever to win the award in two different countries.

• Ronaldo made his international debut for Portugal against Kazakhstan in 2003 and the following year played for his country in their surprise Euro 2004 final defeat by Greece. Captain of Portugal since 2008, Ronaldo is his country's all-time top scorer with 55 goals and the all-time leading scorer in the European Championships with a total of 26 goals at the finals and in qualifiers.

• Arguably the most exciting talent in world football today, Ronaldo is the only player from the Premier League to have been voted World Footballer of the Year, having collected this most prestigious of awards in 2008. After playing second fiddle for some years to his great rival

Lionel Messi, he was delighted to win the award again in both 2013 and 2014.

## WAYNE ROONEY

**Born:** Liverpool, 24th October 1985
**Position:** Striker
**Club career:**
2002-04 Everton 67 (15)
2004- Manchester United 340 (170)
**International record:**
2003- England 107 (50)

When Wayne Rooney scored against Switzerland in September 2015 he became England's all-time leading scorer with 50 goals, passing Bobby Charlton's longstanding previous record of 49.

• **Rooney burst onto the scene with Everton in 2002, scoring his first league goal for the Toffees with a magnificent 20-yarder against reigning champions Arsenal at**

*Wayne Rooney – England's record goalscorer*

Goodison Park just five days before his 17th birthday. At the time he was the youngest ever Premiership scorer, but his record has since been surpassed by both James Milner and James Vaughan.

• After starring for England at Euro 2004 Rooney signed for Manchester United later that summer for £25.6 million, to become the world's most expensive teenage footballer. He started his Old Trafford career in sensational style with a hat-trick against Fenerbahce and has since played a pivotal role for the Red Devils' over the last decade, winning five Premier League titles, two League Cups and the Champions League. His total of 230 goals for the club in all competitions is only bettered by legendary duo Bobby Charlton and Denis Law, while his total of 185 Premier League goals puts him third on the all-time list of scorers.

• **Rooney is the youngest ever England player to play 100 times for his country, reaching the landmark against Slovenia on 15th November 2014 aged 29 and 22 days. He marked the occasion with a goal from the penalty spot in a 3-1 Wembley win.**

• When Wayne Rooney scored his first goal for England, against Macedonia in a Euro 2004 qualifier on 6th September 2003, he was aged just 17 years and 317 days... the youngest player ever to find the net for the Three Lions.

## ROSS COUNTY

**Year founded:** 1929
**Ground:** Global Energy Stadium (6,541)
**Nickname:** The Staggies
**Biggest win:** 11-0 v St Cuthbert Wanderers (1993)
**Heaviest defeat:** 1-6 v Alloa (1968) and v Meadowbank (1991)

Founded in 1929, Ross County played in the Highland league until 1994 when they were elected to the Scottish Third Division along with Inverness Caledonian Thistle.

• **Ross County enjoyed the greatest day in their history in 2010 when they sensationally beat Celtic in the Scottish Cup semi-final. However, there was to be no fairytale ending**

for the Staggies as they went down 3-0 to Dundee United in the final at Hampden Park despite being backed by 17,000 passionate fans.

• Two years later the club won promotion to the SPL for the first time in their history after a glorious campaign which ended with them a record 24 points clear at the top of the Scottish First Division. The Staggies also put together an incredible 34-match unbeaten run, matching a record for the Scottish second tier set by Aidrieonians way back in 1955.

• With a capacity of just 6,541, Ross County's tiny Global Energy Stadium is the second smallest in the SPL.

HONOURS
*First Division champions* 2012
*Second Division champions* 2008
*Third Division champions* 1999

## ROTHERHAM UNITED

**Year founded:** 1925
**Ground:** New York Stadium (12,021)
**Nickname:** The Millers
**Biggest win:** 8-0 v Oldham Athletic (1947)
**Heaviest defeat:** 1-11 v Bradford City (1928)

The club had its origins in Thornhill FC (founded in 1878, later becoming Rotherham County) and Rotherham Town, who merged with County to form Rotherham United in 1925.

• The club's greatest moment came in 1961 when they reached the first ever League Cup final, losing 3-2 on aggregate to Aston Villa. Six years earlier Rotherham had missed out on goal average on promotion to the First Division for the first time in the club's history... the closest they've ever been to playing top-flight football.

• In 1991 Rotherham made history by becoming the first side to win a penalty shoot-out in the FA Cup, defeating Scunthorpe United 7-6 on spot-kicks after a first-round replay.

• Less happily, in 1925 Rotherham failed to keep a clean sheet in 45 consecutive league matches. The run was a record at the time, but Bristol

City extended it to 49 games seven years later.

• At the start of the 2012/13 season the club moved from the Don Valley Stadium in Sheffield to a brand-new ground in Rotherham, the 12,000-capacity New York Stadium. The move proved successful, as the Millers gained promotion from League Two at the end of the campaign and another promotion followed immediately as the Millers beat Leyton Orient on penalties in the 2014 League One play-off final.

• **The Millers received a record £750,000 when they sold winger Kieran Agard to Bristol City in August 2014. In the same month, the Yorkshire side made their record purchase, splashing out £400,000 on Oldham striker Jonson Clarke-Harris.**

HONOURS
*Division 3 (N) champions* 1951
*Division 3 champions* 1981
*Division 4 champions* 1989
*Football League Trophy* 1996

## IAN RUSH

**Born:** St Asaph, 20th October 1961
**Position:** Striker
**Club career:**
1979-80 Chester City 34 (18)
1980-87 Liverpool 224 (139)
1987-88 Juventus 29 (8)
1988-96 Liverpool 245 (90)
1996-97 Leeds United 36 (3)
1997-98 Newcastle United 10 (2)
1998 Sheffield United (loan) 4 (0)
1998-99 Wrexham 18 (0)
1999 Sydney Olympic 2 (0)
**International record:**
1980-96 Wales 73 (28)

One of the most prolific strikers ever, Ian Rush is Liverpool's leading scorer of all time with a total of 346 goals for the club in two spells at Anfield in the 1980s and 1990s.

• **Rush has scored more goals in the FA Cup final than any other player, with a total of five for Liverpool in the 1986, 1989 and 1992 finals. His strikes helped the Reds win all three games, two of them against local rivals Everton. With 44 goals in the competition as a whole, Rush is the second highest scorer in the history of the tournament and the leading FA Cup marksman of the 20th century.**

*Legendary Liverpool goalscorer Ian Rush*

• 'Rushie', as he was known to fans, is also the joint leading scorer in the League Cup with Geoff Hurst, the pair both ending their careers on 49 goals. He enjoyed huge success in the tournament, winning the trophy in 1981, 1982, 1983, 1984 and 1995 to become the first player to collect five League Cup winners' medals.

• **Rush tops the scoring charts for his native Wales, with 28 goals in 73 appearances. However, he never played in the finals of either the World Cup or the European Championships.**

• Rush is the all-time leading scorer in the Merseyside derby with 25 goals against Everton, including a post-war record four goals in a 5-0 thrashing of the Toffees at Goodison Park on 6th November 1982.

• **In 1987 Rush moved from Liverpool to Juventus but had a hard time settling in Turin, telling one reporter, 'It's like living in a foreign country'. After just one season in Serie A he returned to Anfield for a then British record £2.7 million.**

• After hanging up his boots in 1999 Rush briefly became a manager, taking charge of Chester City in 2004. However, after less than a season with the League Two club he resigned after a poor run of results and he now works as a football pundit.

## SACKINGS

A record 10 managers were sacked during the 2013/14 Premier League season, including big names like David Moyes (Manchester United), Andre Villas-Boas (Tottenham) and Michael Laudrup (Swansea City). Fulham showed both Martin Jol and Rene Meulensteen the door, but the Cottagers were still relegated under their third manager of the season, Felix Magath. During the previous season a record 64 managers left their clubs in the four English divisions.

• **In 1959 Bill Lambton got the boot from Scunthorpe United after just three days in the managerial hotseat, an English league record. His reign at the Old Showground took in just one match – a 3-0 defeat at Liverpool in a Second Division fixture. The shortest Premier League reign, meanwhile, was Les Reed's seven-game stint at Charlton in 2006.**

• In May 2007 Leroy Rosenior was sacked as manager of Conference side Torquay United after just 10 minutes in charge! No sooner had the former West Ham and QPR striker been unveiled as the Gulls' new boss when he was told that the club had been bought by a business consortium and his services were no longer required.

• **Crystal Palace have sacked more managers since the Second World War than any other league club. The Eagles have made 47 different managerial appointments since 1945, most recently replacing Tony Pulis with Neil Warnock and then Alan Pardew in the 2014/15 season.**

• However, the Palace job is a model of security compared to being manager of Palermo. Since 2000 the Italian side have got through 32 different bosses!

## ST JOHNSTONE

**Year founded:** 1884
**Ground:** McDiarmid Park (10,696)
**Nickname:** The Saints
**Biggest win:** 13-0 v Tulloch (1887)
**Heaviest defeat:** 0-12 v Cowdenbeath (1928)

St Johnstone were founded in 1884 by a group of local cricketers in Perth who wanted to keep fit in winter.

• **The Saints enjoyed their best ever day in 2014, when they beat Dundee United 2-0 in the Scottish Cup final at Celtic Park. Previously, the club had appeared in two League Cup finals, but lost in 1969 to Celtic and again in 1998 to Rangers.**

• The Saints' record scorer is John Brogan, who hit 114 league goals for the club between 1976 and 1984. Stalwart goalkeeper Alan Main played in a record 361 games for St Johnstone in two spells at McDiarmid Park between 1995 and 2010.

• **Along with Falkirk, St Johnstone have won the Scottish second tier a record seven times, most recently claiming the First Division title in 2009 while going on a club record unbeaten run of 21 games.**

• The Saints have appeared five times in European competition, faring best in 1971 when they reached the last 16 of the UEFA Cup.

HONOURS
*Division 2 champions* 1924, 1960, 1963
*First Division champions* 1983, 1990, 1997, 2009
*Scottish Cup* 2014

## ALEXIS SANCHEZ

**Born:** Tocopilla, Chile, 19th December 1988
**Position:** Winger/striker
**Club career:**
2005-06 Cobreloa 47 (12)
2006-07 Colo-Colo 32 (5)
2007-08 River Plate 23 (4)
2008-11 Udinese 95 (20)
2011-14 Barcelona 88 (39)
2014- Arsenal 35 (16)
**International record:**
2006- Chile 86 (27)

Dynamic Chilean forward Alexis Sanchez became Arsenal's second highest ever signing when the Gunners splashed out £35 million to prise him away from Barcelona in the summer of 2014. In his first season with the north Londoners he notched a career-best 25 goals in all competitions, including a superb one in the FA Cup final against Aston Villa to become the first Chilean since 1952 to score in the final.

• **Sanchez made his name with Italian side Udinese, becoming the first Chilean ever to score four goals in a Serie A match when he filled his boots in a 7-0 thrashing of Palermo on 27th February 2011.**

*Alexis Sanchez's attempt to scare defenders by making faces at them appears to be working...*

• Later that year Sanchez moved on to Barcelona, with whom he won the Copa del Rey in 2012 and La Liga in 2013.

• Sanchez made his debut for Chile against New Zealand in 2006. He impressed at the 2014 World Cup, netting his country's first goal of the tournament against Australia and then scoring the equaliser against hosts Brazil in a last 16 tie which Chile eventually lost on penalties. The following year Sanchez starred in Chile's first ever Copa America triumph, scoring the winning penalty as the hosts beat Argentina on spot-kicks in the final.

## BASTIAN SCHWEINSTEIGER

**Born:** Kolbermoor, Germany, 1st August 1984
**Position:** Midfielder
**Club career:**
2002-04 Bayern Munich II 34 (2)
2002-15 Bayern Munich 342 (45)
2015- Manchester United
**International record:**
2004- Germany 111 (23)

The first German to play for Manchester United, Bastian Schweinsteiger joined the Red Devils in July 2015 from Bayern Munich – a club where he won an incredible eight Bundesliga titles, equalling the record of former Bayern players Mehmet Scholl and Oliver Kahn.

• A powerful player who can perform capably in either central midfield or on the wing, Schweinsteiger has had mixed fortunes in the Champions League. He was a runner-up in the competition with Bayern in 2010, but two years later it was his decisive penalty in the shoot-out against Real Madrid that took the Germans through to another final. Unfortunately, Schweinsteiger missed his spot-kick in the shoot-out against Chelsea and allowed Didier Drogba to clinch the trophy for the Londoners. The following year, though, he helped Bayern win the trophy after a 2-1 victory over fellow German outfit Borussia Dortmund in the final at Wembley.

• A talented all-round sportsman who could easily have become a professional ski racer if he had not chosen to concentrate on football, Schweinsteiger made his debut for Germany in 2004 and is now the fifth highest appearance maker for his country with 111 caps.

• Schweinsteiger starred for Germany at the 2014 World Cup in Brazil, his committed performances helping his country to win the trophy for a fourth time. He was handed the captain's armband after Phillip Lahm retired following the World Cup victory.

Manchester United's World Cup winner, Bastian Schweinsteiger

## TOP 10

### HIGHEST-CAPPED SCOTLAND PLAYERS

| | | |
|---|---|---|
| 1. | Kenny Dalglish (1971-86) | 102 |
| 2. | Jim Leighton (1982-98) | 91 |
| 3. | Alex McLeish (1980-93) | 77 |
| 4. | Paul McStay (1983-97) | 76 |
| 5. | Tom Boyd (1990-2001) | 72 |
| 6. | Kenny Miller (2001-13) | 69 |
| | David Weir (1997-2010) | 69 |
| 8. | Darren Fletcher (2003- ) | 68 |
| 9. | Christian Daily (1997-2008) | 67 |
| 10. | Willie Miller (1975-89) | 65 |

## SCOTLAND

**First international:** Scotland 0 England 0, 1872
**Most capped player:** Kenny Dalglish, 102 caps (1971-86)
**Leading goalscorer:** Denis Law (1958-74) and Kenny Dalglish (1971-86), 30 goals
**First World Cup appearance:** Scotland 0 Austria 1, 1954
**Biggest win:** Scotland 11 Ireland 0, 1901
**Heaviest defeat:** Scotland 0 Uruguay 7, 1954

Along with England, Scotland are the oldest international team in the world. The two countries played the first official international way back in 1872, the match at Hamilton Crescent, Partick, finishing 0-0. Since then, honours have been more or less even between the 'Auld Enemies', with England winning 47 matches, Scotland winning 41 and 20 ending in a draw.

• It took the Scots a while to make an impression on the world scene. After withdrawing from the 1950 World Cup, Scotland competed in the finals for the first time in 1954 but were eliminated in the first round after suffering their worst ever defeat, 7-0 to reigning champions Uruguay.

• Scotland have taken part in the World Cup finals on eight occasions but have never got beyond the group stage – a record for the tournament. They have been unlucky, though, going out in 1974, 1978 and 1982 only on goal difference.

• Scotland have a pretty poor record

in the European Championships, only qualifying for the finals on two occasions, in 1992 and 1996. Again, they failed to reach the knockout stage both times, although they were unfortunate to lose out on the 'goals scored' rule to Holland at Euro '96. More recently, the Scots made a brave attempt to qualify for Euro 2008 but were narrowly pipped by Italy and France despite

beating the French home and away.

• Scotland had a good record in the Home Championships until the tournament was scrapped in 1984, winning the competition 24 times and sharing the title another 17 times. Only England (34 outright wins and 20 shared) have a better overall record.

• Former Aberdeen and Manchester United goalkeeper Jim Leighton kept a record 40 clean

sheets for Scotland, while winning 91 caps between 1982 and 1998.

• Incredibly, when Steven Fletcher scored a treble in a 6-1 hammering of Gibraltar in March 2015 it was the first hat-trick by a Scotland player for 46 years.

| HONOURS |
| --- |
| **World Cup Record** |
| *1930-38 Did not enter* |
| *1950 Withdrew* |
| *1954 Round 1* |
| *1958 Round 1* |
| *1962-70 Did not qualify* |
| *1974 Round 1* |
| *1978 Round 1* |
| *1982 Round 1* |
| *1986 Round 1* |
| *1990 Round 1* |
| *1994 Did not qualify* |
| *1998 Round 1* |
| *2002 Did not qualify* |
| *2006 Did not qualify* |
| *2010 Did not qualify* |
| *2014 Did not qualify* |

## SCOTTISH CUP

The Scottish Cup was first played for in 1873/74, shortly after the formation of the Scottish FA. Queen's Park, who the previous year had competed in the English FA Cup, were the first winners, beating Clydesdale 2-0 in the final in front of a crowd of 3,000 at the original Hampden Park.

• **Queen's Park were the dominant force in the early years of the competition, winning 10 of the first 20 finals, including one in 1884 when their opponents, Vale of Leven, failed**

*Scotland's Steven Fletcher celebrates scoring for his country*

*Inverness Caledonian Thistle lift the Scottish Cup in 2015*

# SCUNTHORPE UNITED

to turn up! Since then, Celtic (36 wins) and Rangers (33 wins) have ruled the roost, although Queen's Park (10 wins) remain third in the list of all-time winners ahead of Hearts (eight wins).

• In 1990 the final was decided on penalties for the first time, Aberdeen beating Celtic 9-8 after a 0-0 draw.

• Incredibly, the biggest ever victories in the history of British football took place in the Scottish Cup on the same day, 12th September 1885. Dundee Harp beat Aberdeen Rovers 35-0 and were confident that they had set a new record. Yet, no doubt to their utter amazement, they soon discovered that Arbroath had thrashed Bon Accord, a cricket club who had been invited to take part in the competition by mistake, 36-0!

• Famous shocks in the Scottish Cup include little Berwick Rangers beating Rangers 1-0 in 1967 and Inverness Caledonian Thistle humbling Celtic 3-1 in 2000.

## SCUNTHORPE UNITED

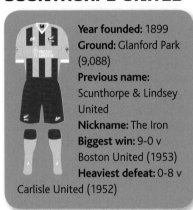

**Year founded:** 1899
**Ground:** Glanford Park (9,088)
**Previous name:** Scunthorpe & Lindsey United
**Nickname:** The Iron
**Biggest win:** 9-0 v Boston United (1953)
**Heaviest defeat:** 0-8 v Carlisle United (1952)

The club was founded in 1899 when Brumby Hall linked up with some other local teams. Between 1910 and 1958 they were known as Scunthorpe and Lindsey United after amalgamating with the latter team.

• Elected to the Third Division (North) when the league expanded in 1950, Scunthorpe won the division eight years later. Their only other honour came in 2007 when the Iron were crowned League One champions under former physio Nigel Adkins. Scunny fans celebrated that triumph by singing, "Who needs Mourinho, we've got our physio!"

• Among the famous names to play for Scunthorpe are England and Liverpool legends Kevin Keegan and Ray Clemence and, somewhat bizarrely, former England cricket captain Ian Botham, who made 11 appearances as a centre-half for Scunthorpe in the early 1980s.

• In two spells at Scunthorpe between 1979 and 1987, Steve Cammack scored a club record 110 goals for the Iron. Defender Jack Brownsword made a record 597 appearances for the club between 1947 and 1965.

• In 1988 Scunthorpe became the first club in the modern era to move to a new purpose-built stadium when they left their former ground, the Old Showground, for Glanford Park.

HONOURS
*Division 3 (North) champions* 1958
*League One champions* 2007

## ALAN SHEARER

**Born:** Newcastle, 13th August 1970
**Position:** Striker
**Club career:**
1988-92 Southampton 118 (23)
1992-96 Blackburn Rovers 138 (112)
1996-2006 Newcastle United 303 (148)
**International record:**
1992-2000 England 63 (30)

Alan Shearer's incredible total of 260 Premiership goals (including a record 11 hat-tricks) for Blackburn and Newcastle is easily a record for the league, none of his rivals having passed the double-century mark. No fewer than 20 of his goals came against Leeds United, a Premier League record for one player against the same opponents.

• Shearer began his career with Southampton, marking his full debut for the Saints in 1988 by scoring three goals in a 4-2 victory over Arsenal. Aged just 17 years and 240 days, he was the youngest ever player to score a top-flight hat-trick.

• In 1992 Shearer moved to Blackburn for a then British record £3.3 million. He helped Rovers win the Premiership title in 1994/95, his impressive tally of 34 goals that campaign earning him one of his three Golden Boots.

• A then world record £15 million move to Newcastle followed in 1996, to the delight of the Geordie faithful. An instant hit at St James' Park, Shearer eventually became the club's all-time record goalscorer, his total of 206 goals in all competitions for the Magpies

eclipsing the 49-year-old record of another Toon legend, Jackie Milburn.

• Strong, good in the air and possessing a powerful shot with both feet, Shearer proved a real handful for international defences, too. His five goals at Euro '96 powered England to the semi-finals of the tournament and won him the competition's Golden Boot. By the time he quit international football after Euro 2000 he had scored 30 goals for his country, a figure only surpassed by five other England players.

• Shearer became a pundit for the BBC after hanging up his boots in 2006, but three years later he sensationally returned to his beloved St James' Park as Newcastle caretaker manager. However, in his eight matches in charge he was unable to prevent the Geordies from dropping out of the Premier League for the first time.

## SHEFFIELD UNITED

**Year founded:** 1889
**Ground:** Bramall Lane (32,704)
**Nickname:** The Blades
**Biggest win:** 10-0 v Port Vale (1892) and v Burnley (1929)
**Heaviest defeat:** 0-13 v Bolton (1890)

The club was founded at a meeting at the city's Adelphi Hotel in 1899 by the members of the Sheffield United Cricket Club, partly to make greater use of the facilities at Bramall Lane.

• The Blades enjoyed their heyday in the late Victorian era, winning the title in 1898, and lifting the FA Cup in both 1899 and 1902. The club won the FA Cup again in 1915, in what was to be the last final to be played before the First World War brought a halt to the sporting calendar. They chalked up another victory in 1925.

• The club's leading scorer is Harry Johnson, who bagged 201 league goals between 1919 and 1930. His successor at centre-forward, Jimmy Dunne, scored a record 41 goals in the 1930/31 season, the most goals ever by an Irishman in the top flight.

• The Blades' home, Bramall Lane, is one of the oldest sporting arenas in the world. It first hosted cricket in

1855, before football was introduced to the ground in 1862. Sixteen years later, in 1878, the world's first ever floodlit match was played at the stadium between two sides picked from the Sheffield Football Association, the lights being provided by two generators.

• During an 18-year career with the club between 1948 and 1966, Joe Shaw made a record 631 appearances for the Blades.

• **Sheffield United hold the record for the most number of points, 90 in 2011/12, for a team failing to win promotion from the third tier.**

• To the dismay of their fans, United have appeared in four play-off finals and lost them all – a miserable record unmatched by any other club. The Blades had another disappointing day at Wembley in 2014 when they lost 5-3 to Hull City in the FA Cup semi-final – only the third time that a semi-final has produced eight goals.

> **HONOURS**
> *Division 1 champions* 1898
> *Division 2 champions* 1953
> *Division 4 champions* 1982
> *FA Cup* 1899, 1902, 1915, 1925

## SHEFFIELD WEDNESDAY

> **Year founded:** 1867
> **Ground:** Hillsborough (39,732)
> **Previous name:** The Wednesday
> **Nickname:** The Owls
> **Biggest win:** 12-0 v Halliwell (1891)
> **Heaviest defeat:** 0-10 v Aston Villa (1912)

The club was formed as The Wednesday in 1867 at the Adelphi Hotel in Sheffield by members of the Wednesday Cricket Club, who originally met on that particular day of the week. In 1929 the club added 'Sheffield' to their name, but are still often referred to simply as 'Wednesday'.

• **In 1904 the Owls became the first club in the 20th century to win consecutive league championships. They did so again in 1929/30, but have not won the league since.**

• In 1935 Wednesday won the FA Cup for the third and last time, striker Ellis Rimmer scoring in every round of the competition.

• **The Owls splashed out a club record**

£5.7 million on Celtic striker Paolo di Canio in 1997. They must have wondered whether they hadn't made a terrible mistake when the volatile Italian pushed over referee Paul Alcock during a match against Arsenal the following year – an action which earned him an 11-match ban.

• Andrew Wilson holds two significant records for the club. Between 1900 and 1920 he played in 501 league matches, scoring 199 goals. No Wednesday player, before or since, can match these figures.

• **In 1991, while residing in the old Second Division, the Owls won the League Cup for the first and only time in their history, beating Manchester United 1-0 at Wembley. It was the last time that a club from outside the top flight has lifted a major domestic cup.**

• On the opening day of the 2000/01 season Wednesday goalkeeper Kevin Pressman was sent off after just 13 seconds at Molineux for handling a Wolves shot outside the penalty area... the fastest dismissal ever in British football.

> **HONOURS**
> *Division 1 champions* 1903, 1904, 1929, 1930
> *Division 2 champions* 1900, 1926, 1952, 1956, 1959
> *FA Cup* 1896, 1907, 1935
> *League Cup* 1991

## PETER SHILTON

> **Born:** Leicester, 18th September 1949
> **Position:** Goalkeeper
> **Club career:**
> 1966-75 Leicester City 286 (1)
> 1975-78 Stoke City 110
> 1978-82 Nottingham Forest 202
> 1982-87 Southampton 188
> 1987-92 Derby County 175
> 1995-96 Bolton Wanderers 1
> 1997 Leyton Orient 9
> **International record:**
> 1970-90 England 125

Peter Shilton is the only player in the history of English football to have played 1,000 league games. He reached the landmark, aged 47, while keeping a clean sheet for Leyton Orient in their 2-0 win over Brighton on 22nd December 1996.

• **Shilton is England's highest capped player with 125 appearances to his name. In his 20-year international career he played at three World**

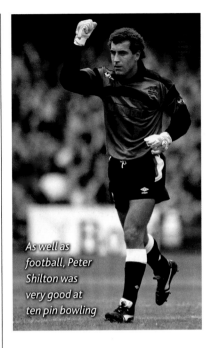

As well as football, Peter Shilton was very good at ten pin bowling

Cups, where he kept 10 clean sheets – a goalkeeping record shared with France's Fabien Barthez.

• A losing FA Cup finalist with Leicester City in 1969 at the age of 19, Shilton had to wait almost 10 years before he collected his first honour, the league championship with Nottingham Forest in 1978. He went on to win two European Cups with Forest before moving on to Southampton in 1982.

• **Shilton is the last goalkeeper to be voted PFA Player of the Year, collecting the award in 1978. The only other keeper to be so honoured was Tottenham's Pat Jennings, two years earlier.**

## SHREWSBURY TOWN

> **Year founded:** 1886
> **Ground:** New Meadow (9,875)
> **Nickname:** The Shrews
> **Biggest win:** 11-2 v Marine (1995)
> **Heaviest defeat:** 1-8 v Norwich City (1952) and v Coventry City (1963)

Founded at the Lion Hotel in Shrewsbury in 1886, the club played in regional football for many years until being elected to the Football League in 1950.

• **Prolific striker Arthur Rowley is the club's record scorer, hitting 152 goals between 1958 and 1965 to complete his all-time league record**

of 434 goals (he also turned out for West Bromwich Albion, Fulham and Leicester City). His best season for the Shrews was in 1958/59 when he banged in a club best 38 goals.

• 'Sir' Mickey Brown is the club's leading appearance maker, playing in 418 league games in three spells at the club between 1986 and 2001. He was 'knighted' by the fans after scoring the winning goal against Exeter on the last day of the 1999/2000 season, thus preserving the club's league status and sending down local rivals Chester City instead.

• **After beating mighty Everton in the quarter-finals of the League Cup in 1961, Shrewsbury came close to reaching the final of the competition but were beaten 4-3 on aggregate by Rotherham in the last four. The Shrews have never made it to a semi-final since.**

• Promoted to League One in 2015, Shrewsbury have won the Welsh Cup six times – a record for an English club.

> HONOURS
> **Division 3 champions** *1979*
> **Third Division champions** *1994*
> **Welsh Cup** *1891, 1938, 1977, 1979, 1984, 1985*

## DAVID SILVA

**Born:** Las Palmas, Spain, 8th January 1986
**Position:** Winger
**Club career:**
2003-04 Valencia B 14 (1)
2004-10 Valencia 119 (21)
2004-05 Eibar (loan) 35 (5)
2005-06 Celta (loan) 34 (4)
2010- Manchester City 161 (33)
**International record:**
2006- Spain 91 (23)

A tricky winger who can wriggle out of the tightest of situations, David Silva is the only Spanish player to have won the Premier League twice after helping his club Manchester City top the table in both 2012 and 2014.

• **Prior to moving to the Etihad stadium, Silva was a key player in the Valencia side that regularly managed** to upset Real Madrid and Barcelona. His best moment with the Spanish side came in 2008, when Valencia won the Copa del Rey after beating Getafe 3-1 in the final.

• In 2010 Silva joined City for £24 million and in his first season in Manchester helped the Sky Blues win their first trophy for 35 years when they beat Stoke City 1-0 in the FA Cup final at Wembley. His most prolific campaign with City was in 2014/15 when he scored 12 goals in the Premier League to help his team finish second behind champions Chelsea.

• **First capped by his country in 2006, Silva was an integral figure in the Spain side that won Euro 2008, but was restricted to just two appearances as the Spanish became world champions in South Africa two years later. However, he returned to the starting line-up at Euro 2012, heading the first goal in Spain's 4-0 thrashing of Italy in the final.**

## SIZE

The heaviest player in the history of the professional game was Willie 'Fatty' Foulke, who played in goal for Sheffield United, Chelsea and Bradford City. By the end of his career, the tubby custodian weighed in at an incredible 24 stone.

• **At just five feet tall, Fred Le May is the shortest player ever to have appeared in the Football League. He** played for Thames, Clapton Orient and Watford between 1930 and 1933. The shortest England international ever was Frederick 'Fanny' Walden, a five feet two inch winger with Tottenham who won the first of two caps in 1914.

• No prizes for guessing who the tallest ever England international is. It is, of course, giraffe-like striker Peter Crouch, who stands six feet seven inches in his socks. Crouch, though, is a full an inch shorter than Sunderland goalkeeper Costel Pantilimon, who claims the record as the tallest ever Premier League player.

• **Kristof van Hout, a goalkeeper with Indian Super League side Delhi Dynamos, is the tallest player in the world at six foot, ten inches.**

> ### IS THAT A FACT?
> Sixteen-stone AFC Wimbledon striker Adebayo Akinfenwa has been ranked as the strongest footballer in the world in various editions of the FIFA videogame series.

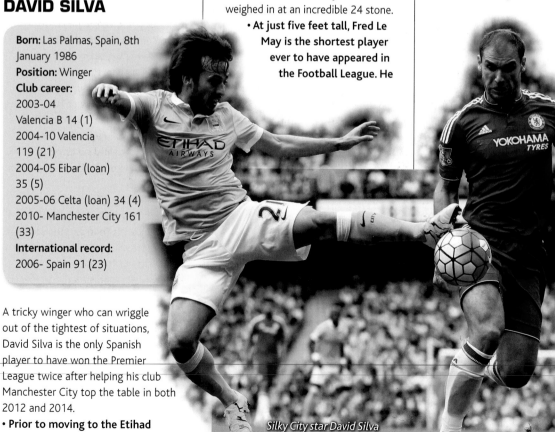

*Silky City star David Silva gets the ball under control*

# MARTIN SKRTEL

**Born:** Handlova, Slovakia, 15th
December 1984
**Position:** Defender
**Club career:**
2001-04 Trencin 44 (8)
2004-08 Zenit St Petersburg 74 (3)
2008- Liverpool 220 (15)
**International record:**
2004- Slovakia 73 (5)

Heavily tattooed Liverpool stopper
Martin Skrtel has been voted Slovak
Footballer of the Year on four occasions, a
record only matched by Napoli playmaker
Marek Hamsik.

• **An aggressive and combative centre-
back who is especially strong in the
air, Skrtel started out with FC Trencin
in Slovakia before moving to Zenit**

St Petersburg in 2004. He won the
**Russian league with Zenit in 2007, a
year before he joined Liverpool for £6.5
million.**

• Skrtel won the League Cup with
Liverpool in 2012, scoring in the final
against Cardiff at Wembley in normal time
before the match was eventually settled
on penalties. The following season was a
poor one for Skrtel, but he bounced back
to become a mainstay of the Liverpool
team which finished second in the
Premier League in 2014. Unfortunately
for the rugged defender, he scored four
own goals during the campaign – against
Hull, West Ham, Swansea and Newcastle
– to set a new record for a single Premier
League season.

• **Skrtel was part of the Slovakia team
which qualified for a first-ever World
Cup in 2010 and surprised many by
reaching the last 16.**

*Well, would you argue with
this man?*

# SOUTHAMPTON

**Year founded:** 1885
**Ground:** St Mary's
(32,505)
**Previous name:**
Southampton St Mary's
**Nickname:** The Saints
**Biggest win:** 14-0 v
Newbury (1894)
**Heaviest defeat:** 0-8 v
Tottenham (1936) and
v Everton (1971)

Founded as Southampton St Mary's by
members of St Mary's Church Young
Men's Association in 1885, the club joined
the Southern League in 1894 and became
simply 'Southampton' the following year.

• **The Saints won the Southern League
six times in the decade up to 1904
and also appeared in two FA Cup finals
during that period, losing to Bury in
1900 and to Sheffield United two
years later.**

• The club finally won the cup in 1976.
Manchester United were hot favourites
to beat the Saints, then in the Second
Division, but the south coast side claimed
the trophy thanks to Bobby Stokes' late
strike. As scorer of the first (and only)
goal in the final, Stokes was rewarded
with a free car... unfortunately, he still
hadn't passed the driving test!

• **Mick Channon, a member of
that cup-winning team and now a
successful racehorse trainer, is the
Saints' leading scorer with a total of
185 goals in two spells at The Dell, the
club's old ground. In Southampton's
Southern League days, Albert Brown
scored a club record seven goals in an
11-0 thrashing of Northampton Town
in 1901.**

• Legendary winger Terry Paine, a
member of England's 1966 World Cup-
winning squad, is Southampton's longest
serving player. Between 1956 and 1974
he wore the club's colours in no fewer
than 713 league games before moving to
Hereford United. Paine's amazing total of
824 league games puts him fourth in the
all-time list, behind Peter Shilton, Tony
Ford and Graham Alexander.

• **England goalkeeper Shilton is the
club's most capped player, winning 50
of his record 125 caps while at The Dell.**

• In August 2013 the Saints forked out
a record £15 million to buy Italian
striker Daniel Osvaldo from Roma. The
following year they received a club

record £30 million when left-back Luke Shaw left the south coast to join Manchester United.

• **Southampton legend Matt Le Tissier was the first midfielder in the history of the Premiership to score a century of goals.** His total of 101 strikes included 25 penalties, a figure only exceeded by Alan Shearer, Frank Lampard and Steven Gerrard in the Premier League era.

• Southampton recorded their biggest ever Premier League win in October 2014, hammering Sunderland 8-0 at St Mary's. Later in the campaign, Saints striker Sadio Mane scored the league's fastest ever hat-trick, taking just two minutes and 56 seconds to complete his treble in a 6-1 rout of Aston Villa.

HONOURS
*Division 3 (South) champions* 1922
*Division 3 champions* 1960
*FA Cup* 1976
*Football League Trophy* 2010

## SOUTHEND UNITED

**Year founded:** 1906
**Ground:** Roots Hall (12,392)
**Nickname:** The Shrimpers
**Biggest win:** 10-1 v Golders Green (1934), v Brentwood (1968) and v Aldershot (1990)
**Heaviest defeat:** 1-9 v Brighton and Hove Albion (1965)

Southend United were founded in 1906 at the Blue Boar pub, just 50 yards away from the club's home, Roots Hall.

• **After joining the Football League in 1920 the Shrimpers remained in the third tier for a record 46 years, before dropping into the Fourth Division in 1966.**

• The club's top appearance maker is Sandy Anderson, who turned out in 452 league games between 1950 and 1962. His team-mate Roger Hollis is Southend's leading marksman, rifling in 120 league goals in just six years at the club between 1954 and 1960.

• **Southend were relegated from the third tier in 1988/89 despite amassing a record points total for a demoted team, 54.**

• Southend were the only Football League club managed by England World Cup-winning captain Bobby Moore, who was in charge at Roots Hall between 1984 and 1986 and also served on the club's board until his untimely death in 1993.

• **Promoted to League One after a play-off victory over Wycombe Wanderers in 2015, Southend put together a club record run of eight consecutive clean sheets during the campaign.**

HONOURS
*League One champions* 2006
*Division 4 champions* 1981

## SPAIN

**First international:** Spain 1 Denmark 0, 1920
**Most capped player:** Iker Casillas, 162 caps (2000- )
**Leading goalscorer:** David Villa, 59 goals (2005-14)
**First World Cup appearance:** Spain 3 Brazil 1, 1934
**Biggest win:** Spain 13 Bulgaria 0, 1933
**Heaviest defeat:** Italy 7 Spain 1, 1928 and England 7 Spain 1, 1931

Spain are the first country in football history to win three major international titles on the trot following their successes at Euro 2008, the 2010 World Cup in South Africa and Euro 2012 in Poland and Ukraine.

• Spain secured their first ever World Cup triumph with a 1-0 victory over Holland at Soccer City Stadium in Johannesburg, midfielder Andres Iniesta drilling home the all-important goal four minutes from the end of extra-time. Despite their entertaining close passing style of play, Spain only managed to score eight goals in the tournament – the lowest total ever by the winning nation at a World Cup.

• Along with Germany, Spain are the only country to have won the European Championships three times. Their first success came in 1964 when they had the advantage of playing the semi-final and final, against holders the Soviet Union, on home soil at Real Madrid's Bernabeu Stadium. Then, in 2008, a single Fernando Torres goal was enough to see off Germany in the final in Vienna. Finally, in 2012, Spain made it a hat-trick of victories after annihilating Italy 4-0 in the final in Kiev.

*Spain's fortunes improved dramatically after the surprise call-up of Zorro!*

• Between 2007 and 2009 Spain went 35 matches without defeat (winning 32 and drawing just three) to equal the world record set by Brazil in the 1990s. The run came to an end when Spain lost 2-0 to USA at the 2009 Confederations Cup, but the Spanish were soon back on form, going into the 2010 World Cup on the back of 18 consecutive victories – including a record 10 in qualification - before they surprisingly lost their opening match at the finals against Switzerland. That setback, though, was soon forgotten as Vicente del Bosque's men went on to lift the trophy, sparking jubilant scenes across Spain from Santander to Seville.

• The cheers turned to tears, however, at the 2014 World Cup in Brazil as Spain were eliminated at the group stage, with their 5-1 drubbing by the Netherlands being the worst ever defeat suffered by the reigning champions at the finals.

The world's largest football arena – Rungrado 1st of May Stadium in North Korea

HONOURS

**World Cup winners** *2010*
**European Championships winners** *1964, 2008, 2012*
**World Cup Record**
*1930 Did not enter*
*1934 Quarter-finals*
*1938 Did not enter*
*1950 Fourth place*
*1954 Did not qualify*
*1958 Did not qualify*
*1962 Round 1*
*1966 Round 1*
*1970 Did not qualify*
*1974 Did not qualify*
*1978 Round 1*
*1982 Round 2*
*1986 Quarter-finals*
*1990 Round 2*
*1994 Quarter-finals*
*1998 Round 1*
*2002 Quarter-finals*
*2006 Round 2*
*2010 Winners*
*2014 Round 1*

## SPONSORSHIP

Manchester United's £45 million-a-year shirt sponsorship deal with US car manufacturers Chevrolet, which started in 2014, is a record for the Premier League.

• **On 24th January 1976 Kettering Town became the first senior football club in the UK to feature a sponsor's logo on their shirts, Kettering Tyres,** for their Southern League Premier Division match against Bath City. The Football Association ordered the removal of the logo, but finally accepted shirt sponsorship in June 1977. Two years later Liverpool became the first top-flight club to sport a sponsor's logo after signing a deal with Hitachi.

• The biggest sponsorship deal in world football was agreed between Manchester City and Etihad Airways in August 2011. The 10-year partnership, which includes stadium naming rights and shirt sponsorship, will boost City's coffers by a staggering £400 million.

• **A kit mix-up in the Tottenham dressing room meant that half the Spurs team wore plain, unsponsored shirts for the 1987 FA Cup final against Coventry City. Needless to say, the Londoners' shirt sponsors, lager manufacturers Holsten, were distinctly unamused.**

• The League Cup was the first major English competition to be sponsored, being renamed the Milk Cup after receiving backing from the Milk Marketing Board in 1982. It has since been rebranded as the Littlewoods Cup, the Rumbelows Cup, the Coca-Cola Cup, the Worthington Cup, the Carling Cup and the Capital One Cup. Since 1994 the FA Cup has been sponsored by Littlewoods, AXA, E.ON, Budweiser, and from the 2015/16 season, Emirates. Meanwhile, the Premier League has been sponsored by Carling, Barclaycard and, until 2016, Barclays.

• **The first competition in England to be sponsored was the Watney Cup in 1971, a pre-season tournament between the highest scoring teams in the different divisions of the Football League.**

## STADIUMS

With a capacity of 150,000 Rungrado 1st of May Stadium in Pyongyang, North Korea is the largest football stadium anywhere in the world. As well as football matches, the stadium also hosts athletic meetings and mass displays of choreographed gymnastics. In the late 1990s a number of North Korean army generals were burned to death in the stadium after being implicated in a plot to assassinate the country's then dictator, Kim Jong-il.

• **Barcelona's Nou Camp is the largest football stadium in Europe with a capacity of 99,786. Old Trafford (76,100) has the largest capacity of any Premier League ground, followed by the Emirates Stadium (60,432) and St James' Park (52,401).**

• Built at a cost of £798 million, Wembley Stadium is the most expensive sporting venue in the world. After years of delays, the stadium finally opened to the public in 2007 and has since hosted 46 England internationals, nine FA Cup finals and eight League Cup finals.

## RAHEEM STERLING

**Born:** Kingston, Jamaica, 8th December 1994
**Position:** Winger
**Club career:**
20012-15 Liverpool 91 (18)
2015- Manchester City
**International record:**
2012- England 16 (1)

Speedy winger Raheem Sterling became the most expensive English player ever when he moved from Liverpool to Manchester City for £49 million in July 2015.

**• Jamaican-born Sterling started his career with QPR, before switching to Liverpool**

for a bargain £600,000 in 2010. He became the third youngest player ever to make his debut for the Reds when he came on as a sub in a 2-1 home defeat against Wigan Athletic on 24th March 2012. Seven months later he became the club's second youngest goalscorer (behind Michael Owen) when he notched his first goal for the Merseysiders in a 1-0 win against Reading.

• A star of Liverpool's magnificent 2013/14 Premier League campaign, Sterling was shortlisted for the PFA Young Player of the Year award but missed out on the prize to Chelsea's Eden Hazard. However, his performances the following season were affected by a contract dispute with Liverpool, which ended with Sterling demanding to leave Anfield.

**• Sterling rose through the England youth ranks to make his senior debut in a 4-2 friendly defeat away to Sweden in November 2012.**

In only his fourth game for the Three Lions he was sent off in a pre-2014 World Cup friendly against Ecuador to become the youngest ever England player to see red.

## STEVENAGE

**Year founded:** 1976
**Ground:** Broadhall Way (6,722)
**Previous name:** Stevenage Borough
**Nickname:** The Boro
**Biggest win:** 7-0 v Merthyr (2006)
**Heaviest defeat:** 1-6 v Farnborough (2002)

The club was founded in 1976 as Stevenage Borough, following the bankruptcy of the town's former club, Stevenage Athletic. In 2010 the club decided to become simply 'Stevenage'.

**• Stevenage rose through the football pyramid to gain promotion to the Conference in 1994. Two years later they won the title but were denied promotion to the Football League as their tiny Broadhall Way Stadium did not meet the league's standards.**

• Stevenage finally made it into the league in 2010 after topping the Conference table with an impressive 99 points. If the club's two victories against Chester City, who were expelled from the league during the season, had not been expunged then Stevenage would have set a new Conference record of 105 points. The following season Stevenage were promoted again, after beating Torquay United 1-0 in the League Two play-off final at Old Trafford, but their three-year stay in League One ended in 2014 when they finished bottom of the pile.

**• In 2007 Stevenage became the first club to lift a trophy at the new Wembley, beating Kidderminster Harriers 3-2 in the final of the FA Trophy watched by a competition record crowd of 53,262.**

• In May 2015 Stevenage brought their biggest ever name to Broadhall Way when they appointed former England international Teddy Sheringham as their new manager.

HONOURS
*Conference champions* 1996, 2010

*Raheem Sterling – the most expensive English player ever*

# STOKE CITY

**Year founded:** 1863
**Ground:** Britannia Stadium (27,740)
**Previous name:** Stoke Ramblers, Stoke
**Nickname:** The Potters
**Biggest win:** 11-0 v Stourbridge (1914)
**Heaviest defeat:** 0-10 v Preston (1889)

Founded in 1863 by employees of the North Staffordshire Railway Company, Stoke are the second oldest league club in the country. Between 1868 and 1870 the club was known as Stoke Ramblers, before simply becoming Stoke and then adding the suffix 'City' in 1925.

• **Stoke were founder members of the Football League in 1888 but finished bottom of the table at the end of the season. After another wooden spoon in 1890 the club dropped out of the league, but returned to the big time after just one season.**

• The club's greatest moment came in 1972 when they won the League Cup, beating favourites Chelsea 2-1 in the final at Wembley, thanks to a late winner by George Eastham - aged 35 and 161 days at the time, the oldest player ever to score in the League Cup final. The Potters had a great chance to add to their meagre haul of silverware in 2011 when they reached the FA Cup final for the first time, but they lost 1-0 to Manchester City. At least their fans enjoyed the semi-final, when Stoke thrashed Bolton 5-0 in the joint-biggest win yet by a club side at the new Wembley.

• **While playing in his second spell at Stoke, the great Stanley Matthews became the oldest player ever to appear in the top flight. On 6th February 1965 Matthews played his last game for the club against Fulham just five days after celebrating his 50th birthday.**

• The legendary Gordon Banks is Stoke's most capped player. The brilliant goalkeeper, a World Cup winner in 1966, won 37 of his 73 England caps while with the Staffordshire outfit.

• **Freddie Steele is Stoke's leading scorer with 140 league goals between 1934 and 1949, including a club record 33 in the 1936/37 season. Stalwart defender Eric Skeels played**
in a record 507 league games for the Potters between 1960 and 1976.

• On 23rd February 1957 Stoke thrashed Lincoln City 8-0 in a Second Division match. Incredibly, Neville Coleman bagged seven of the goals to set a club record which has never been matched since.

• **In August 2015 Stoke splashed out a club record £12 million to bring Swiss international midfielder Xherdan Shaqiri to the Britannia Stadium from Inter Milan. The Potters received a record £8 million in July 2015 when goalkeeper Asmir Begovic joined Chelsea.**

• On 27th January 1974 Stoke became the first top-flight club to host Sunday football when they played Chelsea at their former home, the Victoria Ground. Ignoring the complaints of religious groups, a crowd of nearly 32,000 turned up to see Stoke win 1-0.

• **Stoke recorded their biggest ever Premier League win on the last day of the 2014/15 season, thrashing Liverpool 6-1 at the Britannia Stadium.**

HONOURS
**Division 2 champions** 1933, 1963
**Division 3 (North) champions** 1927
**Second Division champions** 1993
**League Cup** 1972
**Football League Trophy** 1992, 2000

# GORDON STRACHAN

**Born:** Edinburgh, 9th February 1957
**Managerial career:**
1996-2001 Coventry City
2001-04 Southampton
2005-09 Celtic
2009-10 Middlesbrough
2013- Scotland

Appointed as Scotland manager in January 2013, Gordon Strachan saw his team become the first to be officially eliminated from the UEFA 2014 World Cup section, even ahead of real minnows like Andorra and San Marino. However, he then rallied his troops to get off to a good start to their Euro 2016 qualification campaign, the Scots losing just one of their first six games.

• **Strachan's managerial career began at Coventry in 1996 when he was still playing. The following year he became the first outfield player to appear in the Premier League aged 40. He was sacked by the Sky Blues after taking**
them down in 2001, but soon moved to Southampton, guiding them to their first FA Cup final in 27 years in 2003.

• In 2005, Strachan was appointed boss of Celtic. Despite losing his first match, a Champions League qualifier against Artmedia Bratislava, 5-0, the little Scot went on to enjoy huge success in Glasgow. Between 2006 and 2008 he won three successive SPL titles, a feat previously only matched by two other Celtic managers. He resigned his position after Celtic were pipped to the SPL title by arch rivals Rangers on the last day of the 2008/09 season, and then spent an unsuccessful year as Middlesbrough boss before quitting in October 2010.

• **Strachan won a host of honours in his playing days as a tireless midfielder, including the European Cup Winners' Cup with Aberdeen, the FA Cup with Manchester United in 1983 and 1985 and the league title with Leeds in 1992. He also won 50 caps with Scotland.**

# DANIEL STURRIDGE

**Born:** Birmingham, 1st September 1989
**Position:** Striker
**Club career:**
2006-09 Manchester City 21 (5)
2009-13 Chelsea 63 (13)
2011 Bolton Wanderers (loan) 12 (8)
2013- Liverpool 55 (35)
**International record:**
2011- England 16 (5)

A £12 million signing from Chelsea in January 2013, Daniel Sturridge enjoyed a tremendous season with Liverpool in 2013/14, finishing second in the Premier League goalscoring charts behind his team-mate Luis Suarez with 21 goals and earning a place in the PFA Team of the Year. He also became only the second player (after Manchester United's Ruud van Nistelrooy) to score in eight consecutive Premier League games.

• **A fleet-footed striker who never turns down the chance to shoot, Sturridge started out on the books of Aston Villa and Coventry before making his first-team debut as a 17-year-old with Manchester City. During the 2007/08 season he became the first player ever to score in the FA Youth Cup, the FA Cup and the Premier League in the same season.**

• Sturridge joined Chelsea for an initial fee of £3.5 million in 2009, and the following year helped the Blues win the league and cup Double. He spent the second half of the 2010/11 season on loan at Bolton, where he became only the sixth player to score on his first four appearances for a Premier League club. He returned to Chelsea for the start of the 2011/12 campaign, but found his opportunities limited after Roberto di Matteo replaced Andre Villas-Boas in the Stamford Bridge hotseat.

• **Sturridge has played and scored for England at every level from Under-16 upwards. He made his full international debut as a sub against Sweden in November 2011, and in March 2013 notched his first goal for the Three Lions in an 8-0 hammering of San Marino. At the 2014 World Cup he scored England's first goal at the tournament in a 2-1 defeat to Italy.**

## LUIS SUAREZ

**Born:** Salto, Uruguay, 24th January 1987
**Position:** Striker
**Club career:**
2005-06 Nacional 27 (10)
2006-07 Groningen 29 (10)
2007-11 Ajax 110 (81)
2011-14 Liverpool 110 (69)
2014- Barcelona 27 (16)
**International record:**
2007- Uruguay 82 (44)

A quick-witted striker who is famed for his ability to score from the tightest of angles, Luis Suarez became the third most expensive player in football history when he joined Barcelona from Liverpool in July 2014 for £75 million. In a tremendous first season with the Catalans, he helped Barca win the Treble, contributing 25 goals in all competitions including one in the Champions League final against Juventus.

• **Suarez enjoyed a rollercoaster three years with Liverpool after signing for the Merseysiders from Ajax for £22.8 million in January 2011. In his first full season with the Reds he helped them win the Carling Cup but, less impressively, was given an eight-match ban by the FA and fined £40,000 for racially abusing Manchester United defender Patrice Evra.**

*Moving from Liverpool to Barcelona was a challenge Luis Suarez could really get his teeth into*

• The following season Suarez was in hot water again after he bit Chelsea defender Branislav Ivanovic on the arm in an unprovoked attack. The striker, who had been banned for seven games after a similar incident while playing for his previous club Ajax, was hit with a 10-game ban – the fifth longest in Premier League history.

• **However, the Uruguayan appeared to turn over a new leaf in 2013/14 when he topped the Premier League scoring charts with 31 goals, won both Player of the Year awards and became the first player ever to score 10 Premier League goals in a month in December 2013.**

• Sadly for his many admirers, the temperamental Suarez was involved in another shocking incident at the 2014 World Cup when he bit Italy defender Giorgio Chiellini. Despite pleading innocence, the maverick striker was immediately thrown out of the tournament and given a four-month ban from all football activities in the stiffest ever sanction handed out by FIFA at the World Cup for on-field misconduct. In happier days with Uruguay, Suarez was named Player of the Tournament when his country won the 2011 Copa America and two years later he became the South Americans' all-time leading scorer.

## SUBSTITUTES

Substitutes were first allowed in the Football League in the 1965/66 season. The first player to come off the bench was Charlton's Keith Peacock, who replaced injured goalkeeper Mike Rose after 11 minutes of the Addicks' match away to Bolton on 21st August 1965. On the same afternoon Barrow's Bobby Knox became the first substitute to score a goal when he notched against Wrexham.

• **The fastest ever goal scored by a substitute was by Arsenal's Nicklas Bendtner, who headed in a corner against Tottenham at the Emirates on 22nd December 2007, just 1.8 seconds after replacing Emmanuel Eboue.**

• The most goals ever scored in a Premier League game by a substitute is four by Ole Gunnar Solskjaer in Manchester United's 8-1 win at Nottingham Forest in 1999. Incredibly, the Norwegian striker was only on the pitch for 19 minutes. However, Jermain Defoe has scored the most Premier League goals as a sub with 22 for his various clubs.

• **Substitutes were first allowed at the World Cup in 1970, with Holland's Dick Nanninga becoming the first sub to score in the final eight years later. The most goals scored by a sub at the tournament in a single match is three by Hungary's Lazlo Kiss against El Salvador in 1982. Brazilian winger Denilson made a record 11 appearances as a substitute at the finals in 1998 and 2002.**

• The first substitute to score in the FA Cup final was Arsenal's Eddie Kelly, who scored the Gunners' first goal in their 2-1 win against Liverpool in 1971.

• **Former Newcastle forward Shola Ameobi made a record 137 appearances as a sub in the Premier League, while Ryan Giggs was substituted a record 134 times in his long Manchester United career.**

## SUNDERLAND

**Year founded:** 1879
**Ground:** Stadium of Light (49,000)
**Previous name:** Sunderland and District Teachers' AFC
**Nickname:** The Black Cats
**Biggest win:** 11-1 v Fairfield (1895)
**Heaviest defeat:** 0-8 v Sheffield Wednesday (1911), v West Ham (1968), v Watford (1982) and v Southampton (2014)

The club was founded as the Sunderland and District Teachers' AFC in 1879 but soon opened its ranks to other professions and became simply 'Sunderland' the following year.

*Jermain Defoe's goal against Newcastle in April 2015 secured Sunderland's fifth win in a row against their arch rivals*

• **Sunderland were the first 'new' club to join the Football League, replacing Stoke in 1890. Just two years later they won their first league championship and they retained the title the following year, in the process becoming the first club to score 100 goals in a league season. In 1895 Sunderland became the first club ever to win three championships, and their status was further enhanced when they beat Scottish champions Hearts 5-3 in a one-off 'world championship' match.**

• In 1958 Sunderland were relegated after a then record 57 consecutive seasons in the top flight – a benchmark which lasted until Arsenal went one better in 1983/84.

• **Sunderland were the first Second Division team in the post Second World War era to win the FA Cup,**

beating Leeds 1-0 at Wembley in 1973 in one of the biggest upsets of all time thanks to a goal by Ian Porterfield. Incredibly, their line-up featured not one international player.

• Goalkeeper Jim Montgomery, a hero of that cup-winning side, is the Black Cats' record appearance maker, turning out in 537 league games between 1960 and 1977.

• **Sunderland's record victory was an 11-1 thrashing of Fairfield in the FA Cup in 1895. However, the club's best ever league win, a 9-1 demolition of eventual champions and arch-rivals Newcastle at St James' Park in 1908, probably gave their fans more pleasure. To this day, it remains the biggest ever victory by an away side in the top flight.**

• Sunderland last won the league championship in 1935/36, the last time, incidentally, that a team wearing stripes has topped the pile. The Wearsiders' success, though, certainly wasn't based on a solid defence... the 74 goals they conceded that season is more than any other top-flight champions before or since.

• **In 1990 Sunderland became the only team to lose a play-off final yet still gain promotion, the Wearsiders going up to the old First Division in place of Swindon after the Robins were punished for financial irregularities.**

• Inside forward Charlie Buchan is Sunderland's record scorer with 209 league goals between 1911 and 1925. Dave Halliday holds the record for a single season, hitting the target 43 times in 1928/29.

• **Famed for their spending power in the late 1940s and early 1950s, when they were dubbed 'The Bank of England' club, Sunderland coughed up a record £14 million in August 2012 when they signed striker Steven Fletcher from Wolves. The year before the Black Cats sold their previous most expensive signing, Darren Bent, to Aston Villa for a club record £18 million.**

• Sunderland have the worst overall goal difference of any Premier League club, -238 ... a substantial deficit which wasn't helped much when the Black Cats suffered their worst ever Premier League defeat, 0-8 at Southampton, in October 2014.

**HONOURS**

**Division 1 champions** 1892, 1983, 1895, 1902, 1913, 1936
**Division 2 champions** 1976
**Championship champions** 2005, 2007
**Division 3 champions** 1988
**FA Cup** 1937, 1973

## SUPERSTITIONS

Many footballers, including some of the great names of the game, are highly superstitious and believe that performing the same personal routines before every game will bring them good luck. Most Liverpool players, for instance, like to touch the 'This is Anfield' sign in the tunnel on their way onto the pitch.

• **Cristiano Ronaldo believes it brings him good luck if he has a haircut before a big match and he also insists on being the first player in his team to enter the field of play.**

• Kolo Toure's superstition almost cost his then club Arsenal dear in their 2009 Champions League clash with Roma. Believing that it would be bad luck to leave the dressing room before team-mate William Gallas, who was receiving treatment, Toure failed to appear for the start of the second half, leaving the Gunners to restart the match with just nine players!

• **Cameroon assistant coach Thomas Nkono was arrested before the start of the 2002 Africa Cup of Nations semi-final against Mali when he tried to place a lucky voodoo charm on the pitch. In the same tournament, Senegal goalkeeper Tony Sylva was accused of hiring a witch doctor to smear his goal posts with a magic ointment when he went 448 minutes without conceding a goal.**

• Some superstitions are not entirely irrational. For example, Arsenal always make sure that a new goalkeeper's jersey

*Swansea's Bafetimbi Gomis evades a tackle from Sunderland defender John O'Shea*

is washed before it is used for the first time. The policy stems from the 1927 FA Cup final, which the Gunners lost when goalkeeper Dan Lewis let in a soft goal against Cardiff. He later blamed his mistake on the ball slipping from his grasp and over the line as it brushed against the shiny surface of his new jumper.

• **Controversial Cardiff City chairman Vincent Tan prefers to sign players with the number '8' in their birth date. Incredibly, his first 11 signings after buying the club in 2010 all fitted the bill!**

• In a bid to bring them luck at Euro 2012 the Czech Republic squad decided to go unshaven for the duration of the tournament. The 'hairy policy' worked well as the Czechs topped their group before losing to Portugal in the quarter-finals.

## SWANSEA CITY

**Year founded:** 1912
**Ground:** Liberty Stadium (20,827)
**Previous name:** Swansea Town
**Nickname:** The Swans
**Biggest win:** 12-0 v Sliema Wanderers (1982)
**Heaviest defeat:** 0-8 v Liverpool (1990) and v Monaco (1991)

The club was founded as Swansea Town in 1912 and entered the Football League eight years later. The present name was adopted in 1970.

• **Under former Liverpool striker John Toshack the Swans climbed from the old Fourth Division to the top flight in just four seasons between 1978 and 1981, the fastest ever ascent through the Football League. The glory days soon faded, though, and by 1986 Swansea were back in the basement division.**

• In 2011, though, Swansea beat Reading 4-2 in the Championship play-off final at Wembley to become the first Welsh club to reach the Premier League. Again, their rise was a rapid one as they had been in the basement tier just six years earlier.

• **The club's greatest day came in 2013 when they won their first major trophy, the League Cup. The Swans triumphed in fine style, too, demolishing League Two outfit Bradford City 5-0 at Wembley in the**

biggest ever victory in the final.

• Ivor Allchurch is the Swans' leading scorer, banging in 166 goals in two spells at the club between 1949 and 1968. One-club man Wilfred Milne is the Swans' leading appearance maker, turning out in 586 league games between 1920 and 1937.

• **In 1961 the club became the first from Wales to compete in Europe, but were knocked out of the Cup Winners' Cup in the first round by East German side Carl Zeiss Jena. In the same competition the Swans recorded their biggest ever win over Maltese minnows Sliema Wanderers 12-0 in 1982.**

• Long-serving defender Ashley Williams is the Swans' most-capped player, appearing for Wales for the 51st time in a famous 1-0 win over Belgium in a Euro 2016 qualifier in June 2015.

• **The Swans made their record signing in July 2013 when Ivory Coast striker Wilfried Bony moved from Vitesse for £12 million. In January 2015 Bony joined Manchester City for £25 millon, making him also Swansea's record sale.**

• In 1936 Swansea set a Football League record for the longest distance travelled for consecutive matches when they visited Newcastle on Easter Sunday just a day after going to Plymouth.

> **HONOURS**
> *Division 3 (South) champions* 1925, 1949
> *League One champions* 2008
> *Third Division champions* 2000
> *League Cup* 2013
> *Football League Trophy* 1994, 2006
> *Welsh Cup* 1913, 1932, 1950, 1961, 1966, 1981, 1982, 1983, 1989, 1991

## SWINDON TOWN

**Year founded:** 1879
**Ground:** The County Ground (15,728)
**Previous name:** Swindon Spartans
**Nickname:** The Robins
**Biggest win:** 10-1 v Farnham United Breweries (1925)
**Heaviest defeat:** 1-10 v Manchester City (1930)

The club was founded by the Reverend William Pitt in 1879, becoming Swindon Spartans two years later before adopting

the name Swindon Town in 1883. In 1920 Swindon were founder members of the Third Division, kicking off their league career with a 9-1 thrashing of Luton.

• **The Robins' finest moment came in 1969 when, as a Third Division club, they beat mighty Arsenal 3-1 in the League Cup final on a mud-clogged Wembley pitch. Legendary winger Don Rogers was the star of the show, scoring two of Swindon's goals.**

• In 1993, three years after being denied promotion to the top flight for the first time because of a financial scandal, Swindon earned promotion to the Premiership via the play-offs. The following campaign, though, proved to be a miserable one as the Robins finished bottom of the pile and conceded 100 goals… a record for the Premier League.

• **Swindon won the Fourth Division title in 1985/86 with a then Football League best 102 points, a total which remains a record for the bottom tier.**

• John Trollope is Swindon's longest serving player, appearing in 770 league games for the club between 1960 and 1980 – a record for a single club. Harry Morris scored a record 229 goals for the club between 1926 and 1933, including a seasonal best of 47 in the league in his first year with the Robins.

• **On 22nd January 2008 Swindon set an unwanted record when they became the first club to miss all four of their penalties in a shoot-out against Barnet.**

> **HONOURS**
> *Second Division champions* 1996
> *Division 4 champions* 1986
> *League Two champions* 2012
> *League Cup* 1969

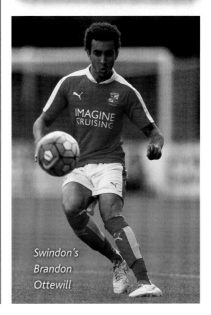

*Swindon's Brandon Ottewill*

## JOHN TERRY

**Born:** Barking, 7th December 1980
**Position:** Defender
**Club career:**
1998- Chelsea 459 (39)
2000 Nottingham Forest (loan) 6 (0)
**International record:**
2003-12 England 78 (6)

In 2015 Chelsea captain John Terry became only the second player (after Manchester United's Roy Keane) to lead his team to four Premier League titles. JT, as he is known to fans and team-mates alike, has also won five FA Cups and three League Cups, scoring in the 2015 final against London rivals Tottenham. In 2012, despite being suspended for the final against Bayern Munich, he added the Champions League to that list, making up for his disappointment four years earlier when he slipped and put his penalty wide in the shoot-out against Manchester United in the final in Moscow.

• A superb tackler who reads the game well, Terry was voted PFA Player of the Year in 2005 after leading the Blues to the first of their back-to-back Premiership titles. With a total of 39 Premier League goals for the club, he is the highest scoring defender in the competition's history.
• After making his England debut against Serbia & Montenegro in 2003, Terry went on to represent his country at Euro 2004 and Euro 2012, the 2006 World Cup – where he was the only England player to be selected for the all-star FIFA squad at the end of the tournament – and the 2010 World Cup.
• **He was first appointed England captain by Steve McClaren in 2006 and retained the role under Fabio Capello. However, in February 2010 Terry was sensationally stripped of the armband following newspaper revelations about his private life. The following year, though, he reclaimed the captaincy only for the FA to take it off him again in February 2012 after he was charged by police for racially abusing QPR** defender Anton Ferdinand earlier in the season. Terry was acquitted at his trial, but when the FA charged him with the same offence he decided to retire from international football.

## THROW-INS

Thomas Gronnemark from Denmark holds the world record for the longest ever throw. Employing a forward hand spring technique he hurled the ball an incredible 51.33 metres on 18th June 2010.
• **The most famous long throw specialist in the modern game is former Stoke midfielder Rory Delap, who could hurl the ball deep into the opposition box even from the halfway line. In the pre-Premier League era Chelsea striker Ian Hutchinson used to cause chaos with his long throws, one of which led to the Blues' winner in the 1970 FA Cup final replay against Leeds United in 1970.**
• The most bizarre goal from a throw-in came in a derby between Birmingham City and Aston Villa in 2002. Villa defender Olof Mellberg threw the ball back to goalkeeper Peter Enckelman and it dribbled under his foot and into the net. Despite Villa's protests, referee David Elleray ruled that the goal should stand because Enckelman had made contact with the ball.
• **Throw-ins were replaced by kick-ins from the touchline in the Diadora League (now the Ryman League) during the 1994/95 season, but the experiment was abandoned at the end of the campaign.**

*What goes up must come down*

## TOTTENHAM HOTSPUR

**Year founded:** 1882
**Ground:** White Hart Lane (36,284)
**Previous name:** Hotspur FC
**Nickname:** Spurs
**Biggest win:** 13-2 v Crewe (1960)
**Heaviest defeat:** 0-8 v Cologne (1995)

The club was founded as Hotspur FC in 1882 by a group of local cricketers, most of whom were former pupils of Tottenham Grammar School. Three years later the club decided to add the prefix 'Tottenham'.

## TOP 10

### CLUBS BY NUMBER OF ENGLAND INTERNATIONALS SUPPLIED

| | | |
|---|---|---|
| 1. | Aston Villa | 73 |
| | Tottenham Hotspur | 73 |
| 3. | Liverpool | 67 |
| 4. | Everton | 66 |
| 5. | Manchester United | 64 |
| 6. | Arsenal | 63 |
| 7. | Blackburn Rovers | 48 |
| 8. | Manchester City | 45 |
| 9. | Chelsea | 44 |
| 10. | Sheffield Wednesday | 43 |
| | West Bromwich Albion | 43 |

• Tottenham were members of the Southern League when they won the FA Cup for the first time in 1901, defeating Sheffield United 3-1 in a replay at Bolton's Burnden Park. Spurs' victory meant they were the first (and, so far, only) non-league club to win the cup since the formation of the Football League in 1888.

• In 1961 Tottenham created history when they became the first club in the 20th century to win the fabled league and cup Double. Their title success was based on a storming start to the season, Bill Nicholson's side winning their first 11 games to set a top-flight record which has not been matched since. By the end of the campaign, the north Londoners had won 31 of their 42 league matches to create another record for the top tier.

• As Arsenal fans like to point out, Tottenham have failed to win the league since those 'Glory, Glory' days of skipper Danny Blanchflower, Dave Mackay and Cliff Jones. Spurs, though, have continued to enjoy cup success, and their total of eight victories in the FA Cup is only surpassed by the Gunners and Manchester United. Remarkably, five of those triumphs came in years ending in a '1', giving rise to the legend that these seasons were particularly lucky for Spurs.

• Tottenham have also enjoyed much success in the League Cup, winning the competition four times. The last of these triumphs, in 2008 following a 2-1 defeat of holders Chelsea in the final, saw Tottenham become the first club to win the League Cup at the new Wembley.

• Spurs have a decent record in Europe, too. In 1963 they thrashed Atletico Madrid 5-1 in the final of the European Cup Winners' Cup, the legendary Jimmy Greaves grabbing a brace, to become the first British club to win a European trophy. Then, in 1972, Tottenham defeated Wolves 3-2 on aggregate in the first ever UEFA Cup final and the first European final to feature two English clubs. A third European triumph followed in 1984 when Tottenham beat Anderlecht in the first UEFA Cup final to be settled by penalties.

• Ace marksman Jimmy Greaves holds two goalscoring records for Tottenham. His total of 220 league goals between 1961 and 1970 is a club best, as is his impressive tally of 37 league goals in 1962/63. Clive Allen, though, struck an incredible total of 49 goals in all competitions in 1986/87, including a record 12 in the League Cup.

• Stalwart defender Steve Perryman is the club's longest serving player, pulling on the famous white shirt in 655 league games between 1969 and 1986, including 613 in the old First Division – a top-flight record for a player at a single club. His team-mate Pat Jennings is the club's most decorated international, winning 74 of his record 119 caps for Northern Ireland while at the Lane.

• In August 2013 Spurs received a world record transfer fee of £86 million from Real Madrid for Welsh winger Gareth Bale. The club's record buy is midfielder Erik Lamela, who cost £30 million from Roma in the same month.

• Tottenham's first title success was in 1950/51 when Arthur Rowe's stylish 'Push and Run' team topped the table just one year after winning the Second Division championship. In the years since, only Ipswich Town (in 1961 and 1962) have managed to claim the top two titles in consecutive seasons.

• Spurs went a Football League record 37 years between 1928 and 1965 without having a single player sent off.

*Tottenham's Nacer Chadli finds himself surrounded*

• Spurs' incredible 9-1 trouncing of Wigan on 22nd November 2009 was only the second time a club had scored nine goals in a Premier League game. Jermain Defoe struck five times after half-time to set a Premier League record for the most goals scored in a single half.

• In 2010 Tottenham became the first team in Champions League history to score two or more goals in all six of their group games.

HONOURS
**Division 1 champions** *1951, 1961*
**Division 2 champions** *1920, 1950*
**FA Cup** *1901, 1921, 1961, 1962, 1967, 1981, 1982, 1991*
**League Cup** *1971, 1973, 1999, 2008*
**Double** *1961*
**European Cup Winners' Cup** *1963*
**UEFA Cup** *1972, 1984*

## YAYA TOURE

**Born:** Bouake, Ivory Coast, 13th May 1983
**Position:** Midfielder
**Club career:**
2001-03 Beveren 70 (3)
2003-05 Matalurh Donetsk 33 (3)
2005-06 Olympiacos 26 (3)
2006-07 Monaco 27 (5)
2007-10 Barcelona 74 (4)
2010- Manchester City 162 (51)
**International record:**
2004- Ivory Coast 95 (19)

Yaya Toure wrote himself into Manchester City folklore when he scored the winning goals in both the FA Cup semi-final and final in 2011, ending the club's 35-year quest for a major trophy. The following season he was a key part of the City side which won the Premier League for the first time, his dynamic displays earning him a place in the PFA Team of the Year. He repeated that feat in 2014 as City won the title again, becoming only the second

midfielder ever (after Frank Lampard) to score 20 Premier League goals in a season.

• A powerful midfielder who likes to switch from a defensive to an attacking role during games, Toure began his professional career in Belgium with Beveren. He later had spells in the Ukraine, Greece (where he won the double with Olympiacos in 2006) and France, before moving to Barcelona in 2007.

• Toure was part of the Barcelona team which won an incredible six trophies in 2009, showing his versatility to good effect when he played at centre-back in the Champions League final against Manchester United. The following year he moved to Manchester City for £24 million, teaming up with his older brother, Kolo Toure.

• Captain of the Ivory Coast side that won the 2015 Africa Cup of Nations, Toure was voted African Footballer of the Year a record four times on the trot between 2011 and 2014.

## ANDROS TOWNSEND

**Born:** Leytonstone, 16th July 1991
**Position:** Winger
**Club career:**
2009- Tottenham Hotspur 47 (3)
2009 Yeovil Town (loan) 10 (1)
2009 Leyton Orient (loan) 22 (2)
2010 MK Dons (loan) 9 (2)
2010 Ipswich Town (loan) 13 (1)
2011 Watford (loan) 3 (0)
2011 Millwall (loan) 11 (2)
2012 Leeds United (loan) 6 (1)
2012 Birmingham City (loan) 15 (0)
2013 QPR (loan) 12 (2)
**International record:**
2013- England 9 (3)

A pacy winger who packs a powerful shot, Andros Townsend is the most loaned out player to ever represent England. By the time the Tottenham star made his full international debut in October 2013 he had spent time on loan at no fewer than nine clubs, including stints with Ipswich, Watford, Leeds and QPR.

*Yaya Toure gives Chelsea's Willian the cold shoulder*

• Uniquely among current England players, Townsend has arguably made more impression with the national team than at club level. Rarely a starter for Tottenham, the Leytonstone-born wideman is nonetheless a favourite of Roy Hodgson's and, when fit, is a regular in the England squad.

• Townsend repaid Hodgson's faith in him by performing superbly on his England debut in a World Cup 2014 qualifier against Montenegro at Wembley, capping his brilliant display in a 4-1 victory with a spectacular strike from the edge of the box. Injury deprived him of a place on the plane to Brazil, but he returned to the England fold to score a stunning equaliser in a friendly against Italy in March 2015.

• Townsend enjoyed his best moment for Tottenham when his penalty gave the Londoners victory over Sheffield United in the first leg of the League Cup semi-final in January 2015. Spurs made it through to the final but Townsend finished on the losing side at Wembley after a 2-0 defeat to London rivals Chelsea.

## TOP 10

### MOST EXPENSIVE TRANSFERS

1. **Gareth Bale** (Tottenham to Real Madrid, 2013) **£86m**
2. **Cristiano Ronaldo** (Manchester United to Real Madrid, 2009) **£80m**
3. **Luis Suarez** (Liverpool to Barcelona, 2014) **£75m**
4. **James Rodriguez** (Monaco to Real Madrid, 2014) **£63m**
5. **Angel Di Maria** (Real Madrid to Manchester United, 2014) **£59m**
   **Zlatan Ibrahimovic** (Inter Milan to Barcelona, 2009) **£59m**
7. **Kaka** (AC Milan to Real Madrid, 2009) **£56m**
8. **Edinson Cavani** (Napoli to Paris St Germain, 2013) **£55m**
   **Kevin De Bruyne** (Wolfsburg to Manchester City, 2015) **£55m**
10. **Radamel Falcao** (Atletico Madrid to Monaco, 2013) **£51m**

## TRANSFERS

The world's most expensive player is Welsh winger Gareth Bale, who moved from Tottenham to Real Madrid in August 2013 for a staggering transfer fee of £86 million. This beat the £80 million which Real paid Manchester United for Portuguese star Cristiano Ronaldo in the summer of 2009.

• The biggest transfer deal in the British game took place in August 2014 when Manchester United paid Real Madrid £59.7 million for Argentinian winger Angel Di Maria.

• The first player to be transferred for a four-figure fee in England was Alf Common, who moved from Sunderland to Middlesbrough in 1905. In 1966 World Cup winner Alan Ball became the first six-figure footballer when he joined Everton from Blackpool, while Trevor Francis broke the £1 million barrier when he moved to Nottingham Forest from Birmingham City for £1,150,000 in 1979.

• The only player to twice change clubs for a world record fee is Diego Maradona. In 1982 the little Argentinian moved from Boca Juniors to Barcelona for a record £3 million, and two years later he joined Napoli for £5 million.

• In the summer of 2011 Chelsea paid Porto £13.3 million for the services of Andre Villas-Boas, a world record transfer fee for a manager. It turned out to be a bit of a waste of money, as the Portuguese boss was sacked midway through the following season!

• Milene Domingues, the then wife of Brazil star Ronaldo, became the most expensive female footballer in the world when she moved from Italian side Fiamma Monza to Atletico Madrid Feminas for £200,000 in September 2002. Chelsea Ladies set a new British transfer record in July 2015 when they bought striker Fran Kirby from Reading for around £60,000.

## TV AND RADIO

The first ever live radio broadcast of a football match was on 22nd January 1927 when the BBC covered the First Division encounter between Arsenal and Sheffield United at Highbury. The Radio Times printed a pitch marked

*Not all big transfers turn out well!*

into numbered squares, which the commentators used to describe where the ball was at any given moment (which some suggest gave rise to the phrase 'back to square one').

• **The 1937 FA Cup final between Sunderland and Preston was the first to be televised, although only parts of the match were shown by the BBC. The following year's final between Preston and Huddersfield was the first to be screened live and in full, although the audience was only around 10,000 as so few people had TV sets at the time.**

• The biggest British TV audience ever for a football match (and, indeed, the biggest ever for any TV broadcast in this country) was 32.3 million for the 1966 World Cup final between England and West Germany. The viewing figures for the match, which was shown live by both BBC and ITV, were all the more remarkable as only 15 million households in the UK had TV sets. The biggest TV audience for an FA Cup final was in 1970 when 28.49 million people watched Chelsea beat Leeds 2-1 in a midweek replay at Old Trafford.

• **The BBC's 'Match of the Day' is the longest-running football programme in the world. It was first transmitted on 22nd August 1964 when highlights of Arsenal's trip to Liverpool were broadcast to an audience estimated to be around 20,000.**

• The current TV deal between Sky, BT and the Premier League which started in the 2013/14 season is the biggest in the history of the game. Under the terms of the deal the two companies will pay £3 billion over three years to show 154 live games per season – a 71 per cent increase on the previous three-year agreement.

## TWITTER

Cristiano Ronaldo has more followers on Twitter than any other footballer in the world, with over 37 million at the last count. His onetime Real Madrid team-mate Kaka is second on the footballers' Twitter leaderboard, the Brazilian's popularity being boosted by his well-known devotion to Christianity. Neither player, though, can compete with the world's most popular Twitter celebrity, the singer Katy Perry, who has more than 74 million followers.

• **The 2014 World Cup semi-final between hosts Brazil and Germany generated an incredible 35.6 million tweets – a record for a sporting event.**

• A record 672 million tweets were sent during the 2014 World Cup, making the tournament as a whole the most tweeted about event in social media history.

• **Chelsea defender Ashley Cole was fined a record £90,000 for a tweet in October 2012, when he posted abusive comments about the FA after the governing body had questioned the truth of his statements in the John Terry race abuse inquiry.**

• The most popular British player on Twitter is Wayne Rooney, who has 11,698, 296 followers – just a couple of hundred behind the Dalai Lama.

## UEFA

UEFA, the Union of European Football Associations, was founded in 1954 at a meeting in Basel during the Swiss World Cup. Holding power over all the national FAs in Europe, with 54 members it is the largest and most influential of the six continental confederations of FIFA.

• **UEFA competitions include the Champions League (first won as the European Cup by Real Madrid), the Europa League (formerly the UEFA Cup) and the UEFA Super Cup.**

• UEFA President Michel Platini, a former captain of France, is the sixth man to fill the role. The longest serving UEFA President is Sweden's Lennart Johansson, who did the job for 17 years between 1990 and 2007.

• **Controversial UEFA decisions in the past include the introduction of penalty kicks to decide drawn European ties (from 1970) and the ban on English clubs competing in European competitions for five years from 1985 after the Heysel tragedy.**

## URUGUAY

**First international:** Uruguay 2 Argentina 3, 1901
**Most capped player:** Diego Forlan, 112 caps (2002-14)
**Leading goalscorer:** Luis Suarez, 44 goals (2007- )
**First World Cup appearance:** Uruguay 1 Peru 0, 1930
**Biggest win:** Uruguay 9 Bolivia 0, 1927
**Heaviest defeat:** Uruguay 0 Argentina 6, 1902

In 1930 Uruguay became the first winners of the World Cup, beating arch-rivals Argentina 4-2 in the final on home soil in Montevideo. The match was a repeat of the Olympic final of 1928, which Uruguay had also won. In terms of population, Uruguay is easily the smallest nation ever to win the World Cup.

• **In 1950 Uruguay won the World Cup for a second time, defeating hosts Brazil 2-1 in 'the final' (it was actually the last and decisive match in a four-team final group). The match was watched by a massive crowd of 199,854 in the Maracana Stadium in Rio de Janeiro, the largest ever to attend a football match anywhere in the world.**

• At the 2010 World Cup in South Africa Uruguay finished fourth, their best showing since Mexico in 1970. However, the South Americans' campaign will mostly be remembered for a blatant handball on the line by striker Luis Suarez, which denied their opponents Ghana a certain winning goal in the teams' quarter-final clash.

• **Uruguay are the most successful team in the history of the Copa America. Winners of the inaugural tournament in 1916, Uruguay have won the competition a total of 15 times, most recently lifting the trophy in 2011 after beating Paraguay 3-0 in the final.**

**HONOURS**
*World Cup winners* 1930, 1950
*Copa America winners* 1916, 1917, 1920, 1923, 1924, 1926, 1935, 1942, 1956, 1959, 1967, 1983, 1987, 1995, 2011
**World Cup Record**
*1930 Winners*
*1934 Did not enter*
*1938 Did not enter*
*1950 Winners*
*1954 Fourth place*
*1958 Did not qualify*
*1962 Round 1*
*1966 Quarter-finals*
*1970 Fourth place*
*1974 Round 1*
*1978 Did not qualify*
*1982 Did not qualify*
*1986 Round 2*
*1990 Round 2*
*1994 Did not qualify*
*1998 Did not qualify*
*2002 Round 1*
*2006 Did not qualify*
*2010 Fourth place*
*2014 Round 2*

*'Behind you!!!' Some would say Manchester United under Van Gaal has been a bit of a pantomime*

## LOUIS VAN GAAL

**Born:** Amsterdam, Netherlands, 8th August 1951
**Managerial career:**
1991-97 Ajax
1997-2000 Barcelona
2000-02 Netherlands
2002-03 Barcelona
2005-09 AZ Alkmaar
2009-11 Bayern Munich
2012-14 Netherlands
2014- Manchester United

Manchester United boss Louis van Gaal is the first non-British or Irish manager to occupy the Old Trafford hotseat. The Dutchman was appointed as successor to the hapless David Moyes in May 2014, shortly before leading the Netherlands to third place at the World Cup in Brazil. His first season with United was a bit patchy, but a fourth place finish was deemed satisfactory by most fans.

• **Formerly a midfielder with Dutch and Belgian clubs, Van Gaal first made his mark in management with Ajax, guiding the Amsterdam giants to three league titles, the UEFA Cup in 1992 and the Champions League three years later following victory over AC Milan.**

• Van Gaal then moved on to Barcelona, replacing former England manager Bobby Robson at the Nou Camp. He won two league titles with a Barça side that included stars like Rivaldo, Patrick Kluivert and Luis Figo, but quit the club after facing heavy criticism for his use of an attack-minded 4-3-3 system traditionally employed by Ajax since the 1970s.

• **After failing to lead the Netherlands to the 2002 World Cup finals and a brief spell back at Barcelona, Van Gaal restored his reputation by taking outsiders AZ Alkmaar to only their second Dutch league title in 2009. He then became the first Dutch manager to win the Bundesliga title when he triumphed with Bayern Munich in 2010, but he was pipped to the Champions League in the same season by Jose Mourinho's Inter Milan.**

## ROBIN VAN PERSIE

**Born:** Rotterdam, Netherlands, 6th August 1983
**Position:** Striker
**Club career:**
2001-04 Feyenoord 59 (15)
2004-12 Arsenal 194 (96)
20012-15 Manchester United 86 (48)
2015- Fenerbahce
**International record:**
2005- Netherlands 98 (49)

Robin van Persie is only the third player – after Alan Shearer and Jimmy Floyd Hasselbaink – to win the Premier League Golden Boot with two different clubs. He first won the award with Arsenal in 2012 and then, following a £24 million move to Manchester United that same summer, retained the trophy in his first season with the Red Devils after his 26 goals powered his new club to the league title.

• **The son of two artists, Van Persie began his career with his local side, Feyenoord, making his first-team debut aged 17 in 2001 and winning the Dutch league's Best Young Talent award at the end of his first season. A UEFA Cup winner the following year, he moved to north London in 2004 for a £2.75 million fee.**

• In his first season with the Gunners, Van Persie fired his new club to the FA Cup final with two goals in the semi-final defeat of Blackburn Rovers. A month later he collected his first medal in English football when Arsenal defeated Manchester United on penalties in the final. His personal best tally of 30 league goals for the Gunners in 2011/12 saw him win both Footballer of the Year awards but, frustrated by the club's lack of success over many years, he jumped at the chance to move north.

• **A clean striker of the ball, especially on his preferred left side, Van Persie made his international debut for the Netherlands in a World Cup qualifier against Romania in 2005 and is now his country's all-time leading goalscorer with 49 goals.**

## THEO WALCOTT

**Born:** Stanmore, 16th March 1989
**Position:** Winger
**Club career:**
2005-06 Southampton 21 (4)
2006- Arsenal 208 (50)
**International record:**
2006- England 40 (5)

Arsenal winger Theo Walcott is the youngest player ever to represent England, coming off the bench to make his debut against Hungary at Old Trafford in 2006 when he was aged just 17 years and 75 days.

• He has continued to set records for England, becoming the youngest player to score a hat-trick for the Three Lions when he notched three goals against Croatia in a World Cup qualifier in Zagreb in 2008, and finishing on the winning side in his first 14 internationals – the best ever such run by an England player. Despite his status as a 'lucky mascot', he was a shock omission from Fabio Capello's squad for the World Cup in South Africa, although the Italian later admitted leaving Walcott out was "a mistake". He did, though, play at Euro 2012, scoring a goal against Sweden before setting up Danny Welbeck's winner in England's 3-2 victory. After an injury-hit campaign, Walcott missed out on the 2014 World Cup in Brazil.

• Walcott began his career at Southampton and is the youngest player ever to appear for the Saints, making his debut as a sub against Wolves in 2005 when he was aged 16 years and 143 days.

• After attracting huge media attention for his dynamic performances for the south coast outfit, Walcott moved to Arsenal for an eventual fee of £9.1 million, making him the most expensive 16-year-old in the history of the British game. He scored his first goal for the Gunners a year later in the Carling Cup final against Chelsea to become the second youngest scorer in the final of the competition.

• Walcott won his first silverware with the Gunners in 2015 when Arsenal beat Aston Villa in the FA Cup final. It was the England striker, too, who opened the scoring in his side's 4-0 victory with a superb left-foot volley that flew past Villa keeper Shay Given.

## WALES

**First international:**
Scotland 4 Wales 0, 1876
**Most capped player:**
Neville Southall, 92 caps (1982-98)
**Leading goalscorer:** Ian Rush, 28 goals (1980-96)
**First World Cup appearance:** Wales 1 Hungary 1, 1958
**Biggest win:** Wales 11 Ireland 0, 1888
**Heaviest defeat:** Scotland 9 Wales 0, 1878

Wales are the least successful of the four British national sides, having qualified for just one major international tournament in their history (prior to the 2016 Euros).

• Their finest hour came in 1958 when a Welsh side including such great names as John Charles, Ivor Allchurch and Jack Kelsey qualified for the World Cup finals in Sweden

**IS THAT A FACT?**
Welsh internationals John Charles (in 1955) and Mel Charles (in 1962) are the only British brothers to have both scored an international hat-trick.

after beating Israel in a two-legged play-off. After drawing all three of their group matches, Wales then beat Hungary in a play-off to reach the quarter-finals where they lost 1-0 to eventual winners Brazil.

• In 1976 Wales made their best ever showing in the European Championships, reaching the quarter-finals before going down 3-1 on aggregate to Yugoslavia. However, after winning five and drawing two of their first seven qualifiers – including a dramatic 1-0 home victory over a star-studded Belgian

*Luckily for Theo Walcott he can jump high as well as run fast*

In September 2015 Wales were higher (9) in the FIFA Rankings than England (10) for the first time ever

team in June 2015 – Wales were in prime position to make it to Euro 2016 for their first experience of the finals proper.

• **Wales winger Billy Meredith is the oldest international in the history of British football. He was aged 45 years and 229 days when he won the last of his 48 caps against England in 1920, a quarter of a century after making his international debut.**

• Wales have the third best record in the British Home Championships with seven outright wins and five shared victories. Their best decade was the 1930s when they won the championship three times.

**World Cup Record**
*1930-38 Did not enter*
*1950-54 Did not qualify*
*1958 Quarter-finals*
*1962-2014 Did not qualify*

## WALSALL

**Year founded:** 1888
**Ground:** Banks's Stadium (11,300)
**Previous name:** Walsall Town Swifts
**Nickname:** The Saddlers
**Biggest win:** 10-0 v Darwen (1899)
**Heaviest defeat:** 0-12 v Small Heath (1892) and v Darwen (1896)

The club was founded in 1888 as Walsall Town Swifts, following an amalgamation of Walsall Swifts and Walsall Town. Founder members of the Second Division in 1892, the club changed to its present name three years later.

• **Walsall have never played in the top flight, but they have a history of producing momentous cup shocks, the most famous coming back in 1933 when they sensationally beat eventual league champions Arsenal 2-0 in the FA Cup. The Saddlers' best run in the League Cup, meanwhile, came in 1984 when they reached the semi-finals before losing 4-2 on aggregate to eventual winners Liverpool.**

• Two players share the distinction of being Walsall's all-time leading scorer: Tony Richards, who notched 184 league goals for the club between 1954 and 1963, and his strike partner Colin Taylor, who banged in exactly the same number in three spells with the Saddlers between 1958 and 1973.

• **In 2015 Walsall played at Wembley for the first time in their 127-year history, but it wasn't a great day for their fans as the Saddlers went down 2-0 to Bristol City in the Football League Trophy final.**

• Striker Alan Buckley, who went on to manage the club, is Walsall's record signing, costing £175,000 when he joined the Saddlers from Midlands neighbours Birmingham City in June

1979. No other Football League club's most expensive purchase goes back as many years, 36 and counting!

**HONOURS**
*Division 4 champions 1960*
*League Two champions 2007*

## WATFORD

**Year founded:** 1881
**Ground:** Vicarage Road (17,477)
**Previous name:** Watford Rovers, West Herts
**Nickname:** The Hornets
**Biggest win:** 10-1 v Lowestoft Town (1926)
**Heaviest defeat:** 0-10 v Wolves (1912)

Founded as Watford Rovers in 1881, the club changed its name to West Herts in 1893. Five years later, following a merger with Watford St Mary's, the club became Watford FC.

• **The club's history was fairly nondescript until pop star Elton John became chairman in 1976 and invested a large part of his personal wealth in the team. With future England manager Graham Taylor at the helm, the Hornets rose from the Fourth to the First Division in just five years, and reached the FA Cup**

*Watford celebrate a goal at Everton on their return to the Premier League in 2015/16*

final in 1984. In the late 1990s Taylor returned to the club and worked his magic again, guiding the Hornets to two successive promotions and a brief taste of life in the Premiership.

• After finishing second in the old First Division in 1983, Watford made their one foray into Europe, reaching the third round of the UEFA Cup before losing to Sparta Prague.

• Luther Blissett, one of the star players of that period, is the club's record appearance maker. In three spells at Vicarage Road the energetic striker notched up 415 league appearances and scored 148 league goals (also a club record).

• In the 1959/60 season striker Cliff Holton scored a club record 42 league goals for the Hornets, helping them gain promotion from the third tier.

• Watford have twice reached the League Cup semi-final, losing to Nottingham Forest in 1979 and Liverpool in 2005.

• In January 2007 Watford received a club record £9.65 million when they sold dynamic winger Ashley Young to Aston Villa. A few months later the Hornets splashed £3.25 million of this cash on West Brom's Nathan Ellington, their

most expensive signing ever.

• In 2015 Watford became the first club to gain promotion to the Premier League after employing four managers during the season. Giuseppe Sannino, Oscar Garcia and Billy McKinlay were all briefly in the Vicarage Road hotseat before former Chelsea midfielder Slavisa Jokanovic steadied the ship and guided the Hornets to second place in the Championship.

> HONOURS
> **Division 3 champions** *1969*
> **Second Division champions** *1998*
> **Division 4 champions** *1978*

# DANNY WELBECK

**Born:** Manchester, 26th November 1990
**Position:** Striker
**Club career:**
2008-14 Manchester United 90 (20)
2009-10 Preston North End (loan) 8 (2)
2010-11 Sunderland (loan) 26 (6)
2014- Arsenal 25 (4)
**International record:**
2011- England 33 (14)

An energetic and quick-thinking striker, Danny Welbeck became Arsenal's record signing from another Premier League club when he joined the Gunners from Manchester United for £16 million in September 2014. He was soon making his mark at the Emirates, becoming only the sixth English player to score a hat-trick in the Champions League in a 4-1 thrashing of Galatasaray.

• A United youth product, Welbeck came to the fore in the 2008/09 season, scoring on his Premier League debut against Stoke City and helping the Red Devils win the Carling Cup. After loan spells at Preston and Sunderland, he returned to Old Trafford to establish himself as Wayne Rooney's main strike partner during the 2011/12 season.

• Welbeck's impressive displays saw him shortlisted for the 2012 PFA Young Player of the Year award, but he just missed out to Tottenham's Kyle Walker. The following campaign, though, was less memorable for the young striker, as he played second fiddle to Robin van Persie and managed just a single Premier League goal.

• The son of Ghanaian parents, Welbeck ironically made his full

England debut against Ghana in a 1-1 draw at Wembley in March 2011. In the Three Lions' first six qualifiers for Euro 2016 he was their top scorer with six goals.

## WEMBLEY STADIUM

Built at a cost of £798 million, the new Wembley Stadium is the most expensive sporting venue ever. With a capacity of 90,000, it is also the second largest in Europe and the largest in the world to have every seat under cover.

• **The stadium's most spectacular feature is a 315m-wide arch, the world's longest unsupported roof structure. Wembley also boasts a staggering 2,618 toilets, more than any other venue in the world.**

• Originally scheduled to open in 2003, the stadium was not completed until 2007 due to a variety of financial and legal difficulties. The first professional match was played at the new venue on 17th March 2007 when England Under-21s met their Italian counterparts, with the first goal arriving after just 28 seconds when Giampaolo Pazzini struck for the visitors. Half an hour later, David Bentley became the first Englishman to score at the new stadium.

• **Chelsea have played at the new stadium a record 14 times, while Arsenal played a record 41 times at the old stadium.**

• The first Wembley Stadium was opened in 1923, having been constructed in just 300 days at a cost of £750,000. The first match played at the venue was the 1923 FA Cup final between Bolton and West Ham, although the kick-off was delayed for nearly an hour when thousands of fans spilled onto the pitch because of overcrowding in the stands.

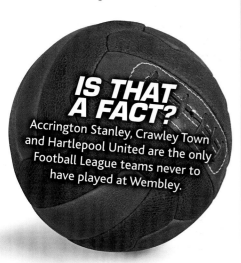

**IS THAT A FACT?**
Accrington Stanley, Crawley Town and Hartlepool United are the only Football League teams never to have played at Wembley.

• Apart from football, the new stadium has also played host to a number of other sports including rugby league, American football and boxing.

• Arsenal and England defender Tony Adams played a record 60 games at Wembley between 1987 and 2000, a total boosted by the fact that the Gunners used the stadium for their home games in the Champions League in the late 1990s.

## ARSÈNE WENGER

**Born:** Strasbourg, France, 22nd October 1949
**Managerial career:**
1984-87 Nancy
1987-94 Monaco
1995-96 Nagoya Grampus Eight
1996- Arsenal

Arsenal boss Arsène Wenger is only the second manager in English football history – after Aston Villa's George Ramsey – to have lifted the FA Cup six times, most recently guiding the Gunners to back-to-back triumphs in 2014 and 2015.

• **After a modest playing career which included a stint with his local club Strasbourg, Wenger cut his managerial teeth with Nancy before moving to Monaco in 1987. He won the league title in his first season there, with a team including English stars Glenn Hoddle and Mark Hateley, and the French Cup in 1991.**

• Following a year in Japan with Nagoya Grampus Eight, Wenger arrived in north London in September 1996. In his first full season at Highbury he became the first non-British manager to win the league and cup Double, and he repeated this accomplishment in 2002.

Arsene Wenger's head exploded when someone suggested he might need to buy a player or two!

• His greatest achievement, though, came in 2004 when his Arsenal side won the title for a third time after going through the entire Premiership season undefeated. Wenger's 'Invincibles', as they were dubbed, were hailed as the greatest team in English football history, not only for their record 49-game unbeaten run but also for their fluid attacking style of play which made the most of exceptional talents like Thierry Henry, Dennis Bergkamp and Patrick Vieira.

• Easily the longest-serving current manager in England, Wenger is one of just four managers in English football to oversee 1,000 matches with the same club. He reached the landmark when Arsenal played at Chelsea on 22nd March 2014 – but it turned out to be a day to forget as the Gunners crashed to a humbling 6-0 defeat.

## WEST BROMWICH ALBION

**Year founded:** 1878
**Ground:** The Hawthorns (26,850)
**Previous name:** West Bromwich Strollers
**Nickname:** The Baggies
**Biggest win:** 12-0 v Darwen (1892)
**Heaviest defeat:** 3-10 v Stoke City (1937)

Founded as West Bromwich Strollers in 1878 by workers at the local Salter's Spring Works, the club adopted the suffix 'Albion' two years later and were founder members of the Football League in 1888.

• The Baggies were the first club to lose two consecutive FA Cup finals, going down to Blackburn Rovers in 1886 and Aston Villa the following year. In 1888, though, West Brom recorded the first of their five triumphs in the cup, beating favourites Preston 2-1 in the final.

• In 1931 West Brom became the first and only club to win promotion and the FA Cup in the same season. The Baggies came close to repeating this particular double in 2008, when they topped the Championship but were beaten in the FA Cup semi-finals by eventual winners Portsmouth.

• **West Brom claimed their only league title in 1920, in the first post-First World War season. The 60 points they amassed that season and the 104 goals they scored were both records at the time. The club's manager at the time, Fred Everiss, was in charge at the Hawthorns from 1902-48, his 46-year stint being the longest in English football history.**

• In 1966 West Brom won the last League Cup final to be played over two legs, overcoming West Ham 5-3 on aggregate. The next year they appeared in the first one-off final at Wembley, but surprisingly lost 3-2 to Third Division QPR after leading 2-0 at half-time.

• **The Baggies, though, returned to Wembley the following season and beat Everton 1-0 in the FA Cup final. West Brom's winning goal was scored in extra-time by club legend Jeff Astle, who in the process became one of just 12 players to have scored in every round of the competition. Astle also found the target in his side's 2-1 defeat by Manchester City in the 1970 League Cup final to become the first player to score in both domestic cup finals at Wembley.**

• In 1892 West Brom thrashed Darwen 12-0 to record their biggest ever win. The score set a record for the top flight which has never been beaten, although Nottingham Forest equalled it in 1909.

• **Cult hero Tony 'Bomber' Brown is West Brom's record scorer with 218 league goals to his name. The attacking midfielder is also the club's longest serving player, turning out in 574 league games between 1963 and 1980.**

• Striker Jiimy Cookson scored a club record six goals in a 6-3 defeat of Blackpool in 1927.

• **West Brom's record purchase is Venezuelan international striker Salomon Rondon, who joined the Baggies from Zenit St Petersburg for £12 million in August 2015. The club's bank balance was boosted by a record £8.5 million when gangly defender Curtis Davies joined local rivals Aston Villa in 2008.**

• West Brom striker William 'Ginger' Richardson scored four goals in just five minutes in a 5-1 win at West Ham on 7th November 1931 – the quickest four-goal haul in English football history.

**HONOURS**
*Division 1 champions* 1920
*Division 2 champions* 1902, 1911
*Championship champions* 2008
*FA Cup* 1888, 1892, 1931, 1954, 1968
*League Cup* 1966

## WEST HAM UNITED

**Year founded:** 1895
**Ground:** Upton Park (35,016)
**Previous name:** Thames Ironworks
**Nickname:** The Hammers
**Biggest win:** 10-0 v Bury (1983)
**Heaviest defeat:** 2-8 v Blackburn (1963)

The club was founded in 1895 as Thames Ironworks by shipyard workers employed by a company of the same name. In 1900 the club was disbanded but immediately reformed under its present name.

• **The biggest and best supported club in east London, West Ham have a proud tradition in the FA Cup. In 1923 they reached the first final to**

*West Brom love to mix up their goal celebrations*

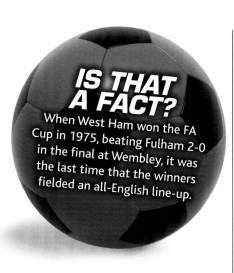

## IS THAT A FACT?

When West Ham won the FA Cup in 1975, beating Fulham 2-0 in the final at Wembley, it was the last time that the winners fielded an all-English line-up.

be played at the original Wembley Stadium, losing 2-0 to Bolton Wanderers.

• The Hammers experienced a more enjoyable Wembley 'first' in 1965 when they became the first English side to win a European trophy on home soil, defeating Munich 1860 2-0 in the final of the Cup Winners' Cup.

• **The following year West Ham were the only club to provide three members – Bobby Moore, Geoff Hurst and Martin Peters – of England's World Cup-winning team. Between them Hurst and Peters scored all four of England's goals in the final against West Germany while Moore, as captain, collected the trophy. The Hammers trio's remarkable contribution to the victory is commemorated by a statue near Upton Park.**

• Striker Vic Watson holds three significant goalscoring records for the club. He is West Ham's leading scorer, with an impressive 298 league goals between 1920 and 1935, including a record 42 goals in the 1929/30 season. In the same campaign Watson hit a record six goals in a match, a feat later equalled by Geoff Hurst in an 8-0 drubbing of Sunderland at Upton Park in 1968.

• **No West Ham player has turned out more often for the club than former manager Billy Bonds. Between 1967 and 1988 'Bonzo', as he was dubbed by fans and team-mates alike, appeared in 663 league games.**

• In 1980 West Ham became the last club from outside the top flight to win the FA Cup. The Hammers, then residing in the old Second Division, beat favourites Arsenal 1-0 thanks to a rare headed goal by Trevor Brooking.

• **The legendary Bobby Moore is the**

club's most capped international. He played 108 times for England to set a record that has since only been passed by Peter Shilton, David Beckham and Steven Gerrard.

• In their long and distinguished history West Ham have had just 15 managers, fewer than any other major English club. The longest serving of the lot was Syd King, who held the reins for 31 years from 1901 to 1932.

• **On Boxing Day 2006 Teddy Sheringham became the oldest player ever to score in the Premier League when he netted for West Ham against Portsmouth aged 40 years and 266 days. Four days later he made his last appearance for the Hammers at Manchester City, stretching his own record as the oldest outfield player in the league's history.**

• In March 2011 West Ham's bid to take over the Olympic Stadium in Stratford after the London Games was approved by the Olympic Park Legacy Committee. Two years later the club signed a 99-year lease to play at the stadium and plan to move in for the start of the 2016/17 season.

• **In October 2014 Hammers striker Diafra Sakho scored in his sixth consective Premier League start to equal a record set by Coventry's Micky Quinn in 1992.**

### HONOURS
***Division 2 champions*** *1958, 1981*
***FA Cup*** *1964, 1975, 1980*
***European Cup Winners' Cup*** *1965*

*At the start of the 2015/16 season West Ham were flying!*

## WIGAN ATHLETIC

**Year founded:** 1932
**Ground:** DW Stadium (25,138)
**Nickname:** The Latics
**Biggest win:** 7-1 v Scarborough (1997)
**Heaviest defeat:** 1-9 v Tottenham Hotspur (2009)

The club was founded at a public meeting at the Queen's Hotel in 1932 as successors to Wigan Borough, who the previous year had become the first ever club to resign from the Football League.

• **After 34 failed attempts, including a bizarre application to join the Scottish Second Division in 1972, Wigan were finally elected to the old Fourth Division in 1978 in place of Southport. The Latics' fortunes, though, only really changed for the better in 1995 when local millionaire and owner of JJB Sports Dave Whelan bought the club and announced his intention to bring Premier League football to the rugby-mad town within 10 years. Remarkably, Whelan's dream was fulfilled exactly a decade later.**

• The greatest day in the club's history came in 2013 when Wigan won their first major trophy, the FA Cup, after beating hot favourites Manchester City 1-0 in the final at Wembley thanks to a last-minute header by Ben Watson. Sadly for their fans, Wigan's eight-year stay in the

**WILSHERE**

Premier League ended just three days after that triumph, meaning that they became the first club ever to win the FA Cup and be relegated in the same season.

· In November 2009 Wigan were hammered 9-1 at Tottenham, only the second time in Premier League history that a side had conceded nine goals. The eight goals the Latics let in after the break was a record for a Premier League half.

· Wigan made their record signing in 2010 when they bought Mauro Boselli from Estudiantes for £6.5 million. Two years later, after the Argentinian had failed to score a single league goal, he was voted the club's worst ever foreign player by unimpressed Wigan fans.

· The club's record goalscorer is Andy Liddell, who hit 70 league goals between 1998 and 2003. No player has pulled on Wigan's blue-and-white stripes more often than Kevin Langley, who made 317 league appearances in two spells at the club between 1981 and 1994.

HONOURS
*Second Division champions* 2003
*Third Division champions* 1997
*FA Cup* 2013
*Football League Trophy* 1985, 1999

## WILLIAN

**Born:** Ribeirao Pires, Brazil, 9th August 1988
**Position:** Winger
**Club career:**
2006-07 Corinthians 16 (2)
2007-13 Shakhtar Donetsk 140 (20)
2013 Anzhi Makhachkala 11 (1)
2013- Chelsea 61 (6)
**International record:**
2011- Brazil 26 (4)

Frizzy-haired winger Willian became Chelsea's third most expensive signing ever when he joined the Blues from Russian side Anzhi Makhachkala for £32 million in August 2013. He has gone on to repay some of that fee by helping the west Londoners win the Premier League and League Cup in 2015.

· Willian Borges da Silva, to give him his full name, started out in his native Brazil with Corinthians before moving to Shakhtar Donetsk in 2007 for around £12.5 million. In his first season

with his new club he won the Ukrainian league and cup double, and went on to win three more leagues and two more cups over the next five years.

· Willian's greatest triumph with Shakhtar, though, came in 2009 when he helped them become the first ever Ukrainian side to win a European trophy, when they beat German outfit Werder Bremen 2-1 in the last ever UEFA Cup final.

· A skilful player with superb close control who loves to

take on and beat defenders, Willian was first capped by Brazil in 2011 in a 2-0 friendly win against Gabon and featured in his country's 2014 World Cup and 2015 Copa America squads.

## JACK WILSHERE

**Born:** Stevenage, 1st January 1992
**Position:** Midfielder
**Club career:**
2008- Arsenal 100 (6)
2009-10 Bolton Wanderers (loan) 14 (1)
**International record:**
2010- England 28 (2)

Arsenal playmaker Jack Wilshere is the only player to have won the BBC's 'Goal of the Season' award

*Jack Wilshere's two stunning goals against Slovenia were his first goals for England*

in consecutive years during the Premier League era. He first topped the poll in 2014 for a deft finish against Norwich following a flowing team move, and then won the award again in 2015 for a thunderous shot against West Brom on the last day of the season.

• **The youngest player to appear for Arsenal in the league, Jack Wilshere was aged 16 and 256 days when he made his Premier League debut for the Gunners against Blackburn in September 2008. Two months later he became only the fifth 16 year old in history to play in the Champions League when he came on as a sub against Dynamo Kiev.**

• After a successful loan spell at Bolton in the 2009/10 season, Wilshere returned to the Emirates to be voted PFA Young Player of the Year the following campaign. He won his first trophy with the Gunners in 2014, when he came on as a sub in their FA Cup final defeat of Hull City, and he repeated the trick the following year against Aston Villa.

• **Then England manager Fabio Capello gave Wilshere his international debut as a sub against Hungary at Wembley in August 2010. He missed Euro 2012 through injury but went to the 2014 World Cup, starting one match against Costa Rica, and the following year scored his first goals for England with two powerful left-foot shots in a 3-2 win in Slovenia.**

## WOLVERHAMPTON WANDERERS

**Year founded:** 1877
**Ground:** Molineux (31,700)
**Previous name:** St Luke's
**Nickname:** Wolves
**Biggest win:** 14-0 v Cresswell's Brewery
**Heaviest defeat:** 1-10 v Newton Heath

Founded as St Luke's by pupils at a local school of that name in 1877, the club adopted its present name after merging with Blakenhall Wanderers two years later. Wolves were founder members of the Football League in 1888, finishing the first season in third place behind champions Preston and Aston Villa.

• **The Black Country club enjoyed**

*Benik Afobe of Wolves might just be having his shirt pulled here*

their heyday in the 1950s under manager Stan Cullis, a pioneer of long ball 'kick and rush' tactics. After a number of near misses, Wolves were crowned league champions for the first time in their history in 1954 and won two more titles later in the decade to cement their reputation as the top English club of the era. Incredibly, the Black Country outfit scored a century of league goals in four consecutive seasons between 1958 and 1961 – the only club to achieve this feat.

• When Wolves won a number of high-profile friendlies against foreign opposition in the 1950s in some of the first ever televised matches they were hailed as 'champions of the world' by the national press, a claim which helped inspire the creation of the European Cup. In 1958 Wolves became only the second English team to compete in the competition, following in the footsteps of trailblazers Manchester United.

• **The skipper of that great Wolves team, centre-half Billy Wright, is the club's most capped international. Between 1946 and 1959 he won a then record 105 caps for England, captaining his country in 90 of those games (another record).**

• Steve Bull is Wolves' record scorer with an incredible haul of 250 league goals between 1986 and 1999. His impressive total of 306 goals in all competitions included a record 18 hat-tricks for the club.

• **Stalwart defender Derek Parkin has pulled on the famous gold shirt more**

often than any other player, making 501 appearances in the league between 1967 and 1982.

• In 1972 Wolves reached the final of the UEFA Cup, losing 3-2 on aggregate to Tottenham in the first ever European final between two English clubs. Two years later the club won the League Cup for the first time, beating Manchester City 2-1 in the final, and in 1980 they repeated that success thanks to a single goal by Andy Gray in the final against Nottingham Forest.

• **Wolves were the first team in the country to win all four divisions of the Football League, completing the 'full house' in 1989 when they won the old Third Division title a year after claiming the Fourth Division championship.**

• After suffering consecutive relegations from the top flight for the second time in their history, Wolves bounced back to the Championship in 2014 by claiming the League One title with an all-time third-tier record 103 points.

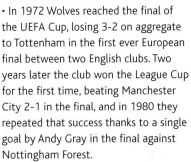

HONOURS

*Division 1 champions 1954, 1958, 1959*
*Division 2 champions 1932, 1977*
*Championship champions 2009*
*Division 3 (North) champions 1924*
*Division 3 champions 1989*
*League One champions 2014*
*Division 4 champions 1988*
*FA Cup 1893, 1908, 1949, 1960*
*League Cup 1974, 1980*
*Football League Trophy 1988*

At the 2015 Women's World Cup in Canada, England's third-placed women achieved the country's best World Cup performance since 1966

# WOMEN'S FOOTBALL

The first recorded women's football match took place between the north and south of England at Crouch End, London in 1895. The north won the game 7-1.

• **The Women's FA was founded in 1969 and the first Women's FA Cup final took place two years later, Southampton beating Stewart and Thistle 4-1. The Saints went on to win the cup another seven times in the next 10 years, but the most successful side in the competition are Arsenal with 13 victories. For the first time, the 2015 final was played at Wembley, Chelsea beating Notts County 1-0 in a disappointing spectacle.**

• In a bid to attract more fans to games the top flight was reorganised in 2011 as a semi-professional summer league consisting of eight clubs, the FA Women's Super League. Arsenal won the first two Super League titles before Liverpool claimed the trophy in 2013 and 2014.

• **The first British international women's match took place in 1972 when England beat Scotland 3-2. In 2005 England recorded their biggest ever win, thrashing Hungary 13-0. Their worst defeat was in 2000 when Norway won 8-0.**

• Midfielder Fara Williams has won a record 145 caps for England, while striker Kelly Smith is the team's top scorer with 46 goals.

• **Between 1987 and 2010 Kristine Lilly won a world record 352 caps for the USA. Powerfully-built American striker Abby Wambach is the leading scorer in women's international football with an incredible 183 goals since making her debut in 2001.**

• Caerphilly Castle Ladies suffered the biggest defeat in the history of British women's football when they were trounced 43-0 by Cardiff Metro University in the Women's Welsh Premier League in 2013 and resigned from the league soon afterwards.

## WOMEN'S WORLD CUP

Since it was first competed for in China in 1991 there have been seven Women's World Cup tournaments. The USA won the first World Cup and have gone on to lift the trophy a record three times, most recently beating Japan 5-2 in the 2015 final in Vancouver at the first tournament to be played entirely on artificial turf. Germany have won the tournament twice, while Norway (1995) and Japan (2011) are the only two other nations to take the trophy home.

• **The top scorer in the World Cup is Marta (Brazil) with 15 goals between 2003 and 2015. Michelle Akers of the USA scored a record 10 goals at the 1991 tournament, including a record five in one game against Chinese Taipei.**

• USA striker Kristine Lilly made a record 30 appearances at the World Cup between 1991 and 2007.

• **Germany hold the record for the biggest win at the Women's World Cup, thrashing Argentina 11-0 in 2007.**

• Switzerland's Fabienne Humm scored the fastest hat-trick in the tournament's history in 2015 when she struck three times in five minutes in her country's 10-1 mauling of Ecuador.

## WORLD CUP

The most successful country in the history of the World Cup are Brazil, who have won the competition a record five times. Germany and Italy are Europe's leading nation with four wins each, the Germans becoming the first European nation to triumph in South America when they beat Argentina 1-0 in the 2014 final in Brazil. Neighbours Argentina and Uruguay have both won the competition twice, the Uruguayans emerging victorious when the pair met in the first ever World Cup final in Montevideo in 1930. The only other countries to claim the trophy are England, France and Spain, the first two countries taking advantage of their host nation status to win the competition in

## IS THAT A FACT?

In May 2014 Portuguese coach Helena Costa was appointed boss of French Ligue 2 outfit Clermont Foot – the first woman to manage at this level in the men's game. However, she resigned after just one month for personal reasons.

## TOP 10

**WORLD CUP FINALS PARTICIPATIONS**

| | | |
|---|---|---|
| 1. | Brazil | 20 |
| 2. | Germany* | 18 |
| | Italy | 18 |
| 4. | Argentina | 16 |
| 5. | Mexico | 15 |
| 6. | England | 14 |
| | France | 14 |
| | Spain | 14 |
| 9. | Belgium | 12 |
| | Uruguay | 12 |

*Including West Germany 1954-90

1966 and 1998 respectively, while the Spanish triumphed in South Africa in 2010 thanks to a 1-0 win over Holland in the final.

• Including both Japan and South Korea, who were joint hosts for the 2002 edition, the World Cup has been held in 15 different countries. The first nation to stage the tournament twice was Mexico (in 1970 and 1986), while Italy (1934 and 1990), France (1938 and 1998), Germany (1974 and 2006) and Brazil (1950 and 2014) have also welcomed the world to the planet's biggest football festival on two occasions each. The next World Cup, in 2018, will be held in Russia.

• Brazil are the only country to have played at all 20 tournaments and have recorded the most wins (70). Germany, meanwhile, have reached a record eight finals, have played the most games (106) and have scored the most goals (224).

• However, Hungary hold the record for the most goals scored in a single tournament, banging in 27 in just five games at the 1954 finals in Switzerland. Even this incredible tally, though, was not quite sufficient for the 'Magical Magyars' to lift the trophy as they went down to a 3-2 defeat in the final against West Germany, a team they had beaten 8-3 earlier in the tournament.

• Hungary also hold the record for the biggest ever victory at the finals, demolishing El Salvador 10-1 in 1982. That, though, was a desperately close encounter compared to the biggest win in qualifying, Australia's 31-0 annihilation of American Samoa in 2001, a game in which Aussie striker Archie Thompson helped himself to a record 13 goals.

• The legendary Pelé is the only player in World Cup history to have been presented with three winners' medals. The Brazilian superstar enjoyed his first success in 1958 when he scored twice in a 5-2 rout of hosts Sweden in the final, and was a winner again four years later in Chile despite hobbling out of the tournament with a torn leg muscle in the second match. He then made it a hat-trick in 1970, setting a sparkling Brazil side on the road to an emphatic 4-1 victory against Italy in the final with a trademark bullet header.

• The leading overall scorer in the World Cup is Germany's Miroslav Klose with 16 goals between 2002 and 2014. He is followed by Brazil legend Ronaldo, with 15 including two in the 2002 final against Germany.

• England's Geoff Hurst had previously gone one better in 1966, scoring a hat-trick as the hosts beat West Germany 4-2 in the final at Wembley. His second goal, which gave England a decisive 3-2 lead in extra-time, was the most controversial in World Cup history and German fans still argue to this day that his shot bounced on the line after striking the crossbar, rather than over it. Naturally, England fans generally agree with the eagle-eyed Russian linesman, Tofik Bahramov, who awarded the goal.

• Germany midfielder Lothar Matthaus made a record 25 World Cup appearances for his country between 1982 and 1998.

*Germany seem mildly pleased to have won the World Cup... again!*

• Forty-year-old Dino Zoff is the oldest man ever to win the World Cup, with Italy in 1982. As captain of the side, he was also only the second goalkeeper to lead his country to glory (after fellow Italian Giampiero Combi in 1934).

• Brazil put together a record run of 11 straight wins at the World Cup between 2002 and 2006. Less impressively, Mexico lost their first nine games at the finals between 1930 and 1958

• **Spain won the World Cup in 2010 despite scoring just eight goals at the finals – the lowest ever total by the winners. Meanwhile, Argentina reached the final in 1990 despite scoring a paltry five goals in six earlier games. To no one's great surprise they failed to hit the target in the final, losing 1-0 to West Germany.**

• Brazil suffered the worst ever defeat by a host nation when they were trounced 7-1 by Germany in 2014 – also the biggest ever win in a semi-final. However, four years earlier South Africa fared even worst, becoming the first hosts to be eliminated in the first round.

• **Robert Prosinecki is the only player to have scored for two different countries at the finals, netting for Yugoslavia in 1990 and Croatia in 1998.**

• El Salvador have the worst record of any country at the finals, losing all six of the games they have played.

**World Cup Finals**
*1930 Uruguay 4 Argentina 2 (Uruguay)*
*1934 Italy 2 Czechoslovakia 1 (Italy)*
*1938 Italy 4 Hungary 2 (France)*
*1950 Uruguay 2 Brazil 1 (Brazil)*
*1954 West Germany 3 Hungary 2 (Switzerland)*
*1958 Brazil 5 Sweden 2 (Sweden)*
*1962 Brazil 3 Czechoslovakia 1 (Chile)*
*1966 England 4 West Germany 2 (England)*
*1970 Brazil 4 Italy 1 (Mexico)*
*1974 West Germany 2 Netherlands 1 (West Germany)*
*1978 Argentina 3 Netherlands 1 (Argentina)*
*1982 Italy 3 West Germany 1 (Spain)*
*1986 Argentina 3 West Germany 2 (Mexico)*
*1990 West Germany 1 Argentina 0 (Italy)*
*1994 Brazil 0* Italy 0 (USA)*
*1998 France 3 Brazil 0 (France)*

*2002 Brazil 2 Germany 0 (Japan/South Korea)*
*2006 Italy 1* France 1 (Germany)*
*2010 Spain 1 Netherlands 0 (South Africa)*
*2014 Germany 1 Argentina 0 (Brazil)*
*\* Won on penalties*

## WORLD CUP GOLDEN BALL

The Golden Ball is awarded to the best player at the World Cup following a poll of members of the global media. The first winner was Italian striker Paolo Rossi, whose six goals at the 1982 World Cup helped the Azzurri win that year's tournament in Spain.

• **Rossi was followed in 1986 by another World Cup winner, Argentina captain Diego Maradona, but since then only one player has claimed the Golden Ball and a winners' medal at the same tournament, Brazilian striker Romario in 1994.**

• The only goalkeeper to win the award to date is Germany's Oliver Kahn in 2002. The most controversial winner, meanwhile, was France's mercurial midfielder Zinedine Zidane, who was named as the outstanding performer at

the 2006 World Cup before the final – a game which ended in disgrace for Zidane after he was sent off for headbutting Italian defender Marco Materazzi.

• **Another much-debated winner of the Golden Ball was Argentina's Lionel Messi, who failed to sparkle in the knock-out rounds at the 2014 finals after a good start to the tournament. Even fellow countryman Diego Maradona described the award as "unfair".**

**World Cup Golden Ball Winners**
*1982 Paolo Rossi (Italy)*
*1986 Diego Maradona (Argentina)*
*1990 Salvatore Schillaci (Italy)*
*1994 Romario (Brazil)*
*1998 Ronaldo (Brazil)*
*2002 Oliver Kahn (Germany)*
*2006 Zinedine Zidane (France)*
*2010 Diego Forlan (Uruguay)*
*2014 Lionel Messi (Argentina)*

## WORLD CUP GOLDEN BOOT

Now officially known as the 'Adidas Golden Shoe', the Golden Boot is awarded to the player who scores most goals in a World Cup finals tournament.

*Even Lionel Messii didn't think he deserved the Golden Ball in 2015*

*Wycombe Wanderers were a minute away from promotion to League One in the 2015 League Two play-offs at Wembley*

The first winner was Guillermo Stabile, whose eight goals helped Argentina reach the final in 1930.

• French striker Just Fontaine scored a record 13 goals at the 1958 tournament in Sweden. At the other end of the scale, nobody managed more than four goals at the 1962 World Cup in Chile, so the award was shared between six players.

• Surprisingly, it wasn't until 1978 that the Golden Boot was won outright by a player, Argentina's Mario Kempes, whose country also won the tournament. Since then only Italy's Paolo Rossi in 1982 and Brazil's Ronaldo in 2002 have won both the Golden Boot and a World Cup winners' medal in the same year.

• The only English player to win the Golden Boot is Gary Lineker, whose six goals in 1986 helped the Three Lions reach the quarter-finals in Mexico.

• At the 2010 World Cup in South Africa Germany's Thomas Muller was one of four players to top the scoring charts with five goals, but FIFA's new rules gave him the Golden Boot because he had more assists than his three rivals for the award, David Villa, Wesley Sneijder and Diego Forlan.

• The 2014 award went to Colombia's James Rodriguez, who scored six goals, including a brilliant volley against Uruguay which was later voted the best of the tournament by fans on FIFA's website.

## WYCOMBE WANDERERS

**Year founded:** 1887
**Ground:** Adams Park (10,284)
**Nickname:** The Chairboys
**Biggest win:** 15-1 v Witney Town (1955)
**Heaviest defeat:** 0-8 v Reading (1899)

Wycombe Wanderers were founded in 1887 by a group of young furniture-makers (hence the club's nickname, The Chairboys) but had to wait until 1993 before earning promotion to the Football League.

• **Under then manager Martin O'Neill** the club went up to the Second Division (now League One) in their first season, beating Preston in the play-off final.

• In 2001 The Chairboys caused a sensation by reaching the semi-finals of the FA Cup where they lost 2-1 to eventual winners Liverpool at Villa Park. Wycombe also reached the semi-finals of the League Cup in 2007, but were beaten 5-1 on aggregate by eventual winners Chelsea.

• **On 23rd September 2000 Wycombe's Jamie Bates and Jermaine McSporran set a new Football League record for the shortest time between two goals when they both scored against Peterborough within nine seconds of each other either side of half-time.**

• In Wycombe's non-league days club legend Tony Horseman played in a record 749 games, scoring an incredible 416 goals to set another record that is likely to stand for a long time.

HONOURS
*Conference champions* 1993
*FA Amateur Cup* 1931

## XAVI

*By the end of his career at Barcelona Xavi was such as star he refused to walk anywhere and had to be carried by his team of personal servantss*

### XAVI

**Born:** Barcelona, 25th January 1980
**Position:** Midfielder
**Club career:**
1997-2000 Barcelona B 61 (4)
1998-2015 Barcelona 505 (58)
2015- Al Sadd
**International record:**
2000-14 Spain 133 (12)

The heartbeat of Barcelona's hypnotic passing game for nearly two decades, slightly-built midfielder Xavi came through the club's fabled youth system

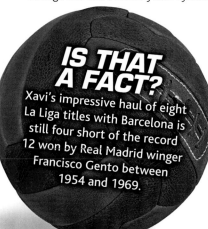

**IS THAT A FACT?**

Xavi's impressive haul of eight La Liga titles with Barcelona is still four short of the record 12 won by Real Madrid winger Francisco Gento between 1954 and 1969.

to head the list of the Catalans' appearance makers, playing in 767 matches in all competitions. No fewer than 151 of those games came in the Champions League, a record for the competition.

• After making his debut for Barça in 1998, Xavi went on to win an Aladdin's Cave of silverware, including eight La Liga titles and four Champions League winners' medals. His outstanding individual contribution to his team's success was recognised in 2010 when he was voted the third best player in the world, behind club-mates Lionel Messi and Andres Iniesta, for the inaugural FIFA Ballon d'Or award. In the same year he was voted World Player of the Year by the readers of World Soccer magazine.

• Xavi first played for Spain in 2000 and is the second highest capped player in his country's history – behind Iker Casillas. In 2008 he was voted Player of the Tournament when Spain won the European Championships and, two years later, he was a key member of the Spanish side that won the World Cup for the first time after beating Holland in the final in South Africa.

• To nobody's surprise he was a vastly influential figure at Euro 2012, setting up two goals in the final as Spain ran riot, thrashing Italy 4-0 to win a third successive international trophy. Two years later he retired from international football after Spain's poor showing at the 2014 World Cup.

### YEOVIL TOWN

**Year founded:** 1890
**Ground:** Huish Park (9,565)
**Previous names:** Yeovil, Yeovil Casuals
**Nickname:** The Glovers
**Biggest win:** 12-1 v Westbury United (1923)
**Heaviest defeat:** 0-8 v Manchester United (1949)

Founded in 1890, initially as Yeovil and then as Yeovil Casuals (1895-1907), the club had to wait until 2003 before finally entering the Football League when they were promoted as Conference champions by a then record 17 points margin.